ALSO BY LANGSTON HUGHES

POETRY

The Panther and the Lash: Poems for Our Times (1967)
Ask Your Mama: 12 Moods for Jazz (1961)
Selected Poems of Langston Hughes (1959)
Montage of a Dream Deferred (1951)
One-Way Ticket (1949)
Fields of Wonder (1947)
Shakespeare in Harlem (1942)
Fine Clothes to the Jew (1927)
The Weary Blues (1926)

FICTION

Something in Common and Other Stories (1963)
The Sweet Flypaper of Life (1955)
with Roy DeCarava (photographer)
Laughing to Keep from Crying (1952)
The Ways of White Folks (1934)
Not Without Laughter (1930)

DRAMA

Five Plays by Langston Hughes (1963)

HUMOR

Simple's Uncle Sam (1965)
The Best of Simple (1961)
Simple Stakes a Claim (1957)
Simple Takes a Wife (1953)
Simple Speaks His Mind (1950)

FOR YOUNG PEOPLE

The First Book of Africa (1960)
The First Book of the West Indies (1956)
The First Book of Jazz (1955)
The First Book of Rhythms (1954)
The First Book of Negroes (1952)
Popo and Fifina (1932)
with Arna Bontemps

Selected Letters of
Langston Hughes

Selected Letters of
Langston Hughes

EDITED BY ARNOLD RAMPERSAD
AND DAVID ROESSEL

with Christa Fratantoro

ALFRED A. KNOPF   New York
2015

THIS IS A BORZOI BOOK
PUBLISHED BY ALFRED A. KNOPF

Copyright © 2015 by The Estate of Langston Hughes
Additional material copyright © 2015 by Arnold Rampersad

All rights reserved. Published in the United States by Alfred A. Knopf, a division of Random House LLC, New York, and distributed in Canada by Random House of Canada Limited, Toronto, Penguin Random House companies.

www.aaknopf.com

Knopf, Borzoi Books, and the colophon are registered trademarks of Random House LLC.

Library of Congress Cataloging-in-Publication Data
[Correspondence. Selections]
    The Selected Letters of Langston Hughes/edited by Arnold Rampersad and David Roessel ; with Christa Fratantoro.
        pages cm
    Includes index.
    ISBN 978-0-375-41379-7 (hardcover)—ISBN 978-0-385-35356-4 (eBook) 1. Hughes, Langston, 1902–1967—Correspondence. 2. Authors, American—20th century—Correspondence. 3. African American authors—Correspondence. I. Rampersad, Arnold.   II. Roessel, David E. (David Ernest), 1954–
    PS3515.U274Z48 2014
    818'.5209—dc23
    [B]   2014014896

Front-of-jacket photograph of Langston Hughes, 1940, by Carl Van Vechten.
Used with permission of the Van Vechten Trust. Print: Yale Collection of American Literature, Beinecke Rare Book and Manuscript Library.
Jacket design by Carol Devine Carson

Manufactured in the United States of America
First Edition

To Judith Jones,
an extraordinary editor

Contents

Introduction

Arnold Rampersad

In an envelope marked:
Personal
God addressed me a letter.
In an envelope marked:
Personal
I have given my answer.
—LANGSTON HUGHES, "PERSONAL," 1933

"Who knows better than I," Langston Hughes once wrote to a friend, "what letter writing entails?" Certainly he knew much about letters. With a crowded life that put him in touch over the decades with thousands of people, the mail was crucial to starting and keeping friendships and to doing business. He admired people who answered letters promptly. His friend Carl Van Vechten, for example, received a flood of mail but usually answered each piece on the day it reached him. Hughes was not so disciplined. In fact, at one point he called himself "the world's worst letter writer." Another time, he confessed to stuffing away a swelling pile of unanswered pieces. "Two drawers are full," he noted, "so I'm moving my sox over." All the same, he wanted to be a faithful correspondent. "I leave you now," he ended a letter in 1944, "to consider the stack of mail on top of mail piled on the bed. I cannot take my rest until I unpile some of it."

Later in life, living near one of the noisier sections of Harlem, he wrote through the night, when the brownstone row house he shared was likely to be quiet. Then, at three or four or five o'clock, or even later, he sat at his type-writer and pounded out letters (more than thirty on many nights) that went all over the world. This was in addition to writing the poems, novels, short stories, plays, autobiographies, histories, translations, opera libretti, song lyrics, children's books, and newspaper columns, as well as editing anthologies and other volumes, that made so many people long to be in touch with him.

Hughes also knew the importance of saving letters. "I guess I never throw anything away ever," he admitted, but he valued letters highly. When Van Vechten founded in 1941 at Yale University an archive devoted to African American culture, Hughes agreed at once to donate all of his papers, including letters to him and also carbon copies of virtually all the letters he wrote. Years passed before he learned that this gift was tax-deductible, but he needed no financial incentive to be diligent about his promise. "I got 30 letters today," he noted in 1958, "which took me all day to read, answer, and get ready for Yale." When Van Vechten complained that too many black people seemed indifferent to the archive, Hughes agreed that most of them were "not collection minded." *He* thought differently. "Those of us who do know and do care," he gently lectured his friend, "will just have to redouble our efforts . . . and include in those efforts . . . the bestirring of others."

His love of letters is also seen in his verse. In "Personal," reprinted above, he refers to the epistolary form with a studied lack of emotion. However, "A Letter to Anne" (1927) is an aching message—"Since I left you, Anne, / I have seen nothing but you"—addressed to a young woman who had stolen his heart in Paris three years before, as he tells us in his autobiography *The Big Sea* (1940). "Dear Lovely Death" (1930) both praises and questions death essentially in the form of a letter (". . . Dear lovely Death, / Change is thy other name"). Also basically a letter is his popular poem "Theme for English B" (1949), in which a young black student from the South, now living in Harlem, turns a teacher's request for a personal essay into a poignant message to him ("You are white— / yet a part of me, as I am a part of you"). In "Letter" (1951), a son writing to his mother from the big city slips $5 into the envelope "to show you I still appreciates you." Political protest seizes the form in "Open Letter to the South" (1932) and in the radical "Letter to the Academy" (1933). War seemed to heighten Hughes's interest in this respect. Covering the Spanish Civil War led him to poems that linked the antifascist cause there to antisegregation efforts at home. These works include "Letter from Spain" (1937) and "Postcard from Spain: Addressed to Alabama" (1938). World War II brought pieces such as "Dear Mr. President" (1943), in which a black soldier denounces racism in Alabama as he and his buddies train there to defend democracy, as well as "Will V-Day Be Me-Day Too? (A Negro Fighting Man's Letter to America)" (1944). A generation later, Hughes's opposition to the war in Vietnam was probably behind "Official Notice" (1967). It begins: "Dear Death: / I got your message / That my son is dead."

The sheer quantity of Hughes's letters, as well as their quality, has much to do with his basic love of people. His choice to live in Harlem when many others were fleeing the "ghetto" starting in the 1950s underscores this point. In 1960, he mocked those who complained that Harlem was a "congested" area. "It is," he agreed. "Congested with people. All kinds. And I'm lucky enough to call a great many of them my friends." He reached out to whites, too. Starting in 1951, he exchanged letters for over ten years with a small-town Kansas housewife who on an impulse—"I had no idea who you were"—had taken one of his books out of her local library. Like all letter writers, Hughes was sometimes manipulative. On the whole, however, he simply liked people. If he was lonely in essential ways, his main response to his pain was to create a body of art that others could admire and applaud. And letters generated mainly by his art, whether ostensibly about business or pleasure, would always be a crucial feature of his life.

Hughes's acute need for other people sprang from his ingrained sense of neglect as a child. His ambitious father, incensed at racism, left his family behind and moved to Mexico when Hughes was an infant. His mother, pursuing her own dreams, often lived so far away that he felt deserted by her as well. Hughes grew up in Lawrence, Kansas, mainly with his maternal grandmother; but she, too, was remote. He recalled her as "old, old" and almost forbiddingly silent as she lived with her memories. Her first husband had died in 1859 fighting alongside John Brown at Harpers Ferry. Her second husband, Hughes's grandfather, who died before Langston was born, had also been a radical abolitionist. Left alone too much of the time, Hughes as a child came to believe "in nothing but books and the wonderful world in books—where if people suffered, they suffered in beautiful language, not in monosyllables, as we did in Kansas."

After his grandmother died in 1915, he spent a year in Lincoln, Illinois, with his mother and her second husband. Then, with a move to Cleveland, Ohio, a new world opened for him there at Central High School. He published poems and stories in its monthly magazine; as a senior, he became editor of the school annual and Class Poet. Graduating in 1920, he spent a year with his father in Mexico, where he had also spent the summer of 1919 after his father suddenly reentered his life. Father and son did not get along. Disdaining both poetry and his fellow black Americans, James Hughes wanted his son to study mining and settle in Mexico. Langston, who wanted to live in New York City to be near or in Harlem ("the Negro capital of the world," someone had jubilantly proclaimed it), applied for admission to Columbia University. Convincing his father to fund at least one year there, he left for New York in September 1921.

Our volume opens with a letter to his father that Hughes mailed that month from New York. Polite on its surface, it hides a truth he faced squarely only later: "I hated my father." Hughes never saw him again. Disenchanted by racism and academic stodginess at Columbia, he withdrew after one year. He then set his sights in a new direction. In June 1921, while still in Mexico, he had published his first poem in a national magazine. This work, "The Negro Speaks of Rivers," had appeared in *The Crisis*, the monthly journal of the New York–based National Association for the Advancement of Colored People (NAACP). From that point, Hughes longed to live by his writings. He also aimed to make African American culture central to his art, even as he reached out to the wider world. Chasing this dream, in the next few years he roamed the United States and the world. In addition to his time in Mexico, he traveled in 1923 up and down the west coast of Africa. He went to Europe, staying for some months in 1924 in Paris. From 1926 to 1929, while he earned a BA at Lincoln University in Pennsylvania, he did not lose his passion for foreign lands, or for poetry. He went to Cuba and Haiti on brief trips; into the South and then out West on a year-long (1931–1932) reading tour; in 1932, to the Soviet Union for a year, with intense months spent in Central Asia; to China and Japan; and around the world before coming home in 1933.

The literary fruit of these years would include two books of poetry, a novel, a landmark essay about the Harlem Renaissance, a play that later reached Broadway, a children's book, and a short story collection. With this work, Hughes laid the foundation of a career that eventually spanned five decades. In the 1930s, he endured poverty at times but published some stunning radical poems; he wrote and saw produced several plays; he was a war correspondent in Spain; he wrote the screenplay for a Hollywood movie; and he finished an autobiography. In the 1940s Hughes worked in support of the U.S. war effort, published three more books of poetry, coedited a major anthology of black American verse, started a weekly newspaper column that lasted twenty years, and collaborated on a successful Broadway opera, in addition to other efforts on the stage.

In the 1950s, even as he endured punishing right-wing attacks, including an appearance by subpoena before Senator Joseph McCarthy's feared sub-committee on "un-Americanism," Hughes became only more productive and versatile. He published additional books of verse, story collections, and children's books; a second volume of autobiography; other opera libretti; and so on. By 1960, as he began the last decade of his life, he was in full flight as an author. Sometimes he wondered if he took on too much in trying to avoid poverty. Signing contract after contract for new projects, he mocked himself about being little more than "a literary sharecropper," toiling away for next to nothing "on a publisher's plantation." Even so, his reputation as a skilled man of letters grew, and the volume of letters destined for Yale swelled accordingly.

In the early 1920s, young Hughes slipped easily from style to style in his letters. According to his mood he could be lyrical, romantic, flirtatious, ironical, sardonic, allusive, casual, objective, or businesslike. Sober or even stony with his father, with someone else he could be, at almost the same time, a blushing ingenue. "I'm stupid and only a young kid fascinated by his first glimpse of life," he ventures in 1923 (at twenty-one) to an older man he wants to charm, even as his compulsive name-dropping shows his anxiety about becoming a man of culture and also being seen as one. "Have you seen Chaliapin in 'Boris'?" he asks breathlessly about the renowned Russian singer in the opera *Boris Godunov.* "It's the experience of a lifetime. And did you see the Moscow Art players? I couldn't get in, so I comforted myself with seeing the 'Chauve Souris' for the third time. . . . I suppose you saw Barrymore's Hamlet, and maybe 'Rain.'" He almost swoons as he writes home from a freighter off the coast of Africa: "And tonight the sunset! Gleaming copper and gold and then the tropical soft green after-glow of twilight, and now stars in the water and luminous phosphorescent foam on the little waves about the ship and ahead the light of Freetown toward which we are steering through the soft darkness." And yet he also shows in other letters written about the same time utter sobriety. The truth seems to be that if he hated his father, he had something of his father's capacity for business and the law. No wonder that his long-time friend Arna Bontemps, a prudent man himself, would note at one point Hughes's "usual thoroughness and feeling for essentials."

Eventually, posturing and purple lyricism would disappear from his letters, making way for a narrower but more mature range of expression in which qualities such as vitality, determination, compassion, and humor dominate. Rage is absent: Hughes remained polite no matter how deeply someone wounded him. In the 1930s, he penned several bitter political poems but even in that period he was considerate in writing to people who offended him. When, for example, an eminent white writer pressed him in 1943 to help the American Red Cross—blithely ignoring its racist practices, which included separating "black" blood from "white" blood in its blood banks and founding segregated Red Cross Clubs abroad—Hughes controlled himself in venting his anger. "Hitler could hardly desire more," he wrote tersely. "General Douglas MacArthur may be right when he says, 'The Red Cross never fails a soldier.' Certainly it has failed thirteen million Negroes on the home front, and its racial policies are a blow in the face to American Negro morale." However, he never went beyond such a rebuke in any of his surviving letters.

Of all the challenges Hughes faced in setting out to be a writer, perhaps the most surprising is one we hardly expect to find in the case of a person so proud to be hailed by blacks as the "Poet Laureate of the Negro Race." This challenge asked Hughes, who had grown up in tiny, isolated communities of blacks, to learn basic truths about African American culture as a whole before he could be at home among those he eagerly saluted in verse as "My People." In a 1929 letter he admitted that almost three years passed at Lincoln University, with its virtually all-black student body, before he felt comfortable facing black strangers: "Only now am I beginning to be at all at ease and without any self-consciousness in meeting my own people." In the early 1920s, Hughes began to rectify this deficiency. Through the agency of letters he met black achievers such as the renowned W. E. B. Du Bois, editor of *The Crisis*; its literary editor, Jessie Redmon Fauset ("my own brown goddess"); Countee Cullen, his congenial major rival among the younger poets; and Alain Locke, the Oxford-trained professor of philosophy at Howard University in Washington who would edit the bible of the Harlem Renaissance, *The New Negro* (1925). Letters also paved the way for Hughes to interact with other writers who were remaking African American literature. These meetings, and those he sought with ordinary folks, emboldened his sense of self as a black American and made possible the decisive cultural force he longed to become.

His relationships with other young black writers would be crucial. Hughes's letters to them underscore above all his refusal to make of their inevitable competition with one another a "Battle Royale" for the scraps that whites tossed at times to artists of color. His letters starting in the 1920s to writers such as Jessie Fauset, Countee Cullen, Wallace Thurman, Zora Neale Hurston, Arna Bontemps, and Claude McKay flesh out the particularities of black life and art in that era but also underscore his generosity and humility. Some of these writers shared his principles, but others did not. Among the finest and longest letters here are those between Hughes and the Jamaican-born poet and novelist Claude McKay. These two men, who loved vagabonding, were also alike in mixing strong race pride with liberal humanism. Intelligent and well read, they hated the snobbery that often marred black middle-class culture. In his letters to McKay, Hughes typically gave a free rein to opinions and expressions he normally kept in check. "This summer I didn't do anything," he confessed in one 1930 message. "Had gotten awfully bored with LITERATURE and WHITE FOLKS and NIGGERS and almost everything else. Borrowed money, and spent it all lying on the beach at Rockaway and sleeping in the sunshine."

Of all the black writers, however, he grew closest to Arna Bontemps. They wrote far more letters to one another—thousands of them—than they wrote to anyone else. Although people often mistook them for one another, they were different in key ways. A Seventh Day Adventist, Bontemps was religious where Hughes was secular to the bone. Bontemps was a family man with several children, while Hughes never married or fathered a child. Hughes roamed the world, but Bontemps generally stayed put, with a long career spent in Nashville as head librarian at Fisk University. But their respect and affection for one another led to several coauthored and coedited books, including children's fiction such as *Popo and Fifina* (1932) and important edited volumes such as the anthology *Poetry of the Negro* (1949). Their letters make up a generally uninhibited, if never sensational, trove of information and opinions about people and events of mutual interest over the greater part of Hughes's life.

Hughes's letters also document his remarkable eagerness to help younger people. Meeting Ralph Ellison (then twenty-three), up from Alabama on his first morning in New York City in 1936, Hughes took pains to unite him with Richard Wright. Through Wright, Ellison would become a fiction writer. Hughes took pride in "discovering" writers, as in the case of Gwendolyn Brooks, Margaret Walker Alexander, and Alice Walker. Approached by Brooks and Walker while they were still teenagers, he read their poems and urged them on. Dazzled on meeting Alice Walker, then twenty-one (she was, he wrote Bontemps, "'cute as a button' and real bright"), he published her first story to appear in print. Brooks and Walker would win the Pulitzer Prize in poetry and fiction respectively, and Ellison would win the National Book Award in fiction. When his novel *Invisible Man* appeared in 1952, Hughes was ecstatic. "Ellison is my protégé!" he exulted. "Dick Wright and I (me first because I introduced him to Dick) started him off writing—and look at him now. Wonderful reviews!"

Some black writers were his friends at first but then were not. A trove of letters here documents the ugly collapse of his friendship with Zora Neale Hurston after she accused him around 1931 of being a liar for claiming coauthorship of their play, *Mule Bone*. A regular guest in Hughes's home, Ellison nevertheless developed a disdain for him as an artist and intellectual. After the grand success of *Invisible Man*, Ellison didn't always hide these feelings. As usual, Hughes refused to strike back in public. Instead, he vented his dismay mainly in occasional bitchy ripostes fired off in letters. "Ralphie is getting real baldheaded," he noted to Arna Bontemps in 1958, "—further proof that he is an intellectual." He had a similar experience with James Baldwin. In 1953, Baldwin took a gratuitous swipe at Hughes in his and Richard Gibson's much noticed article "Two Protests Against Protest." "The young writer," they advised their readers, "might do well to impress upon himself that he is the contemporary of Eliot, Valéry, Pound, Rilke and Auden and not merely Langston Hughes." But although the remark stunned and angered Hughes, he was gallant when he wrote Baldwin about it: "I agree that the more fences young writers jump over, the better. What a bore if they kept on repeating the old! More power to you!"

He was charitable again that year when Knopf sent him the galleys of Baldwin's first novel, *Go Tell It on the Mountain* (1953). Hughes didn't like the book. Baldwin, he told Bontemps, "over-writes and over-poeticizes in images way over the heads of the folks supposedly thinking them." Nevertheless, he sent Knopf a blurb for the dust jacket. In 1956, assessing Baldwin's essay collection *Notes of a Native Son* in *The New York Times Book Review*, Hughes characterized Baldwin as a "thought-provoking, tantalizing, irritating, abusing, and amusing" writer. Baldwin, whose literary stock had soared by this point, probably thought Hughes's tone altogether too jaunty. He bided his time. Three years later, when the roles were reversed and he reviewed Hughes's *Selected Poems* (1959) in the same journal, he opened with a wicked blow: "Every time I read Langston Hughes I am amazed all over again by his genuine gifts—and depressed that he has done so little with them." Furious, Hughes backed away from Baldwin, although they exchanged notes now and then. (Years after Hughes's death, in an interview for a documentary film about Hughes, Baldwin would praise the older man's art as essential to his own understanding of Harlem while he was growing up there.)

Hughes disliked literary pretentiousness, whether in Ellison, Baldwin, or

Melvin Tolson, a learnedly allusive ultra-modernist poet. His objection to Tolson's work probably grew after the reactionary white Southern critic and poet Allen Tate (who previously had refused to meet Hughes or any other black writer while in the South) lavishly praised Tolson's work even as he implicitly dismissed that of Hughes and other blacks. Writing to Bontemps about Tolson's *Harlem Gallery* (1965), Hughes cited arcane lines such as "O Cleobulus / O Thales, Solon, Periander, Bias, Chilo, / O Pittacus, / unriddle the pho[e]nix riddle of this" to ridicule both this kind of poetry and Tolson himself. "I say, MORE POWER TO YOU, MELVIN B.," Hughes chortled. "GO, JACK, GO! That Negro not only reads, but has read!" Nevertheless, Hughes included Tolson in his anthologies—although in one letter here he asks Tolson to change a poem slightly to make it clearer to the reader. (Tolson did so.)

The time would come, ironically, when militant blacks would find Hughes's poetry too tame for their taste. One sticking point would be his relationship with LeRoi Jones, a gifted poet and editor. Jones would change his name to Amiri Baraka as he became the undoubted leader of the aggressive Black Arts movement starting around 1965. Hughes had actively sought out and praised Jones starting in the late 1950s, while Jones was still living with his white wife, Hettie Cohen, in Greenwich Village. Out of the blue, Jones received a fan letter from Hughes that left him amazed and grateful. By 1965, however, Hughes saw Jones somewhat differently. That year, Hughes's column "That Boy LeRoi" in the *New York Post* disapproved of Jones's more shocking, antiwhite new plays, notably *The Toilet*, which is set in a urinal at a boys' school. The column upset some blacks. Addressing one protester, Hughes defended himself with his characteristic grace. "More power to you, too," he replied (at three in the morning, he noted), "for so frankly expressing your opinions. It would be a sad day if the young writers all agreed with the old."

We see Hughes's spirit of inclusiveness again in his many letters sent to Africa as colonial rule ended there, sometimes after bloodshed, in the 1950s and 1960s; or, in the case of South Africa, when the antiapartheid cause badly needed foreign allies. In the course of editing timely anthologies such as *An African Treasury* (1960), or as a judge in literary competitions sponsored by *Drum* magazine of South Africa, he exchanged letters regularly with Africans. At his home, he received so many visiting African writers sent by the United States Information Agency (USIA) that he worried that he had become, unpaid, "the official host of Harlem." He toured Africa privately and on behalf of the United States. (In contrast, Ralph Ellison, for example, declined all invitations to visit Africa.) Hughes was proud to be present in 1960 when Benjamin "Zik" Azikiwe, a former schoolmate at Lincoln University, was sworn in as the first governor-general of independent Nigeria. He corresponded with and met writers whose work would become celebrated, including the poet and president of Senegal, Léopold Sédar Senghor, who saw Hughes's early work as a major inspiration for the Negritude cultural movement he helped to launch; from Nigeria, the novelist Chinua Achebe and the future Nobel Prize winner Wole Soyinka; from South Africa, Ezekiel Mphahlele, Bloke Modisane, and Peter Abrahams; and from Kenya, Ngugi wa Thiong'o. Hughes was a near-legendary figure to these men, but he reached out to them simply as one writer to another. After reading Abrahams's autobiography, *Tell Freedom* (1954), in galleys, he sent Abrahams, still largely unknown, a fan letter. "It's all wonderful!" he gushed. "I love that book! So alive and immediate and real and moving!"

He also reached out to "ordinary" folks in Africa. Impatient with pomp and circumstance amid poverty and repression, he sneered in private at Emperor Haile Selassie of Ethiopia, who presented Hughes with a gold medal in Addis Ababa after Hughes recited a poem he had written in his honor; but Hughes had done so only because U.S. diplomats had begged him to write it. With African commoners he was eager to be friends. As a result, a young Nigerian policeman named Sunday Osuya later became a legatee in Hughes's will. His letters to and about Africans underscore the bond he felt with a continent he had first visited when he was twenty-one. Africa was integral to his broad sense of black identity as well as his expansive sense of humanity. Hughes had kept the faith even as many other black Americans, ashamed of Africa because of Hollywood's consistently demeaning images, wanted little or nothing to do with the "Dark Continent."

If Hughes had to learn about the complexities of black culture, he faced a similar challenge with whites although he had lived among them all of his life. His relationship to them took on a new aspect once he became a grown man and one determined to be a writer. Again and again, he would have to depend, during decades of lawful bigotry in America, on the kindness and the fairness of white strangers as he negotiated the tricky, often treacherous territory of publishers, editors, producers, agents, reviewers, book buyers, booksellers, foundations, and so on. Undoubtedly, Hughes was lucky to have come of age in the decade following World War I. With the war over, a substantial part of the nation began to relax some of its inhibitions and to question some of its viler prejudices. The rising popularity of the blues and jazz, and of musicians such as Louis Armstrong, Duke Ellington, Bessie Smith, and George Gershwin, helped to propel this change. Contradictions, of course, abounded. The Jazz Age was also the era of Prohibition. Racist atrocities, especially lynching, still went on, often with impunity. But certain doors began to crack open in the 1920s that had been shut tight to blacks.

Hughes tapped on these doors carefully but with some confidence. He knew some whites intimately and he had succeeded among them in school. Unlike most blacks, he had never attended a Jim Crow school (Lincoln University did not bar white students, and all of its professors were white). At high school in Cleveland his classmates were mainly white Christians and Jews of immigrant stock; his best friend had been a Polish American boy. But even in college he had felt the sting of racial injustice. In 1921, Columbia had assigned him a room in Hartley Hall only because someone on its staff had blundered. The university let in a tiny number of blacks annually but denied them university housing. At Harvard a year later, President A. Lawrence Lowell publicly vowed to bar blacks from the school altogether rather than allow them to live with whites in the dormitories. It is essential to acknowledge that Hughes, like virtually every other black American, faced racism in one form or another almost every day of his life, even after the Supreme Court in 1954 in effect decreed an end to segregation.

In the 1920s, perhaps the key challenge for an ambitious but principled "Negro" was how to get ahead without losing one's self-respect. Hughes's letters show him proceeding in this regard with an almost princely confidence touched by an appropriate humility. He seemed assured and optimistic when many other blacks were cynical and bitter. When rebuffed, he seemed to shrug off insults. He chose to look ahead. His friendship with the wealthy, sophisticated, and ebullient Carl Van Vechten proved crucial to his future. From their second meeting, when Hughes accepted a poetry prize at a gala event in Manhattan in 1925, they quickly bonded. Within days, Van Vechten had convinced his own publisher, Alfred A. Knopf, to bring out Hughes's first book, *The Weary Blues* (1926). Thereafter, Knopf would be Hughes's main publisher, and Van Vechten would be his friend for life.

Van Vechten's championing of racial integration and of black writers and musicians in particular had been sudden; by 1925 he had become "violently interested in Negroes," he admitted. "It was almost an addiction." Although some blacks, cynical about smiling whites in general, shunned him, Hughes did not. In 1925, when Van Vechten begged for help in preparing an article for *Vanity Fair* on the blues, about which he knew almost nothing, Hughes sent him detailed advice even as Countee Cullen, for one, kept his distance ("I know," he snidely wrote a friend, "that Carl is coining money out of the niggers"). The letters between Hughes and Van Vechten are as entertaining as they are informative. If the colorful Van Vechten set the basic tone, Hughes responded in kind. He even replicated the fey verbal bouquets his friend tossed in closing many letters. "Tulips and jonquils to you!" Hughes signed off once in 1955, more than thirty years after they first met. But Hughes was no sycophant. From the start he showed that he saw them as virtual equals—and himself as superior at times, as when he stated flatly in 1925 that his own taste in the blues was more complex than his friend's ("you like best the lighter ones . . . and I prefer the moanin' ones"). At times they disagreed. In 1933, Van Vechten advised Knopf not to publish a new book of verse Hughes had proposed. Bluntly he wrote Hughes that "the revolutionary poems seem very weak to me. . . . I think in ten years, whatever the social outcome, you will be ashamed of these." No matter—the friendship endured. Now and then Van Vechten saved Hughes by lending him money. His help was crucial in 1938, for example, when Hughes's mother died and he couldn't afford to bury her. (Hughes repaid his loans as soon as he could.)

Another important white friend, with lots of letters between them, was Noël Sullivan of California. Meeting first in 1933 in San Francisco, where Sullivan owned a mansion, they remained friends until Sullivan's death in 1956. He encouraged Hughes to spend a year (1933–1934) living rent-free in a cottage he owned in Carmel. There, Hughes finished the embittered collection of short stories *The Ways of White Folks* (1934). In dedicating the book to Sullivan, Hughes took its epigraph from one of the stories: *"The ways of white folks, I mean some white folks. . . ."* Later, Sullivan sheltered him again for more than a year when Hughes, nearly destitute, was being hounded by his right-wing opponents. Unlike Hughes, Sullivan was a religious man, a Roman Catholic. Liberal on subjects such as civil rights, the death penalty, and cruelty to animals, he was relatively conservative about global politics. However, Sullivan saw Hughes as a brave artist of uncommon integrity, just as Hughes appreciated Sullivan's humanity and generosity.

Perhaps the most important of Hughes's extended contacts with the white world involved editors and publishers. Except for a few newspapers and magazines, all of his publishers were white. Letters show that he had trouble with blacks as well as whites. The black *Chicago Defender* newspaper, where he had a weekly column for over twenty years, tried at one point to break his contract and pay him less because they could sign up syndicated white columnists at a much cheaper rate. For a while, the *Defender* simply stopped paying him. Editors at *The Crisis*, on the other hand, sometimes ignored his wishes about the use of his poems. With white publishers the problems were different. On the whole, they didn't care, as he did, about reaching black readers as a distinct group. He knew that blacks bought far fewer books than whites did, but he wanted his publishers to try harder in this respect. He liked to point out, impishly, that black people would indeed buy books—if the books were brought to them, as he did on his reading tours. Hughes also disliked much of the work of the skilled white artists invariably chosen to illustrate his books. Often he found the drawings demeaning, if unintentionally so.

Undoubtedly his main publishing contact was Blanche Knopf, with whom he exchanged many letters. A brilliant woman living somewhat in the shadow of her lordly husband, Alfred, she signed up most of the writers, especially the foreigners, who made Knopf a prestigious as well as a profitable imprint. In 1925 she had given Hughes his first book contract mainly on Van Vechten's say-so, but she also published several other black authors at a time when many of the other major houses were still reluctant to do so. She edited his work herself when she could have passed him on to an assistant. However, their relationship had its rough patches, in which race and class played roles. After three books by Hughes, she rebuffed his proposal for a volume of his radical verse. (Resentful, Hughes addressed his next letter to "Mrs. Knopf" rather than to his customary "Blanche.") Nevertheless, they worked together smoothly on his next book, *The Ways of White Folks*, with Blanche Knopf unfazed by its bitter tone. A few years later, however, she riled Hughes again when she asked for deep cuts in his autobiography *The Big Sea*. Certain black personalities who meant much to him were of much less consequence to her and, presumably, to the book buyers Knopf depended on, and she wanted them pruned from the text. Backed by Van Vechten, Hughes resisted Mrs. Knopf's request while making some cuts. In the early 1950s, with his books of verse selling weakly, she refused *Montage of a Dream Deferred* (Holt, 1951). She also declined his request for a "Selected Poems" volume—although she brought it out later, in 1959. She also turned down his outline for another volume of autobiography, which later earned good reviews as *I Wonder as I Wander* (Rinehart, 1956).

Despite these rebuffs, Hughes returned to Knopf whenever Mrs. Knopf wanted him back. He knew how much she and her firm had done for his career. Around 1960, after she took over the leadership of the company, she passed Hughes on to an extremely able younger editor, Judith Jones. Together, Hughes and Jones produced his experimental book-length poem *Ask Your Mama: 12 Moods for Jazz* (1961), in a colorful, somewhat complex format that he loved. Jones also saw into print, just after he died, Hughes's snarling *The Panther and the Lash: Poems for Our Times* (1967).

While his way with publishers was relatively smooth, Hughes's dealings with other aspects of the white world were vexed by all sorts of controversies. Some were troubles endemic to the world of art, especially the stage; some were disputes of a political sort that threatened to silence him as an artist; and some, also potentially destructive, were of a more intimate kind.

Much of the trouble came from Hughes's almost fatal attraction to the stage. Constantly at work on dramas, comedies, operas, cantatas, traditional musicals, gospel musicals (a form he said he invented), and the like, he found himself often lunging from one mini-crisis to another. In a 1953 letter to James Baldwin he warned the novelist: "If you want to die, be disturbed, maladjusted, neurotic, and psychotic, disappointed, and disjointed, just write plays! Go ahead!" His letters are rich in evidence of such volatility. They start wrenchingly with Zora Neale Hurston but also include his clashes four years later with Martin Jones, the bigoted white producer of Hughes's first Broadway play, *Mulatto* (1935). Jones made sensational, shabby changes to the script, dared to list himself as its coauthor, and treated Hughes with open contempt. After the first Broadway performance he threw the traditional party but invited neither Hughes nor the star of the show, Rose McClendon, who was the only other black person involved in the production (whites played the other black roles). He also refused to pay Hughes even as the show ran and ran on Broadway. Finally he tendered through an agent a check to Hughes for $88.50, as if to say that Hughes was lucky to get any money at all.

Working with the composer Kurt Weill and the playwright Elmer Rice on the Broadway opera *Street Scene* (1947), Hughes basked in its success until a sudden dispute with Rice over royalties from the lyrics angered him, especially since his contracted share of the profits, 2 percent, was unusually low for a Broadway lyricist. Although Hughes fought Rice over his claims, he was as diplomatic as ever in doing so. Eventually he and Rice reached an agreement. Not so with the moody black composer William Grant Still. For years their relationship had been cordial. "Really, you are unique among collaborators," Still had lauded Hughes in 1945. But their friendship died in 1949 just after their opera *Troubled Island*, about the Haitian Revolution, opened at the City Center in New York. When newspaper critics panned Still's music as derivative and lackluster, he took out his resentment on Hughes by refusing to speak to him. Hughes was hurt but not astonished. Writing to Bontemps in

1948 about Still and another composer with whom he was working, Hughes noted dryly: "Both of my opera people are behaving as though they smoked reefers between every note. . . . I am not given to displaying temperament. I just sit calmly and let them blow their tops."

That other composer was the German émigré Jan Meyerowitz. Their first opera, *The Barrier,* based on the play *Mulatto,* reached Broadway in 1950 but flopped there. Nevertheless, the men kept working on other projects. Over the years, Hughes was called upon to weather Meyerowitz's many stormy fits of rage. (Hughes's respected drama agent dumped Hughes as a client after she refused to deal anymore with Meyerowitz.) Finally, in a 1960 letter, Hughes told Meyerowitz that he was done working as a librettist—although, characteristically, he made no mention of his friend's outbursts. "I see no point," he wrote instead, "in spending long hours of thought, and weeks of writing seeking poetic phrases and just the right word—and then not enough of the librettist's lines are heard for anybody to know what is being sung. . . . And NO money is made."

Politics, however, presented perhaps the most dangerous threats to Hughes's career. He had been a socialist sympathizer ever since high school in Cleveland, when delirious kids at Central High, most of them of East European immigrant stock, had celebrated the 1917 Bolshevik Revolution in Russia by parading a red flag around the grounds. His radicalism in the 1930s led him to compose fierce poems—and, later, to a campaign of retribution waged against him by anticommunists. It began in earnest in 1940 with the noisy picketing of a major literary luncheon at a hotel in Pasadena, California, intended to capitalize on the appearance of *The Big Sea.* Frightened, the sponsors canceled the event on the day itself. His enemies tried to make sure that Hughes paid dearly for poems such as "Goodbye Christ," "Good Morning Revolution," and "One More 'S' in the U.S.A." ("Put one more s in the U.S.A. / To make it Soviet"). In 1953, summoned before Senator Joseph McCarthy's feared subcommittee, Hughes was forced to surrender. In a televised hearing, he repudiated his radical past. His sheer relief when the ordeal was over comes through in a letter he sent to Frank D. Reeves, his main lawyer in Washington. "No words—and certainly no money," Hughes wrote, "(even were it a million dollars) could in any sense express to you my gratitude or from me repay you for what you've done for me in a time of emergency. Without your able help and kind, considerate, patient, and wise counsel, I would have been a lost ball in the high weeds or, to mix metaphors, a dead duck among the cherry blossoms!"

This letter gives us a glimpse of the deep-seated sense of vulnerability that

Hughes's persistent graciousness never fully concealed. On the whole, his letters, especially after he became a radical, give only an oblique sense of his emotional core, insofar as one can identify with certainty that core in anyone. As for intimate feelings, we have little to go on. We have a few mildly romantic letters to or about women, notably those to Sylvia "Si-Lan" Chen (Leyda), the Trinidad-born dancer he met in Moscow in 1932–1933 and who later married the noted American film historian Jay Leyda and settled in America. But such letters don't tell us much. The absence of love letters is puzzling. Was Hughes's devotion to his work so complete that he had no time for love? Did he destroy such letters, denying them tenure at Yale? Or did he ask others to destroy them upon his death? (No one has said that he did so.) In any event, we have a paucity of love letters to women, and none to men, if Hughes ever wrote any of those.

In this respect, perhaps the most telling documents here are a series of drafts of letters Hughes wrote around 1930. These drafts suggest depths of self-doubt and self-loathing seen nowhere else in his correspondence— although they are clearly reflected in many of his poems. Critics have generally ignored these bleaker, nonracial, and nonpolitical poems even though they make up a substantial part of Hughes's poetic output. Works such as "Exits" (1924) or "A House in Taos" (1926) reflect the stark quality of emotional or existential bleakness with which Hughes lived—and fought—much of his life.

These drafts (the letters themselves are lost) were addressed to the major patron of his life, the wealthy, elderly, inspiring, but also somewhat terrifying Mrs. Charlotte Mason, or "Godmother," as she made some of her dependents call her. For at least two years Mrs. Mason lavished money, praise, and what seemed like love on Langston. She gave him a generous monthly stipend, decked him out in fine clothes, entertained him at her luxurious home on Park Avenue, visited him at Lincoln University when he studied there, and let him squire her to fancy Manhattan functions such as the opera. All the while, she sought to drive him to artistic heights that would reflect what she, a prophet, saw as the unique spiritual essence of Africa.

Hughes evidently fell in love with Mrs. Mason, as a son loves his mother. (His relationship with his real mother was almost always vexed, and he perhaps hated her, just as he hated his father.) And when Mrs. Mason suddenly threw him out, without a real explanation, he became violently ill. Cast off, he pleaded desperately for reinstatement. "I am not wise, Godmother," Hughes wrote in one particularly agonized appeal. "The inner soul is simple as a fool, sensitive as a sheltered child, at odds too often with the reasons of the mind, a coward hiding in the dark, wrapping itself in the cloak of art when, too sick with loneliness, it must go out for air or die. The soul is deaf and dumb, and the body cannot speak for it. . . . The body lies too often to itself. The soul looks on in silence—and moves away. There are too many things it does not understand." But Godmother never changed her mind. Broken, Hughes spent months recovering from this crisis—if indeed he ever recovered fully from it.

Selected Letters of Langston Hughes offers a body of writing invaluable to our understanding of a writer once seen by critics as essentially shallow. To most of them, he was at best a charming brown minstrel boy who, going off to the big war against white racism, beat his drum bravely but plaintively, ineffectually. They judged him as lacking a complex inner life and the ability to produce enduring art.

The truth, as his letters suggest, is that Hughes's life was a struggle that he won. He emerged victorious by virtue of his unfailing commitment to art, his unconditional devotion to black America, and his democratic desire to embrace all people. He created a body of work that is uneven in quality, to be sure, but also invaluable in the end. He also possessed a compelling emotional and intellectual integrity. His brief poem "Personal," which forms the epigraph to this introduction, was written near the middle of his life. In its modest way it captures something essential about his sense of himself. It suggests a being living afloat in a dangerous but also wondrous world. He lives on, buoyed both by a sense of the power of the uncanny absolute and also by his faith in the redeeming power of artistic language, as well as the integrity of honest silence.

Editorial Preface

The correspondence of Langston Hughes is so vast that it could easily fill almost twenty large volumes. Given the cold realities of modern scholarly publication, it is highly unlikely that anyone will attempt in the foreseeable future a project to publish all of these letters. Instead, we offer here a single volume, carefully chosen. Selecting from such riches was not an easy task. We made our decisions about what to include and what to exclude keeping in mind the goal of offering "a life in letters." We aimed to create an epistolary companion to the life story Hughes tells in his autobiographical works, *The Big Sea* and *I Wonder as I Wander* (although these works go only up to about 1938, and so do not cover the three decades before his death in 1967), as well as biographical work by, most prominently, Arnold Rampersad and Faith Berry. We want these letters to illuminate as clearly as possible the wonderfully rich and valuable life that Hughes lived. The main themes of his poetry, plays, and fiction—indeed, of all his writing—are also the main themes we sought to capture here. To read the letters written by Hughes as he lived his life from day to day, month to month, year to year, is crucially important to any true understanding of his life and art. Ideally, the letters together comprise a continuously fresh perspective on Hughes by sharing with the reader the intimacy of his immediate involvement in events as they were happening.

We also aimed for representativeness over the course of his artistic career, and so decided to begin in the year 1921, the year Hughes published "The Negro Speaks of Rivers," his first poem in a national journal. Three correspondents stand out above all others by virtue of the quantity of letters he sent to them: Carl Van Vechten, Noël Sullivan, and Arna Bontemps. But the amazing vitality and variety of Hughes's life and career insist on many other voices being heard, and variety is of the essence here. Many important persons enter and then exit fairly quickly, leaving their mark behind. Our first letter here is from Hughes to his father, a man he hated and with whom he eventually was forced to break. The writers Countee Cullen and Alain Locke enrich the early 1920s but then become less frequent or vanish altogether. Other fascinating characters take their place, including Zora Neale Hurston, Amy Spingarn, Claude McKay, Blanche Knopf, Ezra Pound, Maxim Lieber, Richard Wright, Margaret Walker Alexander, Elmer Rice, Carl Sandburg, Gwendolyn Brooks, James Baldwin, Cassius Clay (Muhammad Ali), LeRoi Jones (Amiri Baraka), Judith Jones, Martin Luther King, Jr., and Wole Soyinka. These are only a sampling from the long list of Hughes's acquaintances, collaborators, editors, agents, antagonists, and friends to whom he sent letters over the course of his life.

Unfortunately, some of Hughes's most desirable letters have vanished. He did not begin to keep carbon copies of his letters in a systematic fashion until the 1940s, when he started sending material regularly to Yale for the James Weldon Johnson Memorial Collection of Negro Arts and Letters founded by Carl Van Vechten in 1941. Except for a few copies he saved, most of his letters to the extraordinary Zora Neale Hurston are lost, a casualty perhaps of her anger at him around 1931, when she accused him of dishonesty over the authorship of a play. (Her letters to him, on the other hand, are safely housed in his papers at Yale.) In another case, his letters to their patron Charlotte Mason, with whom he had perhaps the most harrowing relationship of his life, are also lost. Fortunately, Hughes kept some drafts of these letters, drafts without parallel in revealing the depths of his anguish and his fears about himself. We have chosen to publish some of those drafts. We have been careful here to include all evidence of Hughes's alterations of his texts, including his scratching out of words or even lines, as he struggled to express himself under enormous personal pressure. A draft of a letter to the poet Vachel Lindsay also appears with all of Hughes's in-process editing and rewriting of words and lines shown.

Inevitably some readers will think that certain themes and personalities have been neglected or misrepresented in what is necessarily a small selection. They will also have to deal with certain hard truths about Hughes's life. For example, although several of his poems are blisteringly radical, he rarely displayed that anger or revolutionary zeal in his correspondence except in the case of some letters he sent from the Soviet Union in the early 1930s. On the rare occasions in which he did express himself as a radical in letters, we have made every effort to include rather than exclude such evidence. Readers looking for exposure of Hughes's sexual identity and experience may also be disappointed. Hughes virtually never revealed anything of such an intimate nature in the letters that have survived. We also have no evidence whatsoever that he censored or destroyed any letters he received, or that other people destroyed or suppressed revealing letters that he sent them.

Hughes was by no means fastidious about most of the letters he sent out, unless they were strictly about business. This lack of fastidiousness is part of the charm and, indeed, the integrity of the man. However, this "looseness" often presents editorial challenges. Where possible, we have transcribed here the text of the original letter that Hughes wrote and put in the mail. In certain instances, as stated, we have been compelled to use carbon copies preserved by him in his papers at Yale. Most were written on a typewriter. For letters where Hughes made a handwritten correction or addition, we have enclosed this text with angle brackets: < >. Our editorial insertions of words or punctuation into the text of the letter are enclosed in vertical bars: | |. At the beginning of each letter, we indicate our source for the text. "ALS" signifies an autograph (handwritten) letter signed by Hughes; "AL" a handwritten letter unsigned; "TLS" a typed letter signed; and "TL" a typed letter unsigned.

We tried to let Hughes's letters stand as he wrote them. Each letter appears in its entirety; all occurrences of ellipses and serial periods within the letters are Hughes's own punctuation. We have made silent corrections only when it was clear Hughes had unintentionally misspelled a word or the name of a person or place, for example. Our guiding principle in making these silent corrections has been to do so when we believed that leaving the letters untouched would mislead the reader or otherwise mar his or her experience of the letters. With thousands of extant letters and with space at a premium, it did not seem appropriate for us to include comprehensive textual and annotative material here. However, we also have made it an absolute priority to identify, wherever we could do so, virtually each of the individuals and incidents mentioned in the letters, the better to illustrate the world in which Hughes lived.

We have not depended unquestioningly on the work of earlier scholars working in Hughes's letters, and in every case have relied on our own firsthand research to ascertain the accuracy of the material. Nevertheless, we are grateful to them for their pioneering efforts. They include the late Charles Nichols, who edited a selection of letters between Bontemps and Hughes (published in 1980); Emily Bernard, who did the same with letters between Hughes and Carl Van Vechten (2001); and Shane Graham and John Walters, whose center of interest was Hughes's correspondence with certain South African writers (2010). Some of the letters here appeared in these earlier editions. We hope that other editors will bring their skills to bear on Hughes's correspondence so that the world can profit as much as possible from his extraordinary efforts to express himself intimately as a poet, to illuminate black American culture and also American culture in general, and to encourage his ideal vision of human dignity and unity.

One sustaining hope in imagining this project and carrying it on through the years of its duration is that in these letters you will meet the author of his beloved poem of 1924 "I, Too." The poem begins: "I, too, sing America." Hughes indeed sang America, and he sang America in his letters as well as in his verse.

I, too, sing America.

I am the darker brother.
They send me to eat in the kitchen
When company comes,
But I laugh,
And eat well,
And grow strong.

Tomorrow,
I'll be at the table
When company comes.
Nobody'll dare
Say to me,
"Eat in the kitchen,"
Then.

Besides,
They'll see how beautiful I am
And be ashamed—

I, too, am America.

PART I

We Have Tomorrow

1921 to 1931

Hotel America

145-155 WEST 47TH STREET

New York

September 5, 1921

Dear father:

I arrived last night after a fine trip. The sea was very calm all the way and none of the passengers were sea-sick so we enjoyed the voyage. I am here at the Hotel America for a day only as the boat arrived so late yesterday that the inspection was not passed untill nearly 10 P.M. and, not knowing New York, I came here with a number of other travelers from Mexico and Cuba as this Hotel is the center of Spanish speaking travelers. This morning, however, I found a room at the colored Y.M.C.A at 181 West 135th St. where you can write me, Room 422. I shall not stay there long if I can find any place cheaper as they charge $7.00 a week, but the secretary tells me that it is

Hotel America

145-155 WEST 47TH STREET

DIRECCION CABLEGRAFICA
"BERUTICH"

EXECUTIVE OFFICE

JUAN M. BERUTICH,
MANAGER

New York

difficult to find anything much cheaper in a decent house as Harlem is very crowded and those having rooms to rent charge high. He will help me, tho, to find another place, unless I can enter the school dormitory soon. Today being Labor Day the University is closed so I can find out nothing until tomorrow, when I shall go up there. However send my mail to the Y.M.C.A. address until I get in school and if there are any letters in Toluca for me send them, too, please. I will write you again tomorrow giving you the name of a bank where you may send the money and tell you whether I am to be admitted or not.

Mr. Medina was at the docks with me in Vera Cruz. His brother was to leave for Spain on the 1st of this month.

Write soon.

Love,
James Langston Hughes

Langston Hughes, c. 1924. Portrait by
James L. Allen

I've known rivers:
Ancient, dusky rivers.

My soul has grown deep like the rivers.
—"THE NEGRO SPEAKS OF RIVERS," 1921

Nineteen years old, Langston Hughes published "The Negro
Speaks of Rivers" in the June 1921 issue of *The Crisis*. For the
first time, his work appeared in a national journal. In a real sense,
his career as a writer had begun. "The Negro Speaks of Rivers" would
become his signature poem. He usually chose it to end each of his
many public readings in the years to come.

In September of that year, Hughes arrived in New York City to
attend Columbia University. He did so with financial support from his
father, who had suddenly reentered his life in 1919 after many years

of estrangement. Soon after his birth in Joplin, Missouri, in 1902, his father moved to Mexico. An attempted reconciliation in Mexico failed, and Hughes's parents divorced when he was five. With his mother often away, he spent most of his childhood in the care of his grandmother in Lawrence, Kansas. After her death in 1915, he joined his mother and her second husband in Lincoln, Illinois, and then in Cleveland, Ohio. There he attended Central High School (1916–1920), where he published his first poems and stories in the school magazine. In 1921, after a year living with his father in Toluca, Mexico, following his high school graduation, he set off to attend Columbia.

Hughes lasted only one year (1921–1922) at Columbia, which he found generally unfriendly, before withdrawing from the school. He then worked at various odd jobs, including delivering flowers in Manhattan and as a gardener on a vegetable farm on Staten Island. He also sought out members of the African American community in Harlem, which later would become central to his life. From 1921 until 1923, living in or near New York City, he worked steadily at his verse even as he befriended other gifted African American writers such as Jessie Fauset, Countee Cullen, and Alain Locke of Washington, D.C.

TO JAMES NATHANIEL HUGHES   [ALS]

[On Hotel America, 145-155 West 47th Street *stationery*]

September 5, 1921

Dear father:*

I arrived last night after a fine trip. The sea was very calm all the way and none of the passengers were sea-sick so we enjoyed the voyage. I am here at the Hotel America for a day only as the boat arrived so late yesterday that the inspection was not passed until nearly 10 P. M. and, not knowing New York, I came here with a number of other travelers from Mexico and Cuba as this Hotel is the center of Spanish speaking travelers. This morning, however, I found a room at the colored Y.M.C.A. at 181 West 135th St. where you can write

------

* In 1903, James Nathaniel Hughes (1871–1934) began work at the American-owned Pullman Company in Mexico City. Fired without explanation in 1907, he moved to Toluca in 1909 to work for the American-owned Sultepec Electric Light and Power Company. Eventually, he owned property in Mexico City, a house in Toluca, and a ranch in the mountains nearby.

me, Room 422. I shall not stay there long if I can find any place cheaper as they charge $7.00 a week, but the secretary tells me that it is difficult to find anything much cheaper in a decent house as Harlem is very crowded and those having rooms to rent charge high. He will help me, tho, to find another place, unless I can enter the school dormitory soon. Today being Labor Day the University is closed so I can find out nothing until tomorrow, when I shall go up there, however, send my mail to the Y.M.C.A. address until I get in school and if there are any letters in Toluca* for me send them, too, please. I will write you again tomorrow giving you the name of a bank where you may send the money and tell you whether I am to be admitted or not.

Mr. Medina was at the docks with me in Vera Cruz. His brother was to leave for Spain on the 1st of this month.

Write soon.

Love,
James Langston Hughes

TO JAMES NATHANIEL HUGHES   [ALS]

Oct. 6, 1921

Dear father,

I have received no letters from you whatever since being here. The one in which you say you sent the money has not been received in New York according to the Post Office. After paying my preliminary fees and a twenty-five dollar deposit on my dormitory room for ten days, which was up yesterday, I had nothing left to pay on my tuition and the balance due on my room which I was lucky enough to get. Expecting to receive money from you at any moment I procured a postponement of payment until Oct. 3 and then when nothing came had to ask for another postponement until Wednesday when my dormitory fees were also due. I sent you a telegram on Saturday and another on Tuesday from which I received no answers, so, unable to wait any longer, I called upon Mr. C. L. Rossiter† at his offices, explained matters, and he was

---

* His father, who wanted Langston to become an engineer and settle in Mexico, agreed to fund one year of study at Columbia, with the prospect of further support if he did well as a student. Father and son got along poorly. Writing about the summer of 1919, which he had spent with his father in Toluca, Hughes later declared in *The Big Sea* that it was "the most miserable I have ever known. I did not hear from my mother for several weeks. I did not like my father. And I did not know what to do about either of them."

† C. L. Rossiter was a New York–based executive of the Sultepec Electric Light and Power Company.

kind enough to send a check for $100 and a personal letter to the school asking them to grant me another postponement, which they did until Oct. 20. The money loaned by Mr. Rossiter covered my dormitory fee and $37.50 of my tuition, leaving $120.50 to be paid. I was also compelled to borrow $10 from a person I met here in order to eat and buy the most necessary books, altho there are several such as the "Physics" which cost 3.00, which I cannot get until I receive money, and so am afraid I shall be behind in my classes. Please send me enough to pay the remainder of my fees before the twentieth for if I have to drop the course, all the amounts I have paid will be lost. It is very strange about your registered letter. If you will send me the number of your stub the P.O. here may be able to trace it. Please write to Mr. Rossiter about the money he let me have due to Mr. Danley's[*] signature on my application. His address is 30 Vesey St. I am taking dinner with a family I met in Cleveland until I can afford to eat here at school where board averages about seven a week. I hope to hear from you at once as I wish to pay back the money I have borrowed and buy my books and laboratory materials. In my next letter I will let you know about the school, and the exact amounts paid for fees, books, etc. Now I must go to class. Write me at 111 Hartley Hall, Columbia University.

Your son,
Langston Hughes

TO JAMES NATHANIEL HUGHES [ALS]
[On Hartley Hall, Columbia University, New York stationery]

October 27, 1921.

Dear Father:

Your letter of 13 inst. was received and I was certainly very glad to hear from you. The Post Office here has not yet received your registered letter as I have just inquired there, as well as at the Y. M. C. A. I think it must have gotten lost. It cannot be traced from this end as the P.O. here has no record of its arrival. I have not received the forwarded letter either but they do not matter. If you cannot trace the drafts and wish to send me the duplicates I will pay Mr. Rossiter and deposit the remainder with the school until I need it, as they keep funds for the students here.

Mrs. Danley was very kind about delivering the $250. She came over here

---

[*] R. J. M. Danley, another official of the Sultepec Electric Light and Power Company, was an American colleague of James Hughes in Mexico. He and his wife also made a personal loan to Hughes of $250 (see letter dated October 27, 1921).

to the University but could not find me, so left a note which I did not get until two days later as I was not expecting to receive letters at the school and had not called at the Office. However, I went to her home in Brooklyn where she had it for me.

The poem of mine in the June "Crisis" was copied in the "Literary Digest" of July 2 on their poetry page.* I am unable to get an old number or would |have| sent it to you. It was also copied by the "Topeka Daily Capital." I understand that some other newspapers published it, too, but I have not seen them. I just received today an invitation from Miss Fauset, Literary Editor of "The Crisis," to take lunch with her next Tuesday.†

I am trying out for "The Spectator," the daily newspaper published here at Columbia.‡ The candidates receive 3 classes a week in newspaper work free.

I hope to hear from you soon.

Affectionately,
Langston Hughes

TO JAMES NATHANIEL HUGHES [ALS]

[On Hartley Hall, Columbia University, New York *stationery]*

February 14, 1922.

Dear Father:

I am sorry to tell you that the draft for $300 which you sent me on December 26 will not be sufficient to last me through the present term. I have now only enough money for my expenses until the end of March. Unless you are able to help me then, please send a letter to the Dean of the College asking that I be allowed to withdraw. I cannot do my best work here as long as I have to worry

---

* Founded in 1910 by W. E. B. Du Bois (1868–1963), *The Crisis* is the monthly magazine of the National Association for the Advancement of Colored People (NAACP). This appearance marked Hughes's first publication in a national magazine with an adult readership (in January, his poems "Fairies" and "Winter Sweetness" had appeared in *The Brownies' Book*, a magazine for black children, with ties to *The Crisis*). The poem was reprinted later that year in *The Literary Digest*, which had a mainly white readership.

† Jessie Redmon Fauset (1882–1961) was the literary editor of *The Crisis* from 1919 to 1926, and the author of *There Is Confusion* (1924) and three other novels. Hughes wrote in *The Big Sea* that Fauset, along with Charles S. Johnson and Alain Locke, had "midwifed the so-called New Negro literature into being. Kind and critical—but not too critical for the young—they nursed us along until our books were born."

‡ The student-run Columbia University *Spectator* published four poems by Hughes using the pseudonym "LANGHU" or "LANG-HU." However, as Hughes wrote in *The Big Sea*, "when I tried out for the *Spectator,* they assigned me to gather frat house and society news, an assignment impossible for a colored boy to fill, as they knew."

about my expenses, work after school, and stay up half the night washing my clothes. As this may be my last year in college I should like to get all that I can out of it and make a good record in case I should get a chance to return or to enter another school.

I did very well last term. According to my French instructor, my paper, which received an "A" mark, was the best one given to him in the final examinations. I received an "A-" on my term's report. In Contemporary Civilization I also received an "A" on the three hour examination. It gave me a B+ on the report. As you will see when you receive it, my other marks were a "B" in English, a "B" in Physical Education, a "B-" in Oral French and a "C" in Phy. Ed A3 (Hygiene). I have been chosen this term as a member of a picked group of students (supposed to be the best) who are to do more advanced work in English than the other pupils, and are to receive the best instructors.

Have you read "Batouala?" You know the work of René Maran,* the Negro, who received the Prix de Goncourt lately in France and is being so widely discussed. I have just borrowed a copy from Mr. Dill† and find its French not hard to read.

I hope I shall be able to remain here until June.

Sincerely,
Your Son,
Langston.

TO JAMES NATHANIEL HUGHES   [ALS]

March 2, 1922

Dear Father: I have your letter of Feb. 21. Enclosed you will find the itemized statement which you wish and also a letter which I received from the Dean

---

* When the French writer René Maran (1887–1960) received the Prix Goncourt in 1921 for his novel *Batouala*, he became the first person of African descent to win it. Since 1903, the Prix Goncourt has been awarded annually for the best new book of prose written in French. Hughes would meet Maran in Paris in 1924 (see letter dated July 4, 1924).

† Augustus Granville Dill (1881–1956) was the Harvard-educated business manager of *The Crisis* until 1928, when his mentor W. E. B. Du Bois summarily fired him after his arrest by the police for alleged homosexual activities. In *The Big Sea*, Hughes loyally described Dill as "a short, voluble man of middle-age who, besides running the magazine, was a fine musician on the pipe organ and the *piano forte* (as he always said) as well. He attended the Community Church, where John Haynes Holmes preached, and sometimes played the organ for services there. He told them of my poetry, and that church was, I believe, the first church in which I was invited to read my poems."

showing that I have done good work here. The amounts which I received from you and which are not listed on the statement were used for food, laundry, and incidental expenses. I should need $150 to finish the term which ends June 14.

Please don't think that I am trying to cheat you or am spending your money foolishly. If you think that, I had rather you give me nothing. Besides I never like to ask you for funds because I feel that you do not wish or cannot afford to give them, as I know you care very little about my going to college here and that you are not interested in what I want to study. You probably think that I am a bad investment and that you have more valuable things in which to put your money, so, as I stated in my letter of February 14, if you are unable to or do not desire to keep me here until the end of term, please send a request for my withdrawal to the Dean immediately and the amounts which I have paid for tuition for the rest of the semester will be reimbursed to you. That is fair, is it not? I don't want to burden you if you can't keep me in school. Besides, I cannot study and worry at the same time about every cent of money I must spend.—Your magazine subscriptions have been paid, the $2.25 was sent to the firm in Chicago, and your several letters of the dates to which you referred were received.

Sincerely Yours,
Langston

TO JAMES NATHANIEL HUGHES [ALS]

2289 Richmond Avenue,
Staten Island, New York,
June 22, 1922.

Dear Father:
I was very glad to get your letter and to hear that you are able to be about again.[*]
I still have the one hundred dollars you sent me last which I will return to you if you need it. If not I will keep it for my classes next fall which I want to take in extension. I did rather well in college but I don't want to go back. My final grades were three "B's" and a "C". In trigonometry I failed. Columbia was

---

[*] In May, James Hughes suffered a severe stroke. Although he made a substantial recovery, his right arm remained paralyzed.

interesting.* Thanks for the year there. I am working on Staten Island for the summer but will be back in New York in the fall as I want to continue some of my classes in Columbia's extension. Next spring I hope to go to France. I wish I could come to Mexico, if I could be of any help to you, but I don't like Toluca. Take good care of yourself until you are well again and don't overwork even then. Don't send me anymore money. I have had enough; and do not worry about things—rest, get well.

Write to me soon. I hope you are regaining your health rapidly and that you will have completely recovered in a little while. Give my regards to the Fräu.† Tell her I would write her but I am afraid she wouldn't answer.

Affectionately, your son,

Langston.

TO JAMES NATHANIEL HUGHES [ALS]

2289 Richmond Avenue,
Staten Island, New York,
August 20, 1922.

Dear Father:

I have your letter of July 30th and was indeed glad to hear from you, but I am sorry to know that your arm does not seem to be improving with more rapidity. One must have patience though, I suppose.

Perhaps, by this time you have received the German paper which I sent you, but if not, its name, as nearly as I can spell it from memory is "Vossiche Zeitung."‡ The Fräu can probably tell you. It is a Berlin daily and my poem appeared as the conclusion to an article called "The American Negro" in the issue for Saturday, April 1st.

An interesting bit of news here at present is that Negro theatrical attractions are very much the vogue in New York now. After "Shuffle Along"§ closed

---

* In *The Big Sea*, Hughes wrote: "I had no intention of going further at Columbia. . . . I felt that I would never turn out to be what my father expected me to be in return for the amount he invested. So I wrote him and told him I was going to quit college and go to work on my own, and that he needn't send me any more money. He didn't. He didn't even write back."
† Bertha Schultz was James Hughes's housekeeper. She became his wife in January 1924.
‡ A German liberal newspaper published from 1911 to 1934.
§ The landmark musical *Shuffle Along*, which opened in 1921, helped to launch the Harlem Renaissance. It was written by Flournoy Miller and Aubrey Lyles, with music and lyrics by Noble Sissle (like Hughes, a graduate of Central High in Cleveland) and Eubie

a run of a year and two months (the record for a colored show), there have been four Negro companies playing in white theatres down town this summer, and one of them, after meeting with great success in a small house, has moved to the newest and, according to reports, the finest theatre in the city. "Shuffle Along" has gone to Boston for the summer. Then it will do Chicago, after which they have contracts for Europe. Its authors have signed to produce a play a year for the 63rd Street Theatre here for five years, besides doing numerous supper shows for the New York and Atlantic City cabarets. So the Negro theatrical world is booming. Bert

James Nathaniel Hughes, c. 1930

Williams, did you read in the papers, left some $200,000 according to his will.* Reports in Harlem say there is more, but it is being kept secret in order to avoid income tax.

Did I tell you that Miss Fauset has been reading my poems in the New York City high schools in her lectures on modern Negro poetry? They seem to take them seriously. Ha! Ha!

Please do not write me here after the third of next month as my month ends the tenth and I am returning to New York. What's my job here?—You'd never guess—farming!!! Yes, a real 43 acre farm for me to exercise my talents on.†

Love,

Langston

Blake. The four men comprised the first African American team to develop a successful Broadway show.

* Bert Williams (1874–1922) was one of America's greatest vaudeville stars. After the death of his partner, George Walker (c. 1873–1911), who had been a childhood friend of Hughes's mother in Lawrence, Kansas, Williams pursued a successful solo career. He joined the Ziegfeld Follies as its only black performer and became its highest-paid star.

† Despite his year at Columbia, the color line barred Hughes from many jobs before he was hired to work on a vegetable farm on Staten Island belonging to two Greek brothers and their wives. In *The Big Sea*, he wrote that they "didn't care what nationality you were just so you got up at five in the morning and worked all day until it was too dark to see the rows in the field." Despite the long hours, he found this job deeply satisfying.

TO ALAIN LOCKE   [ALS]

S.S. West Hassayampa,*
Jones Point, N. Y.
February 6, 1923.

Dear Mr. Locke:†

I have had your delightful letter for a long while and I have wanted to answer you sooner, but so many things have intervened, a bad cold and a birthday,—I am twenty-one! And then I am a terrible correspondent. But I should like to know you and I hope you'll write to me again.

It is too bad I am not living in New York anymore. I am missing so many interesting people. I am chasing dreams up here, though, and that's an infinitely more delightful occupation even than being in New York, where all my old dreams had been realized; college, (horrible place, but I wanted to go), Broadway and the theatres—delightful memories, Riverside Drive in the mists, and Harlem. A whirling year in New York! Now I want to go to Europe. Stay for a while in France, then live with the gypsies in Spain (wild dream, isn't it?) and see the bull-fights in Seville. My Spanish is good from having lived in Mexico and there's no sport in the world as lovely as a "corrida de toros," to those who like them.

Jeritza is wonderful, isn't she?‡ I fell in love with her last year and waited at the stage door for a smile and a rose. But have you seen Chaliapin in "Boris"?§ If you haven't, please do. It's the experience of a lifetime. And did you see the Moscow Art players?¶ I couldn't get in, so I comforted myself with seeing

---

* In mid-October of the previous year, Hughes had started to work as a mess boy at Jones Point. The U.S. Shipping Board mothballed a large fleet of vessels there (109 during Hughes's tenure) after World War I. Hughes served aboard the *Oronoke*, the *Bellbuckle*, and the *West Hassayampa*.

† With degrees from Harvard and some years at Oxford, where he had been a Rhodes scholar, Dr. Alain Locke (1886–1954) was the chair of the Department of Philosophy at Howard University in Washington, D.C., from 1921 until his retirement in 1953. His books include *The New Negro* (1925), *The Negro in Art* (1941), and (with Bernard J. Stern) *When Peoples Meet: A Study in Race and Culture Contacts* (1942). Sent Hughes's address by Countee Cullen, Locke wrote in February to tell him that each of Hughes's friends "insists on my knowing you. Some instinct, roused not so much by the reading of your verse as from a mental picture of your state of mind, reinforces their insistence."

‡ The Austrian American soprano Maria Jeritza (1887–1982), who sang the part of Marietta in the first Vienna performance of Erich Wolfgang Korngold's *Die tote Stadt* in 1920, reprised the role at her Metropolitan debut in 1921.

§ The Russian operatic bass singing star Feodor Chaliapin (1873–1938) performed the title role of Modest Mussorgsky's *Boris Godunov* at the Metropolitan Opera House in 1921.

¶ The Moscow Art Theatre was founded in 1898 by Constantin Stanislavsky and Vladimir

the "Chauve Souris"* for the third time, and Jane Cowl's Juliet.† I suppose you saw Barrymore's Hamlet,‡ and maybe "Rain."§ I have been telling all my friends to see it—"Rain"—but none of them take my advice. For me, it's the finest thing, aside from "Hamlet," I've seen this season, and stands out in my mind as "Anna Christie"¶ from last year's plays.

Countee** told me about seeing the "World We Live In"†† with you. He has been doing some very beautiful poems lately, hasn't he?

Jones Point is about forty miles up the Hudson from New York—a little white village almost pushed into the water by the snow-covered hills. And the Hassayampa is one of five "mother ships" anchored in the river in a forest of masts and cables belonging to a hundred other long old sea-going boats waiting for the Subsidy to pass, or something to happen to take them back to the sea. The sailors up here are the finest fellows I've ever met—fellows you can touch and know and be friends with. And after the atmosphere of college last year, being up here on the long ships is like fresh air and night stars after three hours in a dull movie show.

No I haven't a single dramatic sketch.

I would be glad to hear from you again and to enjoy your friendship.

Sincerely,

Langston Hughes

Nemirovich-Danchenko. Their innovative approach to theatrical production helped to create modern theater. The Moscow Art Theatre began its American tour with an eight-week engagement in New York City that opened at Jolson's 59th Street Theatre on January 8, 1923.

* The Chauve-Souris, or the Bat Theatre of Moscow, was a theater group led by Nikita Balieff (1876?–1936), a vaudevillian and former member of the Moscow Art Theatre. On February 3, 1922, Balieff and his troupe began an engagement lasting seventeen months in New York City. The Chauve-Souris gave its four hundredth performance on January 4, 1923, in honor of the recent arrival of the Moscow Art Theatre company in America.

† A playwright and actress, Jane Cowl (1883?–1950) appeared as Juliet in Shakespeare's *Romeo and Juliet* at Henry Miller's Theatre on 43rd Street in Manhattan in 1923.

‡ John Barrymore (1882–1942) performed the title role of Shakespeare's *Hamlet* at the Sam H. Harris Theatre on Broadway from November 1922 to February 1923.

§ *Rain: A Play in Three Acts* (1923) is John Colton's adaptation of W. Somerset Maugham's short story "Miss Thompson," later called "Rain" (1921).

¶ *Anna Christie* won Eugene O'Neill the Pulitzer Prize for Drama in 1922.

** Countee Cullen (1903–1947), Hughes's close friend and literary rival, was a major poet of the Harlem Renaissance. Unlike Hughes, he preferred traditional forms, such as the villanelle and sonnet, and found his main inspiration in the European classics. He won several literary prizes for poems that appeared in periodicals such as *Opportunity, The Crisis, Harper's,* and *The American Mercury.* In 1925, Harper & Brothers published his first volume of poetry, *Color.*

†† *The World We Live In,* also known as *The Insect Comedy* or *The Insects,* was written by the Czech brothers Josef and Karel Capek. It ran on Broadway at Jolson's 59th Street Theatre from October 1922 to February 1923.

TO ALAIN LOCKE

[ALS]

Dear Mr. Locke:

I am writing this very hurried note because I want you to get it before you leave for New York. It would be inconvenient for you to come up to Jones Point and I can't come down to the city just now, so I am afraid we will have to postpone our meeting until some other time. This is the most out of the way place and our ship is at the very end of the fleet, a good half mile of slippery gang-planks and icy decks from the shore landing. And then, at the end of your journey, you would find a very stupid person because I am always dumb in the presence of those whom I want to be friends with. You have written me such an understanding letter that I would like to know you, but I'd rather you wouldn't come up here to see me.

I shall write you again soon.

Sincerely,
Langston Hughes

S.S. West Hassayampa,
Jones Point, New York,
February nineteenth, 1923.

TO COUNTEE CULLEN

[ALS]

Dear Countee:

Certainly it is very kind of you to offer to read my poems for me at the library and very beastly of me not to have written a single line since returning from New York. I'm an absolutely shameless person, am I not? But, anyway, I hope you liked some of the poems I sent you but if you didn't, and would like to, you may read some of my old things,—"The Negro" or "The Negro Speaks of Rivers," or the group of poems from last March's "Crisis," or any of the published stuff that you choose. Miss Fauset can send them to you. "Our Land" and "Dreams," though, are going to be used in "The World Tomorrow" so perhaps you'd better not read them. "Joy" and "Tragedy" were sent out a month ago to "The Bookman"* but I've heard not a word about them, nor have they been

---

* *The Bookman*, a prominent American review published from 1895 to 1933, accepted neither "Joy" nor "Tragedy." "Joy" first appeared in *The Crisis* in February 1926. "Tragedy"

returned, you may use them, if you like. But please don't read "Fascination." But does that leave you enough to choose from? I wrote Miss Rose, in answer to her letter, that I had sent my material to you, and that you had very kindly offered to read for me.[*] You know, I wouldn't dream of reading anything, if I were there.

What's happened to "Kelley's"[†] and have you or I had anything in "The Crisis" recently?

Thanks a lot for your "To a Brown Boy." I don't know what to say about the "For L.H." but I appreciate it, and I like the poem. I'm glad it was accepted.

Ridgely Torrence wrote me asking if I would send something for a special Negro number of "The World Tomorrow".[‡] They returned my "Three Poems of Harlem," but kept "Dreams," "Our Land" and another that I don't believe you have,—"Poem for the Portrait of an African Boy after the Manner of Gauguin." (Terribly long title, isn't it?) I was surprised at their keeping them as I was afraid they weren't quite the thing that they'd want.

I've had another delightful letter from Mr. Locke. Did you see him in New York over the holiday week-end? He wrote me that he would be there and that he wanted to come up here, which frightened me stiff. He writes such charming letters that I would be afraid to meet him because I know he'd find me terribly stupid.

Have you seen the Moscow Art Theatre yet? I see they're staying for an extra four weeks.

I haven't written Donald.[§] I have had so very much to do. We are moving from one ship to another. And it takes me hours to write a decent letter. Then, too, I've been working on my poems, copying manuscripts and getting them together as I may be moving soon. You know, spring's coming and I feel the

---

(its first lines are "Pierrot / Took his heart / And hung it / On a wayside wall") was retitled "Heart" and first appeared in *One-Way Ticket* (1949).

[*] Ernestine Rose (1880–1961), a white librarian and social activist, organized popular evenings of poetry readings, lectures, and social events at the 135th Street Branch Library in Harlem.

[†] William M. Kelley (1894–1958) was the editor of the Harlem-based *New York Amsterdam News*. The paper published the poems "A Black Pierrot" and "Justice" in its April 4 and April 24, 1923, issues.

[‡] Ridgely Torrence (1874–1950), a white poet, dramatist (the landmark *Three Plays for a Negro Theater*, 1917), and editor of *The New Republic* from 1920 to 1924, prepared a special number on blacks for the magazine *The World Tomorrow* (May 1923). He chose three poems by Hughes ("Dreams," "Our Land," and "Poem: For the portrait of an African boy after the manner of Gauguin"). This marks the first time Hughes's work (apart from reprintings) appeared in a journal circulated mainly to a white audience.

[§] Probably Donald Duff, a close friend of Countee Cullen and Harold Jackman, with ties to the leftist magazine *The Liberator*. Cullen dedicated his poem "Tableau" to Duff.

call of the road, or shall it be the sea this time. Do you know that poem of
Edna St. Vincent Millay's, "Travel," I believe it's called, that closes:

> "My heart is warm with the
> friends I make
> And better friends I'll not be
> knowing
> Yet there isn't a train I
> wouldn't take
> No matter where it's going."

Don't you ever get that feeling sometimes? To go somewhere, anywhere,
just to be going. I suppose that's one of the reasons why I couldn't stay in college. I spent more time last spring on South Street looking at the ships than
I did in the Dorms.

Say, there's a most beautiful Pierrot cover on La Vie Parisienne* for February third. If you're ever down on Sixth Avenue some time stop in one of the
little French bookshops and see it. The copy we have up here is the Swede's or
I'd send it down to you.

Write me soon.

Sincerely,
Langston

Box 37
Jones Point, N.Y.
March 4, 1923.

TO COUNTEE CULLEN   [ALS]

Dear Countee:
I am sorry, but I have not another thing that you can read unless you want to
be divertingly original and give them this:

SYLLABIC POEM
Ah ya!
Ah ya!

---

* *La Vie Parisienne* was an erotic French magazine.

Ky ya na mina,
Ky ya na mina.
So lee,
So lee nakyna.
Ky ya na mina,
Ky ya na mina.

Tell them that it is the poetry of sound, pure sound, and that it marks the beginning of a new era, an era of revolt against the trite and outworn language of the understandable. Wouldn't that be amusing? Then they could discuss the old question as to whether artists and poets are ever sane. I doubt if we are. But, seriously, I haven't anything else decent to send you. Read my old things, if that would help you any.

Tell me about the programme.* Who's on and who's coming?

If you wanted me to come, I'm sorry that I won't be able to. But I may perhaps be in New York anyway soon. The Subsidy failed to pass so our fleet may be left alone to rust.†

Your friend,
Langston

Box thirty-seven,
Jones Point, New York,
March seventh, 1923.

TO ALAIN LOCKE [ALS]

Box Thirty Seven
Jones Point
April Sixth, 1923

Dear Friend,

I am sorry I have been so long in writing you but it seems that letters are always my hardest tasks—not the actual writing of them, but the getting ready to write them. And the time slips by so rapidly! But I did enjoy your last

---

* Cullen read some of Hughes's poems as well as some of his own at a poetry reading at the 135th Street Branch Library.
† Hughes asserts in *The Big Sea* that he left because "I thought it was about time to leave the dead ships and find a vessel that was moving. So I quit the fleet and went back to New York, determined now to get on a boat actually going somewhere."

letter a great deal and I believe that you are a <u>Sympathetic</u> friend. So many friends aren't. They are only well meaning.

I can quite understand why you like the Germans. I like them, too,—those whom I have known. I met a number of them in Mexico (our housekeeper happened to be a German lady and they were delightful people).

Do you teach Greek or the classics? I have read nothing but the Odyssey and a few of the tragedies but love them. They were the only things college gave me, (other than a supreme dislike for college). But I am glad that I've known Telemachus and the beauty of Homer's wine dark sea. The Odyssey is truly a marvelous thing!

Up here I have been reading Nietzsche and Conrad, Walt Whitman and Pio Baroja.* Down in New York I saw "Will Shakespeare," Jane Cowl's "Romeo and Juliet," Nazimova's "Salome"† and the Moscow Art Players do "The Lower Depths".‡ Did you ever see Duse§ in Europe? I want to. And did you ever see Mimi Aguglia? She and Grasso¶ gave some very fine performances at the Irving Place Theatre last winter. I saw them do Benavente's "Malquerida." I didn't get to hear a single opera this winter, and I wanted to, especially those of the "Ring".** But I did both hear and see "Liza" and it's a perfect diamond of joy!†† Didn't you think so?

Tell me sometime about the Howard Players and your work with them.

Do you know a young fellow at Howard by the name of Moon (Edward, I believe) from Cleveland?‡‡ We both graduated there in the same year. And

---

* Pío Baroja (1872–1956) was a Spanish author whose trilogy of novels, *La Lucha por la Vida* ("The Struggle for Life"), published between 1922 and 1924, depicts the world of the Madrid slums.

† The world-famous Russian-born actress Alla Nazimova (1879–1945) partially financed, produced, and starred in *Salomé*, a silent screen adaptation of Oscar Wilde's play of the same name. The film was released in February 1923.

‡ *The Lower Depths*, first produced by the Moscow Art Theatre in 1902, is perhaps the best-known play by the Russian writer Maxim Gorky (1868–1936).

§ Eleanora Duse (1858–1924) was a renowned Italian actress. At Jones Point, Hughes had read Gabriele D'Annunzio's novel *The Flame of Life* (1900), in which he drew on his intimate friendship with Duse. Later that year, when Hughes attended the premiere of Duse in Ibsen's *La Donna del Mare* at the Metropolitan Opera House, he was disappointed: "She seemed just a tiny little old woman, on an enormous stage, speaking in a foreign language, before an audience that didn't understand."

¶ Mimi Aguglia (1884–1970) and Giovanni Grasso (1873–1930) were Italian actors and two of the founders of the Sicilian Theatrical Company.

** Richard Wagner's four epic operas *The Ring of the Nibelungen* (1853) are often called *The Ring Cycle*.

†† *Liza*, an all-black musical comedy, introduced the dance sensation called the Charleston to New York during its run on Broadway from November 1922 to April 1923.

‡‡ Probably Henry Lee Moon (1901–1985), a friend from his teenage years in Cleveland who later worked as a prominent journalist for the *New York Amsterdam News* and as editor

do you know Jean Toomer?* I have liked some of his work very much in "The Liberator" and "The Crisis."†

An Easter card from Countee |Cullen| in Washington told me that he was having a delightful time. You must be a charming friend for poets. And you say that we are reaching the poet's dangerous age. I don't know, but anyway I do want your help, and friendship, and criticisms. And how good you are to offer them to me! So I am sending you an envelope of poems to read. I am afraid that none of them are particularly good, but if you should like any of them well enough to send out for me, I would be very glad. I had thought of Poetry and the Little Review, but then I was afraid |they weren't| good enough for one nor eccentric enough for the other.

I shall perhaps be here only a month or so more, until the spring comes over the high hills and down to the river's edge. There are fruit trees all along the west bank waiting for flowers. I've had a glorious winter. I've made strange friends for whom I care a great deal and met many poets, although they never write their poems, and potential artists, who do not develop their talents (but I have persuaded one to take a correspondence course and another to try to enter an art school when he goes to New York). And there have been nights of sailor's chanties and songs in Swedish and German, Italian and Spanish, and games, and stories of days on sailing ships, and trips around the Horn, and nights in Bombay and Cape Town. Do you wonder that of my four volumes, Nietzsche and Conrad, Walt Whitman and Pio Baroja, I have finished and well read but one? Of course, I'm stupid and only a young kid fascinated by his first glimpse of life, but then after so many years in a book-world and so much striving to be a "bright boy" and an "intelligent young man" it's rather nice to come here and be simple and stupid and to touch a life that is at least a living thing with no touch of books.

But I am boring you, no? Anyway, I hope you'll write me soon.

Sincerely,

Langston Hughes

---

of *The Crisis*. Moon also accompanied Hughes and twenty other young African Americans on a visit to the Soviet Union in 1932 to work on a film (soon abandoned) about American race relations.

* Jean Toomer (1894–1967) was an influential African American poet and fiction writer. Published that year (1923), his book *Cane* is a collection of poems and stories about black life in Washington, D.C., and in the rural South. The sections of *Cane* that appeared in *The Liberator* are "Georgia Dusk" (September 1922), "Carma" (September 1922), and "Becky" (October 1922). "The Song of the Son" appeared in *The Crisis* (June 1922).

† *The Liberator* was the successor to the Greenwich Village left-wing magazine *The Masses*.

TO COUNTEE CULLEN   [ALS]

Dear Countee:

I was very glad to receive both your letter and your card from Washington, where you must have had a delightful time. Tell me about it. You visited Howard, of course. How is it? What else did you do? Is Mr. Locke married? I have just written to him and mailed off an envelope of poems.

Thanks so much for your criticisms. I'll bet Donald |Duff| was the friend who checked the poems, wasn't he? For who else could have liked just those things? So the Poetry Evening came off nicely? Who all were there? Mr. |Augustus Granville| Dill must have been as he writes me that he's heard of my being in town numbers of times and not even calling him up. He says that Hall Johnson, the violinist, has written for permission to do a musical setting for my "Mother to Son" and wonders what my "reaction to that will be."* Have you seen Miss Fauset lately?

At last, I've heard from Kelley's. He's keeping my stuff for the Amsterdam News. But not a word from The Bookman yet. Isn't that a scream of a poem over my "Black Pierrot"? I'd rather have written it.

Seen any new plays lately? I haven't done a thing intellectual since returning from New York, except to write a few verses, and attempt to discover (to my financial embarrassment) the secret of luck in poker. Now I shall be here until sometime in May.

I am sending you an envelope of things—Miss Fauset's article on color from last year's Negro Number of the "World Tomorrow," an article on your beloved Housman from the Lib,† a Sailor's Song that I rather like, and a song from Andalusia that I translated myself. And two poems of my own in rhyme. How's the "chansons vulgaires" for vulgar songs? Is it good French? I have another beauty of a cabaret poem that came to me in New York <unfranc ish>.

---

* Hall Johnson (1888–1970), an African American choral director, composer, and violinist, set Hughes's poem "Mother to Son" to music. Passionate about preserving the spirituals, he founded the renowned Hall Johnson Choir in 1925.
† A. E. (Alfred Edward) Housman (1859–1936) was an acclaimed British classics scholar and poet. His collection of lyrical verse *A Shropshire Lad* (1896) brought him international fame. Floyd Dell's article "Private Classics," which appeared in the January 1923 issue of *The Liberator*, discusses Housman's volume *Last Poems* (1922).

Do you ever visit any of those little cellar places? They're interesting and very Harlemish.

Write to me soon. Where's the poem you were going to send?

Sincerely,

Langston

Box thirty seven,

Jones Point, N.Y.

April seventh, 1923.

TO ALAIN LOCKE [ALS]

|c. May 1923|

Dear Mr. Locke:

I was very glad indeed to receive your letter and interested by what you told me about my poetry, and about your summer plans,—Knickers and sandals on the German roads, then Egypt, the tombs and the pyramids. How wonderful! I wish I were going with you.

I have read a little about the German Youth Movement and I remember seeing a motion picture showing a band of young folk tramping to an old baronial castle for a holiday. By the way, did you read about Countee |Cullen|'s speech to the League of Youth in New York?

You are right that we have enough talent now to begin a movement. I wish we had some gathering place of our artists,—some little Greenwich Village of our own. But would our artists have the pose of so many of the Villagers? I hate pose or pretension of any sort. And especially sham intellectuality. I prefer simple, stupid people to half-wise pretenders. (But perhaps it's because I'm stupid myself and half ashamed of my stupidity. I don't know. I never studied psychology. I wish that I had.)

I am going to have some pictures taken this week, (one for Mr. Kerlin's "Negro Poets")* and I shall send one to you. Then if we meet on some strange road this summer we shall recognize one another. I think that I should know

---

* Robert T. Kerlin (1866–1950), a controversial white professor of English and History, edited the landmark anthology *Negro Poets and Their Poems* (1923), which includes Hughes's poem "Negro." In 1921, the Virginia Military Institute fired him because of his various publications on behalf of black rights.

you although I have never seen you. Perhaps it's because I do know you and like you that makes me feel as though I have already seen you.

Have you ever been to Spain? It must be a gorgeous land. I've always dreamed of going there.

Have you ever read D'Annunzio's "The Flame of Life"?[*] It is pagan and very lovely, filled with the beauty of Venice in autumn, and half-dead myths.

Do you like Walt Whitman's poetry? His "Song of the Open Road" and the poems in "Calamus"?[†] I do, very much. And have you read, or tried to read, Joyce's much discussed "Ulysses"?

I shall see the Chicago Players in "Salome" when I go down for the pictures. Thanks for telling me about them as I hadn't heard before.

Write to me again soon.

Sincerely,
Langston Hughes

Jones Point, New York,
Thursday

TO ALAIN LOCKE [ALS]

|c. May 1923|

Dear friend,

Your charming and generous letter has been on my table for the last two weeks and I have not been able to bring myself to answer it,—disappointingly, at least for me. But I can't go with you this summer. My "I wish I could go with you" did really mean so, but for more than one reason, I must work the entire summer. Even at that, though, I may get to Europe or northern Africa as I hope to work on a freighter going to the Mediterranean. Perhaps, some fine day, we may even meet in Piraeus or Alexandria. I shall try to let you know what ports I touch. And how delightful it would be to come surprisingly upon one another in some Old World street! Delightful and too romantic! But, maybe,—who knows?

Anyway, I am sending you the promised picture. It does look something like me. I am not autographing it for you, but I will, if you wish it, when I

---

[*] Gabriele D'Annunzio (1863–1938), an Italian poet and playwright, was the author of the novel *The Flame of Life* (1900). See also letter of April 6, 1923, fourth footnote.

[†] Whitman's group of poems called "Calamus," introduced in the 1860 edition of *Leaves of Grass*, is often noted for its homoeroticism.

come to Howard, as I hope to, for a visit at least, if not to continue my suddenly and gladly (though sadly) interrupted education.

Please write to me soon as I shall not be here much longer. The hills are at their loveliest now and I do not like to go, but then there are other rivers in the world to see besides the Hudson. And Oh! so many dreams to chase!

Your friend,
Langston Hughes

Jones Point, New York,
Friday

With Jessie Fauset and Zora Neale Hurston at
the statue of Booker T. Washington, Tuskegee
Institute, 1927

And the tom-toms beat,
And the tom-toms beat,
And the low beating of the tom-toms
Stirs your blood.
—"DANSE AFRICAINE," 1922

In 1923, Hughes secured a job as a mess boy on the *West Hesseltine*, a freighter bound for Africa. On June 13, as the ship put out to sea, he decided to throw all of his books overboard. He recalls the moment in *The Big Sea:* "It was like throwing a million bricks out of my heart— for it wasn't only the books that I wanted to throw away, but everything unpleasant and miserable out of my past: the memory of my father, the poverty and uncertainties of my mother's life, the stupidities of color-prejudice, black in a white world, the fear of not finding a job, the bewilderment of no one to talk to about things that trouble you, the feeling of always being controlled by others—by parents, by employers, by some outer necessity not your own. All those things I wanted to throw away." In an earlier draft of *The Big Sea*, however, Hughes wrote that he saved one book, his copy of Whitman's *Leaves of Grass*: "I had no intention of throwing that one away."

On another voyage the following year, he crossed the North Atlantic to Rotterdam, where he jumped ship and headed to Paris. There he found a job washing dishes in a jazz club in Montmartre. These two adventures seemed to inspire him as a poet. After a month-long stay in Italy, he was about to return to the United States when thieves stole his money and passport. As a result, he was stranded in Genoa for more than a month. This ordeal moved him to write one of his best-known poems, "I, Too."

TO CARRIE CLARK [ALS]

Lagos, Nigeria,
July 21, 1923,
S/S West Hesseltine.*

Dearest Mother:†
We are at Lagos, British Nigeria, now, just eight ports from the end of our trip.‡ This is the first town since Dakar at which we have had shore leave or a chance to mail letters.

---

* Hughes had left Jones Point on June 4 to take the job as a mess boy on the ship.
† Born Carolina Mercer Langston, Carrie Clark (1873–1938) was the daughter of the abolitionist and businessman Charles Langston (1817–1892) and his wife, Mary Sampson Patterson Leary Langston (1837?–1915). Passionate about novels, poetry, and the theater, Carrie aspired in vain to become a successful actress. Her letters show that she used various forms of her first name, from Caroline to Carolyn to Carrie, as well as alternately spelled Clark with and without a final "e." Hughes's own "full and legal" name, as he wrote on January 21, 1960, to Arna Bontemps, is James Langston Hughes and not "James Mercer Langston Hughes," as he called himself once, and is often called.
‡ The *West Hesseltine* called at ports from the Azores to Lobito Bay on the Angola coast, including Lagos in what was then the British colony and protectorate of Nigeria.

I'm having a delightful trip and, you won't believe it, but it's cool over here, really cool. This is the rainy season and the weather is fine, and at sea always a continuous breeze.

We've about a hundred and fifty on board now,—our regular crew and passengers, and a gang of African helpers—Kru boys. I have two, both about the age of Gwyn*—but wonderful little workers—and smart! Their father is a head-man. The kids aren't paid, but the men get two shillings a day, and each and every human consumes about ten pounds each of rice a meal!

Our one colored passenger is getting off here. He is a tailor and enthusiastic about business prospects in Africa. He is going to open a shop here and a school. The white missionaries are going clear down to the Congo, about two weeks yet. There we are going to load mahogany logs and palm oil and start back. I'm going to get the monk there, too.† There are two on board already doing all sorts of pranks. I'll write you again soon. Hope you got all my letters. Lots of love to you. One kiss.

Langston

TO COUNTEE CULLEN [ALS]

S. S. Hesseltine,
Lagos, Nigeria,
July 21, 1923

Dear Countee:

This is our sixteenth port, Lagos, just where the coast curves south again. From here we go to Duala, and then ninety miles up the Congo to Boma and Matadi. We've had no shore leave since Dakar so about the most I've seen of Africa has been the orange-yellow sands of the coast and the roofs of white houses hidden in groves of cocoanut trees. We usually anchor out and our

---

* Gwyn Clark was Hughes's stepbrother. After her divorce from Hughes's father, his mother, Carrie, married a sometime cook, Homer Clark, who had a son, Gwyn, by a previous union. Rebellious and a weak student, Gwyn "Kit" Clark was often a source of worry to Hughes, who nevertheless loved him as a brother. In Sierra Leone, the *West Hesseltine* took on men and boys from the Kru tribe to unload and load cargo as well as perform various other chores aboard the ship.

† On October 21, Hughes returned to New York with a large red monkey named Jocko, which he had acquired in the Congo as a gift for Gwyn Clark. He writes about Jocko in *The Big Sea*.

cargo is taken by surf boats in charge of eight oars-men whose paddles are three-pointed like Father Neptune's fork and the oars-men themselves gorgeously naked save for a whisp of loin-cloth.

We have about sixty Kru boys from Freetown on board now as workers, so everyone has a helper. I have two kids who work excellently well, but who eat better. They each consume a dish pan full of rice at every meal, chewing untiringly, and then are not full.

Our own ship's crew is a mixed lot. The engine room gang, from the chief down, are Irish, the sailors mostly of the "white-headed race" with a Porto Rican and a few Americans mixed in. The "old man" himself is a Dutchman whose breeches are a yard wide and his pipe almost as long. And the steward and the galley men Phillipinos. And we four, the mess-boys—one from San Juan, one from Kentucky, one from Manila, and I—where am I from?

I'll write again at Matadi.

Sincerely,
Langston

TO COUNTEE CULLEN   [ALS]

Freetown, Sierra Leone,
October 1, 1923,
S/S West Hesseltine.

Dear Countee:

We are homeward bound. Only one more port and then across to Manhattan—and Harlem. We are a month late now but then we have almost a full cargo—palm oil, cocoa beans, and mahogany logs, and here we load ginger and pepper. And then we've been everywhere—up rivers, branch rivers and creeks, surf ports and harbor ports, and visited about every colony on the West Coast. We have had delightful weather all the whole summer, too, but now the hot season is beginning, so I am glad we are getting away. I have had a very interesting trip, though, and have seen more of Africa than I ever expected to see. And tonight the sunset! Gleaming copper and gold and then the tropical soft green after-glow of twilight, and now stars in the water and luminous phosphorescent foam on the little waves about the ship and ahead the light of Freetown toward which we are steering through the soft darkness.

I'll be up to see you soon after this letter. I am anxious to be back again. Just a little bit homesick for New York.

Sincerely,
Langston

Be in about November first.*

TO ALAIN LOCKE   [ALS]

|February 4, 1924|

Dear Friend:

Forgive me for the sudden and unexpected message I sent you.† I'm sorry. I should have known that one couldn't begin in the middle of the term and that I wasn't ready to come anyway. But I had been reading all your letters that day and a sudden desire came over me to come to you then, right then, to stay with you and know you. I need to know you. But I am so stupid sometimes.

However I am coming to Howard and I want to see you and talk to you about it.

I am sailing again tomorrow but you may write me in Holland—

S/S McKeesport,
c/o Agent, Cosmopolitan Line,
Rotterdam, Holland.‡

I was so pleased to get your card from Cairo.

Sincerely,
Langston

* The *West Hesseltine* docked in Brooklyn on October 21.
† On February 2, 1924, Hughes had sent Locke a telegram asking for help to start at once as a student at Howard University in Washington: "MAY I COME NOW PLEASE LET ME KNOW TONIGHT WIRE LANGSTON HUGHES 234 WEST 131 ST CARE CULLEN." Not receiving a response (Locke had mailed a letter, which apparently never arrived), Hughes sent this apology.
‡ On February 5, Hughes departed on his second stint as a mess boy aboard the *McKeesport*, a freighter that sailed regularly between Rotterdam and New York. He observed in *The Big Sea* that his "second trip across was as bad as the first, so far as weather went. And worse in other respects. Several very unfortunate things happened aboard." These things included the death of the chief engineer from pneumonia, an accidental scalding of another mess boy, and a mental breakdown of their wireless operator.

TO COUNTEE CULLEN [ALS]

Paris
March 11 |1924|

Dear Countee:

I am in Paris. I had a disagreement on the ship, left, and came to Paris purely on my nerve, as I knew no one here and I had less than nine dollars in my pocket when I arrived.* For a week I came as near starvation as I ever want to be, but I got to know Paris, as I tramped from one end to the other looking for a job. And at last I found one and then another one, and yet another!

Happily or not, I have fallen in to the very whirling heart of Parisian night life—Montmartre, where topsy-turvy, no one gets up before seven or eight in the evening, breakfast at nine, and nothing starts before midnight. Montmartre of the Moulin Rouge, Le Rat Mort, and the famous night clubs and cabarets!

I myself go to work at eleven pm and finish at nine in the morning. I'm working at the "Grand Duc" where the culinary staff and the entertainers are American Negroes. One of the owners is colored, too. The jazz-band starts playing at one and we're still serving champagne long after day-light. This is my second cabaret job within the last two weeks. I'm vastly amused. But at my first place glasses and even bottles were hurled too often for me. The "Grand Duc" is not so wild and then our folk are quite chic. Last night we had a prince in the house and his party.

But about France! Kid, stay in Harlem! The French are the most franc-loving, sou-clutching, hard-faced, hard-worked, cold and half-starved set of people I've ever seen in life. Heat—unknown. Hot water—what is it? You even pay for a smile here. Nothing, absolutely nothing is given away. You even pay for water in a restaurant or the use of the toilette. And do they like Americans of any color? They do not!!! Paris—old and ugly and dirty. Style, class? You see more well dressed people in a New York subway station in five seconds than I've seen in all my three weeks in Paris. Little old New York for me! But the colored people here are fine,

Hughes doodled this streetlamp in the margin of his letter to Cullen.

* Hughes argued with the ship's steward, who apparently refused to give him a piece of leftover chicken because chicken was reserved for officers. When the *McKeesport* reached Rotterdam on February 20, Hughes paid for a visa to enter France and took a train to Paris.

there are lots of us. I'll tell you in my next letter. Please write me now. I did not get your Rotterdam letter.

Sincerely,
Langston Hughes

Address:
15 Rue Nollet,
Paris XVIIe, France.

Be sure to use the XVIIe or else I doubt if anybody in the world could find this street.

I've just had tea over in the Latin Quarter with three of the most charming English colored girls!*—Claude McKay† just left here for the South—Smith‡ is in Brussels—Roland Hayes§ is coming.

TO ALAIN LOCKE   [ALS]

15 Rue Nollet,
Paris (XVIIe) France,
April 23, 1924

Dear Mr. Locke:

It's two months today since I came to Paris and I am just now beginning to like the city a little. Perhaps because it's the fourth day of sunshine in the whole two months, and Parisian houses are so cold! But the gardens were lovely Sunday and the young leaves are coming out on the trees along the

---

* In Paris, Hughes met Amy and Gwen Sinclair, two sisters from Jamaica, and, from London, Anne Marie Coussey, with whom he fell in love, according to his account in *The Big Sea*.

† Claude McKay (1889–1948), a poet, novelist, and editor, moved from Jamaica to the United States in 1912 and studied agriculture in Kansas and at Tuskegee Institute in Alabama. Aiming for a career as a writer (he had published two books of poetry in Jamaica), he settled in Harlem in 1914. His novel *Home to Harlem* (1928) is considered a major work of the Harlem Renaissance.

‡ Hughes was a devoted fan of the African American singer Bessie Smith (1894–1937). Known as the "Empress of the Blues," she has been called the most influential vocalist in the history of the blues.

§ The tenor Roland Hayes (1887–1977) was the first African American man to earn international fame as a classical concert performer.

boulevards. Never, though, until this week, had I missed the sun so much before. And French people! (Mon dieu!!) I can't ever love them. Yesterday I heard Raquel Meller* sing and the old desire of seeking the sun in Spain came over me. But I think I'd better stay here for a while. Paris is still amusing. And then I have a "jazzy" job in a Montmartre cabaret where one gets a sort of back stage view of "the gay life,"—the other side of the smile, so to speak.†
It's interesting.

Please tell me, how's chances for me at Howard? I should like very much to come there next September. (If I save my fare. If not I shall go on to Spain.) If I come, I shall have to depend entirely on myself for all expenses. I can do almost all sorts of work now and perhaps tutor Spanish or French. Please, dear friend, let me know about this. I do want to come.

Are you coming over this summer|?| If so, of course I will see you. I hope so.

Write to me,

Sincerely,
Langston

TO HAROLD JACKMAN [ALS]

Paris, France,
15 Rue Nollet (XVIIe)
May 25, 1924.

Dear Harold:‡
Stay home! Europe is the last place in the world to come looking for a job, and unless you've got at least a dollar for every day you expect to stay here, don't come! Jobs in Paris are like needles in hay-stacks, for everybody, and espe-

---

* Raquel Meller (1888–1962) was a Spanish actress and singer whose films include *Violettes Impériales* (1923) and *Carmen* (1926).
† Hughes worked for Bruce, the colorful cook at Le Grand Duc nightclub in Montmartre. The club, managed by a black American, attracted a clientele that included American celebrities and even the occasional royal. Late at night, musicians and entertainers from other clubs would gather at Le Grand Duc for what Hughes describes in *The Big Sea* as "a jam session until seven or eight in the morning—only in 1924 they had no such name for it. They'd just get together and the music would be on."
‡ Harold Jackman (1901–1961) was a notably handsome and urbane African American schoolteacher, lover of the arts, and close friend of Countee Cullen and Carl Van Vechten. With degrees from New York University and Columbia University, he taught Social Studies in the New York public school system for thirty years.

cially for English-speaking foreigners. The city is over-run with Spaniards and Italians who work for nothing, literally nothing. And all French wages are low enough anyway. I've never in my life seen so many English and Americans, colored and white, male and female, broke and without a place to sleep as I have seen here. Yet if you'd give them all a ticket home tomorrow, I doubt if ten would leave Paris. Not even hunger drives them away. The colored jazz bands and performers are about the only ones doing really well here. The rest of us, with a dozen or so exceptions, merely "get along." The others, in "hard luck" beg, borrow, gamble, or steal for a living until something better turns up. And to be broke in Paris is a "pain." Then a franc (six cents) over here is harder to get than a dollar in New York.

The French colored people, and there are many, seemingly live and work under about the same conditions as other Frenchmen. But those conditions are bad enough. Personally, I think I had rather be a colored worker in New York than a colored or white worker over here, as far as wages, hours, and conditions are concerned.

About mademoiselles—one will live with you forever if you only pay the room rent.* Girls' wages are so low here that they can't afford to live alone. And in Montmartre, at least, nobody ever takes the trouble to get married.

If I were you, tho, I wouldn't come over, unless you've got the dollars to back you up. As far as—working on boats goes,—it's a tough life, kid. Neither you nor Countée |Cullen| is enough of a "bum" to enjoy it. And getting a boat is not so easy unless you've had experience. You see I did six months on the laid-up fleets before I went to sea.

I am sorry if I am discouraging you with all my would-be good advice. But if you're like me you'll do as you want to do, anyhow. I always do as I want, preferring to kill myself in my own way rather than die of boredom trying to live according to somebody else's "good advice." Besides, adventure is two-thirds uncertainty. Had I been sure about Paris, I wouldn't have been nearly as thrilled as I was when I came here with eight dollars, and wondered how Fortune would let me live. But then I'm a "nut." You needn't be one. It's better to stay home.

Sincerely,
Langston

---

* In *The Big Sea*, Hughes recalls living for a while in a similar arrangement with a young woman he calls Sonya.

TO COUNTEE CULLEN [ALS]

Paris, France,
15 Rue Nollet,
June 27, 1924

Dear Countee:

Thanks for your letter. I certainly do like to hear from you. Your letters are a breath of home. But your <u>Suicide Chant</u> doesn't excite me. The me and the seed, and the weed and the deed don't quite hang together.* If it were not for the title I wouldn't know what it's all about. Really, I think it is the worst thing you've ever done. Most of your poems are beautiful but this one isn't. The fourth verse is nice, but the rest—Oh, mon Dieu!. . . . Excuse me! As to my own poem,—people are taking it all wrong.† It's purely personal, not racial. If I choose to kill myself, I'm not asking anybody else to die, or to mourn either. Least of all the whole Negro race. But it's all right, the Pittsburgh Courier's giving me a bit of free advertising anyway, aren't they?

And have you also heard from the Boston gentleman who is also issuing a book on Negro poetry—a Dictionary |or| Negro Anthology he says?‡ We'll have plenty of books, won't we?

I'm very anxious to see Mr. Locke, tho I came near leaving Paris yesterday,—had a sudden notion that I wanted to see the sea again. But I am going to try to stay until he comes, besides I've got a wonderful idea for a story that I want to work out with the night life of Montmartre as a background and colored characters. Did I tell you about my meetings with Barnes and Guillaume?§

---

* "Suicide Chant" appeared in *Color* (1925), Cullen's first book of poetry. The poem begins: "I am the seed / The Sower sowed; / I am the deed / His hand bestowed / Upon the world."

† Hughes's "Song for a Suicide" appeared in *The Crisis* of May 1924.

‡ A proper Bostonian, William Stanley Braithwaite (1878–1962) was an African American poet and the editor of a respected annual collection of American magazine verse. Although he did not produce a volume such as the one mentioned in this letter, he included four poems by Hughes in his *Anthology of American Magazine Verse* for 1926. Countee Cullen dedicated his own anthology of African American verse, *Caroling Dusk* (1927), to Braithwaite.

§ Locke had arranged for Hughes to meet Dr. Albert C. Barnes, described in *The Big Sea* as "the Argyrol [a popular antiseptic] magnate, who had the finest collection of modern art in America at his foundation in Merion, Pennsylvania." Their lunch at the Café Royale near the Louvre went poorly because the business-obsessed Barnes reminded Hughes of his father. However, Barnes arranged for Hughes to visit the home of Paul Guillaume, a well-known French collector of African art. Barnes's art collection is now housed in a museum in central Philadelphia.

There's a new colored paper here in French which the Prince is putting out.* I've been asked to call at the office but haven't had a chance yet. If they want to use any of our stuff I'll let you know so you can send something you especially like.

I think you've done fine with the junk I left with you. Here's a $ to cover past postage. Keep the <u>Southern Workman</u>† until I come. Don't send to the Crisis. I've sent them some poems of which I'm enclosing a list. If any of them happen to be ones you have sent out, (I've forgotten exactly what I gave you), or ones which have been published, please notify "The Crisis" so they won't re-use them. Don't worry with my stuff this summer. Take a vacation.

Mother's staying at 1200 Arctic Ave. I know she'd be glad to see you. Locke says he just missed her in Washington.

The French are very slow. After two weeks of waiting Flammarion notifies me that no more copies of |René| Maran's first two books of poems are to be had. They're out of print. So I'm sending you the only one I could get "Le Visage Calme." And I'm returning Edna St. Vincent |Millay|. I hate to do it, but I imagine you like her as much as I do. Thanks. Write to me soon.

Sincerely,

Langston

TO COUNTEE CULLEN　　　　　　　[ALS]

Paris

July 4

1924

Dear Countee:

I've just met René Maran and the colored prince, Kojo Tovalou. Maran says that he hasn't even any copies of his first books himself, but that he is going to try to get them for you. He's a darned nice fellow,—reminds me a bit of you. And talk! I don't get a third of what he says. But it's good practice in French so

---

* Prince Kojo Tovalou Houénou was the nephew of the deposed king of Dahomey (now the Republic of Benin). René Maran, a French writer of African descent, helped the prince edit *Les Continents*, France's first black newspaper.

† *The Southern Workman* was published by the Hampton Normal and Agricultural Institute in Virginia (now Hampton University), one of the country's major historically black colleges. The periodical sought to document the achievements of African American educators from the end of the Civil War to the early twentieth century. Hughes's "Danse Africaine" appeared in the April 1924 issue.

I'm going to see him often. He may come to the States to lecture next winter. I hope he does.

Send me two or three poems that you like real well. I think I can get them in "Les Continents," and write me a little article about yourself to go along with them.* I've told them who you are but I don't know just what you'd want in a little note to go with your poems.

The Paris "Midnight Shuffle Along" opens tonight—20 colored artists. American sailors and colored Frenchmen have had several rows lately. Fists & knives. Write me, Langston

I didn't intend for "Dream Variations" to be in The Crisis at all. I sent it to Mr. Dill in a personal letter!x*!? Now I'll have to give Locke something else for "The Survey."†

TO HAROLD JACKMAN [ALS]

|August 1, 1924|

Dear Harold:

It's fine to hear from you. I'm sorry you didn't get over, in a way. The gardens at Versailles are worth coming from China to see,—but then home isn't bad. And I'm glad that "ol' divil sea" said, "—you!" Wait until you save $300 then come over and stay a few months. Don't give up coming but let the sea alone. She's a wicked creature.

Mr. Locke is here and we've been having a jolly time.‡ I like him immensely. And I've just about "done" everything in Paris except the "Louvre" and an airplane ride over the city. I'm afraid I'll miss those, though, because I'm going to Italy next week.

Do not write me here again. And forgive me for not writing you a longer

---

* The July 15, 1924, edition of *Les Continents* included poems by Hughes ("The Negro" and "A Black Pierrot"), Countee Cullen, and Claude McKay.

† Locke was then editing a "Negro" number of *Survey Graphic*, a special yearly supplement of *The Survey*, an influential monthly magazine devoted to national and international social problems. Locke was eager to include poems by Hughes. Although "Dream Variations" had appeared in *The Crisis*, Locke republished it in his special issue, which became the basis of his acclaimed anthology *The New Negro* (1925).

‡ After corresponding for eighteen months, Alain Locke and Hughes met for the first time in Paris in late July. Locke sought to introduce Hughes to the main cultural treasures of Paris beyond the nightclubs of Montmartre.

letter now, but I have such a pile of correspondence in front of me. If I get it all answered by next August I'll be doing well.

My "little love" from London has gone back to Piccadilly.* And tho our hearts may be broken, they still beat.

A woman of charm is right! Miss Fauset is my own brown goddess!

Eric's review is a terribly childish and badly written thing. And the curt impertinence of the last two sentences tempts one to want to punch him in the eye.†

I'll send you "Song for a Banjo Dance" from my next stopping place, (wherever that might be). So long!

Sincerely,

Langston

TO COUNTEE CULLEN   [ALS]
[Postcard]

Desenzano, Lago di Garda‡

August 13 |1924|

Dear friend: This is where I take my daily dip. You wouldn't believe such colors anywhere but on a post card, yet it really is here. And the sun—oh! what sun! I'm in love with Italy. This is an old up-hill town full of simple, kind people. I'd like to stay here forever,—almost. But I think I shall leave by the first.—Maran's address: René Maran, 82 Rue de la Huchette, Paris, France.

Sincerely,

Langston

---

* In the spring of 1924, Hughes enjoyed a close friendship with Anne Marie Coussey, the daughter of a prosperous West African–born resident of London. He describes this friendship vividly in *The Big Sea* (1940).

† Eric Walrond's review of Jessie Fauset's first novel, *There Is Confusion* (1924), appeared in the July 9 issue of *The New Republic*. His review ends: "Mediocre, a work of puny, painstaking labor, *There Is Confusion* is not meant for people who know anything about the Negro and his problems. It is aimed with unpardonable naïvete at the very young or the pertinently old."

‡ Romeo Luppi, a waiter at Le Grand Duc in Paris, had invited Hughes to spend August (when the club was closed) with him at his mother's home in Desenzano on Lake Garda in northern Italy.

TO ALAIN LOCKE   [ALS]

Desenzano, Brescia,
Lago di Garda, Italy,
August 24 |1924|.

Dear friend:

I understand how much the attractiveness of Italy depends upon color. Cloudy days here are as empty and devoid of beauty as those in any ordinary place. Even the lake turns gray. But when the sun shines everything is brilliant. Today there was a rare sunset, the kind that you would love. (And only the second really lovely one since I've been here.) The color changes lasted for more than an hour, until the various mountain ranges became merely shadows behind shadows. And the lake always a changing jewel,—blue-gold, blue, dark blue, purple, gray. If you want to stop off here for a day maybe there will be another sunset like that. Then we could go to Verona for a few hours to see the tomb of Romeo and Juliet and the arena where Duse appeared, and on to Venice.*

I wish you were here now. Your company in Paris has spoiled me for being alone.

Romeo |Luppi|'s friend from Turin is coming down tomorrow and they are expecting to leave about the twenty-ninth. If we are going to Venice, I do not want to return all the way to Turin, as that would only be a waste of good railroad fare. So I hope I hear from you soon.

You won't forget to get my letters for me when you pass through Paris. And my book from Maran. And see that Countée |Cullen| gets some copies of the number in which his poems appear. Please.

I have just finished Madame Bovary, and think that the best thing Emma did was to kill herself. She should have done it before.

I suppose you're enjoying the London Exposition. There must be a number of monkeys there in the African sections!

Yours sincerely,
Langston

*P. S. Your letter from Paris just came, also Claude |McKay|'s. We'll skip Venice, if you say so, and do the Blue Coast instead so as to see McKay. But let me know. I hope he's better.

---

* After Hughes met Locke in Verona at the end of August, they traveled together to Venice.

TO ALAIN LOCKE   [ALS]

Genoa[*]

Wednesday |September 1924|

Dear Friend,

How much I hated to see you leave yesterday! We really were having a delightful time together. Certainly our week in Venice was as pleasant as anything I
can ever remember.

But I wish you had seen the Albergo Popolare before you left, then you
wouldn't doubt me when I say that it's a wonder. For twenty-one lira a week
one has one's own room, a baggage locker, tax and service. And it's very clean.
Lots of German hikers are here. And it has a beautiful view. It's on the hill
way at the other side of the fort from where we were. And its windows look
straight out to sea, with the harbor at one side below.

I've found a restaurant where it's impossible to eat more than a five lira
meal. And that's from soup to cheese. And lovely wine. It's a sort of family
place. Yesterday my luncheon and dinner came to but seven eighty. So I'm
good for at least a month here. If nothing turns up. But I worked today on
the "City of Eureka." Hung over the end on a swinging stage and painted
the stern. It was fun—trying to keep from falling into the water. And I'm as
"painty" as can be tonight.—$2.08.

But I like Genoa. And there's nearly |a| full moon again. You should hear
them play guitars here! Write to me. Till next time, dear friend,

Langston

* Hughes's passport and wallet were stolen while he was traveling by train to France by
way of northern Italy. Unable to reenter France without a passport, he left the train in
Genoa with Alain Locke, who gave Hughes some money and headed home. Stranded,
Hughes stayed in Genoa, living by his wits at times while he sought passage back to the
United States.

TO ALAIN LOCKE   [ALS]

Genoa, Italy
The Sailors' Rest,
15 Via Milano,
September 25 |1924|

Dear Friend:

Still on the beach. Five of the original six have gone, so there's only two of us here now—Americans. But there's a wonderfully varied assortment of other beach-combers here. And of colored fellows, all the way from Porto Ricans to Abyssinians. Each with a long adventurous tale. One doesn't have to read to be entertained here. And they have the most amusing ways of "bumming" people! One Irishman always takes off his shoes, puts them under a park bench, and runs bare-footed after the tourists. Yesterday, in his haste, he threw his breakfast away (a sandwich) thinking he was going to make a good haul. But they happened to be Germans who had no money for alms,—and no extra shoes!X! The sun's still wonderful here, but they say it gets cold soon, and begins to rain. I could have gone to India yesterday if I'd have been a cook and a baker,—but I'm not.

I had a long letter from Claude |McKay| today, and the September <u>Crisis</u>. He probably won't come down. He has too much baggage to carry. (My own is growing lighter all the time. I put the alarm clock up for sale today. And gave a shirt away to a Porto Rican friend who hadn't any—it's getting a bit cool.)

I've been reading Emerson's essays and my Greek plays. I've done a couple of new poems. I have no more paper so I'm sending you one on the back of this letter.*

Be happy, dear friend. Write to me,—c/o Sailors' Rest.

Love,
Langston

---

* On the back of this letter Hughes wrote the text of his popular poem "I, Too."

With his mother Carrie Clark at graduation,
Lincoln University, 1929

I got the Weary Blues
And I can't be satisfied.
Got the Weary Blues
And can't be satisfied—
I ain't happy no mo'
And I wish that I had died.
—"THE WEARY BLUES," 1925

Returning to the United States in November 1924, Hughes lived
with his mother and stepbrother in Washington, D.C., for just over

a year. While he worked at various low-paying jobs, he continued to explore the blues, jazz, and other African American forms in his verse. In 1925, "The Weary Blues" won the top prize for poetry in a contest run by the magazine *Opportunity*. From that moment Hughes was seen as one of the stars of the Harlem Renaissance. His first book of poetry, *The Weary Blues*, appeared in 1926, the same year that he enrolled in Lincoln University, a historically black school in Pennsylvania. While critics liked his first book, some were scathing about his second, *Fine Clothes to the Jew* (1927), because of its sympathetic emphasis on "low-class" black culture. But Hughes was defiant on this matter. In the June 23, 1926, issue of *The Nation*, he had proclaimed his rebellious credo in his most famous essay, "The Negro Artist and the Racial Mountain." He declared: "We younger Negro artists who create now intend to express our individual dark-skinned selves without fear or shame. If white people are pleased we are glad. If they are not, it doesn't matter. . . . If colored people are pleased we are glad. If they are not, their displeasure doesn't matter either. We build our temples for tomorrow, strong as we know how, and we stand on top of the mountain, free within ourselves."

TO HAROLD JACKMAN   [ALS]

1917—3rd Street N.W.,
Washington, D.C.,*
December 14, 1924.

Dear Harold:

What's the New York news?

I've got another job since you left. I'm working on the "Washington Sentinel" now, one of the colored weeklies here, breaking in on a newspaper.† The work's all right, just so it yields the bucks.

---

* On October 5, after a tough month stranded in Genoa, Hughes was put aboard the *West Cawthorn* as a "consular" passenger working for the ship in return for his passage home. Arriving in Harlem in late November, he went to see Countee Cullen, who gave Hughes a letter from his mother, Carrie Clark. In it, she invited him to join her in Washington, D.C., where she was then living with prosperous relatives. One of her uncles, John Mercer Langston (1829–1897), had been an abolitionist, a U.S. congressman, a U.S. diplomat in Haiti, and the first dean of the Howard University law school.

† Hughes had taken a job at the *Washington Sentinel*, a weekly for which he sold advertising space on commission. He did poorly and soon left the newspaper.

Did you get home safe and sound? Teaching yet? Why don't you go South and get a school? It would be warm down there (in more ways than one!). But seriously, you're the type of young man they need down there, and you'd be doing more racial good spreading culture where culture isn't, than you would teaching in New York City or Washington. Don't you think so? And there they need you.

Oh—How I love to give advice! Take it!

Write to me soon.

Sincerely yours,
Langston Hughes

TO HAROLD JACKMAN   [ALS]

Dear Harold:

Very glad to get your letter. Thanks, too, for the one you sent on. It contained lots of news from Europe.

No news at all over here. Except that I have a new job—about the twenty-third since you left. I'm with the Associated Publishers now, Dr. Woodson's Journal of Negro History, you know.* It's a "position," if you please! with very decent hours. I think I'm anchored here forever.

I hope you'll be teaching during the new term.

Sincerely,
Langston

1749-S-Street, N.W.,
Washington, D.C.,
January thirteenth |1925|.

* Quitting his job at the Washington Sentinel, Hughes worked in a wet-wash laundry and as a pantry man in an oyster house. He then joined the staff of Dr. Carter G. Woodson (1875–1950), a Harvard-trained African American historian, a founder of the Association for the Study of Negro Life and History, and the editor of its Journal of Negro History. He also founded, in 1926, Negro History Week (which later became Black History Month). Hughes's main task was to help prepare for publication Woodson's current project, Free Negro Heads of Families in the United States in 1830, a list of some thirty thousand names.

TO CARL VAN VECHTEN   [*TLS*]

1749 S Street, N. W.
Washington, D.C.
May 15, 1925.

Dear Friend,*

I would be very, very much pleased if you would do an introduction to my poems. How good of you to offer. I am glad you liked the poems in the new arrangement and I do hope Knopf will like them, too. It would be great to have such a fine publisher!

About your paper on the Blues,†—Sunday I am going to type some old verses for you that I used to hear when I was a kid, and that you may or may not have heard. You probably have. On the new records I think the Freight Train Blues (one of the many railroad Blues) is rather good, and Reckless Blues, and Follow the Deal on Down. Did you ever hear this verse of the Blues?

> I went to the gypsy's
> To get my fortune told.
> Went to the gypsy's
> To get my fortune told.
> Gypsy done told me
> Goddam your un-hard-lucky soul!

I first heard it from George, a Kentucky colored boy who shipped out to Africa with me,—a real vagabond if there ever was one.‡ He came on board five minutes before sailing with no clothes, nothing except the shirt and pants he had on and a pair of silk sox carefully wrapped up in his shirt pocket. He

* Carl Van Vechten (1880–1964), a prominent writer suddenly enthralled by black culture, first met Hughes at a benefit party on November 19, 1924, in Harlem. He later introduced Hughes to Alfred and Blanche Knopf (of Alfred A. Knopf, Van Vechten's main publisher). Van Vechten persuaded them to bring out Hughes's first book of poems, *The Weary Blues* (1926). He also befriended and promoted the careers of several other major figures of the Harlem Renaissance, including Zora Neale Hurston and Wallace Thurman.
† Van Vechten's essay "The Black Blues: Negro Songs of Disappointment in Love: Their Pathos Hardened with Laughter" was published in *Vanity Fair* (August 1925) as part of a series of articles on African American songs that he wrote for the magazine.
‡ Hughes writes about George in *The Big Sea*.

didn't even know where the ship was going. And when somebody on board gave him a suit he traded it in the first port to sleep with a woman. He used to make up his own Blues,—verses as absurd as Krazy Kat[*] and as funny. But sometimes when he had to do more work than he thought necessary for a happy living, or, when broke, he couldn't make the damsels of the West Coast believe love |was| worth more than money, he used to sing about the gypsy who couldn't find words strong enough to tell about the troubles in his hard-luck soul.

I did like the Blind Bow-boy. I hope you will send Peter Whiffle.[†] Do you know any Negro Pauls in Harlem—those decorative boys who never do any work and who have some surprisingly well-known names on their lists? In a really perfect world <,though,> people who are beautiful or amusing would be kept alive <anyway> solely because they are beautiful and amusing, don't you think?

About the story of my life,—I don't know what you want it for, and for me to sit down seriously and think about it and write it would take a long, long time. I mean,—to show cause and effect, soul-peregrinations, and all that sort of thing. <How serious it sounds!> But I will send you an outline sketch of external movements; an essay I did for the Crisis Contest on the Fascination Of Cities;[‡] and a semi-autobiographical poem I did for the Crisis, but which I don't think they're publishing. Out of all that junk you'll perhaps get something. And then if you would know more, just ask me, and I'll be glad to answer.

I'm having some pictures taken here, but they may not be as good as the Muray[§] ones, so perhaps you'd better get him to give you one of his if you wish one.

I am anxiously awaiting the June Vanity Fair. I like the magazine, and Countee |Cullen| does such lovely things. What's become of John Peale Bishop?[¶]

---

* The comic strip Krazy Kat, created by George Herriman in 1913, ran in many American newspapers through the mid-1940s.
† The Blind Bow-Boy (1923) and Peter Whiffle: His Life and Works (1922) are novels by Van Vechten.
‡ Hughes's autobiographical essay "The Fascination of Cities" won second prize in the August 1925 Crisis essay competition. The Crisis published it in January 1926.
§ Born Miklós Mandl, Nickolas Muray (1892–1965) was a Hungarian-born photographer based in New York City. By the mid-1920s, he had become widely admired for his portraits in Harper's Bazaar and elsewhere.
¶ John Peale Bishop (1892–1944), a former managing editor of Vanity Fair, published many critical essays, four books of poetry, a volume of short stories, and a novel.

I liked his work and I don't believe I've read anything of his lately. And Nancy Boyd's clever essays?*

Remember me to Harlem.

Sincerely,
Langston

TO CARL VAN VECHTEN   [*TLS*]

Thursday |June 4, 1925|

Dear Carl,

I have been thinking about what you said concerning the histoire de ma vie and the making of a book out of it. I would rather like to do it and yet there are a number of reasons why I wouldn't like to do it. The big reason is this: There are so many people who would have to be left out of the book, and yet they are people who have been the cause of my doing or not doing half the important things in my life, but they are or have been my friends, for that reason I couldn't write them up as I would like to. Besides most of them are still very definitely connected with my life in a negative or positive way. So you see, unless I showed effects without causes, or else fictionalized a good deal (which might be interesting) the book wouldn't be all that it ought to be. Do you get me? And then I'm tired. I've had a very trying winter and don't feel like doing anything all summer except amusing myself. And writing prose isn't amusing after a day of reading censuses in an office. I can't be bored both night and day and I don't want to be driven back to sea from sheer boredom. I ought to give college another trial. Besides, I think I will like Howard.

I've just discovered a number of little bars here frequented by southern Negroes where they come to play the banjo and do clog dances. There may be a chance to pick up some new songs and one certainly sees some interesting types.

When you mentioned Bessie Smith you reminded me that I once wrote a Blues for her but never did anything with it. It's nothing unusual but I'm sending it to you. If you see her ask her if she likes it. She used to be quite amusing when she was doing her old act in small-time houses. And when she sang He May Be Your Man at the big anniversary performance of Shuffle

---

* Edna St. Vincent Millay (1892–1950), deeply admired as a poet by Hughes, published prose under the pseudonym Nancy Boyd.

Along in New York (were you there?) she was a "riot," but the last time I saw her she didn't seem so good. But I like her records,—and speaking of Blues, have you heard Clara Smith[*] sing <u>If You Only Knowed</u>? It's a real, real sad one! Do hear it. But I believe our tastes in Blues differ. You like best the lighter ones like Michigan Waters and I prefer the moanin' ones like Gulf Coast and Nobody Knows the Way I Feel This Morning. Have you seen one Ozzie McPhearson?[†] She does a low-down single that is really good, but I expect she'll cut half the rough stuff when she plays New York and then she won't be so funny. When will your paper on the Blues appear? And is Campaspe in Firecrackers?[‡] I hope so.

I believe Vanity Fair is using some of my stuff. They sent me a telegram for some more. Otherwise I haven't heard from them. I'm glad if they liked some of it.

Zora Neale Hurston is a clever girl, isn't she?[§] I would like to know her. Is she still in New York?

What a magnet New York is! Better to be a dish washer there than a very important person in one's own home town seemingly. A young student friend of mine <from Mexico> has finally arrived there,—to work in a hotel. And yesterday a letter came from Africa, from a boy in Burutu, saying that he intends to stowaway for New York the first chance that offers! And half the Italian boys I knew in Desenzano swear that in a few years they will all be waiters at the Ritz!

Thanks for telling me what the songs are in They Knew What They Wanted.[¶] And for the suggestions toward writing the book.

I sent you one of the new pictures. Out of four poses I am not sure it is the best, but perhaps you will like it. It looks somewhat like me anyhow. But to relieve the seriousness I am enclosing some snapshots taken with the office girls here.

---

[*] Clara Smith (1894–1935), a groundbreaking African American blues singer, was sometimes called "Queen of the Moaners."

[†] In 1925, blues singer Ozie McPherson recorded the songs "You Gotta Know How" and "Outside of That He's All Right with Me" for Paramount Records in Chicago.

[‡] Van Vechten's *Firecrackers: A Realistic Novel* (1925) features Campaspe Lorillard, who also appears in his novels *The Blind Bow-Boy* (1923) and *Nigger Heaven* (1926).

[§] Zora Neale Hurston (1891–1960), from Eatonville, Florida, was an African American folklorist, playwright, and fiction writer who studied anthropology at Columbia University under Franz Boas and received a BA from Barnard College in 1928. Her most influential works include the novel *Their Eyes Were Watching God* (1937) and her autobiography, *Dust Tracks on a Road* (1942).

[¶] Sidney Howard (1891–1939) won the Pulitzer Prize in 1925 for his play *They Knew What They Wanted*.

I would like to come up to New York again but can't make it for at least two months yet. My expenditures are always ahead of my income and my monthly check is gone before it comes. But I am going to exercise economy, as I have been so often advised, if I can find anything to exercise it on. Being broke is a bore. That's one reason why I like the sea,—the old man always advances money in port and at sea one doesn't need any, but on land one needs money all the time and I don't believe I've ever had enough money at any one time to last me more than a day. If it's a quarter it goes, if it's fifty dollars it goes just the same, and the next day. . . . one looks for some more. Today is only the fourth yet my pockets show no signs of having received anything on the first. And June is a long month. All months are.

Write to me soon.

I send pansies and marguerites to you, too,*

Sincerely,
Langston

TO CARL VAN VECHTEN [TLS]

Friday |October 9, 1925|

Dear Carl,

I have been trying to write you for the last two weeks. I have a new job now working in a hotel.† The hours are longer but I have the whole afternoon off. Almost every day some one comes in, tho, so I get nothing done. I wished I lived in an apartment like you with a hall boy so I could telephone down: Nobody home. . . . When one gets real famous one must have to be bored with a lot of uninteresting people,—no?

A few days ago I sent you some new Blues. I want to dedicate the best one to you, if any of them are ever published,—and if you like it. I think the Po' Boy Blues is the best and if you know anyone who would like to do music for one or two of them, please hand them over to them. I've got any number of verses, but haven't been able to put anything together that I think The Mercury‡

---

* Van Vechten closed his letter to Hughes of June 4 with the wish "pansies and marguerites to you!" Similar closing flourishes are common throughout their correspondence.
† Hughes worked as a busboy at the Wardman Park Hotel in Washington at a salary of $55 per month.
‡ The iconoclastic magazine *The American Mercury* was founded by H. L. Mencken and George Jean Nathan in 1924. Van Vechten contributed several articles to the periodical in 1925 and 1926, but it published none of Hughes's poems.

would like. I wish I could. I don't think they'd want just a plain song like I sent you, do you?

Jessie Fauset was down here for a week-end a short time ago. She is enthusiastic about your book on cats.* Says it's the best thing of yours she has read. Everybody here likes your article on the Negro theatre in Vanity Fair, too. Locke wishes he could have had it for his book. I like your suggestions for improving the revues, especially the one about the choruses: why they don't use black choruses for a colored show, I don't know. They can usually sing better and certainly work harder than the yellow girls. A cabaret scene would be a scream, too, if they'd do it right. Irvin Miller† did have one in one of his shows once. Did you see it, where a black man kept following a high yellow girl around the cabaret floor until his shoes wore out?

The autobiography is coming. I believe it is going to be interesting. I want to have it ready by the first of the year. What's the news about my other book, do you know? And your Negro novel?. . . . . Are you still thinking of going abroad? . . . How did Hotsy-Totsy go in Paris?‡

Would Knopf object to my reading the Weary Blues over the radio? There's a bare chance of my getting an engagement at a rate that would be more than a month's salary at the hotel. The man has asked to see my poetry and is thinking of arranging a Blues accompaniment for The Weary Blues, so I have been told.

Your article with my poetry in Vanity Fair has brought me a number of letters from the various places where I used to live. And there was quite a piece in the Lincoln, Ill. paper about me, followed later by a letter from one of my former teachers telling about how well she remembered me and what a bright boy I was in her classes. You'd think I was famous already! Lots of people seemed to like the Fantasy in Purple.§

Did I tell you in my last letter that Hall Johnson had done the music for a new show that they hope to put on Broadway? I believe it is ready for rehearsals now.

Today is pay-day, so I must go back to work early before the money runs out. Last time I left half my pay in my locker and somebody stole it. This

---

* Van Vechten's *The Tiger in the House* was published in 1922.
† Irvin C. Miller (1884–1967), a Fisk University graduate, was a writer, producer, and actor. He wrote the book for and performed in the musical comedy *Liza* (1923).
‡ "Hotsy-Totsy" alludes to *La Revue Nègre*, an all-black revue produced by Caroline Dudley Reagan that made Josephine Baker an overnight star in Paris. The show opened there at the Théâtre des Champs-Elysées on October 2, 1925.
§ Four of Hughes's poems, including "Fantasy in Purple," appeared with an introduction by Van Vechten in the September 1925 issue of *Vanity Fair*.

time I shall not be so stupid. I shall buy some new Blues records and pay my rent. . . . The place I work is quite classy. There are European waiters and it caters largely to ambassadors and base-ball players and ladies who wear many diamonds. It is amusing the way they handle food. A piece of cheese that everybody carries around in <his> hands in the kitchen needs two silver platters and six forks when it is served in the dining room.

Write to me soon.

This time purple asters and autumn leaves,

Sincerely,

Langston

<1749 S Street,
North west.>

TO THE DEAN OF LINCOLN UNIVERSITY [ALS]

1749 S Street, N.W.,
Washington, D.C.,
October 20, 1925.

Dean of the College,
Lincoln University, Pa.

Dear sir,

I wish to become a student at Lincoln University.* I am a graduate of Central High School, Cleveland, Ohio, and I have been for one year at Columbia College in New York City. I was forced to leave Columbia for lack of funds, but since then I have worked my way to Africa, have spent seven months in Paris and three months in Italy, and on the vessel in which I earned my passage home I visited many of the Mediterranean ports. I have also spent some time in Mexico where, after my high school graduation, I taught English. I have a fair knowledge of both French and Spanish.

My high school record admitted me to Columbia without my taking the entrance examinations. Some of my offices and honors in high school are as

---

* Founded in 1854, Lincoln University was the first historically black college or university to offer degrees. With an all-white faculty, it attracted some of the best students in the United States and beyond. Its many distinguished alumni include Justice Thurgood Marshall of the U.S. Supreme Court (1908–1993) and Kwame Nkrumah (1909–1972), the first president of Ghana.

follows: Member of the Student Council, President of the American Civic Association, Secretary of the French Club, First Lieutenant Cadet Corps, a letter for work on the track team, and in my senior year, Class Poet and Editor of the Year Book.

For some time I have been writing poetry. Many of my verses have appeared in "The Crisis" and "Opportunity."* "The Survey Graphic," "The Forum," "The World Tomorrow," "Vanity Fair," "The Messenger,"† and "The Workers' Monthly,"‡ as well as a number of news papers have also published my poems. Some of them have been copied by papers in Berlin, London, and Paris. A poem of mine, "The Weary Blues," received first prize in the recent Opportunity Contest and, in the Amy Spingarn Contest conducted by The Crisis, my essay received second prize. Early in the new year Alfred A. Knopf will publish my first book of poems.

I want to come to Lincoln because I believe it to be a school of high ideals and a place where one can study and live simply. I hope I shall be admitted. Since I shall have to depend largely on my own efforts to put myself through college, if it be possible for me to procure any work at the school, I would be deeply grateful to you. And because I have lost so much time, I would like to enter in February if students are admitted then. I have had no Latin but I would be willing to remove the condition as soon as possible. I must go to college in order to be of more use to my race and America. I hope to teach in the South, and to widen my literary activities to the field of the short story and the novel.

I hope I shall hear from you soon.§

Yours very sincerely,

Langston Hughes

---

* *Opportunity* magazine was founded by the National Urban League in 1923 and edited initially by Charles S. Johnson (on Johnson, see note for letter of February 27, 1928).
† *The Messenger,* a socialist monthly magazine edited by A. Philip Randolph (1889–1979) and Chandler Owen (1889–1967), ran from 1917 to 1928. Hughes's first published short stories (apart from those in his high school magazine), as well as sixteen of his poems, appeared in *The Messenger.*
‡ *The Workers Monthly* was a leftist magazine published by the Chicago-based Workers Party from November 1924 until February 1927. Hughes published five poems in the journal in 1925: "Drama for Winter Night" in March; "Poem to a Dead Soldier," "Park Benching," and "Rising Waters" in April; and "To Certain 'Brothers'" in July.
§ Acting at once, the dean wrote on October 22 to admit Hughes.

TO VACHEL LINDSAY   [TL]
[Surviving draft of a letter]

|c. December 1925|

Dear Vachel Lindsay,[*]

I have <been> a long time writing to thank you for your gift.[†] I had been away from the hotel with a severe cold and when I came back it was there for me. I don't know just how to thank you. But perhaps if I say,—and if you will believe me sincere,—that the gift, which you gave me in the ~~way~~ quiet way you did, is one of the most delightful things my poetry ever brought me. ——→ (You will understand how much I value it.) And certainly I am deeply pleased, and honor* by the beauty of your giving.

Taken soon after Hughes met Vachel Lindsay at the Wardman Park Hotel, Washington, D.C., 1925

Something of what you tell me in your letter on the fly leaves I already knew. I have long admired Amy Lowell and have read several ~~of her booksx~~ of her books of verse but none of her prose. Thank you for telling me about them and for giving me the John Keats which I had wanted to read but never hoped to own.

Thank you |for| the advice too. I <u>am</u> wary of lionizers. I <<u>do</u>> avoid invitations to receptions and teas. I'm afraid of public dinners. And people who tell me my verse is good I seldom believe. I see no factions to which I could belong and if I did I think should p<r>efer to walk alone,—to be myself.[‡] Don't be afraid. I will

* In November 1925, when the famed poet Vachel Lindsay (1879–1931) came to the Wardman Park Hotel to give a public reading, Hughes quietly slipped him the texts of three poems. On stage, Lindsay announced dramatically that he had discovered a genuine poet working as a busboy at the hotel. As proof, he then read aloud the three poems. The resulting publicity included a widely circulated photograph of Hughes hoisting a tray on the job.
† The poet Amy Lowell (1874–1925) had published that year a two-volume biography of John Keats (1795–1821). Lindsay elaborately inscribed a copy as a gift to Hughes.
‡ In his message (dated December 6, 1925) handwritten on the fly leaves of the biography, Lindsay warned Hughes: "Don't let lionizers stampede you. Hide and write and think. I know what factions can do. Beware of them. I know what flatterers can do. Beware of them."

not become conceited. If anything is important, it is my poetry not ~~myself~~ <me>. I do not want ~~people~~ <folks> to know me but if they know and like some of my poems I am glad. Perhaps the mission of an artist is to interpret beauty to the people,—the beauty within themselves. That is what I want to do, if I con<s>ciously want to do anything with poetry. I think I write it most because I like it. With it I seek nothing except not to make work out of it for so much |as| a line |of| propaganda for this cause or that. I want to keep it for the beauty<ful> thing it is.

Many of you of the "New Poetry" <movement> ~~have~~, yourself, Carl Sandburg,* Lola Ridge† have helped me to feel the worth of expressing beauty. I thank you <all> for that. And I thank <u>you</u> again for your kindness and your generousity to me here.

May you make many more beautiful poems.

In all sincerity,

TO AMY SPINGARN   [ALS]

1749 S Street, N.W.,
Washington, D.C.
December 29, 1925.

My dear Mrs. Spingarn,‡
I have been thinking a long time about what to say to you and I don't know yet what it should be. But I believe this: That you do not want me to write to you the sort of things I would have to write to the scholarship people. I think you

---

* The poet Carl Sandburg (1878–1967) was already noted for his lively use of free verse and American vernacular forms, including blues and jazz. He later wrote the biographies *Abraham Lincoln: The Prairie Years* (1926) and the Pulitzer Prize–winning *Abraham Lincoln: The War Years* (1939). He was a major early influence on Hughes, who later recalled him as "my guiding star."
† Lola Ridge (1873–1941) was a well-known poet and anarchist whose first collection, *The Ghetto and Other Poems*, appeared in 1918.
‡ The daughter of a rich businessman, Amy Einstein Spingarn (1883–1980) was an artist and a poet (she published a poem in 1924 in *The Crisis* under the name Amy Einstein) who had studied art history, literature, and foreign languages at Barnard College and Columbia University and in Europe. She successfully proposed marriage to Joel Elias Spingarn (1875–1939), at that time a stellar professor of literature at Columbia University, with whom she would have four children. She quietly enlisted in the suffragette and civil rights causes after he left Columbia in 1911 and became an NAACP leader. Hughes sent her a thank-you note after winning two cash prizes in the August 1925 *Crisis* literary contest that she had funded. Mrs. Spingarn then invited him to her Manhattan home at 9 West Seventy-third Street. At this meeting, Hughes told her about his wish to attend historically black Lincoln University, and about his need for money to do so.

understand better than they the kind of person I am or surely you would not offer, in the quiet way you do, the wonderful thing you offer me.* And if you were the scholarship people, although I might have to, I would not want to accept it. There would be too many conditions to fulfill and too many strange ideals to uphold. And somehow I don't believe you want me to be true to anything except myself. (Or you would ask questions and outline plans.) And that is all I want to do,—be true to my own ideals. I hate pretending and I hate untruths. And it is so hard in other ways to pay the various little prices people attach to most of the things they offer or give.

And so I am happier now than I have been for a long time, more because you offer freely and with understanding, than because of the realization of the dream which you make come true for me. . . . Words are clumsy things. I hope you understand what I mean.

I do want to go to Lincoln in February. But I had not expected to be able to do so. Strange that in the middle of a seemingly hopeless winter you should be the person to make "trees grow all around with branches full of dreams." But that is what you have done. You are surely the spirit of Christmas.

From February to June all expense at Lincoln may be covered by $200 or $225. A room deposit of $15 must be made before January 15th. The rest due the school may be paid upon entrance. I am very, very glad I am going to be able to go and the school wants me to come there.

I liked your little book immensely. You must have a number of good poems in order to be able to select twelve such very nice ones. I particularly like the Campanile one, L'Harmonie, and Change. Blue Water is lovely,—Round Lake, too,—and Pain is fine and true. It is an entirely beautiful little book. Thank you so much for letting me see it.

I am glad you liked my play for the children.† I am sending you some new poems. One, A House in Taos, nobody understands.

If you've ever wanted anything, and then have stopped wanting it because you were sure you wouldn't get it, then you maybe understand how glad I am, and how surprised, about going in February to Lincoln.

I <u>am</u> happy. What can I say to you to make you understand how very happy?

Sincerely,

Langston Hughes

---

* Amy Spingarn surprised Hughes with a letter offering him a loan of $300 to attend Lincoln. Her letter reached Hughes on Christmas Eve 1925.
† "The Gold Piece," Hughes's one-act play for children, appeared in the June 1921 edition of *The Crisis*.

TO HENRY BLOCK   [*TLS*]

1749 S St., N.W.,
Washington, D.C.,
January 16, 1925 |1926|.

Dear Block,*

Thanks for your letter and those announcements of the reading. They are beauties. The program last night went off well and there was a fair sized crowd in spite of four definitely conflicting gatherings: the annual meeting of the Penguin Club from which I would have drawn the larger part of my white attendance, the annual meeting of the N.A.A.C.P. which subtracted from my colored audience, a student council party at Howard which held the students, and a big society ball. But it wasn't so bad at that. There was a gang of teachers there and it took me longer to shake hands with everybody than it did to read my poems. We had a Blues interlude between the two sections of the reading,—that is between my jazz poems and The Weary Blues, and it went well. If you could get a real Blues piano player to play said Interlude at the New York reading it ought to be a wow! But he ought to be a regular Lenox Avenue Blues boy. The one we had here was too polished. The powers behind the tickets didn't want the one I had chosen so they got a nice piano player who knew how to read Blues but not play them. Result: nice music, but nothing grotesque and sad at the same time, nothing primitive, and nothing very "different." But maybe |Alain| Locke was right when he said our audience wouldn't get Blues in the rough. . . . . The Blues in between relieves the monotony of so much reading and gives the proper atmosphere for my cabaret poems too. Would you like to have it in New York? Carl |Van Vechten| ought to be able to help you find a player and it would be a novelty. Poetry recitals are usually such darn dull affairs.

Locke is coming to New York tonight. If you see him don't tell him I didn't like his Blues player. <I told him.>

It's one in the morning and I am very tired so I won't write any more. I've gone back to bussing dishes again. Had to. Rent day came, passed, and had been long gone and I haven't yet paid the lady.

I have an offer to read in Baltimore soon, also in Cleveland. And another in New York at the Civic Club on February 28th. So you see last night was good practice.

* Henry C. Block, known as "Harry," was a senior editor at Knopf.

I like my book. I hope you will let me autograph a copy for you when I come to town.

Sincerely

Langston

<See Locke's review of "The Weary Blues" for Palms* which I am sending Mrs. Knopf.>

TO CARL VAN VECHTEN [ALS]

February 21, 1926

Lincoln University, Pa.

Dear Carl,

Because I wanted to have time to sit down and write you a decent letter, I haven't written you at all. When I came back from New York I got in just in time to make a dinner engagement and from then on it was something every day and every night until I left. Negro History Week, with the demand for several readings, the public dinner at the "Y" in honor of |Alain| Locke's book and mine, the before leaving parties given by people who wouldn't have looked at me before the red, yellow, and black cover of the Weary Blues hit them in the eye, teas and telephones, and letters! Golly, I'm glad to get away from Washington.

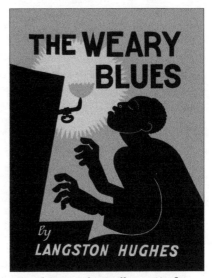

I read last Saturday night in Baltimore for Calverton and "The Modern Quarterly" group.† Had quite a nice time, stayed with them Sunday, and came on over here. They want to use some Blues, too.

Miguel Covarrubias's illustration for the dust jacket of *The Weary Blues*

---

* *Palms,* an American poetry magazine, was published in Mexico from 1923 to 1940. The work of several writers of the Harlem Renaissance appeared there.

† V. F. Calverton (1900–1940), a Baltimore leftist (whose real name was George Goetz), founded the influential *Modern Quarterly* in 1923 and edited it until his death. Calverton invited Hughes to give a public reading in Baltimore, which Hughes did on Saturday, February 13. He later sent Calverton several blues poems, but *Modern Quarterly* used only "Listen Here Blues" (May–July 1926).

I had a letter from Handy a couple of weeks ago about doing music for them.* I have said nothing yet. We can talk it over this week-end when I come up. I think I'm reading for the Civic Club next Sunday.

Hall Johnson tried music for the Midwinter Blues. It's the only one anyone has attempted. So Lament Over Love that you gave Rosamond,† or any of the others, are free. . . . . I hear The Reviewer is no longer being published, but if it is, I'm glad you've given them five of my Blues.‡ I hope that leaves some for a try at Poetry.§

I like the school out here immensely. We're a community in ourselves. Rolling hills and trees and plenty of room. Life is crude, the dorms like barns but comfortable, food plain and solid, first bell at six-thirty, and nobody dresses up,—except Sunday. Other days old clothes and boots. The fellows are mostly strong young chaps from the South. They'll never be "intellectuals,"—probably happier for not being,—but they have a good time. There are some exceptions, though. Several boys from Northern prep schools, two or three who have been in Europe, one who danced at the Club Alabam'. And then there are the ones who are going to be preachers. They're having revival now. But nothing exciting, no shouting. No spirituals. You might find it amusing down here, tho, if you come. I room with the campus bootlegger. The first night I was here there was an all night party for a departing senior. So ribald did it become that the faculty heard about it and sent five Juniors "out in the world." And are trying to find out who else was there. There is perhaps more freedom than at any other Negro school. The students do just about as they choose.

I think I'll be in New York Friday. Of course, I want to come see you some time during the week-end, if you'll let me. Miss Sergeant said something about my meeting Mable Dodge,¶ too, and also this trip I am supposed to

* William Christopher Handy (1873–1958), an African American composer and musician, is often called the "Father of the Blues" because of his historic standardization of this form when he published "Memphis Blues" (1912). In 1914, Handy wrote the renowned "St. Louis Blues." He set Hughes's "Golden Brown Blues" to music in 1927.

† John Rosamond Johnson (1873–1954), a singer, pianist, and composer, was the brother of James Weldon Johnson, also a skilled musician as well as a diplomat and writer. In 1899 the brothers composed "Lift Ev'ry Voice and Sing," which is often called the black American national anthem.

‡ From 1924 to 1925, Paul Green (1894–1981) and his wife, Elizabeth, edited The Reviewer in Chapel Hill, North Carolina. Green was a noted white playwright who explored African American themes with success; his In Abraham's Bosom won the Pulitzer Prize in 1927. The Greens turned The Reviewer into one of the few avant-garde, progressive journals in the South. Later it was folded into The Southwest Review of Dallas.

§ The Chicago-based monthly Poetry: A Magazine of Verse published four blues or blues-influenced poems by Hughes in November 1926 ("Suicide," "Hard Luck," "Po' Boy Blues," and "Red Roses").

¶ Elizabeth Shepley Sergeant (1881–1965), a journalist, was a friend of Mabel Dodge

meet A'Lelia Walker.* Last time she sent two books for me to autograph for her, but I didn't get to see her.

Miguel† and |Harry| Block and Walter‡ made it very pleasant for me last trip, and I enjoyed the dinner and evening with you immensely.

Did Meta§ get her book? I sent it.

I'm anxious to see "Lulu Belle."¶ Some of my poems were in the Herald Tribune last Sunday, I heard, but I didn't see it out here. However a check came so they must a been there.

Sincerely,

Langston

TO HENRY BLOCK [*ALS*]

March 9, 1926
Lincoln University

Dear Harry

Nothing exciting's happened since my return. Only I have been swamped by letters and have been working overtime to get them answered. . . . Still in love with the school and shall probably be eight years in graduating,—if I keep on cutting classes. By that time I'd be writing bucolics. That's what one writes in the country, isn't it? . . . There's a good review of my book in the Messenger

---

Luhan (1879–1962), herself a patron of the arts and a friend of Van Vechten. Although Hughes's bleakly modernist poem "A House in Taos" is often taken to be about Luhan's home there, it was published in November 1925, long before he had a chance to meet her or see the house.

* A'Lelia Walker (1885–1931), daughter of Madame C. J. Walker (1867–1919), was probably the richest black woman in America in the 1920s, thanks to the success of her late mother's pioneering hair-care business aimed at the needs of black women. A patron of the Harlem Renaissance, A'Lelia Walker established in a part of her Harlem home a tearoom salon named "The Dark Tower," after Countee Cullen's popular poem "From the Dark Tower."

† Miguel Covarrubias (1904–1957) was a popular Mexican artist and caricaturist whose work appeared regularly in *The New Yorker* and *Vanity Fair*. Covarrubias, at the behest of Van Vechten, illustrated the dust jacket of Hughes's *The Weary Blues*.

‡ Blond and blue-eyed but proudly African American, the Atlanta-born Walter White (1893–1955) was a major figure in the NAACP. From 1931 to 1955 he led the organization. He was also a writer. In 1924 Knopf published *The Fire in the Flint*, his novel about racial violence in the South.

§ Hughes refers to Meda Fry, the Van Vechtens' housekeeper.

¶ In February 1926, the Broadway production by David Belasco (1853–1931) of *Lulu Belle*, a melodrama of Harlem street life, featured the white actress Lenore Ulric appearing in blackface along with several black actors. The play contributed to Harlem's sudden popularity with adventurous whites.

this month. Have you seen it? Let me know if anything interesting comes out of the New York papers. And when the New Republic uses my Blues*. . . . I'm reading in Trenton Saturday and may get on up to New York, but don't think so. Better save the bucks for Easter. . . . . Have been reading around the country-side with the college quartet making a few dollars and some country meals that didn't taste so bad. . . . Have got a lot of clippings from the Southern papers (white papers) that have been publishing The Weary Blues. And even a front page story in a Georgia paper. Maybe you saw it. . . . Had to turn down the Indianapolis reading because we couldn't get the dates fixed. Wasn't anxious about going to that far-off town anyway. Walter White's going out April 12th, they told me, to speak.

I'm enclosing the publicity dope I promised. Hope you will be able to get something out of it,—if you're on publicity. Are you? It's written up in outline for someone else to make the story from. Put in a good word for the school.

I'm reading in Cleveland on April 16th at the Y.M.C.A. auditorium. Could you get some advance publicity stories in the Cleveland papers? And would you send whatever advertising material you can, along with a picture, or a cut,—not that dopey looking one,—and a mat of Miguel |Covarrubias|'s cover such as you used on the New York bills to the man in charge: Mr. Sidney B. Thompson, 2216 East 40th Street, Cleveland, Ohio, as soon as possible. You might also have them asked how many books they wish to sell that evening. . . . . Could you have sent, too, a copy of the Borzoi Broadside† with the Negro books checked to Mr. Peter Thomas, Lagos, Nigeria, British West Africa. They tell me he's a big book buyer. . . . And please have half dozen Weary Blues sent to me here. Some of the boys want to buy them. Have them billed against my royalties. . . . And while you are sending out reading pictures might as well get one to Susie Elvie Bailey, Johnson College, Oberlin, Ohio, who is in charge of arrangements there‡. . . . . I'm sorry to bother you with all of this.

Say Howdy to Covarrubias and help him finish that Blues drawing for

* *The New Republic* published "Midwinter Blues," "Gypsy Man," and "Ma Man" in its April 14, 1926, issue.

† Blanche Knopf designed the original Borzoi, or Russian wolfhound, as the logo for Alfred A. Knopf, Inc. The *Borzoi Broadside* was a monthly magazine aimed at publicizing Knopf books.

‡ Susie Elvie Bailey (1903–1996) had invited Hughes to speak at Oberlin College. In 1928, she hosted him again at Hampton Institute in Virginia, where she taught music. There she introduced him to another young instructor, Louise Thompson (Patterson), who became one of his lifelong friends. In 1932, Bailey married the noted black theologian Howard Thurman (1899–1981).

Vanity Fair. And if review copies of Poppy Juice* are being sent out to the world, or if there are any extra proof sheets lying around, I'd like to get a slant at it. If it touches South Sea folks or Negroes anywhere I could review it.

See you Easter—Sincerely—Langston

TO CARL VAN VECHTEN   [ALS]

Dear Carl,

Yesterday brought a nice telegram from Lenore Ulric thanking me for The Weary Blues I sent her.† This morning one of my classmates committed suicide, or tried to, with a razor. He isn't dead yet. "Negroes are 'posed to cut <u>one</u> <u>another</u> with razors, but when they start to cuttin' themselves, they're gettin' too much like 'fay folks," is the most expressive comment of the student body on the case. I'm hoping the poor boy dies if he wants to, but naturally they had to tie his neck up and try to save him.

|W. C.| Handy sent me what I believe to be a good contract for setting music to my Blues. I'll let you read it when I come up. . . . Hall Johnson's singers came off well at their recital, he tells me. He said you were there.

Some copies of the second printing of my book came to me this week. . . . I read in the Times where Vachel Lindsay was giving a talk on it Tuesday in New York. Also see where it was put out of the library in Jacksonville, Fla. . . . The Times review last Sunday was interesting. I can't see, though, why they chose "Poëme d'Automne" to illustrate my troubadour-like qualities.

In Trenton where I read for the colored Teacher's Association a couple of weeks ago I called them "intellectuals" in saying that they might not "get" my cabaret poems, but that night they retaliated by giving a Charleston party to show me how wild they could be. . . . Are you still in New York! I think I'll be in town Thursday for the Easter week-end. I'm due to read at Martin's Book Shop on Friday. Will there be any chance of meeting Rebecca West?‡ I'd like to. I think I'll be staying at Hall Johnson's, but I'll give you a ring soon as I get in. I'm broke but hope to get a ride up on the mushroom trucks that go to market nightly, or else borrow from the school. They are good about lending

---

* Probably "Poppy Juice," a dramatic narrative poem by Genevieve Taggard (1894–1948). First published in *Words for the Chisel* (Knopf, 1926), "Poppy Juice" tells a story of hula girls, smugglers, opium, and leprosy.

† Lenore Ulric (1892–1970) had recently played the lead in *Lulu Belle* (see Hughes to Van Vechten, February 21, 1926).

‡ Rebecca West (1892–1983) was an English novelist whose work was published frequently in *The New Republic* and *The New Yorker*.

money out here. Lincoln is more like what home ought to be than any place I've ever seen.

I hope "Nigger Heaven"'s successfully finished.* It is, isn't it?

Tulipanes à tu,

Langston

March 26, 1925 |1926|
Lincoln University, PA

TO BLANCHE KNOPF   [ALS]

Lincoln University, Pa.,
April 27, 1926.

Dear Mrs. Knopf,†

I am sorry about being so late in returning the Bryn Mawr Alumnae book which you sent me to sign but it came while I was away,—Cleveland, Oberlin, and Indianapolis, giving readings, and a slight auto accident kept me out there a few days overtime to get patched up. The book was sent, too, to my Washington address, which I am no longer using, so please have it taken off your files.

The readings were all successful. Good crowds, good publicity in the local papers, an interview in Cleveland, forty-five books sold in Indianapolis, and return dates for next winter. I met Mary Rennels of Burrow's in Cleveland, whom I think you know, and signed several books for Beach's Book Shop in Indianapolis.

The New Orleans Times Picayune devotes nearly a column to a review of my book (April 4th).‡ Unusual for a Southern paper I thought. Several other good reviews have come in recently.

Did you find the foreign list of folks to whom I suggested sending books? I hope so. "The Weary Blues" and "Jazzonia" appeared in French translation in an excellent article on Negro poetry recently in a Liège paper. The colored

---

* Knopf published Van Vechten's controversial, best-selling novel of Harlem life, *Nigger Heaven*, later that year.

† The daughter of a Viennese-born jeweler in New York, Blanche Wolf Knopf (1894–1966) was vice president of the publishing house named after her husband, who incorporated the firm with her in 1918. She was crucial to its success, seeking out foreign authors such as Sigmund Freud, Albert Camus, Jean Paul Sartre, Simone de Beauvoir, André Gide, and Thomas Mann. She remained Hughes's editor there until she succeeded Alfred as president of the firm in 1957.

‡ The *Times-Picayune*, which traces its origins to 1837, is a distinguished, white-owned newspaper based in New Orleans.

papers and magazines copy foreign write-ups, so they make good publicity over here.

I'd like, if there is another printing, to have corrected an error made in the second printing. In the poem "Negro Dancers" (Page 26) the quotation marks (") should be placed after the sixth line of the poem, at the end of the verse, and <u>not</u> after the third line.

And would you please have sent me, here at the school, six copies of "The Weary Blues." Merci.

Sincerely,
Langston Hughes

TO ALAIN LOCKE   [ALS]

Tuesday,
Lincoln University, Pa.
|January 1927|

Dear Locke,

Here's Mulatto.* My book will be ready this week.† Then you will have all the poems from which to make a selection. Exams begin soon so I won't be in New York anymore until the 29th. Will you be there then, too?

Did I tell you about the Knopf's party New Year's? Yasha Heifitz,‡ Ethel Barrymore,§ Steffansson,¶ Fannie Hurst,** and almost everybody was there.

I'm doing six short stories with the West African coast and a steamship as the background. I haven't been able to do anything else but write on them

---

* Hughes's poem "Mulatto," on one of the most compelling themes in his writings, appeared in *The Saturday Review of Literature* on January 29, 1927. It helped to shape a major short story ("Father and Son") in *The Ways of White Folks* (1934), his Broadway play *Mulatto* (1935), and his Broadway opera *The Barrier* (1950).

† *Fine Clothes to the Jew*, Hughes's second book of poems, published by Knopf in January 1927.

‡ Jascha Heifetz (1901–1987) was a Russian-born American violin virtuoso.

§ Ethel Barrymore (1879–1959), an Academy Award–winning actress and Broadway performer, was a member of one of America's best-known acting families.

¶ Probably Harold Jan Stefansson, the nephew of the explorer Vilhjalmur Stefansson (1879–1962). The younger Stefansson lived at this time in Harlem with his close friend Wallace Thurman at 267 West 136th Street. Zora Neale Hurston dubbed their home "Niggeratti Manor" because it attracted many of the younger black writers and artists. Stefansson helped Thurman produce the only issue of the magazine *Fire!!* (1926).

** Fannie Hurst (1889–1968) was an American novelist most famous perhaps for her *Imitation of Life* (1933), about a pale-skinned "black" woman who tragically defies and denies her mother in passing for white. Zora Neale Hurston worked as Hurst's assistant during Hurston's early years in New York.

for the past week. Two are finished. I wish the ideas hadn't struck me just at exam time,—and a million of unanswered letters lying around, too.

If you want to do me a grand favor ———▶ you can mail me a ten $ until the first when my royalties come due again. Otherwise my strength may fail me, and I won't get my stories done. (Where do you suppose I can sell them? They're about sailors, and missionaries' daughters, and port-town girls.)*

Hope I'll see you in New York.

Sincerely,
Langston

TO WALTER WHITE

|February 1927|

Dear Walter,

Here's a note for your publicity service,—I've been invited to read my poems at Walt Whitman's house in Camden on March first. Invitation comes from the Walt Whitman Foundation and because I admire his work so much it seemed a great honor for me to read my humble poems in the house where he lived and worked.

"Fine Clothes" has been getting some good reviews.†

Hope you've gotten rested up. You looked tired when I saw you.

"Hello" to Jane and Gladys.‡

Langston

---

* These stories were "Luani of the Jungles" (*Harlem*, November 1928) and, appearing in *The Messenger*: "Bodies in the Moonlight" (April 1927); "The Young Glory of Him" (June 1927); and "The Little Virgin" (November 1927).

† In a wan reference to pawnbrokers serving the black poor, *Fine Clothes to the Jew* (1927) took its title from the last two lines of the first stanza of Hughes's poem "Hard Luck." He later conceded that "it was a bad title, because it was confusing and many Jewish people did not like it. I don't know why the Knopfs let me use it, since they were very helpful in their advice about sorting out the bad poems from the good, but they said nothing about the title." In fact (unknown to him) the Knopfs, who were Jewish, disliked the title but gave in after Van Vechten vigorously defended it. Almost certainly, as with *The Weary Blues*, Van Vechten himself had suggested the title. While reviews by whites of *Fine Clothes to the Jew* were positive, most notices in the African American press were extremely hostile because of its championing of lower-class black culture.

‡ Gladys White was married to Walter White, and Jane was their daughter.

TO CLAUDE MCKAY   [ALS]

Lincoln University, Pa.
May 28, 1927.

Dear Claude,

It's a shame to answer your letter on such paper,—that <u>mighty welcome</u> letter I had been waiting for so damn long,—but I'm in the midst of packing up to leave here for The South,—Nashville (Fisk), Marshall and Hollister, Texas, where I'm to read poetry to student groups, and then "on the bum" through the flood district* to New Orleans, and then back up to New York (working my way on the fruit-boats). This will take all summer, I guess, and ought to yield some grand experiences. I've never been South before, and I've always wanted to go. Am still pretty broke, but what I make from the readings ought to help me through. They only last (I'm glad to say) till June 15th, then I'm free for the summer . . . . . . That's great about your novel. I hear the jacket has already been designed by Aaron Douglas.† I'm surely glad you're better and things are going pretty well again. I know how it is about writing, and didn't think you had forgotten me at all,—only I was worried about you,— and ashamed because I've been broke all the time, too, and couldn't help you any. . . . Tried writing lyrics for Broadway shows but none of them have been put on so far. . . . The best of the lot, now in rehearsal, I had to drop on account of school and their unwillingness to give an advance to make it worthwhile losing a semester. The theatre is too unsure a place to work in. . . . Thanks for what you say about my book |*Fine Clothes to the Jew*|. Colored critics razed it to death, but the big papers and magazines were very kind. It goes into another edition this month. "Weary Blues" will always be the most popular book, I think. It's more "poetically" poetic. . . . . Didn't leave N.Y. last summer. . . . Hope you do come home soon. Lord knows I'd like to see you. . . . Write c/o Alfred A. Knopf, Inc., 730 Fifth Avenue, N. Y. When you get this I'll be in Texas which must be a lonesome place! Think about me.

   Good luck, ole boy!

Langston

---

* In April 1927, the swollen Mississippi River flooded more than 23,000 square miles in the most destructive inundation in American history.
† Aaron Douglas (1899–1979) is the illustrator, painter, and muralist most closely identified with the Harlem Renaissance. He designed the cover of Wallace Thurman's magazine *Fire!!* in 1926 and the dust jacket for McKay's novel *Home to Harlem* (1928).

TO CARL VAN VECHTEN [ALS]

Memphis,*
June 11, |1927|

Dear Carl,

Last night at a revival I heard what was to me a brand new train song with this refrain:

> "We's bound fo' de
> heavenly depot,
> "Where de angel
> porters wait."

It's the first time I'd ever heard angels referred to as Red Caps!

Beale Street is not what it used to be according to its present inhabitants. But it's still full of Blues coming out of alleys and doorways. Yesterday I spent the afternoon in a barrel house at 4th and Beale where three musicians, all of whom claimed to have been with |W. C.| Handy, played all kinds of Blues until they were overcome with gin. And the girl who won the amateur contest at the vaudeville show last night sang a Flood Blues something like Bessie |Smith|'s on the record.

"The National Grand United Order of Wise Men and Women of the World" meets nightly just across the street in front of my windows, over the Yellow Pine Cafe. The "P.Wee Saloon" is just down the block.

Tomorrow I'm going to Vicksburg, Miss. and the flood region, then on to New Orleans. My address there for mail will be

3444 Magnolia St.,
c/o Mrs. Jackson.

"Ain't gonna sing it no mo',"—

Langston

* After reading his poems in June at Commencement at Fisk University in Nashville, Hughes stopped in Memphis to explore Beale Street and the notorious blues district around it. He also visited Cuba and New Orleans, before returning north in a car driven by Zora Neale Hurston.

TO CARL VAN VECHTEN   *[ALS]*

Havana, Cuba,*
July 15, 1927.

Dear Carl,

Havana is not all it might be at this time of year, yet I've rather enjoyed it so far. There is a marvelous Chinatown here where I went last night with some of the Chinese fellows from our crew. They have cousins there waiting to be smuggled into New Orleans or New York. We had some very good food and a jar of Chinese whiskey (and I'm bringing a jar to you, if it ever gets there. It ought to make grand cocktails.—I hope you haven't stopped drinking again.) Then we went to a house where there are girls in little shuttered rooms built around an open courtyard. There are three floors, and literally hundreds of Chinese walking around and around looking at them. It's right near the Chinese theatre and is always crowded. . . . I am the only "colored"

colored person on my ship. The crew is all mixed up,—Spaniards, German, South Americans, Philipinos and Chinese. The confusion of languages is amusing. We are loading sugar here and I think we're going directly back to New Orleans in a few days. . . . Just the day before I sailed I met Walter |White|'s brother-in-law and he told me about the little new Carl.† Great!. . . . I'm glad it was a boy and that it has been so well named. . . . . Walter's brother-in-law is a very nice fellow. I'm going to see him when I go back. . . . . By the way, I was in New Orleans three weeks without meeting a single "dicty" person,—then someone took me to the Aristocrats Club, I believe the

Carl Van Vechten, 1932

---

* Eager to see Cuba, Hughes sailed from New Orleans to Havana as a mess boy aboard the freighter *Munloyal.* He returned to New Orleans on July 20.
† Walter and Gladys White had named their baby Carl in honor of their friend Van Vechten.

name was, and then invitations began to come in to go places,—and the next day I got this job to Cuba,—so I'm saved. . . . There's a street called Poydras Street where one can hear Blues all night long,—and most of the day, too. A stevedore called Big Mac is particularly good and seems to know a thousand verses. I never heard any of these before:

> Did you ever see peaches
> Growin' on a watermelon vine?
> Did you ever see peaches
> On a watermelon vine?
> Did you ever see a woman
> I couldn't take for mine?
>
> If you shake that thing I'll
> Buy you a diamond ring.
> If you shake that thing I'll
> Buy you a diamond ring,—
> But if you don't shake it
> I ain't gonna buy you a thing.
>
> Yo' windin' and yo grindin'
> Don't have no 'fect on me.
> Yo' windin' and grindin'
> Don't have no 'fect on me
> Cause I can wind and grind
> Like a monkey climbin' a cocoanut tree.
>
> Throw yo' arms around me
> Like de circle round de sun.
> Throw yo' arms around me
> Like de' circle round de sun
> and tell me, pretty mama,
> How you want yo' lovin' done.

I lived for a week on Rampart Street which is the Lenox Avenue down there, then I moved into the Vieux Carré just in front of St. Louis Cathedral, in a house with stone floors, wooden blinds, an open court and balconies,—a very old place and quite charming. . . . . To me, New Orleans, seems much like a southern European city. Everything is cheap, and every-thing is wide open. There is good wine at 30¢ a bottle and even whiskey at 5¢ a drink in some bars. . . . I met the caretakers of the old St. Louis Cemetery,—Creole fellows who do little work and can be found any after-noon behind some cool tomb, with a few bottles of white wine at hand. They took me to meet their families and to several jolly Creole parties and gumbo suppers.

Write to me c/o Mrs. A. C. Johnson, 3444 Magnolia Street, N.O. or else to Tuskegee after July 25. . . . . Wish you'd send me Eddie Wasserman's address, too, so I can drop him a card.* I'm not sure I remember it correctly. Tell him "hello" for me.

Pañal and Bacardi to you,

Langston

P.S. You can buy all sorts of voodoo stuff in Poydras Street, too,—Follow Me Powder, War and Confusion Dust, Black Cats' Blood, etc. I thought I'd bring you a bottle of Good Luck Water, but I think you'd rather have the Chinese licker.

* Eddie Wasserman, reputedly an heir to a banking fortune, was a noted bon vivant and a close friend of Carl Van Vechten. In *The Big Sea*, Hughes mentions the lively interracial parties that Wasserman hosted.

In Haiti, 1931

What right has anyone to say
That I
Must throw out pieces of my heart
For pay?
—"POET TO PATRON," 1939

In 1927, in what would prove ultimately to be a major disaster, Hughes met an elderly white philanthropist, Charlotte Louise Mason (1854–1946) of Park Avenue in Manhattan. She soon won his heart through an outpouring of maternal love and support he had never before experienced—including a handsome monthly stipend to encourage his growth as a black writer. Hughes clearly fell in love with "God-mother," as she asked her various protégés to call her. Widowed since 1903, Mrs. Mason (born Charlotte Louise Van der Veer Quick in New Jersey) had devoted herself to a variety of interwoven causes involving ethnicity, spirituality, art, and humanity. Her intensity of vision would both inspire and bewilder Hughes. While Godmother wanted him to be a "primitive" poet true to her idealized vision of Africa, he had other interests, including leftist politics, which she found tiresome. Generally obedient and sympathetic to her goals, he was caught virtually naked emotionally and psychologically when in 1930 she suddenly, ruthlessly, broke with him. This rupture would also ruin his friendships with Alain Locke and Zora Neale Hurston, fellow "godchildren" of Mrs. Mason. Reeling from these losses, Hughes would flee in 1931 to the Caribbean to brood about them and about his prospects without her.

TO ALAIN LOCKE [ALS]

January 3, 1928

Dear Alain,

It was great to see you in New York and I was sorry you had to leave so soon. . . . I came back to school yesterday but I am still sleepy. I'm writing you this note, though, as Godmother* wishes you to have a memorandum of facts about Gwyn.†

Here goes:

13 years old
Sixth grade
Tendency to colds
Needs good food
Family where there are other children desirable
Also New England preferred because of schools
Change him if possible around end of Jan. when his school term ends.
In no case mention her or myself.

---

* In *The Big Sea*, Hughes describes Mrs. Mason: "My patron (a word neither of us liked) was a beautiful woman, with snow-white hair and a face that was wise and very kind. She had been a power in her day in many movements adding freedom and splendor to life in America. . . . Now she was very old and not well and able to do little outside her own home. But there she was like a queen. Her power filled the rooms."
† When Godmother asked Locke to find Hughes's stepbrother, Gwyn "Kit" Clark, a home and a school, Locke secured Gwyn a home in Springfield, Massachusetts, under the roof and care of a woman named Eva Stokein, as well as enrollment in a nearby school. Godmother paid the bills.

Bills to be paid thru you.

Write Godmother as soon as you have a place.

She is also trying thru a <u>Negro</u> doctor.

I know you must be very busy and I am sorry to put this extra task on you. Don't bother writing me until you have news.

Hope you're liking Fisk and are not too tired after the rush of getting moved.

I've started the New Year off gloriously by getting up in time for breakfast this morning.

Sincerely,

Langston

TO ALAIN LOCKE   [ALS]

Lincoln University, Pa.,

February 27, 1928.

Dear Alain,

Thanks for your card from my home state. I hope you enjoyed it out there. I had a delightful time at Lynchburg with Anne Spencer,*—and the best food,—waffles with honey, baked Virginia ham, and various other Southern delicacies. Then I went to New York for the rest of the week-end with God-mother. She has her victrola now and a great collection of records,—all of Robeson,† I believe, and almost all the best Blues. She loves the "Soft Pedal" and even the "Yellow Dog." And they sound marvelous on her machine. . . . The party for Madariaga was quite a success, I think.‡ Just about everybody was there, even Eugene Gordon§ down from Boston and Georgia Douglas¶

---

* Anne Spencer (1882–1975) was an African American modernist poet whose work appeared in various journals and in Locke's *The New Negro* (1925). While in Lynchburg, Virginia, Hughes stayed at the home Spencer shared with her husband.

† A graduate of Rutgers University and Columbia Law School, Paul Robeson (1898–1976) was an athlete, singer, actor of stage and screen, and civil rights activist.

‡ Jessie Fauset threw a party on February 8 for Salvador de Madariaga (1886–1978), a prominent Spanish diplomat who was then professor-elect of Spanish at Oxford University.

§ Eugene Gordon (1891–1974), an African American journalist, was an editor and a feature writer for *The Boston Post* from 1919 until 1940.

¶ A published poet, Georgia Douglas Johnson (1877?–1966) opened her home in Washington, D.C., mainly to other African American writers and their friends on Saturday evenings. Among the regulars at various times were Rudolph "Bud" Fisher, Richard Bruce Nugent, and Alain Locke. Her books of verse include *The Heart of a Woman* (1918), *Bronze* (1922), and *An Autumn Love Cycle* (1928).

up from your home town. He's a witty and amiable gentleman and kept the evening alive and humorous. But it was the most polite and bored gathering you ever saw before he came in. He had been with Johnson* to Porgy and after Jessie |Fauset|'s we went to Small's,— but it was no good.

Countée's wedding is going to be very grand.† He wants me to be an usher,— so I'll be in it, too,—with a swallow-tail coat on! Do be there to see it. . . . . He and Yolande are both getting fat. . . . . Claude |McKay|'s book is out in a few days as I guess you know. Also Nella Imes' soon.‡ Carl |Van Vechten| has finished a new one for next fall about Hollywood. . . . Bledsoe§ has had appendicitis, too, but didn't die. . . . I'm going to read a few Blues at Princeton next month with our Glee Club. . . . Some Dr. Anna Nussbaum of Vienna sends me a review from "Tageblatt" with two of my poems done in German.¶ She wants the exclusive right to translations in that language. Wonder if you know who she is? I don't.

I've just read Congaree Sketches and find it tremendously amusing and Negroish**. . . . Your African books were fascinating, too. Thanks so much for lending them to me. I discover therein that one had almost as well be civilized,—since primitiveness is nearly as complex. Godmother gave me Sandburg's Lincoln for my birthday. . . . I'm afraid it will take me years to read all the books I've been given in the last three months. . . . Yesterday I went to Philly with the boy from Haines.†† He says your prodigy is about 16 or 17, raised cane in Augusta, stayed out all night any time, and was smarter than any body

* Charles S. Johnson (1893–1956) was a University of Chicago–trained sociologist. As director of research for the National Urban League, he edited its monthly magazine *Opportunity*, which also encouraged black writers. In 1927, Johnson became the chair of the Department of Social Research at Fisk University. In 1946, he became its first black president.
† On April 9, Countee Cullen married Yolande Du Bois, daughter and only surviving child of W. E. B. Du Bois, in one of the most extravagant events (stage-managed by the bride's father) seen that year in Harlem. The marriage was short-lived.
‡ Nella Larsen (1891–1964) was the child of a black father from the Caribbean and a white mother from Denmark. From 1919 to 1933, she was married to Elmer Imes, an African American physicist. Knopf published her first novel, *Quicksand*, in 1928.
§ The African American actor and baritone Jules Bledsoe (1897?–1943) originated the role of Joe (who sings the show-stopping lament "Ol' Man River") in *Show Boat*, the Broadway musical by Jerome Kern and Oscar Hammerstein II based on Edna Ferber's novel of the same name.
¶ Anna Nussbaum, a socialist scholar, translated thirty-seven of Hughes's poems into German for publication in her anthology *Afrika Singt: Eine Auslese Neuer Afro-Amerikanischer Lyrik* ("Africa Sings: A New Selection of Afro-American Poetry") (1929).
** *Congaree Sketches* (1927) by Edward C. L. Adams, a white physician, is a collection of black folklore gathered from people living in the region around his home near the Congaree River in central South Carolina.
†† Haines Normal and Industrial Institute was located in Augusta, Georgia.

else, right on. . . . Met my mother in Philly and saw the new Miller & Lyles show which is <u>terrible.</u> All the old stuff done over again, even the blue overalls for the chorus, the cotton fields scenery, and the comedy of stealing from one another. . . . Little brother seems to be doing fine in Springfield,—likes the people and the schools. I'm very glad about it and deeply appreciative for what you've done. I'd rather have the kid happy than to be happy myself. I think he's going to be very smart,—anyhow, let's hope he's a "credit to the race". . . . I've written <u>The Crisis</u> about my poems but they haven't answered. . . . <u>The Tattler</u>, under Lewis, is becoming a kind of Harlem <u>New Yorker</u>,—quite smart and sophisticated, I think*. . . . Guess you know Club Ebony closed. . . . |Carter G.| Woodson spoke out here at Lincoln and made a big hit. . . . Do you know any body who might be inclined to give a scholarship to a very splendid fellow out here who suddenly finds himself broke? He is one of the few <u>real</u> people on the campus and it would be a shame if he has to leave while the 90 and 9 less worthy ones remain. . . . You ought to hear "Trouble in Mind" on the O.K. and Gene Austin's "Lonesome Road" on the Victor. And when you come to New York see "Simba," a marvelous picture of the African bush. . . . When are you coming back anyway? And when do you sail? . . . I've decided now I'd rather stay over here and get some work done. So far, I'm rather behind,—but I got a ② in math last semester,—which is an achievement of great worth in my life. You see, I'm getting smart!

Remember me to the Jones', the Gordons', Miss Watts, and Johnnie. And come on home before you get the Northern Blues. . . . Yee-hoo!

Langston

TO ALAIN LOCKE   [ALS]

March 1. | 1928|

Dear Alain,

Thanks immensely for <u>The African Saga</u>.† It's one of the new books I've wanted. It's a grand birthday gift. . . . . Just finished Claude |McKay|'s <u>Home to Harlem</u> and am wild about.‡ It ought to be named <u>Nigger Hell</u>, but I guess

* *The Inter-State Tattler,* a weekly black gossip sheet, was first published in 1925.
† *The African Saga* (1927) is an American translation of *Anthologie Nègre* (1921), a collection of African folktales and stories compiled by Blaise Cendrars (1887–1961), a Swiss-French poet, novelist, and soldier. Cendrars's main sources were accounts by European travelers, especially missionaries.
‡ Although publicly condemned by W. E. B. Du Bois for its celebration of lower-class hab-

the colored papers will have even greater spasms than before anyhow.* It's the best low-life novel I've ever read. Puts Francis Carco and Pio Baroja,—and even Gorky, in the shade,—for that kind of thing.† Up till now, it strikes me, that Home to Harlem must be the flower of the Negro Renaissance,—even if it is no lovely lily. . . . Can't ask my mother for $40. She hasn't got it.

Su seguro servidor,

Langston

TO CLAUDE MCKAY [ALS]

Lincoln University, Pa.,

March 5, 1928.

Dear Claude,

I was mighty pleased to have your letter and right on the heels of it came your book,—which is the most exciting thing in years. Undoubtedly, it is the finest thing "we've" done yet. And I don't mean limited by the "we". It's a very fine novel,—as fine as Baroja writing about Madrid, or Ibañez in his early stories of the poor of Valencia,‡ or Carco in Paris. . . . Lord, I love the whole thing. It's so damned real!. . . . Has there ever been another party anywhere in literature like Gin-Head Susy's? I thought that was marvelously well-done. . . . Jake and Ray and Rose and the landladies, and the dining car folks are all too alive to be in a book. . . . . . . I'm enclosing what I wrote to Ruth Raphael about it as publicity comment. I hope it will be a great sales success, too. . . . It's going to be amusing reading what the colored papers will say about it. They will want to tear you to pieces, I'm sure, but since they used up all their bad words on Nigger Heaven, and the rest on me,—I don't know what vocabulary they have left for you. . . . Didn't Keats say "Beauty is Truth"?. . . . But I don't suppose a one of the Negro editors will see that Home to Harlem is beauty. . . . But maybe you've done it so well that they can't help themselves. I hope so.

its and values, Claude McKay's *Home to Harlem* (1928) remains one of the defining novels of the Harlem Renaissance.

* Hughes is referring to the uproar among many blacks caused by the title of Carl Van Vechten's novel *Nigger Heaven* (1926).

† Francis Carco (1886–1958) was a French writer whose works describe the street life of Montmartre in Paris. Pio Baroja depicted the slums of Madrid (see also Hughes's letter to Locke of April 6, 1923). Maxim Gorky (1868–1936) wrote about the lives of the lower classes in Russia.

‡ Vicente Blasco Ibáñez (1867–1928) was a Spanish activist and novelist. In his early novels, such as *Flor de Mayo* (1895) and *La Barraca* (1898), he wrote graphically about farm life in Valencia.

I suppose you'll have a deluge of letters for the next few months, but if you can write me before summer, let me know where you are. I may be over when school closes. Not certain yet, though. . . . I guess you know most of the literary news over this way: A |René| Maran novel due; Bud Fisher novel, comedy vein, for fall;* Nella Imes novel, slight and delicate, this spring; a play and novel by Wallace Thurman next season,† I think. . . . And God knows how many books by white people about Negroes due soon, and due to be due. . . . . Your novel ought to give a second youth to the Negro vogue. Some said it would die this season. . . . . Have you seen Walter White around your way? What you doing from now on,—still remaining an expatriot?‡ . . . Couldn't you do a play, maybe? Our theatre's way behind the rest of our world. Are you all healthy again and happy? You deserve to be. . . . Wish I were in town so I could send you papers and magazines once in a while. We're two hours and more from Philly so I only see them in the library . . . The Colored press is always amusing. But the best thing lately has been an interview which Ethel Waters§ gave to a white paper in Cleveland in which she said (quite truthfully) that the most successful Negroes on the American stage got to be that way by playing just what they are,—darkies. . . . Of course, the best people are about to expire over that. They are so delicate! |Alain| Locke is at Fisk for a term. . . . Artist from Chicago, Motley, is holding the first Negro one-man show in a down town gallery.¶ His pictures are selling. . . . Countée |Cullen| in this month's Opportunity says it isn't always good to tell the truth. . . . He's to be married at Easter. I'm going to be an usher with a swallow-tail coat on. It'll be grand. . . . . Enjoy yo' damn self!

Sincerely,
Langston

---

* Rudolph "Bud" Fisher (1897–1934), a physician with a special interest in radiology, was also a noted writer of the Harlem Renaissance. Knopf published his first novel, *The Walls of Jericho*, in 1928.

† Hughes described Wallace Thurman (1902–1934) as "a strangely brilliant boy, who had read everything, and whose critical mind could find something wrong with everything he read." His books include the novels *The Blacker the Berry: A Novel of Negro Life* (1929) and *Infants of the Spring* (1932).

‡ The Jamaican-born Claude McKay was then living in France.

§ Ethel Waters (1896–1977) was an Academy Award–nominated actress and an acclaimed jazz singer also known for her popular rendition of the religious song "His Eye Is on the Sparrow." In 1951, Waters published an autobiography of the same name.

¶ Archibald J. Motley, Jr. (1891–1981), was praised for his paintings of black life in Chicago. Although he never lived in New York, his work became associated with the art of the Harlem Renaissance.

TO CLAUDE MCKAY   *[TLS]*

Lincoln University, Pa.,
September 13, 1928.

Dear Claude,

I am always sorry I answer letters so badly. I think of you so often and write you so seldom,—which seems to be my way with all the people I care anything about! Letters from people I never heard of always get answered regularly and promptly,—but I take all that as a part of helping my publishers sell my books,—which I have discovered is much more work than writing them. . . . . I no longer read my poetry to ladies clubs, Y. W. C. A., and the leading literary societies in places like Columbus,—as I did for two winters. I began to hate my own stuff as much as I do Browning or Longfellow. And being "an example" to little kids in schools and listening to teachers telling what a model to pattern after I am rather shamed me,—because I have never felt like a good example,—and am worse at making inspirational speeches than I am at answering letters. I like to read to kids, though. They always strike me as having much more sense than grown-ups, but I don't like being exhibited before them like a prize dog. Did you ever have to go through anything like that when you were first published? I don't suppose you'd have stood it, would you? I don't see how I did it either, but sometimes I wanted the fifty dollars and sometimes I thought I was helping charity or race relations or some other dull cause, or again I didn't like to say "No" to a friend or old schoolmate. And last summer it was the only way I could discover to get my fare paid into the South,—but once there I threw my books away and lived in New Orleans almost a month before anybody who wore a necktie discovered I was there,—and when they did I got a job to Cuba on a tramp and failed to appear at the club meeting called in my honor. . . . . Did you ever visit the Chinatown in Havana where thousands of them sleep on shelfs in warehouse-like boarding places waiting for a chance to come to the States? Or visit the whore-houses like kids visit the zoo, standing for hours in groups gazing at one woman and them moving on to the next doorway to gaze for a while at another? . . . . . You've been at Tuskegee, haven't you? Do you remember the power house dynamo that can be heard at night beating and pulsing like a hidden tom-tom at the heart of the place? And the nice Negroes living like parasites on the body of a dead dream that <was alive> once for Booker Washington? I want to do an article, or even a novel, about that place. I suppose it will be a

great university sometime with the Veterans Hospital for a med school. . . . .
This summer I went North for awhile,—Provincetown and Boston. I liked
the beaches at Cape Cod and the clams,—but the artists are awful!. . . . . In
Boston I didn't go anear Harvard,— although I went there largely to see what
the old place looked like,—but I met a colored lady who looked like she possessed six degrees, wore nose glasses and all,—and had been in jail eighteen
times and in the pen once for robbing her clients,—Chinese laundrymen and
white clerks,—but she was still operating undaunted. I never saw so digni-
fied a daughter of joy before, but she said she had always worn pince-nez, and
Boston has a cultural atmosphere,—even if the cops don't want colored ladies
to associate with white gentlemen!

I've just come from New York, so I'll give you the news. I may hit some-
thing that |Wallace| Thurman or some of the other guys haven't told you
yet. . . . . Anyway, the white woman who took Josephine Baker to Europe is
now after Paul Robeson with the law because he refuses to come back from
London to be in a revue which I once wrote for her years ago and which I can't
much blame him for not wanting to perform in.* However, she has him under
contract,—but their social success in London, according to Mrs. Robeson has
been amazing,—teas with duchesses and cocktails with Lords,—so they don't
want to come back. The show is all being done over a la Broadway, anyhow,
and I can't stay in town to work on it now that college is open so I suppose
I'll have little left in it when it is produced, if ever it is produced, so I don't
particularly care whether Paul comes back or not. . . . . Porgy opens in London
Easter Monday after a winter tour here. Almost every production on Broadway
has a Negro or two in it these days and almost anybody who looks niggerish
can get a job. . . . . But leading men must still be white blacked up, if the play
calls for their speaking to white ladies on the stage. Such is the case in "Goin'
Home," laid in France after the war when the colored troops were on their
way back leaving the little Francaises behind. The play is pure hokum done
in chocolate, but rather amusing and simple minded. . . . . The New York theatre, the part that isn't gone black, has gone in for gangwar and underworld
stuff, and is producing some amazingly life-like and tremendously entertaining pictures of modern Chicago and Tenth Avenue scarcely less melodramatic
than the reality. . . . . The papers are full of real gangwar stuff this week. And

---

* Hughes had worked with Caroline Dudley Reagan (see also letter of October 9, 1925) on
the review *O Blues!*, which Reagan hoped to stage with Paul Robeson as its star. However,
following the success in London of *Show Boat*, in which Robeson created a sensation with
his rendition of "Ol' Man River," he backed out of his agreement with Reagan.

THE GRAPHIC seems to be always on the spot with its cameras whenever a victim is popped off.* Yesterday the whole front page was devoted to a picture of a falled crook dying in a saloon door. . . . . A troupe of colored actors have gone to the coast, too, and the rumor is that all the big companies are planning a colored production or so soon. . . . . Grant Still has set a song of mine called THE BREATH OF A ROSE that is so modern that nobody can sing it†. . . . . VOODOO, a Negro opera by Freeman,‡ opened Monday. Everybody in Harlem expected it to be punk like most of Freeman's former things, but the SUN gave it an amazing review, so maybe it's good. Anyway I hope so. This Johnny Spielt Auff or whatever it is that the Met is putting on this winter sounds awful,—but it's supposed to be a jazz opera.§ I can't imagine those fat singers at the Met waddling around in a jazz opera made in Berlin. But if it isn't good, I guess it will at least be funny. . . . . Did you like Bud Fisher's book |*Walls of Jericho*|? Too much surface,—is the verdict of the niggerati. They expected better things of Bud, they say, and the colored papers don't seem to have gotten insulted over it yet. Or maybe you killed all the critics with your brick. Nella Larsen is said to have finished another novel;¶ Walter White a book on lynching;** Eric his Panama Canal volume;†† and Wallie his "The <Blacker> the Berry" which is due out in January‡‡. . . . . Harlem cabarets are disgracefully white. The only way Negroes get in nowadays is to come with white folks, whereas it used to be the other way around. . . . . Too bad you missed Countee |Cullen| and Harold |Jackman|. |Alain| Locke was

---

* The *New York Evening Graphic* (1924–1932) was a periodical known for its confessional and true detective stories and also its "cosmographs," sketches of court scenes with photographs of the heads of the participants pasted in.
† William Grant Still (1895–1978) was an acclaimed African American composer who set Hughes's poem "Breath of the Rose" to music in 1928. In 1935, Still began work with Hughes on *Troubled Island*, an opera about the Haitian revolution. It was finally performed in 1949 in New York City.
‡ The composer H. Lawrence Freeman (1869–1954) received the 1929 Harmon Award for musical achievement. His opera *Voodoo* was produced in New York in September 1928.
§ Austrian-American Ernst Krenek (1900–1991) composed the jazz opera *Jonny Spielt Auf* ("Johnny Strikes Up"), which failed on its Metropolitan debut in 1929.
¶ Nella Larsen's second novel, *Passing*, was published by Knopf in 1929.
** Walter White's *Rope and Faggot: A Biography of Judge Lynch*, a study of lynching in America, was published in 1929.
†† Supported by a Guggenheim Foundation fellowship, the British Guiana–born short story writer Eric Walrond (1898–1966) left the United States in 1928 to work on a novel about the Panama Canal. Although he never finished the novel, his 1926 collection of stories, *Tropic Death* (which includes stories about the canal), was admired by other writers.
‡‡ Wallace Thurman's novel *The Blacker the Berry: A Novel of Negro Life*, mainly about color consciousness among black Americans (Macaulay, 1929).

in Spain but I guess you didn't see him. . . . . The phonographs are turning out some marvelous Negro records this year. Have you got a vic over there? I hope you aren't bothered with radios very much. All the lunch rooms and restaurants in Harlem have them now so one no longer eats in peace. They let them run wide open, picking up anything from the Buffalo Jazzers to the lectures on the correct way to write a social letter. . . . . The prohibition war over here is too funny for words,—and the licker is too bad to drink! I don't think it's worth the raids,—but the cops seem to like it. They take all they can get for themselves. . . . . Niggers and machines,—what's going to happen when they really get acquainted? Have you read Paul Morand's MAGIE NOIRE?* I just got it. . . . . Did you ever discover if Carco was really rotten or not as a writer?

Do you like bull fights? I loved them. . . . . Do you want to come back to New York? I imagine it would bore you sick now. . . . . I don't quite know why I'm so tired of it. . . . . This is my last year at Lincoln. You see, I didn't go to Howard while I was in Washington, so with only a year at Columbia, I had to do three more here. I don't mind it so much, since I have nothing more amusing to do anyway. There's no self-discipline to it,—no more than it takes for me to remain anywhere six months straight. . . . . I don't suppose you mind what Du Bois says? Who does? Some of the things the CRISIS does are too stupid to repeat,—so I'm not amazed at your poem story. After I had asked for the return of all my kid poetry they kept right on printing it. And after a second request for its return they even printed one poem with —'s in place of my name!† It amused me so much that I didn't get angry. They must have needed it badly or something. But it was so awful. . . . I suppose you saw Allison Davis's article last month. I had to send a letter about that,—not that I cared what he said about me or my work,—but I didn't think he ought to blame Mr. Van Vechten for my defects because if I'm ruined, I ruined myself, and nobody else had a hand in it, and certainly not Mr. Van Vechten whom I hadn't met when many of the poems were already old‡. . . . . But otherwise

* *Magie Noire* (1928), a collection of stories by French diplomat and writer Paul Morand (1888–1976), appeared in English as *Black Magic* in 1929 and includes illustrations by Aaron Douglas.
† The poem, "Nonette," appeared in *The Crisis* of June 1928.
‡ In the July *Crisis*, the black academic William Allison Davis (1902–1983) charged that Van Vechten had subverted Hughes's talent. Hughes then pointed out that he had written the poems in *The Weary Blues* before he met Van Vechten. An anthropologist, Davis would become the first African American to hold a full faculty position at a major white institution when the University of Chicago appointed him in 1942.

who cares what people say about your work? When I'm done with a poem or a book I can't be bothered arguing over it forever. I imagine if I ever wrote a play I would be bored sick if I ever had to look at it more than once. . . . . I don't see how artists stand their own pictures on their own walls. I like to create things but I don't like them around afterwards. . . . . Writing is like traveling,—it's wonderful to go somewhere but you get tired of staying, and I've never stayed six months in any one place I've ever wanted to go back to,—except New York and if there were any other place at all like it, I wouldn't want to go there again. . . . . Did HOME TO HARLEM come out in England, too? I was awfully glad about its success. It's so alive! I love it as much as any book I know. . . . . I imagine your second one will be great. When does it come out? Do you know yet? And where are you going from Barcelona? And why?

I'm doing a dozen or so short stories and some articles which I may sell later on. I wrote a few poems this summer, too, but I seem to enjoy prose more now.

|Wallace| Thurman is married, too,—a very nice girl who was teaching at Hampton,—and a very efficient typist,* which isn't a bad combine for a literary man who doesn't like to copy his own manuscripts. . . . . There seems to have been some hold up on Wallie's play† but I'm hoping it will be put on soon because it sounds like a good one. And he has two others on the road to completion to bring forward if the first one is a hit.

Best of luck to you. I'm anxiously awaiting the new novel.

Sincerely,
Langston

* Louise Alone Thompson (Patterson) (1901–1999), later one of Hughes's closest friends, graduated with a degree in economics from the University of California in Berkeley in 1923. Later she studied at the New York School of Social Work before joining the faculty at Hampton Institute. Forced out of Hampton for opposing its conservative leadership, she worked at first as a typist for various Harlem writers, including Wallace Thurman, to whom she was briefly married. In 1940, Thompson married William L. Patterson, a lawyer and prominent communist.
† Wallace Thurman wrote his first play, *Harlem: A Melodrama of Negro Life in Harlem*, with a white collaborator, William Jourdan Rapp. Their play opened on February 20, 1929, at the Apollo Theater in Harlem.

TO CHARLOTTE MASON [ALS]
[Surviving draft of a letter]

Lincoln University,
February 23, 1929.

Dearest Godmother,

All the week I have been thinking intensely of you and of what you have done for me.[†] And I have written you several letters but I have not sent them because none of them were true enough. There were too many words in them, I guess. But all of them contained in some form or other these simple statements:

I love you.

I need you very much.

I cannot bear to hurt you.

Those are the only meanings in all that I say here. You have been kinder to me than any other person in the world. I could not help but love you. You have made me dream greater dreams than I have ever dreamed before. And without you it will not be possible to carry out those dreams. But I cannot stand to disappoint you either. The memory of your face when I went away on Monday is more than I am able to bear. I must have been terribly stupid to have hurt you so, terribly lacking in understanding, terribly blind to what you have wanted me to see. You must not let me hurt you again. I know well that I am dull and slow, but I do not want to remain that way. I don't know what to say except that I am sorry that I have not changed rapidly enough into what you would have me be. The other unsent letters contained more words than this one. They were much longer. They were more emotionally revealing, perhaps, and there were explanations and promises. But I do not know how to write what I want to say any simpler than it is said here. Words only confuse, and I must not offer excuses for the things in which I have failed. Your face was so puzzled and so weary that day. I shall never forget it. You have been my friend, dear Godmother, and I did not want to disappoint you. If I can do no better than I have done, then for your own sake, you must let me go. You must be free, too, Godmother. At first we had wings. If there are no wings now for

---

* All of Hughes's letters to Charlotte Mason have been lost, apparently. In their absence, we include here several surviving drafts of letters from him to Mason.

† On Monday, February 18, after what seemed to him a pleasant lunch, Mrs. Mason exploded at Hughes. She accused him of ingratitude and insincerity, of taking money and doing virtually nothing in return. Her fury, and her visible weariness once it was spent, deeply upset him.

me, you must be free! You can still fly ahead always like the bright dream that is truth, and goodness. Free!

Always my love to you, and my truth
Langston

You have been so good to me.

TO CHARLOTTE MASON   [ALS]

[Surviving draft of a letter]

Lincoln University,
February 23, 1929.

Dear Godmother,

This is another letter in which there are some little, less important things that I want to tell you. . . . . About Monday. When I left you, I took the Third Avenue "L" and rode in a sort of daze until, when I looked out the window for my station, I found that I had gone way past it, and was then in some strange section of the Bronx where I had never been before. . . . . It was after eight o'clock when I got to my mother's. She was in bed, but insisted that she was only slightly bruised and very nervous from the accident, but she refused to have a doctor because she said we could not afford it.* However, I told the lady where she was stopping to get one for her if she did not feel well the next day. . . . . It was too late then to get to Lincoln so we stayed in New York until an early morning train. I had a very good time in Harlem over the week-end,—or rather a very interesting time. I met so many new people. . . . . It seems that a new life-period is centering about me. You know I told you about the period of books,—how all my childhood, lonely, I spent reading up until the time I went to sea. Then I told you how, suddenly, the very sight of books made me ill, and I threw the ones I possessed into the sea. After that came what I guess one could call a period of solitary wandering, looking out of myself at the rest of the world, but touching no one, nothing. "The Weary Blues" belongs to that period. But I think my second book marks an unconscious turning toward this third state, for there many of the poems are outward, rather than inward, trying to catch the moods of individuals other than myself. In Washington I realized fully how terrible it was to live alone, unlike the folks about. And I came to Lincoln. For the first time in my life I found myself in some way

---

* The nature of the accident or injury to Hughes's mother is not known. Carrie Clark was then living in Atlantic City, New Jersey, with her stepson, Gwyn.

belonging to a group. But it took me a very long time (and my work interfered often) to learn to live with them. Only now am I beginning to be at all at ease and without self-consciousness in meeting my own people. Lincoln has done that for me, and I value it immensely. The football trips this fall, I guess, were what one might call the beginning of a "social state," in contrast to the state of books, and that of observation. I wonder if I am analyzing my inner moods toward life correctly as they seem to have changed! I'm trying to do so. But I am not, at the moment, so interested in watching myself as I used to be. Maybe that is why I enjoyed Harlem so much this time. Things seemed so fresh, alive, and new.

|Miguel| Covarrubias has an amusing caricature on African Art in the current "Vanity Fair." And I know you must have seen the love letters of |Abraham| Lincoln that have been running in the "Atlantic Monthly." These are the third installment, but I have only just now seen them. . . . . I noticed yesterday a good review of "Harlem" in the Times. It seems to have made a hit.

I meant to tell you in New York what a very beautiful, dark, rich brown my Christmas bag has become by the use of the saddle soap. It is a splendid thing to look at now. . . . . Luncheon with you was very nice last Monday. I haven't been hungry since I came back to college, but I have been thinking I might like to eat if there were some of your mushroom soup here.

You have been so awfully good to me, dear Godmother. If there is anything in my other letter to hurt you, it is not because I want it to be there. It is only that I want to say what is best for you. If I make you unhappy, then I cannot come to see you anymore. If I am too heavy, too slow, then you must not give me your strength. There are too many beautiful things in the world for you to do, too many others who need you. You must be strong and well for them. That is what I mean. Because I love you, I must try to tell the truth. We agreed upon that, didn't we? Do not misunderstand me, dear Godmother. Of course I need you terribly,—but you must be free to live for all the others who love you, too. If I am too much for you, you must not have me.

Langston

TO CARL VAN VECHTEN   [ALS]

Dear Carlo,`

It was very good of you to write me before you sailed away again. Of course, I'm sorry you're leaving New York, if it's going to be for a long time, but I'm hoping, and I'm sure, you'll have a delightful sojourn abroad, and that you'll find little Harlems now almost everywhere you go. (I'm enclosing what the Literary Digest copies from a Berlin paper this week)..... And you were a mighty big part in starting it all...... Lately, now that another period in my life is about to come to an end, I've been thinking about the people who've been so very good to me the last four years, and who helped me when I came back from the continent with neither sous nor lire nor pesos, and certainly no dollars..... Well, you're person No. 1,—the first human being to whom I received a formal introduction after my hard return to native shores,—the night I landed,—in Happy Rhone's cabaret, the very middle of the dance floor. Don't you remember? The first person, too, to see my poems in any sort of collected form, to send them to a publishers, and to be happy with me (by wire) over their appearance. But you know all that, and the rest, too. And I don't want to bore you with thanks. You've been a mighty good friend, Carl, so I want you to have a great time in Europe.

I've been awfully busy the last two months or so making a survey of Lincoln as a sociology class assignment (but mainly for myself). It's finished now, was read here, and has produced some sensational but unintended results,—as we who made it didn't mean for it to get to the papers. I'm enclosing one clipping, but there were several more, besides editorials, etc. Its effect here at Lincoln was upsetting enough to the staid contented Presbyterians who have been easing along in delightful mediocrity for the last 40 years, not caring much if the students improved or not, with the result that Lincoln became a charming winter resort and country club, but not much of a college. (Lovely for me,—but not so good for the serious-minded boys who want and need something else.) The survey covered everything,—faculty, curriculum, buildings and grounds, student thought and activities, etc. (2 upper classes) and various complicated looking charts and tabulations were made. (The Afro succeeded in getting only a small part of the material that had been posted in the sociology room.)* But it would take a whole paper to tell you all about it. Anyway, it was interesting work, and I feel that we've got down some important figures and data concerning some of the grave problems facing Negro education today in schools dominated by white philanthropy, well-meaning but dumb.

This summer I'm going to stay here again and finish up my book. (Wish you could read it before I send it in.) Six weeks or so more I think will do it. Then I'm free again. Had some offers to teach, Tuskegee among others, but

---

* Since 1892, the weekly newspaper *Baltimore Afro-American,* commonly called *The Afro,* has served the black communities especially in the Baltimore and Washington, D.C., metropolitan areas.

haven't taken them so far,—so I'm liable to meet you in Hong Kong if you keep on round the world.

Tell Fania* Hello for me and both you all enjoy yo' selves to de utt'most! Remember me to Paul and Essie,† too,—and the kid.

Saluti e bacci,

Langston

Lincoln University,

May eighth,

1929.

Another envelope <u>for enclosures.</u>

TO CLAUDE MCKAY‡   [ALS]

Lincoln University,

June 27, 1929

Dear Claude,

This time there is no bell to ring calling me to class, no lessons to get, no students to knock, no hundred and one little, pressing, unimportant things to be done: I'm quite graduated, have the "A. B." in my trunk, and am now, as the boys say, "out in the world." All I've got to do is—do something. Classes and all are over, but I'm staying here for the summer to do a little writing,—at least until August. I've just been in New York for 2 weeks and came back, so maybe you'd like to hear the news—(friends and enemies, those you know and those you don't): |Wallace| Thurman and Louise |Thompson Patterson| are being divorced and he's using up all his "Harlem" money paying alimony,—so he writes me. He's in Santa Monica, California. In fact, gangs of N.Y. whites and colored are out there now getting in on the talkies which have recently become the big racket. Wallie's play "Harlem" was good atmosphere made exciting in the Broadway manner by his Jewish collaborator. Murders, and so on, that belong to melodrama, but not necessarily to Negroes. But it made a good stage

---

* Fania Marinoff (1890–1971), Van Vechten's wife, was a Russian-born actress with a successful career on Broadway and in silent films.
† Eslanda "Essie" Cardozo Goode Robeson (1895–1965) was a trained chemist, writer, and civil rights activist. She published *Paul Robeson, Negro*, the first biography of her husband, in 1930.
‡ Written on the back of the envelope of the June 27, 1929, letter:
Cats in the alley fighting over guts
<u>Women in whorehouses</u> " " nuts

show. It has closed now in both N.Y. and Chicago. In Chi, I guess you read, the leading Negroes razzed it and begged the police to close it because it was "low down,"—anything that's not about high-yellow angels is, you know!.... Well, anyhow,—went to see Kid Chocolate box [(also Al Brown)* but the kid is most marvelous] with Aaron Douglas, Alta, his wife, and Arna Bontemps, the poet.† They're all going West for the summer, Alta and Aaron to Kansas. Arna (a man, if you don't know) to California. Aaron did the drawings for the American edition of Paul Morand's "Magie Noire," and is booked to illustrate a de luxe edition of "Nigger Heaven" next spring. . . . . All the world is writing novels. Taylor Gordon, singing partner of Rosamond Johnson, has written a 1st person narrative of himself in humorous vein.‡ Miguel Covarrubias is doing pictures for it. (I guess you know his drawings of Negroes. Miguel is a very nice Mexican boy whom you would like a lot. Maybe you've met him in Paris.) . . . . . . Awfully bad colored shows are being put on Broadway every week or so now. They fail,—as they deserve to. Some of the colored victrola records are unbearably vulgar, too. Not even funny or half-sad anymore. Very bad, moronish, and, I'm afraid, largely Jewish business men are exploiting Negro things for all they're worth. You can't blame the "nice" Negroes much for yelling, in a way, even when some of us are sincere! We do get a lots of racial dirt shoved on the market.

Ethel Barrymore is to play in black face next season—Scarlet Sister Mary!.... The Hall Johnson Negro Choir sings in the Stadium with the Symphony Orchestra in July. . . . . The "Porgy" people are back from London.

Colored New Yorkers are not liking "Banjo" so much as your first novel. They didn't like my second book so much either. Maybe second books are due to be—second books—when the first makes too much noise. And "Home to Harlem" was the grandest thing in years. Dancing and swift and alive. I guess every one expected another book on the same order. "Banjo" is, seemingly, a lot more thoughtful and, I think, very good in its way, but not at all the same thing. Certainly, I feel it important for the white world to know a lot of the "colored" thoughts that are in "Banjo." And the picture of Marseilles is

* The boxers Kid Chocolate (1910–1988), born Eligio Sardiñas Montalvo in Cuba, and Panama Al Brown (1902–1951), born Alfonso Teofilo Brown, became world champions in their respective weight classes in 1931.

† Arna Bontemps (1902–1973), a novelist and poet, served as head librarian at Fisk University from 1943 to 1966. After Hughes met Bontemps in 1924, the two men developed a lifelong friendship and exchanged thousands of letters. They also collaborated on several anthologies and children's books, published and unpublished.

‡ Taylor Gordon (1893–1971), a specialist in spirituals, joined the versatile musician J. Rosamond Johnson to form a singing duo in the mid-1920s that toured the United States, France, and England. In 1929, Gordon published an autobiography, *Born to Be*.

superb. Good God! I can feel the very air of it. Liked your beach scenes, too,—but lemme ask you—was there ever a ship that gave away lettuce? Real good, fresh lettuce to beachcombers? That struck me like the two West Indian girls fighting naked in Harlem, did some of your former critics. But maybe it <u>did</u> or <u>could</u> happen!

Are you still in Paris? Do you know Nora Holt?[*] She's rather a nice person I think, especially when she's playing and singing. She was due for our revue, too. . . . . You got Anita right.[†] Droves of society ladies will be in Paris this summer. Half the colored folks I know are going over. . . . . Harold |Jackman| sails again. Countée |Cullen|, he says, is to remain another year . . . . . . Carl Van Vechten is there now, I think. . . . . Alain Locke sails next week. He was to have gone the 11th but missed his sailing due to a bad tooth. . . . . I'm the least fashionable of all the literary crew—but I haven't got any money, and I've sailed enough on as—"moon", at least, in that direction. Next time I want to go to Asia.

Dudley Murphy, young modernist director, is to make a talkie of "The St. Louis Blues" with Bessie Smith doing the woman.[‡] It ought to be great.

I've never felt so unpoetic in my life. I think I shall write no more poems. I suppose I'm not quite miserable enough. I usually have to feel very bad in order to put anything down,—and terrible to make up poems. How did you have to feel?

Aren't you going to publish another volume of poetry? I thought those unpublished things I once saw were awfully good. Please think about bringing them out, if you can.

Tell me the Paris news when you write. . . . . Are your North African sketches to appear in Harper's? I'm anxious for them to come out. They ought to be great.

You know, I was very happy to get your fine letters last winter and ashamed

---

[*] Nora Holt (1895?–1974) was a well-known African American singer who also served as a respected music critic for *The Chicago Defender*.

[†] Probably Anita Thompson (1901–1980), a film actress and model who was involved with McKay in Paris at this time. She appears as "Carmina" in McKay's autobiography, *A Long Way from Home* (1937). On May 14, 1929, McKay had written that Thompson "says she knows you and has often visited Lincoln," adding that she was "the society type that takes up bohemianism because it is smart to do so!" Her memoir was edited and published posthumously by George Hutchison as *American Cocktail: A "Colored Girl" in the World* (Harvard University Press, 2014).

[‡] Dudley Murphy (1897–1968) cast Bessie Smith in the leading role of his short film *St. Louis Blues* (1929), which provides the only recorded footage of Smith performing.

for not writing. But I'm really very bad at that. . . . . I hope you're far enough away not to be flooded with mail from unknowns who want everything from an autograph, a picture, to your life's history, and your personal affection. Ladies, even by mail, can be very persistent.

Bien à toi, old man. Hope you're happy and that the wine still tastes good. Write soon.

Sincerely,
Langston

TO WALLACE THURMAN [TLS]

Monday July 29, 1929 (full date for benefit of literary historian)
Lincoln University, Pa., Box 36, (full place, ditto)
<Signed by my own hand. L.H.>

Dear Wallie,

I am sorry to hear about your being ill—but anyway I see you're still able to use the typewriter so that's something. Zora |Neale Hurston| has been sick in a Florida hospital, too. Thought it was her stomach but discovered it was her liver, at the last moment, so she's on the road to recovery now. Two of my friends and classmates who graduated with me, immediately had a nervous breakdown the week following and are still suffering. I have tried in vain for two years to have one and can't—so that I could rest. I recall with ever recurring pleasure my three weeks in the hospital that time I got mad at my father in Mexico and all my red corpuscles turned white. I never enjoyed myself so much before nor since, being waited on and wheeled about by lovely nurses, and having nothing, absolutely nothing, to do. Not even the necessity of being bored. I don't suppose I shall ever be in a hospital again for so trivial a cause. It seems I can't get anything wrong with my heart either. Nothing will fail me. I'm trying now to cough every morning, but without much success. I think a nice long hospital would do me so much good. There being no more nice, long colleges to do nothing in . . . . . . Poor |Alain| Locke had a heart attack, lay on the floor all night, and missed his sailing. I think I told you. It seems that all the niggerati's going under—then going off and resting. He's on his way to Mannheim now to take the cure (plus baths), you're in Salt Lake being cared for, hand and foot, no doubt by a darling grandmother. . . . And here am I broken hearted—not even in love anymore. She's gone home to her people taking several of my books and one ring (that someone else had given me.)*. . . . . Even my kid brother refused to go |to| summer school, as dumb as he is, because he felt that he need<ed> the outdoor air of a Massachusetts summer camp. And my mother has wearied her ankles working, so she is going home to Kansas day after tomorrow!. . . . . I think I shall sit out in the sun for the next week and get a sun-stroke, then see if the black intelligentsia will rally to the aid of a poor New Negro (still quite young). I'm doing my best to keep literary. . . . . Did I tell you that someone tried to rob, assault, or otherwise molest me when I first returned from N. Y.? I live in the oldest, largest, darkest, and most remote dormitory on the campus, third floor north-east corner, by myself. (Said residence donated to me by the University for literary purposes.) Well, I hadn't been here any time before, about midnight one evening while I was still up, some prowler or other by unlocking the door tried to get into my room, but in reality the door was already unlocked so what they did in turning the key was really to lock it, and when I got up and yelled hearing the key turn, they fled leaving the key in the lock and I was locked in all night, until <next> morning I called the campus janitor to let me out. (Wasn't anxious to get out beforehand, anyway.) You see, the villagers think I'm rich because I spend the summer here and do nothing, so maybe they planned, whoever it was, to take my cash, my typewriter, or my I know not what. But anyway I now lock up securely every night and play Bessie Smith on the victrola so I wouldn't hear them if they came. . . . . In the day time I occasionally practice on prose technique while waiting for information, <(I mean inspiration)> to descend upon me like a dove and lift me above mere writing. But the appearance of two or three nice checks recently from book reviews and German translations of Blues (God knows how they did it—perhaps if I could read them, I would get sick) lead me to think of seeking the sea shore or the mountain heights for the rest of the season. Or the eastern shore of Maryland across the Chesapeake Bay, which they tell me is like Georgia, it's so remote, and its Negroes are so nappy-headed. And they eat oysters all the year around. It's not far away. All one does is go to Baltimore and take a Jim Crow boat to the land of miscegenation where every colored lady has at least six little halfbreeds for practice before she gets married to a Negro. And where the word Mammy is still taken seriously, and the race is so far back that it has illimitable potential—like me!. . . . . Yes, I do intend to teach in the remote future when hunger and old age and dire necessity come upon me. (The fall is quite remote!) And as for Harlem, alas, all the cabarets have gone white and the

* "She" is Laudee Williams, a young woman with whom Hughes had apparently fallen in love the previous November.

Sugar Cane is closed and everybody I know is either in Paris or Hollywood or sick. And Bruce* wears English suits!. . . . . Finish your talkie, if need be, but for crying out loud, don't die if cod liver oil can save you. I detest talkies, but funerals are even worse. I think I shall be cremated and put in a jar, then sent on a trans-Atlantic flight . . . . . . Will you kindly write more about the renaissance of the race in the West, and who's connected with which in the Hollywood scramble. . . . Or will I have to come out there to see for myself?. . . . . God what a child I have been. . . . . (When?). . . . . The German papers say I'm still quite young. . . . . But I'm in no mood to wax eloquent over trifles and I can only think about what I wouldn't write if the doctor would let me. . . . . Who is a nice family doctor in New York? I may need one. . . . . How much do divorces cost and what are the grounds? (Why must it be grounds—Oh, Lord, the bitter dregs!—says he who drains the cup.). . . . I believe I'll go to Canada instead of Maryland where licker's still what it used to be.† Even the owner of Small's Paradise summers in Quebec. . . . . I think my nerves need wine. . . . . Are you taking the waters at the Salt Lake . . . . . . Don't be like that! <If you need anything I can send you, let me know. (This last is real!)>

<Sincerely, your friend,

Langston

(Hughes—for the sake of literary history. This letter guaranteed authentic— price to museums, $15,000 cash.!>

TO CHARLOTTE MASON [ALS]

[Surviving draft of a letter]

May 28, 1930

I am deeply sorry—but I feel that I must keep my promise about Washington.‡ I am terribly sorry about everything. You have been more beautiful to me

---

* Richard Bruce Nugent (1906–1987) was an illustrator, short story writer, poet, playwright, and bohemian personality. Born in Washington, D.C., where he met and became fast friends with Hughes in 1924 or 1925, Nugent moved to Manhattan to join the Harlem Renaissance. With Hughes's help, he published poems in Countee Cullen's anthology *Caroling Dusk* (1927), in *Opportunity* magazine, and in *Fire!!*

† On August 15, Hughes went to the Eastern Shore of the Chesapeake Bay. Around September 1, he continued on to Canada.

‡ Late May 1930 marks the beginning of the end of Hughes's relationship with Mrs. Mason. He believed that their break resulted in part from Godmother's dissatisfaction with the slowness of his writing and the fact that he was not "primitive" or "African" enough for her. As he puts it in *The Big Sea*, "I was only an American Negro—who loved the surface of Africa and the rhythms of Africa—but I was not Africa. I was Chicago and

than anybody in the world, and my own failure is miserable beyond speech, so I will say no more about it. If I ~~mistakenly~~ have said the wrong things, already I am ~~humbly~~ deeply sorry. I offer you the most sincere apologies. I did not want to hurt you. I wanted only to be true to your love for me, but human words ~~even when most carefully selected,~~ have too many meanings other than the single meaning of the heart.

Here is my love and faith and devotion to all that you have taught me. If ever I can serve you in any way, I shall be only too happy. The truths of your spirit live with me always in light and beauty, that is why I cannot bear for anything else ~~to xxxxx~~ to come between us.

I want to be your spirit-child forever,

L.

TO CHARLOTTE MASON   [AL]
[Surviving draft of a letter]

June 6 |1930|

In all my life I have never been free. I have never been able to do anything with freedom, except in the field of my writing. With my parents, with my employers in my struggle for food, in all the material circumstances of life, I have been forced to move this way and that—only when I sat down for a moment to write have I been able to put down what I wanted to put down, to say what I've wanted to say, when and where I choose . . . . . . As long as I worked on my novel, dear Godmother, I think we were One—we both wanted it finished soon, we both agreed about what was being done.* But when you told me that I should have begun my writing again the week after I returned from Cuba†—I must disagree with you. I must never write when I do not want

---

Kansas City and Broadway and Harlem. And I was not what she wanted me to be. So, in the end it all came back very near to the old impasse of white and Negro again, white and Negro—as do most relationships in America." In this draft, Hughes alludes to their latest quarrel, which was precipitated by his decision to keep a commitment in Washington, D.C., rather than stay home and write. Seeing this decision as evidence of his disloyalty and ingratitude, she reminded Hughes how much she had spent to support his writing while he had given her almost nothing in return.

* Hughes wrote *Not Without Laughter* (Knopf, 1930) with Mrs. Mason's generous financial support and intense encouragement.

† After submitting the manuscript of *Not Without Laughter* to Blanche Knopf on February 17, Hughes decided to seek a Cuban musician to collaborate with him on a new project, a "singing play." Godmother liked this plan and gave him $500 to fund his trip. Hughes traveled to Cuba aboard the Cunard ship *Caronia*, which arrived there on February 25. He left Cuba on March 6, after making friends among the local literati but without finding a

to write. That is my last freedom and I must keep it for myself. . . . Then when you tell me that you give me more than anybody ever gave me before—($225⁰⁰ a month—my allowance and half of Louise)*—and that I have been living in idleness since the first of March—I must feel miserably ashamed. I must feel that I have been misusing your kindness and that it would be wrong ~~to you~~ for me to take your help any more when I cannot write—when I cannot do what you believe I should be doing—when I am afraid of making you unhappy because you have been ~~kind~~ good to me—and when I know that I cannot write ~~at all~~ on any sort of pre-arranged schedule. The nervous strain of finishing the novel by a certain time has shown me that. Almost all of one's life must be measured and timed as it is—meals every day at a certain hour; if I am working for a salary—to work at a certain time; to bed at a certain time ~~in order~~ to get enough sleep; letters to be answered by a certain time in order to avoid discourtesy or loss of business. So far ~~in this world~~, only my writing has been my own, to do when I wanted to do it, to finish only when I felt that it was finished, to put it aside or discard it completely if I chose. For the sake of my physical body I have washed ~~restaurant~~ thousands of hotel dishes, cooked, scrubbed decks, worked 12 to 15 hours a day on a farm, swallowed my pride for the ~~sake~~ help of philanthropy and charity—but nobody ever said to me "You must write now, you must finish that poem tomorrow. You must begin to create on the first of the month." Because then I could not have ~~have written, I could not have~~ created anything. I could only have put down empty words at best. . . . . . The creative urge must come from within, ~~always~~ as you know dear G.,—or it is less than true. . . . . So I am sorry if you feel that I have been unnecessarily idle. And, I am ashamed beyond words, if I have misused your generousity. I did not want ever to do that. And if I have misunderstood your ~~words~~ advice, your kind and sincere talks with me the last few weeks, blame only my stupidity, ~~Godmother,~~ not my heart. My love and devotion are yours always, and my deepest respect and gratitude, and my willingness ~~always~~ to listen to you in the future as in the past and to be guided by you as nearly as I can. But I must tell you the truth so that there will be no wall between us.

---

suitable composer. Returning to his residence in Westfield, New Jersey, he did not begin writing immediately. When news of his inactivity reached her (probably through Alain Locke, who had become her well-paid, principal advisor on black American culture), Godmother became angry.

* Louise Thompson (Patterson) had been hired by Mrs. Mason in September 1929 to be Hughes's typist. (For information on Thompson, see note for letter of September 13, 1928.)

TO CHARLOTTE MASON [AL]

[Surviving draft of a letter]

<Sent to G.—Aug. 15, 1930 from Rockaway.>[*]

I ask you to help the gods to make me good, ~~and~~ to make me to make me clean, ~~and~~ to make me strong and ~~to make me~~ fine that I might stand aflame before my people, powerful and wise, with eyes that can discern the ways of truth. I am nothing now—no more than a body of dust ~~possessing no~~ without wisdom, having no right to see. Physically and spiritually I pass through the dark valley, a dryness in my throat, a weariness in my eyes, fingers twisted into strange numb shapes when I wake up at night, the mind troubled ~~and confused~~ in the face of things it does not understand, the mouth silent because there is no one to talk to, the ~~cool~~ sweet air burning the lungs, the hot sun cold to the body. Too far away the spear of Alamari.[†] Too far away the ~~young and~~ gentle hands of Sandy's faith.[‡] If you ~~will~~ understand, perhaps it will not be so hard to climb toward the hills again. Your letter has been a great help to me, sending with it the rays of the morning sun, that touch the ~~hill tops~~ summits always before they reach the valley. Godmother, for your sake I am sorry. For myself—so many life-destroying things have happened to me before—~~to seek relief in self pity is stupid and futile~~ I ~~can~~ only lie still and wait. ~~till strength comes to move again.~~ I could not go to sea because I couldn't have passed the physical exams, or eaten the galley-food, or done the work. I had hoped to be better by now, but two ~~enervation heavy~~ severe summer colds have kept me doped with enervating medicines. It's been a crazy season for me, with the stomach turning over and over like a ~~churn~~ machine whenever the mind displeased it by attempting to think seriously.[§] You can

---

[*] Hughes spent the dog days of August on the beach in Far Rockaway, New York. His mother was working as a maid near this popular resort city.

[†] Mrs. Mason sometimes poetically referred to Hughes as "Alamari." The origin of the name is unclear, although it is perhaps linked to a reputed West African warrior dance of the same name.

[‡] Modeled in part on Hughes himself, Sandy is the main character of his novel *Not Without Laughter*.

[§] In *The Big Sea*, Hughes recalls his final meeting with Godmother: "I cannot write here about that last half-hour in the big bright drawing-room high above Park Avenue one morning, because when I think about it, even now, something happens in the pit of my stomach that makes me ill. . . . Physically, my stomach began to turn over and over—and then over again. I fought against bewilderment and anger, fought hard, and didn't say anything. I just sat there in the high Park Avenue drawing-room and didn't say anything."

understand why I have not written you. It would have been wrong to add my self to the burdens of your morning mail. It isn't that I don't love you, Godmother. The thousands of ~~beautiful~~ good and generous things you have done for me come back to me always in loveliness and beauty: the time you bought the saddle-soap for my bag; the times you came to Lincoln to see me; the time you said we would write the play together. And I never read a letter in praise of the novel—what they call its simplicity and lack of propaganda—but that I think "they do not know who helped me write it—Godmother." And every criticism in the papers must inevitably bear comparison with the superior and flaming criticism ~~which~~ that you wrote long ago when the book was only half finished. . . . You have been continually in my thoughts this summer, and continually I've been trying to puzzle out what happened between us, and what I ~~can~~ must do to keep it from ever happening again. We could not bear it. Love has no armor against itself. ~~If only I could understand.~~

I am not wise, Godmother. ~~in myself. The mind speaks truth. In myself I am not wise. I am not wise.~~ The inner soul is simple as a fool, sensitive as a sheltered child, at odds too often with the reasons of the mind, ~~The soul's~~ a coward hiding in the dark, ~~putting~~ wrapping itself in the cloak of art ~~about itself~~ when, too ~~much alone~~ sick with loneliness, it must ~~walk~~ go out for ~~breath of~~ air or die. The soul is ~~xxxxx~~ deaf, and dumb, and the body cannot speak for it. ~~afraid of its own body and the body thinks its xxxxx afraid of all the other bodies the soul but it is not so In the world The mind knows all these things about the soul. The soul knows nothing about itself—and yet the soul can kick the mind about, and~~ armour armour ~~make of reason a lackey in the house, and cry for love, and when love is not found, refuse to listen to the mind that~~ ~~"again again. It's yet again and maybe you will find~~ The body lies too often to itself. The soul looks on in silence—and moves away. There are too many things it does not understand.

~~The~~ Last week my kid brother |Gwyn Clark| was with me here at the beach ~~for a week~~ on his way home to Cleveland. One day he rescued a girl from drowning. She had been caught in the under-

Charlotte Mason, "Godmother," c. 1925

tow at the end of the jetty. . . . I'm enclosing a letter to show you something of his record at camp. He's a good little chap and I want to help him all I can. Mother is planning to keep house in Cleveland so he will go to school there next year. He wants to take a course in electricity at the Technical High School and, at the same time, study for entrance to the college in Springfield where he can ~~study~~ prepare for xxxxxx athletic and recreational work. He hated to leave ~~there~~ |the camp| and the people there were loath to give him up. They seemingly had a very tearful time about it. Mother and I are deeply grateful to you for the helpful years which you gave him[*] ~~there~~ in an environment that has surely been of great benefit to him, in health and character, and that has given him a fine foundation for his adolescent years.

novel.[*][†]

~~house—at 3 least, is seems so now . . . . . . I have not dared to think of the play~~

[*]I've had a friendly note from Mr. Paul Chapin. Mrs. Biddle[‡] has written me a lovely letter about the novel, saying that you have read it all aloud. I am ~~glad that~~ grateful that my poor people ~~have~~ known the blessings of your voice even as they knew the strength of your ~~love~~ devotion when they were coming into being. The book is yours as well as mine. Whatever beauty ~~and truth~~ it may have travels on the wings of your love as long as its ~~remains in print~~ pages hold together.

May the Gods be kind to you. May the summer bring you strength and life. May the tall pines protect you in beauty.

With my love,[§]

---

[*] Mrs. Mason's financial support of his stepbrother, Gwyn Clark, is discussed in earlier letters to Alain Locke (see those of January 3, 1928, and February 27, 1928).

[†] Hughes included this asterisk to indicate the insertion of text (also marked with an asterisk) that he had written on a separate sheet, with a different pen. The crossed-out line preceding the asterisk appears at the top of this separate sheet.

[‡] The poet Katherine Garrison Biddle (1890–1977) and her sister Cornelia Chapin (1893–1972), a sculptor, served as assistants to Mrs. Mason. L. H. Paul Chapin, a businessman (1888–1938), was their brother.

[§] The following incomplete text appears on a page that Hughes crossed out with a large "X":
"When I read the letters that come to me expressing surprise and admiration at its simplicity and lack of propaganda, I say "They do not know who helped me to write that book." And I never read a review but that I ~~Iv~~ remember the flaming and ~~superior~~ finest criticism which you wrote for me when the book was only half finished.
I wish we could work on the play together, Dear Godmother.
Every day for hours ~~here on the~~ lying in the sun on the beach, I try to puzzle out what has happened to me recently that has"

TO CLAUDE MCKAY   [*TLS*]

[*On* Hedgerow Theatre Moylan-Rose Valley, PA. *stationery*]*

Home address:
P.O. Box No. 94,
Westfield, N.J.,
September 30, 1930.

Dear Claude,

I've been owing you a letter for months. How time can pass! I hope this one finds you. Wonder if you're still in Spain? Anyway, I asked my publishers to send you a copy of my novel there. I hope it reached you somewhere, and that it won't bore you. I haven't read it for months to see what it's like. I got rather fed up with it in the re-writing stage and couldn't bear the sight of it for a while. It's had good reviews, though—only a couple of slams so far—and the sale isn't bad considering the book slump and summer and a market flooded with "Negro" stuff mostly by white people. I want to do another novel. This time with a city back-ground. Maybe I'll start on it soon. . . . . This summer I didn't do anything. Had gotten awfully bored with LITERATURE and WHITE FOLKS and NIGGERS and almost everything else. Borrowed money, and spent it all lying on the beach at Rockaway and sleeping in the sunshine. . . . . Now I'm sort of visiting out here at Jasper Deeter's theatre near Philadelphia. Rose McClendon,† the colored actress, is here, and three colored fellows who are resident members of the company. (They keep <u>Othello</u> and <u>The Emperor Jones</u>‡ in the repertory, and had planned a series of Negro plays

* In June, Hughes had been invited to the Hedgerow Theatre in Rose Valley, Pennsylvania, the first residential repertory theater in America. Its director, Jasper Deeter (1893–1972), a former member of the Provincetown Players, founded the Hedgerow Theatre in 1923 with a commitment to staging experimental and progressive plays. Deeter had planned a season of six plays with black or integrated casts and wanted a black playwright in residence. Hughes arrived in Moylan–Rose Valley, Pennsylvania, on September 15.

† Rose McClendon (1884–1936) was one of the most accomplished black actresses of her time. While at the Hedgerow Theatre, Hughes showed McClendon an early draft of "Cross: A Play of the Deep South," a drama about miscegenation that he later renamed *Mulatto*. When *Mulatto* was produced on Broadway in 1935, McClendon played the part of Cora Lewis, the black common-law wife of a Georgia plantation owner, Colonel Thomas Norwood, until her final illness forced her to leave the cast.

‡ Eugene O'Neill's *The Emperor Jones* (1920) tells the story of Brutus Jones, a black American porter who is jailed for fighting but escapes to an island in the West Indies, where he establishes himself as emperor. At the Provincetown Playhouse premiere on November 1, 1920, the African American actor Charles S. Gilpin (1878–1930) performed the title role while Jasper Deeter played Smithers, a white colonial opportunist.

for the fall, but it seems that the money didn't come through or something, so they probably won't come off.) Anyway, it's a pretty spot down in a lovely little valley, and I'm getting a sort of inside slant on the theatre, watching the rehearsals and the plays every night. . . . . What's the news with you? I haven't seen any of the returned natives this fall, so I haven't heard whether any one ran into you over there or not. |Countee| Cullen's back, I hear, and |Alain| Locke is due back soon, and at least ten million colored school teachers have been, seen Paris, and returned. . . . . You're more or less right about the Negro intellectuals. (After all these months, I could hardly expect you to remember just what you said in that last letter, but anyhow much of it concerned your reputation after it had gone through the mouths of the niggerati and back to earth again.) Sure, they say bad things about you. They say bad things about anybody unless you're right there when they're talking. But who cares? Certainly there are a lot of half-baked beans in the intellectual pot, but they don't make me sick any more like they used to. Maybe it's because I see so little of them—and am not concerned about whether I have a reputation or not.

I've been translating some lovely Cuban poetry lately. There's a Chinese-Negro poet in Havana named Regino Pedroso[*] who works in an iron foundry and writes grand radical poems and Chinese revolutionary stuff and mystical sonnets, and there's another boy named Nicolas Guillen who has recently created a small sensation down there with his poems in Cuban Negro dialect with the rhythms of the native music,[†] sort of like my blues here,—the first time that has been done in Latin-America. I've translated some of the revolutionary poems, and some of Guillen's straight Spanish, because neither the sonnets nor the dialect could I do over very well into English. There's a charming little Mexican poetess, too, whose things I want to try to put into English.[‡] She was dancing in Havana last winter when I was there . . . . . . I had a swell time down there. Don't believe I ever wrote and told you, did I? Met all the literary people in the capital, and lots of grand Negroes, and lots

* Regino Pedroso (1896–1983) was a Cuban writer of African and Chinese descent whom Hughes met on his second trip to Cuba. Hughes helped Pedroso to place his poem "Alarm Clock" in the New York–based *Poetry Quarterly*.
† Hughes encouraged the Afro-Cuban poet Nicolás Guillén (1902–1989) to employ black Cuban vernacular forms, including speech, songs, and dance rhythms, in the same way that Hughes had used blues and jazz in his own poetry. Shortly after Hughes left Cuba in March 1930, Guillén created a sensation in Havana with the publication of *Motivos de Son*, eight poems that used the popular *son* dance rhythm rooted in Cuba's black culture.
‡ Graziella Garbalosa (1896–1977) was a prolific Cuban poet and avant-garde writer. In 1920, she published a volume of poetry entitled *La juguetería de amor* ("The Toy of Love").

of players in the native orchestras. Brought back a bongó and maracas, and all sorts of things to play on—and can't play any of them! I'd love to go back to Cuba again this winter, or somewhere South. I hate cold weather. . . . . Are you coming this way ever, Claude? You said something about being in New York when you finished your next book. I hope it's coming along well. Wish you could sell something to the movies and make lots of money. That's what all the white writers are doing. Selling their books months before they come out even. . . . . . . Well, there isn't any news to speak of that I could tell you. The annual hundred colored shows have started rehearsing for Broadway. Maybe three or four will get there. Ethel Barrymore is reported a black-face flop in her opening in Scarlet Sister Mary* out in Columbus, an all white company in all Negro parts, bound for New York. The new Paul Green Negro play, The Potter's Field† may be one of the first Meyerhold‡ productions when he arrives in New York. It seems that it is a semi-impressionistic play or something that would suit his manner of doing things—or so they think. Countee |Cullen|'s going to write a novel, so says rumor. Clarence Cameron White is writing an opera.§ Fisk University has a new library. At least a nigger a week is being lynched in the South this season, the color line is getting tighter and tighter, even in New York, but in books and the theatre the Negro is still muy simpatico. Dance, damn you, dance! You're awfully strange and amusing!

> Un abrazo, compadre,
>
> Langston

---

* *Scarlet Sister Mary*, Julia Peterkin's play based on her Pulitzer Prize–winning novel of the same name, opened in Columbus, Ohio, on September 22, 1930, and in New York on Broadway on November 25, 1930. Peterkin (1890–1961) was a successful white writer known for her portrayals of black folk life in the South Carolina Low Country.

† *Potter's Field: A Symphonic Play of the Negro People* was the first musical drama written by the white North Carolina playwright Paul Green.

‡ Vsevolod Emilevich Meyerhold (1874–1940) was an avant-garde Russian theatrical producer, director, and actor important in the Moscow Art Theatre until he left it in 1902. Although Paul Green had been told that Meyerhold would arrive in October 1930, Meyerhold did not come to the United States in 1930 or 1931, nor did he produce *Potter's Field* in New York.

§ Clarence Cameron White (1880–1960) was an African American concert violinist who studied composition in Great Britain with the black musician Samuel Coleridge-Taylor. In 1932, White created the opera *Ounga* with John F. Matheus, his colleague at West Virginia State University. *Ounga* tells the story of Jean-Jacques Dessalines (1758–1806), the slave turned revolutionary who declared himself emperor of Haiti in 1804.

TO ARTHUR SPINGARN   [ALS]

Box No. 94,
Westfield, N.J.*
December 6, 1930.

Dear Arthur Spingarn,†
I didn't know any of the things you told me about Sheridan Leary‡ in your letter. I am mighty glad to have those facts, and it was surely good of you to look them up for me. I wish I had been old enough to learn more from my grandmother before she died.

You remember, I was ill when I last saw you? Well, the doctor has just found out the cause: it is, of all things, a tapeworm!§ The kind you get from eating infected beef. So now I am going in the Sanitarium on Tuesday for a few days to have him killed off. . . . . Will see you when I come out, I hope.

The name of that bibliography is: The Black Man's Point of View (It lists magazines articles, too) and was compiled by Miss Josephine De Witt, and

Amy Spingarn's sketch of Hughes

---

* Hughes left the Hedgerow Theatre in late October to return to his home in Westfield, New Jersey.
† Arthur B. Spingarn (1878–1971), the brother of Joel E. Spingarn, was Hughes's lifelong attorney and friend. A tireless advocate for black rights, he served as president of the NAACP from 1940 until 1965.
‡ Lewis Sheridan Leary (1835–1859) was the first husband of Hughes's maternal grandmother, Mary Langston. A member of John Brown's insurrectionist band, Leary was killed in the Harpers Ferry raid.
§ Soon after writing this letter, Hughes visited a Park Avenue specialist (recommended by Spingarn), who rudely dismissed the tapeworm diagnosis. In The Big Sea, Hughes acknowledges that anger had made him sick: "Violent anger makes me physically ill, I guess, although I've only been that angry twice in my life. All that day I had kept trying not to feel angry or hurt or amazed or bewildered over the morning on Park Avenue—and I didn't feel any of those things consciously—for I had loved very much that gentle woman who had been my patron and I wanted to understand what had happened to us that she had sent me away as she did."

financed by the Acorn Club for the library. It may be gotten from the Oakland Free Library, Oakland, Cal.*

I'm glad you like Mrs. Amy's drawing of me.† I do, too—quite as well as any of the drawings I've had of myself.

I had a nice time at your house that night in spite of the tapeworm.

With best regards to Mrs. Spingarn, as ever,

Sincerely,

Langston

P.S. Do you know an old Negro novel <u>Unfettered</u> (Orion Pub. Co., Nashville, 1902) by Sutton E. Griggs?‡ I've borrowed it to read lately—but haven't yet.

TO ZORA NEALE HURSTON   [*TLS*]

<Third letter from me to Miss Hurston>

4800 Carnegie Ave.,

Cleveland, Ohio.

January 19, 1931.

Dear Zora,

I'm sorry the Guild turned down MULE BONE§—but I'm also sorry it went to them in such a shape, and in such a way¶. . . . . This is the Cleveland situation:

---

* This bibliography was published by the Oakland Public Library, following (according to the library) "a suggestion from Mrs. Delilah Beasley." There are three copies at the Oakland Public Library.

† Amy Spingarn sketched a portrait of Hughes, which was used as the frontispiece for their booklet *Dear Lovely Death* (1931).

‡ Sutton E. Griggs (1872–1933), the son of a former slave, was a Baptist minister, orator, and writer. His five published novels, written between 1899 and 1908, are generally considered early works in the Black Nationalist literary tradition. The first and best known is *Imperium in Imperio* (1899).

§ In the spring of 1930, Hughes and Zora Neale Hurston began to collaborate on a folk comedy they called "Mule Bone." The basic plot comes from a story collected by Hurston entitled "The Bone of Contention." Once the best of friends, Hurston and Hughes quarreled over the authorship of the comedy (see also letters dated January 30, 1931, and February 7, 1931). Because they could not resolve their dispute, "Mule Bone" was not produced in their lifetimes. It was finally staged, with only limited success, at Lincoln Center in New York City on February 15, 1991.

¶ Around May 1930, with "Mule Bone" almost finished, Hurston suddenly left Westfield and moved to Manhattan. Whenever Hughes tried to reach her to discuss the future of the play, she evaded him. The following February, while visiting his mother in Cleveland, Hughes was stunned to learn that the Gilpin Players, a local amateur theater group, had received a script of "Mule Bone" that credited Hurston as the sole author. In October 1930, with Hughes at the Hedgerow Theatre, Hurston had copyrighted the play in her name only.

The Gilpin Players here are probably the best Little Theatre Negro group in the country, and for ten years have been producing plays successfully.* Each year they do a downtown season. In the past they have used such plays as Roseanne,† In Abraham's Bosom, etc. They do try-out plays for New York producers also, and have been offered try-outs of plays the Guild was considering. New York scouts and agents attend their openings. This year they are to open downtown at the Theatre of Nations under the auspices of The CLEVELAND PLAINDEALER, leading white paper out here, which would mean a great deal of assured publicity right there. Then later they will move to the OHIO, one of the leading legitimate downtown theatres here. All of which means an assured two-weeks run. This would in no way hurt a New York production. In fact, it would help it, because if the play is well-received out here, New York managers will be sure to bid for it—and I think that is our best bet, now that the Guild is out of the running. I hope you will agree for it to be done here, as I think it will mean much to us both. . . . . I was in touch by phone today, through Mrs. Jelliffe, manager of the Gilpin Players, with Barrett Clark, the reader who handled your play. He thinks it will be swell when whipped into shape. Mrs. Jelliffe explained the entire situation to him, and he also promised to get in direct touch with you about it. I have also written two letters to Carl |Van Vechten|, since the play seems to have reached the agent and eventually Cleveland through him‡ . . . . . . Since the Gilpin Players must open on the 15th of February, some word from you by wire at once would be appreciated. I haven't your letter yet. . . . . As you know, the comedy reached here entirely without my knowledge, but since it did get here, and since the

* The Gilpin Players (which would stage several plays by Hughes) were a mainly black amateur theater group founded and led in Cleveland by Rowena Woodham Jelliffe (1892–1992) and Russell Jelliffe (1891–1980). In 1915, the Jelliffes, a young white couple, established an interracial settlement house in Cleveland based on Jane Addams's Hull House in Chicago. They also started the Dumas Drama Club, but renamed it in 1923 after a visit from the outstanding African American actor Charles S. Gilpin. In 1927, when the Gilpin Players acquired a theater adjacent to the settlement house, they called it Karamu House, karamu being Swahili for "a place of joyful meeting."

† Roseanne is a romantic three-act drama with Negro spirituals written by Nan Bagby Stephens, a white playwright. First produced in 1923 with an all-white cast made up in blackface, it was then revived with greater success in 1924 with a black cast. The revival attracted outstanding performers: Rose McClendon starred in the 1924 touring production opposite Charles S. Gilpin, who was later replaced by Paul Robeson.

‡ In November 1930, Hurston (implicitly claiming sole authorship) had sent Carl Van Vechten a finished version of "Mule Bone." Charmed by it, Van Vechten passed along the play to Barrett Clark of the Theatre Guild in New York. The Guild rejected it, but in his capacity as an associate of the prominent Samuel French Agency, Clark then recommended the comedy to the Gilpin Players.

Players are anxious to do it, I would be interested in seeing it go through. They would be glad to have you come out for rehearsals and the opening if you cared to do so. . . . . In any case, I do not think it would be a bad beginning for our first play, and for the first Negro folk-comedy ever written. . . . . Let's not be niggers about the thing, and fall out before we've even gotten started. Please wire me.

Sincerely,

L. Hughes

TO ARTHUR SPINGARN   [ALS]

4800 Carnegie Ave.,

Cleveland Ohio,

January 30, 1931.

Dear Arthur Spingarn,

Thanks for your letters. Am in bed with the grippe, so I haven't been so quick with an answer. I do not understand Dr. |Alain| Locke's zeal in upholding Miss Hurston's position—except that they are both employed by the same patron. Miss Hurston has probably claimed Mule-Bone as entirely her own before Dr. Locke and their patron; and Dr. Locke, knowing only one side of the story, chooses to back Miss Hurston.* So far as I can recall, I have never spoken to Dr. Locke about our comedy, nor was I aware, until I heard from you, that he even knew Miss Hurston and I had worked on a play together. I wired him asking for an explanation of his statement to you. His answer was: "Congratulations on the Harmon Award† but what more do you want.". . . . . Isn't that annoying?. . . . . Yesterday Mrs. Jelliffe received a letter from Mr. Paul Banks, one of the Gilpin Players at present visiting in New York for some few weeks or so. Mr. Banks had just called on Miss Hurston. He quotes her as saying that I have been stupidly untruthful about the play; that she has convinced you that I am wrong; that you are very much disillusioned about me; and that you will no longer represent me in New York; and that she has Dr.

---

* Probably eager to maintain his own lucrative ties to Mrs. Mason, Locke had assured her that he would support Hurston's claims against Hughes in the controversy.

† The Harmon Foundation, established in 1922 by William E. Harmon (1862–1928), a white real estate developer and philanthropist, promoted black participation in the fine arts. The Harmon Gold Award (a gold medal and $400) honored distinguished achievement in seven areas, including literature. Nominated apparently by Alain Locke, Hughes received the award in 1930.

Locke on her side. Further, that she will shortly leave for Cleveland, but that she absolutely refuses to associate my name with the production.

Of course, all this excited Mrs. Jelliffe anew. She tried to reach both you and Miss Hurston yesterday by phone but failed—so she tells me today that she has written you. The play is in rehearsal here and has been announced by The Plaindealer as a Negro comedy by myself and Miss Hurston. Miss Hurston, as I told you, authorized the production by her two wires Okay and Proceed Good Luck. Now Mrs. Jelliffe does not know what might happen from her present attitude as expressed to Mr. Banks. Miss Hurston has never ordered the production stopped here—but seemingly after I told her I had put the matter in your hands she became angry and decided to go back to her strange and stubborn policy of not admitting our collaboration. Mrs. Jelliffe feels that she had better get expert legal advice here to prevent any thing happening at this late date which would disrupt and spoil their downtown season, for that reason she asks me to get from you all correspondence of which I kept no copies: i.e. Miss Hurston's two letters to me, and anything else you may have, marked in red "Please return." So would you kindly send letters so marked back to me. . . . . Also if you can aid me by giving Mrs. Jelliffe some expert advice about her tangle here when you answer her letter, I would appreciate it immensely, since I know nothing more to do or say about it myself. The check for Miss Hurston's fare to Cleveland has been sent her—so maybe the face to face conference can be held soon. I hope so—as this strange and unpleasant business is beginning to get on my nerves. Judging from Mr. Banks' letter, New Yorkers are beginning to think that I am the robber, instead of the robbed! Well, sir!! What next?

Sincerely,

Langston

(over)

P.S. Would the copyright office be likely to copyright the same play twice thru mistake? Is it possible to discover whether or not Miss Hurston did copyright Mule-Bone last October by asking the question of the Register of Copyrights? If the play has been copyrighted twice, once by Miss Hurston with herself as sole author, again by myself this month with both of us as authors, what bearing would that have on the situation here regarding the impending Gilpin production—should it come to a matter of injunctions, etc. from Miss Hurston or her agents? The play was once tentatively called "The Bone of Contention"—and that's what it really has become. Miss Hurston has evidently decided to bluff her way through on the false stand that she has taken. Or else she is ashamed to back down before her New York friends. I'm sorry about the whole matter.

<P.S. Am sending the II & III acts of the comedy as prepared for the Gilpins' production using the I and III acts done in collaboration last spring, and the II as revised from the version Miss Hurston did last summer in the South with the use of my spring notes for its construction, and following my outline as to scenes and action, except that in her version <u>the turkey</u> incident was used instead of <u>the girl</u>. This had to be removed to conform with our original two acts. This is really a 2nd draft version of our collaborated play. I had wanted to work it over once more with Miss Hurston before we tried to sell it, or even tried it out here.>

TO LOUISE THOMPSON (PATTERSON)   *[TL]*

4800 Carnegie Avenue,
Cleveland, Ohio,
February 7, 1931.

Dear Lou,

As you probably know by now, Zora |Neale Hurston| has been here. And how! There were two conferences, both with the Jelliffes, one on Monday, another on Tuesday. The Monday one was fairly agreeable. Zora and I went off alone in the front office, settled our private affairs (or so I thought) came out, and she admitted I had had a part in the play, that she would collaborate, and that she and I would both sign the contract for the production here (if the Gilpins were going to do the comedy, as they had voted the night before Zora's arrival to drop it as no one could get a sensible answer from her, or her new agent Elizabeth Marbury.) However—overnight the change took place. In the early dawning Zora called up Mrs. Jelliffe and proceeded to attempt to bawl her out by phone for daring to put my name beside hers on the play, for taking your word for anything as you were this-that-and-the-other, etc. Mrs. Jelliffe said you were a friend of theirs, that she wouldn't listen to any more over the phone, and that we could all meet again at five. I was in bed with tonsillitis, so everyone came to my house. Zora brought a young man, Paul Banks, with her, one of the Gilpin Players who had been in New York and had made the trip back with her in her car. He, of course, was strongly on her side, and had previously written here that I had been stupidly untruthful since he knew I had had nothing to do with the play, and furthermore Zora said that my law-

yer* was so disillusioned with me that he wouldn't even represent me! . . . . . .
Well, anyhow, this young man was with her, the Jelliffes, my mother, and me.
And such a scene you cannot imagine. The young man, of course, said nothing. But Zora pushed her hat on the back of her head, bucked her eyes, ground
her teeth, and proceeded to rave. She called Mrs. Jelliffe a dishonorable person, said she, Zora, had not come all the way to Cleveland to be made a fool
of, implied that everybody was trying to pull sly tricks on her and she knew
it, said who was you that anybody should take your word, (here again Mrs. Jelliffe said you were her friend). I said that you had nothing to do with the point
under discussion anyway. Zora then shook manuscript in my face and dared
and defied me to put my finger on a line that was mine, and that what had
been mine in there, she had changed in her "new" version, and furthermore,
the whole third act had been written by herself alone while you and I were "off
doing Spanish." Yes, I had helped some with the characterization—but what
construction was there to it? And the story was hers, every line of dialog was
hers except one line at the end of the first act, and she took that out. I was just
trying to steal her work from her!!! And so on and on until Mr. Jelliffe asked
his wife to no longer remain to be further insulted, whereupon they all left,
Zora without even saying Goodbye to Mother or I. The whole scene on her
part was most undignified and niggerish. Nobody else quarreled. And whenever she was asked to explain her wild statements she would say she hadn't
come to be questioned or made a goat of . . . . . . That was Tuesday. . . . . I have
not seen her since, but on Thursday who had the astounding nerve to attend
a party given by the Omegas for me, but to which I could not go on account
of my throat.† There Zora, I understand, told everyone that I was stealing her
work, as well as saying some very unpleasant things about you. She has started
a great swirl of malicious gossip here about all of us, the Jelliffes as well. The
Gilpins have split up into groups some for the Jelliffes, some against, and
the whole thing has developed into the most amazing mess I ever heard of.
The Gilpins, of course, had to cancel their downtown date. Mrs. Jelliffe has
been terribly upset about the matter, as she and I both had been as nice and as
tactful as possible with both Zora and her agents, and with Zora herself when
she arrived. Certainly none of us expected such a performance from the lady!
It seems that now Zora chooses to be not only contrary and untruthful, but

---

* Arthur Spingarn represented Hughes's legal interests in the "Mule Bone" controversy.
† Hughes had joined the nationally prominent black Omega Psi Phi fraternity while
attending Lincoln University.

malicious and hurtful as well. (I have received the most insulting note I have ever heard tell of from 399.* How she thinks of such ungodly things to say, I don't know.)..... Anyway, the Jelliffes feel that something should be done to stop Zora's irresponsible and malicious statements, even to the point of asking my lawyer to threaten a libel suit if she insists further on saying publicly that I have tried to steal her play.

Personally, I think Zora must be a little off, as in all my letters to her, or talks here with her, I have been agreeable to further collaboration, and I have made no attempt, nor threatened to make one, to dispose of any part or parts of the play without her knowledge or consent. (She's the one. I kept quiet about it, now she's spreading the opposite tale.) So all that she is saying is crazy and without foundation in fact. She could not prove any of it—but how can people know that? So we all feel that you must be warned against her in New York..... She contends that I wanted you to have a large interest in the profits of the play, therefore she withdrew..... Can you imagine it?..... I think I had better tell everyone of my friends in New York the story of the play now, because with both |Alain| Locke and Zora on the lying line, God knows what will get about. (I think I wrote you of Locke calling on |Arthur| Spingarn to back Zora up.) I wired him for an explanation and his answer was CONGRATULATIONS ON THE HARMON AWARD BUT WHAT MORE DO YOU WANT?...... I think they all must be quite mad!

Anyhow, Louise, why Zora should be so ungodly sore at you for, is something I don't know. But you certainly have to know all this, at least in self defense..... Have you ever seen such amazing niggers or white folks either. I'm glad you have another job and that I have my new book well in mind. They can all go to the nether regions as far as I am concerned..... Best of luck to you, and love to Mother. I am going to write her..... Take care of that cold you said you had, and find yourself a mule-bone because the free-for-all is on.

Sincerely,

---

* Charlotte Mason's address in Manhattan was 399 Park Avenue.

TO CARL VAN VECHTEN   [ALS]
[On L.H. monogrammed stationery]

(Air Mail)
Poste Restante,
Cap-Haïtien, Haiti,*
May 27, 1931.

Dear Carlo,

Have been laying off to write you for weeks, but we've been moving so fast and rough that I haven't had a chance, but at last we come to a stopping place—with the sight of the Citadel† 20 miles away on a mountain top. We came across Cuba in old cars that continually broke down, and camions full of peasants and chickens; took deck passage on a French ship at Santiago for Port au Prince and rode in the open for three days with the sugar-cane workers coming home, while the boat went all around southern Haiti picking up cargo. The last night a storm came up and we slept in the hole with the Haitian crew. Port au Prince struck us as being little more than a collection of wooden huts with tin roofs, gangs of Marines, badly lighted streets, and everything at American prices or higher, so we left for the North. Half way to the Cape the spring floods held us up for nearly two weeks, but we had a swell time. Stayed at St. Marc where there is a splendid beach, mountains all around, and lots of Congoes on week-ends, drums sounding everywhere. (The Congo is a simplified Cuban rumba with a more monotonous rhythm, a more primitive pattern—men and women dancing alone or together as they choose, all circling round and round a sort of Maypole in the middle of a thatched roof, singing and throwing hips.)

    We reached the Cape last week, found a grand hotel on the water-front, for seamen and Santo Domingan revolutionaries—a place where they play bisique‡ and dominoes all day, and dance to Cuban records, talk revolutions,

---

* Remaining in Cleveland after Hurston left, Hughes finished the revision of his play "Cross" and renamed it *Mulatto*. Distraught after Godmother took Hurston's side in the "Mule Bone" dispute, he decided to escape to the Caribbean. On April 1, he and his traveling companion and driver Zell Ingram left for Florida in a car owned by Ingram's mother. From Miami, they took a train to Key West, where they went by boat to Havana. After about two weeks in Cuba, the men traveled by boat to Port-au-Prince, Haiti, and then via bus to Cap-Haïtien in the north.
† La Citadelle Laferrière is a spectacular fortress (the largest in the Western Hemisphere) approximately seventeen miles south of Cap-Haïtien. Built between 1805 and 1820 from pieces of stone hauled up a three-thousand-foot mountain, it was designed to resist French attacks on the newly independent republic.
‡ Bezique is a card game for two players.

and drink copoise half the night. The Cape is charming, full of old ruins from the days of the French. Pushed into the sea by the hills, it's much cooler, less full of mosquitoes, and not nearly so ugly as Port au Prince. Our windows and balconies look out on the ancient embankments, the bay and the mountains beyond. Room and meals for only $25 each a month! All the native crew from the ship we took at Santiago live here at the Cape, so we have plenty of friends (in fact, they told us of this hotel). They take us to Congoes, cockfights, dances, and bars; also out on the bay in their fishing boats. (We're hoping for a Voodoo dance this Saturday of which they have told us.) Last week we went to a grand Congo at the foot of the mountains, got tight on sugarcane rum, and Zell* outdanced the natives. (The snakehips† was a new one to them.) The next morning the musicians came to our hotel and we bought both their drums, the "Mama" and the "Baby." Need only a "Papa" drum now to have a full set, but it seems that between the priests and the Marines (both of whom try to stop the dances and confiscate the drums), "Papa" drums are pretty scarce, and probably can only be found way back in the hills. . . . . Zell had made some nice heads in Cuban and Haitian woods, and a few watercolors. Every body down here takes him for a boxer, and the prettiest woman I've seen in town, so far, has taken him for her own personal property. . . . . We had a swift and glorious time in Havana. I was surprised at the amount of publicity our visit got—reporters and flashlights at the pier, with pictures and a front page story next morning; later a full account of my reading at the Cercle Francais; and the front page again when we were arrested at the beach where we went to meet a professor at the University and Addison Durland, a most amusing Cuban-American rich boy who makes swell pictures.‡ (You must meet him when he comes to New York again).

They wanted to charge us $10.00 each to come in the beach, refused to let us wait for our friends at the entrance, and when we stopped outside, had us arrested and charged with "escandolo"—disturbing the peace. They testified next day that we had bathed inside, put our feet on the beach chairs and refused to take them down, and generally misbehaved. Of course, this was

---

* Rozelle "Zell" Ingram (1910–1971) was a young African American artist at Karamu House who worked in prints, woodblocks, and theater scenery. In 1931, he and Hughes traveled together to Cuba and then to Haiti. In *I Wonder as I Wander*, Hughes describes Ingram as "a solid, amiable, easygoing fellow who had grown up, as I had, in the slums of Cleveland."

† The entertainer Earl Tucker (1905–1937), dubbed the "Human Boa Constrictor," was also known by the name of the sinuous dance he invented, "Snakehips."

‡ Addison Durland was the child of a Cuban journalist and a New York banker. He became an NBC executive who later worked in Hollywood to improve the presentation of Latin Americans in the film industry.

absurd as they didn't let us in. The judge, who knew of the frequent attempts at discrimination there against Cubans of color, rebuked the beach authorities, cleared us, and made a long oration on the rights of all people of whatever color under Cuban law to go freely to all public places . . . . . . With the rainy season coming on, and boats from Haiti to the outward islands very difficult to get, we've decided to go no further South this trip, but to take a sailing vessel from here thru the Bahamas, thence Miami, and home. Zell has a summer job in sight; and I want to do my novel. The next island of distinctive interest would be Martinique—and it's a long ways. . . . . I haven't had any mail from the states for about six weeks, (nor have I seen an American paper in Haiti) so I don't know what's happening. However, I trust Harlem is still there; and that you're O.K. I hope you got over the trouble with your leg all right. . . . . I haven't done any work. Been trying to wear my troubles off my mind . . . . . . Saw <u>Nigger Heaven</u> & <u>Magic Island</u>* (French editions) in the only bookshop at Port au Prince where I bought my Anthologie de Poesie Haitienne. Creole patois is marvelous—like Chinese—full of little tunes and half notes . . . . . . Stars over the black mountains to you,

Langston

TO JAMES NATHANIEL HUGHES   [TLS]

Cap-Haïtien, Haiti,
June 30, 1931.

Dear Father,

I was most happy to have your letter, as well as the book which you sent me. It was good to have direct news of you. Some years ago I wrote you, c/o of the American Consulate in Mexico City, but the letter finally came back. I saw Aunt Sallie in Indianapolis (1716 Blvd. Place) a few years back, and I hear from her occasionally.† She always asks about you, and I know she would be glad to hear from you, if you wanted to write her. . . . . I was interested in what you had to say about my novel. It had a great critical success, the reviews in both the English and American press being almost uniformly good. The sales exceeded those of the average first novel, my January first statement showing a sale of some five thousand copies for the first five months of publication. It was published in Moscow this spring, and will probably appear in Paris in

* *The Magic Island* (1929) is a study by Alexander King B. Seabrook of Haitian social and religious customs.
† Mrs. Sarita "Sallie" J. Garvin (d. 1935) was the sister of Hughes's father.

the fall as the French translation rights have been sold . . . . . . In one way or another, directly or indirectly, enough money has come to me from my books to live, but to make a good steady income from literature takes a long time, as one must slowly build up a buying public, or else sell a great deal to the magazines, or the movies. . . . . I am certainly sorry to hear that you have had such a difficult time with your health, and I wish that something could be done about it. I was sorry I couldn't come to you that time when you first became ill, but I wanted to make my own way in the world—which has proven quite exciting, although I have nothing to show for it except three books and practically no money. I have traveled quite a lot, however—as you advised me. Last March I started on a trip through the West Indies with another fellow, but so far, we have gotten no farther than Haiti, where we have been for two months here in the shadow of the Citadel built by the black king Christophe.* Twenty miles away on a mountain top, it stands a magnificent ruin, the grandest thing in Haiti—for the people today are asleep in the sun. The Marines are here, and all the money goes into white pockets. . . . . The news which you give me of Mexico is very interesting. Miguel Covarrubias, the Mexican artist, is a good friend of mine in New York, and he tells me, too, of the progress which the country is making . . . I would like very much to read that book on the American Negro.† You must send it to me when I get back to the States in August. Please do not destroy the books you say you do not want, as I would like to have them. . . . . Have you seen the magazine OPPORTUNITY, and a new one called ABBOTT'S MONTHLY, published by the man who owns the Chicago Defender?‡ They are both interesting, and I will send you copies when I get back, also any other books or papers which you feel you would like to have. You must have a great deal of time on your hands now to read, so if there is anything from the States you want, let me know. . . . . You ask me several questions I can't answer. I don't know about Dr. Sweet.§ The Binga Bank,

* Henri Christophe (1767–1820), a former slave and revolutionary, was elected president of the Northern State of the republic of Haiti in February 1807. His election followed the 1806 assassination of Jean-Jacques Dessalines, who had crowned himself emperor of Haiti in 1804. On March 28, 1811, Christophe proclaimed the Northern State as the Kingdom of Haiti and himself as King Henri I.

† In his letter of January 13, 1932, James Hughes offered to send Langston a copy of the rabidly anti-black *The American Negro: What He Was, What He Is, and What He May Become* (1901) by William Hannibal Thomas (1843–1935). Thomas was himself African American, born free in Ohio.

‡ Robert Sengstacke Abbott (1870–1940) printed the first edition of his weekly newspaper *The Chicago Defender*, aimed mainly at an African American readership, on May 5, 1905. In October 1930, Abbott launched the short-lived magazine *Abbott's Monthly*.

§ After Ossian H. Sweet, a black physician, moved his family into a previously all-white Detroit neighborhood in 1925, unruly whites targeted his house. Dr. Sweet, members of

it seems, went down in the general crash with hundreds of other small banks in the country caught in the Depression—frozen assets, etc.* When I left the States the papers said a reorganization was on foot. The DuBois-Cullen match seemed to have been a marriage without love, the two concerned not being very friendly on the day of the wedding, so they probably had little intention of living together long. No one in New York knows why they married, unless pressure had been brought to bear on the part of one or the other of the parents as the engagement had been so long announced . . . . . . Rhinelander married Alice, knowing her to be the daughter of a colored coachman. His parents forced a separation. There were counter-divorce suits. She came out best, receiving a large settlement of money†. . . . . Do you know the Murray's in Mexico City, a colored family from New York? Mrs. Murray is the sister-in-law of Walter White, head of the N. A. A. C. P. She was in New York on a visit just before I left. . . . . I have been in Havana twice in the last two years. My poems are known there, many of them having been translated in their magazines and papers. Am enclosing a clipping. . . . . <Will send later. Left in Port au Prince.> Give my love to the Patiños,‡ and write to me whenever you have the time. You can always reach me c/o of my publishers, Alfred A. Knopf, Inc, 730 Fifth Avenue, New York. That is the best address. If I make a lot of money from my next book, I will come down and see you. . . . . Thanks for all the good advice. I'm sure you're right.

Affectionately,

Langston

---

his family, and some visitors to the house were brought to trial after an incident in which gunfire from inside the house killed a demonstrator. With support from the NAACP, the famed lawyers Clarence Darrow and Arthur Garfield Hayes defended them. At the second trial (the first ended with a deadlocked jury), Henry Sweet, who had admitted to firing the fatal shot, was acquitted. The prosecution then dropped charges against the other defendants.

* Jesse Binga (1865–1950) opened the Binga State Bank on January 3, 1921, to serve the black business community in Chicago. In July 1930, the bank closed as a result of the Depression as well as bad loans and investments.

† In 1924, a wealthy New Yorker, Leonard "Kip" Rhinelander, sensationally sued for divorce Alice Jones Rhinelander, his wife of six weeks. He charged that she had fooled him into believing she was white. Her attorney had her disrobe behind closed doors for the white, all-male jury to see evidence of her "colored blood." The jury ruled in favor of Alice Rhinelander.

‡ The Patiños—Dolores, Refugio, and Rafaela—were old friends of Hughes's father. In *The Big Sea*, Hughes describes them as "three charming Mexican ladies who were his friends—three unmarried sisters, one of whom took care of his rents in the city. They were very Latin and very Catholic, lived in a house with a charming courtyard, and served the most marvelous dishes at table. . . . These three aging ladies were, I think, the only people in the whole world who really ever liked my father."

PART II

Let America Be America Again

1931 to 1939

On tour with Radcliffe Lucas, 1931

Christ is a nigger,
Beaten and black:
Oh, bare your back!

Mary is His Mother:
Mammy of the South,
Silence your mouth.

God is His Father:
White Master above
Grant Him your love.

Most holy bastard
Of the bleeding mouth,
    Nigger Christ
    On the cross
    Of the South.
—"CHRIST IN ALABAMA," 1931

At the suggestion of Mary McLeod Bethune, and with money from the Rosenwald Fund, Hughes toured the South and then the western United States (1931–1932) reading his work in schools and churches, taking poetry to the people. This tour helped to solidify the connection between him and a wide African American audience that would last the rest of his life. His readings would also provide him with a modest but sustaining income as he struggled to continue writing. Hughes's commitment to the left deepened with his support of the Scottsboro Boys, nine black youths accused of raping two white women in Alabama in 1931.

TO JAMES WELDON JOHNSON   [TLS]

Y.M.C.A.,
181 West 135th St.,
New York, New York,
August 14, 1931.

Dear Mr. Johnson,*

Just recently back from Haiti, and I found your note with the enclosure waiting for me the other day when I went after my mail. I have a lot to tell you about my impressions of the Black Republic. Would also like to talk over with you a reading tour of the South which I hope to do this fall and winter if dates and a Ford can be procured. In a Ford we came all the way from Miami for less than $20.00, so I know such a tour by car could be done cheaply. I want to help build up a public (I mean a Negro public) for Negro books, and, if I can, to carry to the young people of the South interest in, and aspiration toward, true artistic expression, and a fearless use of racial material. I am asking the Rosenwald Fund if it wishes to help me in that and in the writing of some of

---

* James Weldon Johnson (1871–1938) was a highly respected poet, novelist, and lawyer who served as field secretary and general secretary of the NAACP from 1916 to 1930. His books include the novel *The Autobiography of an Ex-Coloured Man* (1912), the volume of poetry *God's Trombones* (1927), the urban study *Black Manhattan* (1930), and an autobiography, *Along This Way* (1933).

the many things I have in mind to do.* I would appreciate it immensely if you would allow me to use your name should they ask me for recommendations, etc., as I suppose they will. . . . . I hope your summer has been an enjoyable one. I know I remember with delight the afternoon I spent at your lovely place last year with Amy Spingarn. . . . . I send all good wishes and best regards to Mrs. Johnson.

Sincerely,
Langston

TO AMY SPINGARN   [ALS]
[On L.H. monogrammed stationery]

181 West 135th St.
New York, N.Y.,
September 24, 1931.

Dear Mrs. Spingarn,

I was happy to hear that you were back in the East again. I'm home, too, and have a lot to tell you about Haiti. I hope you had another profitable and happy time in California this year. Haiti was beautiful and strange, but depressing and very poor. . . . . Mr. Spingarn tells me our booklet may soon be underway, and that Zell Ingram's drawing made a nice cut.† He is in town for the winter now, going to the League,‡ and making studies of Negro dancers. When you come to town I'd like both of you to see each other's work. . . . . If I can help any on the booklet, please let me know. . . . . In November I'm going South on a lecture tour. The Rosenwald Fund has given me a thousand dollars to buy a Ford! Isn't that swell? . . . . And I'm working on a new play. And am

---

* Julius Rosenwald (1862–1932), the president of Sears, Roebuck and Company from 1909 to 1924, established the Rosenwald Fund in October 1917. It operated until June 1948. The fund built schools for black children in the rural South, awarded fellowships to African American scholars and artists, and also gave money to public schools and libraries. On September 17, 1931, Hughes learned that the fund had awarded him $1,000 for his proposed tour.

† In October 1931, Amy Spingarn's private Troutbeck Press published a limited edition of *Dear Lovely Death*, a booklet of Hughes's poems with a cover designed by Zell Ingram. ("Troutbeck" was the name of Joel and Amy Spingarn's estate in Dutchess County, north of Amenia, New York.)

‡ Since its founding in 1875 on West 57th Street, the Art Students League of New York has provided classes for aspiring artists at modest fees.

doing a children's book on Haiti with another fellow.* And have a pamphlet of dramatic recitations on racial themes coming out soon—intended for a non-literary public—with some broadsides, too.† (You gave me the idea—with Barrel House!)‡ This has been a tremendously busy month for me since my return. . . . . Please let me know when you're in town. I have something for you.

Sincerely,

Langston

TO NANCY CUNARD   [TLS]

Dear Nancy Cunard:§

Thought your article in the CRISIS was swell.¶ Also your idea of doing an international book on COLOR which I hope you will succeed in filling with new and exciting material from all quarters.** Have been terribly busy since I got back from Haiti, and am about to leave New York again for a lecture tour of the South starting in November, but if I can help any more, I'd be happy to. Here are a lot of things enclosed from which you may select whatever you might like. Also some addresses that might be useful to you. I think there's a lot of Negro talent in Havana, and the Cuban "son" music is grand. Zell Ingram has <many> good drawings that you might like. Write him. A girl

---

* Hughes wrote *Popo and Fifina* (Macmillan, 1932) with Arna Bontemps.
† Hughes refers to *The Negro Mother and Other Dramatic Recitations* (Golden Stair Press, 1931), with illustrations by a young white artist, Prentiss Taylor (1907–1991).
‡ Amy Spingarn made a typeset print of his poem "Barrel House: Northern City" on her own printing press. A handwritten note on the back of the print in the Moorland-Spingarn Research Center at Howard University reads: "Very rare Langston gave it to me and I printed it on my press I don't know if it ever appeared among his poems AES." The *Lincoln News* had first published the poem (a series of three sonnets) in 1928 with the title "Barrel House: Chicago." It first appeared in book form in *One-Way Ticket* (1948) as "Juice Joint: Northern City" and that title has been used in all subsequent reprintings.
§ The British writer and political activist Nancy Cunard (1896–1965) was an heir to the fortune derived mainly from the Cunard fleet of luxury ocean liners. In 1920, Cunard moved to Paris, where her interest in modernist writers and in African and African American cultures deepened. Her book *Black Man and White Ladyship: Anniversary*, about her intimate relationship with the American musician Henry Crowder, was published in 1931.
¶ "Does Anyone *Know* Any Negroes" appeared in the September 1931 issue.
** Nancy Cunard's anthology *Negro* (London: Wishart & Co., 1934) is a massive collection of writings on black history, culture, and social and political conditions as well as reviews of music, poetry, and the other arts. Among the contributors are Hughes, W. E. B. Du Bois, Alain Locke, Zora Neale Hurston, Samuel Beckett, and Ezra Pound.

named Pauline Murray, 437 Manhattan Ave., New York, has some poems and stories that I liked.* Never been published. Not racial stuff, but might be worth your seeing, if she'd send you something. Also young artist, Charles H. Alston, 1945 Seventh Avenue, New York, has done some decorations for my WEARY BLUES poem that show an interesting talent.† Completely unknown, but if you could make a few discoveries, or introduce some youngsters in your book, it mightn't be a bad thing to do, and I believe these two show promise.... James L. Allen, 213 West 121st Street, N. Y., is probably the best photographer of Negroes in the world‡. . . . . This month's POETRY contains some

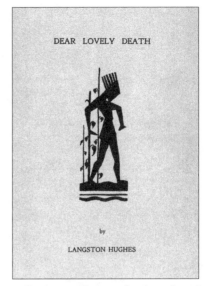

Zell Ingram's drawing for the jacket of *Dear Lovely Death*

new poems of mine from which you may select, too, if you like any of them. And of-course, you can use any from my books, if you care to, with the permission of my publishers, Alfred A. Knopf, Inc, 730 Fifth Avenue, N.Y. . . . . . I'm sorry I wasn't here when you were in America. Better luck <for me> next time . . . . . . With best wishes for the book,

Sincerely,

Langston Hughes

P.S. Aaron Douglas is in Paris. Perhaps you've met him by now.

181 West 135th Street, N.Y.

September 30, 1931.

---

* Hughes helped Pauli Murray (1910–1985) to place her first published poem, "The Song of the Highway," in Nancy Cunard's *Negro*. A civil rights lawyer and legal scholar, Murray also published an admired memoir, *Proud Shoes* (1956). In 1977, she became the first African American woman to be ordained as an Episcopal priest.
† Charles Henry Alston (1907–1977) started his career as a commercial artist but became a noted painter, teacher, and sculptor.
‡ James Latimer Allen (1907–1977) was a well-known commercial photographer whose work remains an important record of Harlem life.

TO WALTER WHITE   [*TLS*]

On Tour*
High Point, NC
Dec. 8, 1931

Dear Walter,

You have my greatest sympathy in the recent death of your father. I have just heard about it from the papers.

Our engagement here in High Point has been most pleasant. This morning, I read to the various colored schools, and at the white high school. Sold gangs of books (Thanks, to you and Miss Randolph† for the tip.). . . . Had a swell time in Chapel Hill, too. Paul Green had a little party for me after the reading to meet some of his friends. Then Larry Flynn (Andrew Mellon's nephew, I learned later) opened a million bottles of home brew in my honor (Southern white ladies present at both functions). I ate dinner in one of the largest restaurants in town with the editors of Contempo. Nothing happened.‡

Tomorrow Orangeburg, S. C., then return engagement at Augusta, Ga., then Florida, and, just before Xmas, your home-town Atlanta. We're traveling every day, poeticizing at night—so haven't much time to write. Here's best regards to Gladys and the youngsters. Don't work too hard. (I'm showing your picture every day to the youth of the race as one of the biggest men. That's part of my road show.) So don't let the race and its problems work you to death—even tho a great man becomes even greater when he dies.

Sincerely,

Langston

* On November 2, 1931, Hughes and W. Radcliffe Lucas, a schoolmate from Lincoln University who served as both business manager and chauffeur, left New York on a poetry reading tour. With money from the Rosenwald Fund, Hughes had bought a new Model A Ford car. They returned to New York City on March 24, 1932. A few days later, Hughes resumed the tour when he headed for Texas with a new driver. (Hughes never learned to drive a car.)
† Richetta G. Randolph (1884–1971?) held numerous administrative positions at the NAACP, including office manager and private secretary to James Weldon Johnson and Walter White.
‡ Paul Green invited Hughes to read at the University of North Carolina in Chapel Hill. During his trip, Hughes dined with Anthony Buttita and Milton Abernethy, the young white editors of Contempo, in the dining room of a prominent café there. In I Wonder as I Wander, Hughes recalls some of the reaction to this defiance of Southern racial etiquette: "At succeeding stops in other Carolina towns my audiences were overflowing. Negroes were delighted at my having, so they said, 'walked into the lion's den, and come out, like Daniel, unscathed.'"

TO HELEN SEWELL   *[TL]*

LANGSTON HUGHES
c/o The Crisis
69 Fifth Avenue
New York City

On Tour
Tuskegee Institute
Alabama
February 15, 1932

Miss Helen Sewell*
18 West 16th Street
New York City

My dear Miss Sewell:
I am very glad you are going to illustrate my book of poems for young people.
Miss Power† and the Knopfs are happy also.
    Miss Hayes‡ suggests that I write you although I do not know anything

These illustrations by Helen Sewell appear in *The Dream Keeper.* Hughes had asked
Sewell to draw "beautiful people that Negro children can look at and not be ashamed to
feel that they represent themselves."

* Helen Moore Sewell (1896–1957), a noted author and illustrator of children's books,
provided drawings for Hughes's volume of poetry for young readers *The Dream Keeper and
Other Poems* (Knopf, 1932), which he dedicated to his stepbrother, Gwyn Clark.
† Effie Lee Power (c. 1872–1969) was director of work with children at the Cleveland Pub-
lic Library and an authority on children's books. After she suggested that Hughes publish
a selection of poems for young readers, he sent her a draft of the manuscript that became
The Dream Keeper and Other Poems (1932). Power later wrote the introduction to the book.
‡ Most likely, Miss Hayes was employed at Knopf.

that I could tell you that would help with the illustrations. Of course, if there is anything that I could tell you, you can feel free to request the information of me. The only thing I might say now is that we all hope the book will have quite a sale in the Negro schools of the South. I have been lecturing in many of those schools this winter. It seems to me that one of the great needs of Negro children is to have books about themselves and their lives that can help them to be proud of their race and to not accept the inferiority complex that many of them living in this white civilization of ours experience. I hope then that if you picture Negro children or black people in your photographs you will make them, not the usual kinky headed caricatures that most illustrators put into books of Negro child life, but I hope that they can be beautiful people that Negro children can look at and not be ashamed to feel that they represent themselves. But then I am sure you are a fine sympathetic artist and that I need not tell you this.

Sincerely yours,

LH:h

TO MARY MCLEOD BETHUNE   [TL]

Tuskegee Institute
Alabama
February 15, 1932

Mrs. Mary McLeod Bethune
Bethune-Cookman Institute
Daytona Beach, Florida

Dear Mrs. Bethune:*
Of course I have been thinking about you a great deal since I left Bethune-Cookman. I am sure you must have known how I hated to leave so pleasant a

---

* Mary McLeod Bethune (1875–1955), an acclaimed pioneer in the field of African American education, opened the Daytona Normal and Industrial Institute for Negro Girls in 1904. After her school merged in 1923 with one for boys, the Cookman Institute of Jacksonville, to form the coeducational Bethune-Cookman College, she remained its president until retiring in 1942. In *I Wonder as I Wander*, Hughes recalled the drive northward with Bethune and Zell Ingram in 1931 on his return from Haiti: "We shared Mrs. Bethune's wit and wisdom, too, the wisdom of a jet-black woman who had risen from a barefooted field hand in a cotton patch to be head of one of the leading junior colleges in America, and a leader of her people. She was a wonderful sport, riding all day without complaint in our cramped, hot little car jolly and talkative, never grumbling."

place. I did not even feel like telling you goodbye that day in the dining room. I felt more like staying.

My lecture schedule has been pretty strenuous for the last month. Among other things I did ten days through Mississippi over some of the worst roads in the world, but meeting some of the most responsive groups of Negro students it has been my pleasure to read before.

At Fisk I had a long talk with James Weldon Johnson about your book and about possible people who might assist you in bringing it to pass. As to Mr. Johnson himself, there are several reasons why he cannot undertake the task. One is that he has considerable work of his own already in progress—enough, he says, for the next two or three years; another is that he feels that a woman writer might be able to do your book with greater sympathy and understanding. He suggests very strongly that you think about Jessie Fauset in connection with the matter. He feels that Miss Fauset has a thorough mastery of her style and the proper touch for an inspirational autobiography such as yours should be. Of course, she has a name in the literary world and her last book, THE CHINABERRY TREE, has been receiving splendid reviews from some of the papers. I think he might be right in his suggestion concerning your consideration of her as a person to write your book or else to work with you in doing it. Mr. Johnson feels that it would be a splendid thing to have a book about one great Negro woman by another Negro woman who has made a name for herself as a writer.

I don't know what you will think about this yourself. I have been turning over in my mind the thought of your book in relation to myself, and whether or not I might be able to do it. This is what I think: that I could not do your book as an impersonal study of your life and do it well and with complete objectivity. I am afraid, too, that if I did it, having a personal style and tone of my own, people might expect to find the personal flavor and my own analyses of your work and your position therein. You know, of course, that I have tremendous admiration for you, but a life such as yours connected so closely with the general problems of Negro education would, if I wrote about it directly and personally, demand from me, I feel, a critical treatment that, while not in any way touching your own splendid position, might hold up to too unpleasant a criticism our entire American system of philanthropic and missionary education for the Negro, since I am becoming very critical of that system from my observation on this tour. Not that it isn't doing good; it is. But I feel it a great pity that any group of people should have to beg for their education, and it is a worse defect in our public education systems, of course.

I feel, however, that if you would like to do your book as your own under your own name, for example, with such a title as this:

MARY MCLEOD BETHUNE

MY STORY

with, if you wish, a note or sub-title perhaps stating "as recounted to Langston Hughes", (or whoever did most of the actual writing), that I could be of help to you in that way. The advantage of this method would be that the whole story of your life and work would have the effect of coming from your own lips and could then carry as much of the flavor of your own powerful and inspiring personality as your speeches have when you stand before an audience. At least I hope it could be written in a fashion which would convey your own force, simplicity and great sincerity. It would be then much like Jane Addams' books,* and I think, would perhaps have even more value to the youth than if it were written as a study of your life by someone else. Many autobiographies, you know, are not actually written by the subjects themselves. Sometimes credit is given to the actual writer, and sometimes not. In my own case, if I were to do your book in that way, it would be entirely up to you as to whether you thought it wise to name myself or not. In any case, believe me only too happy to be of service to you, if I can, in any way that I can, and certainly I hope that your book will get under way soon.

Please let me know what you think of these two ideas and whether or not you are planning to get in touch with Miss Fauset. Perhaps should the book be done in the personal manner (as your own story) Miss Fauset might be, even then, the person to do it. Being a woman, perhaps she would have greater power of putting into words some situations in your life which maybe only a woman could truly understand. Anyway I would be happy to know what you yourself think about all this.

I am enclosing my forwarding addresses for the |next| two weeks, so that you can write me without writing through New York if you would like to.

I shall never forget the cordial reception accorded me on your campus, and I send my regards to my many friends there.

With my love, I am

Sincerely yours,

LH:h

enc.

---

* Jane Addams (1860–1935), a pioneering social worker and winner of the Nobel Peace Prize, is best known for developing Hull House, the settlement house in Chicago that became the model for many such ventures. She published two autobiographies: *Twenty Years at Hull-House* (1910) and *The Second Twenty Years at Hull-House* (1932).

TO PRENTISS TAYLOR   *[TLS]*

Care "The Crisis"
69 Fifth Avenue,
New York City

On Tour
Wiley College
Marshall, Texas
February 23, 1932

Mr. Prentiss Taylor*
23 Bank Street
New York City

Dear Prentiss:

A note regarding the possibility of a Scottsboro pamphlet of your declarations <I dictated "decorations!"> and my poems combined:† Would there be a sale for such a pamphlet, or would we be doing it because we want to do it? I like the idea very much, but I would not like to do it from a commercial angle. If it were so, and I made anything from it, I would like to have it known that the proceeds were going toward either the comfort or the defense of the Scottsboro boys. Would that be agreeable to you?

As to the content, I believe I have four poems that might be included, one article, and (if you thought wise) the Scottsboro play. The booklet would hardly be, all told, as large as the "Negro Mother." It would include, I hope,

---

* Prentiss Taylor (1907–1991) was an illustrator and artist known for his surrealist lithographs. With a $200 loan from Carl Van Vechten, he and Hughes founded the Golden Stair Press, which was based in Taylor's home in Greenwich Village. Their first booklet was *The Negro Mother and Other Dramatic Recitations* (1931), which included works by Hughes and illustrations by Taylor (see also letter dated September 24, 1931).

† Golden Stair Press produced a booklet consisting of Hughes's play *Scottsboro, Limited*, along with four poems and four lithographs on the same theme. The Scottsboro Boys were nine African American males of various ages who were falsely accused of raping two white women on a train in March 1931. After a hasty trial in April, eight of the "boys" were sentenced to death in Scottsboro, Alabama. Their case sparked international outrage. In a series of trials between 1931 and 1938, four of the defendants were acquitted. The other four were found guilty and sentenced to prison. The last was released on parole by 1950. One was pardoned by Governor George Wallace in 1967, while the other three were granted posthumous pardons by the state of Alabama in 2013.

The cover of *Scottsboro, Limited*
(Golden Stair Press, 1932)

the very powerful Scottsboro drawing which you sent me at Christmas.*

The questions in my mind are these: Would Carl |Van Vechten| want to back its publication? Through what channels would we sell it? Would you like me, if we are thinking seriously of doing it, to get in touch with Theodore Dreiser's Committee for the Defense of Political Prisoners,† of which I am a member, or with the I.L.D.,‡ to see if they would care to help us with the sales or publicity? Or would you bring it out as a limited edition with only a certain number of signed copies to sell for a price that would cover the edition and still leave something over for me to send these Scottsboro boys—if only a few cartons of Lucky Strikes?

The interest which such a booklet might help to arouse in the case would, I suppose, outweigh under any circumstances the financial returns; and that, along with the artistic reason, would be why I would especially like to do the booklet. Not being in New York, I can't talk over these things with you, and I am so busy these days that I hardly have time to write a decent letter, but if you want to do the booklet, let me know and I shall get the material together at once. Maybe the play is too red to be included. If so, we shall use only the other things, maybe just the poems. Did you see in the Negro press the little story I wrote about visiting the boys at the prison a few Sundays ago?§ If not, I shall send you a copy.

I hope I shall receive the third edition of the "Negro Mother" soon, as we

---

* The cover of *Scottsboro, Limited* features an illustration that Taylor dated November 1931 on a postcard he sent to Hughes. This may be the drawing to which Hughes refers in his letter.
† The novelist Theodore Dreiser (1871–1945) was chairman of the National Committee for the Defense of Political Prisoners, which actively defended the Scottsboro Boys.
‡ The International Labor Defense (ILD) was the legal arm of the communist Workers Party of America.
§ A version of Hughes's story about visiting the defendants appeared later as "Brown America in Jail: Kilby" in *Opportunity* (June 1932).

are all sold out. I didn't answer your wire because I had just sent you a letter a day or so before, so I trust that everything is OK.

    With best wishes to you, I am

Sincerely,
Langston
Langston Hughes

LH: GA

<Pardon a dictated note—but you ought to see the mail I have to answer. And no time. Mon Dieu, alors!>

<Answer at:

1227 School St.,
Y.W.C.A. Branch,
Des Moines, Iowa.>

TO EDWIN R. EMBREE   [TL]

Forwarding address:
THE CRISIS,
69 Fifth Avenue
New York.

On tour,
Kansas City, Mo.,
March 5, 1932.

Mr. Edwin R. Embree,[*]
Julius Rosenwald Fund,
Chicago, Illinois.

My dear Mr. Embree,

On November 3rd I left New York City on my present tour of the South. With the $600.00 advanced me by the Rosenwald Fund, I bought a Ford, paid for the preliminary expenses of the tour, and started out. Since then, the tour has been paying for itself, and there has been a profit, as you see from the enclosed report, A. An itemized list of the way in which the money was

---

[*] Edwin Rogers Embree (1883–1950) was president of the Rosenwald Fund.

expended is indicated on sheet B. And the tour route, with the states that I have covered, on sheet C. A full account of all tour incomes and expenditures has been kept, and is open to you, should you care to see it. Under separate cover, I am sending you press notices and programs in regard to the tour.

I feel that for the first time, I have met the South. I have talked with many white Southerners, and thousands of Negroes, teachers, students, and towns people. I know now attitudes and complexes I had not realized before. One is that the white people are afraid of one another in regard to things Negro: A white man of wealth speaking, "We would do a lot of things for the Negroes of this county, but the crackers won't let us." . . . . . . A white teacher calling me Mister in private; but Professor, Doctor, anything but Mister before her students. . . . . Amusing and tragic, the little things like Mister |are| not really important except as they reveal the minds behind the peonage, jim-crow schools, and lynchings. . . . . I spent Christmas at Huntsville where the Scottsboro girls |the accusers| live and where there are plantations all around where the Negroes haven't been paid in a blue moon. I visited one of them Christmas day with a man who wore a red cross button in order to gain admittance to distribute fruit to kids who didn't even know it was Christmas day.

The Negro students everywhere have been most kind to me, and seemingly intensely interested in what I had to offer them. My fees for a lecture reading of my poems have been from nothing at many grammar and high schools to $10.00 for places like Trinity that could only afford to pay expenses, to $25.00 at colleges like Rust and Piney Woods, to $50 top price for places like Talladega and Morehouse and New Orleans. Splendid crowds everywhere, and usually quite a number of white people present, even in Mississippi. I have come up now for a few engagements in the mid-west, but will return shortly to the South through Oklahoma and Texas. In April I go to California for probably ten lectures. When those are finished I want to settle down to work on my novel; then two plays; and a series of articles and short stories. There's plenty I want to do. If the Rosenwald Fund would care to help me on a year's creative work, I trust something worthwhile would come out of it. The main thing is to be able to pay a few months rent without worry, and to have help on typing—which takes up a great deal of time better devoted to creation. I have found several amazingly cheap cities in which one can live. They say California is cheap, too. I shall see when I get out there.

I want to thank you for your BROWN AMERICA.* All over the South I have heard people saying good things about it; the colored students, that it is full of inspiration for them; the white people, that it is revealing and thought provoking in many ways. So you have written a book that has a meaning for both races . . . . . . Unfortunately, I haven't read anything this winter except the poems and the manuscripts of the hundreds of brown youngsters in the South who want to be writers. I still have a brief case full of them with me now, awaiting comment. I have found a few who are really good. But your book, Miss Ovington's† and all the Negro novels of the season are still to be read. My tour companion reads them every night while I lecture, and tells me what they're all about. . . . . He liked yours.

There is little need to say how deeply we all feel the loss of Julius Rosenwald, friend of America and of my people. Little children all over the South looked at his picture that week and were sad to know that he had gone. May my present tour, which his generosity helped to bring about, produce something worthy of his name, for I must always remember him with personal as well as racial gratitude.

On March 19th, I am to be at the C. A. & N. University, Langston, Oklahoma. I would be happy to have you send me there half of the remaining amount of my fellowship, $200.00, that I might apply it on the balance of $266.00 due on my Ford.

My New York address while on tour is: c/o THE CRISIS, 69 Fifth Avenue, New York, N.Y.

Sincerely yours,
Langston Hughes

---

* In *Brown America: The Story of a New Race* (Viking Press, 1931), Embree examined areas such as education, industry, and the arts. He theorized that a new brown race, a "hybrid" people who were different physically and culturally from their African ancestors, existed in America.
† *Portraits in Color* (Viking Press, 1927), Mary White Ovington's collection of biographical essays about prominent African Americans, includes one on Hughes. In 1909, Ovington (1865–1951), a white woman, had helped to found the NAACP. She served for several years as its executive secretary.

TO WALLACE THURMAN

[Western Union Telegram March 12, 1932]

C339 45 NL=FG KANSAS CITY MO 12
Wallace Thurman=
316 138 St. New York City

YOU HAVE WRITTEN A SWELL BOOK* PROVOKING BRAVE AND VERY
TRUE YOUR POTENTIAL SOARS LIKE A KITE BREAKING PATTERNS
FOR NEGRO WRITERS I LIKE PARTICULARLY EUPHORIA'S STORY
OF HER LIFE THE DONATION PARTY THE FIRST SALON AND YOUR
INTROSPECTION. IT'S A REAL BOOK WALLIE THANKS=

LANGSTON.†

TO NOËL SULLIVAN   [ALS]

On tour,
San Antonio,
Texas
April 8, 1932

Dear Mr. Sullivan,‡

I should be happy to spend a few days with you when I come to Los Angeles (I
mean San Francisco). Many of my friends have spoken so beautifully of you.
As yet I do not know my coast itinerary as the bookings have been arranged

---

* Thurman's novel *Infants of the Spring* (Macaulay, 1932) was based in part on his life at
the colorful Harlem residence (at 267 West 136th Street, dubbed "Niggerati Manor" by
Zora Neale Hurston) that he, Bruce Nugent, and others had once shared. It includes a
satirical portrait of Hughes as "Tony Crews," who had published two books of poetry "pre-
maturely." Crews hardly ever spoke but winked and smiled a lot. He was either hopelessly
shallow or "too deep for plumbing by ordinary mortals."
† A handwritten postscript, in French, from Carl Van Vechten appears on the telegram:
"Mon cheri ami, je suis trés desolé que tu n'es pas ici mais quand je te verrai je tu donnerai
les petites livres! Merci bien Van." ("My dear friend, I am very sorry that you're not here
but when I see you I will give you the little books! Thanks a lot Van.")
‡ Noël Sullivan (1890–1956), a wealthy bachelor from a prominent San Francisco family,
lived in the old Robert Louis Stevenson residence on Russian Hill. A supporter of causes
such as civil rights for blacks, the abolition of the death penalty, and animal welfare, he
was also a devout Roman Catholic, a trained singer, and a lover of classical music. In early
March, Sullivan wrote to Hughes and invited him to stay at his home. Hughes arrived at
2323 Hyde Street on May 15, 1932.

by someone out there, but I will write you soon as to the time of my coming to San Francisco, as I hope to have my schedule next week.

Some of the same poems which Carpenter* sent have also been set to music in Germany. Have you seen them? I shall bring them along.

Sincerely,
Langston Hughes

At Los Angeles
April 21st on:
c/o Loren Miller
837 East 24th Street.

TO EZRA POUND   [TL]

On tour
837 East 24th Street
Los Angeles, Calif.
April 22, 1932.

Mr. Ezra Pound†
Via Marsala 12 Int. 5
Rapallo, Italy.

Dear Mr. Pound:
I am sorry to have been so long about answering your letter but I have been on a lecture tour of the South all winter. I was very much interested in what you had to say about Frobenius.‡ Certainly I agree with you about the desirability of his being translated into English and I have written to both Howard and Fisk Universities concerning what you say and |am| sending them each a copy of your letter that was sent to Tuskegee.

---

* John Alden Carpenter (1876–1951) was an American composer. Sullivan, a basso, had recently sung in concert a poem by Hughes that Carpenter had set to music. Among Carpenter's works is *Four Negro Songs* (1926), a setting of four poems by Hughes.
† Based in Europe, the American poet Ezra Pound (1885–1972) was a founder and key figure of literary modernism. He influenced and supported certain major writers, including W. B. Yeats, James Joyce, and T. S. Eliot.
‡ Leo Frobenius (1873–1938) was a prolific German ethnologist who had traveled to Africa to study its myths and folklore. Pound, who admired Frobenius and his work, had asked Hughes whether black colleges in America might wish to underwrite an English translation of Frobenius's volume *Und Afrika sprach* ("And Africa Said") (c. 1913).

Tuskegee is a very wealthy industrial school but I am afraid they have little inclinations toward anything so spiritually important as translations of Frobenius would be to the Negro race. I am enclosing here the letters with which Howard and Fisk have answered me. So you can see what they seem to think about it. They are our largest and most important Negro Universities.

Some weeks ago I sent you my books in care of INDICE.* I hope you have received them.

I have known your work for more than 10 years and many of your poems insist on remaining in my head, not the words, but the mood and meaning, which, after all, is the heart of a poem. I never remember 10 consecutive words of anybody's, not even my own, poems.

Thank you for bringing this great German's work to the attention of American Negroes. I hope something will come of your suggestion and if I can do any more about it I assure you that I will.

Very sincerely yours,
Langston Hughes

---

* *L'Indice* was a literary newspaper based in Genoa. After Pound responded that "the *Indice* went bust" and that he had not received the books, Hughes re-sent them to Pound's home.

Aboard the *Europa* en route to Moscow with the Meschrabpom film group, 1932

Good-morning, Revolution:
You're the very best friend
I ever had.
We gonna pal around together from now on.
—"GOOD MORNING REVOLUTION," 1932

Like many other writers and artists in the 1930s, Hughes reacted with indignation and a warm embrace of radical socialism to the onset of the Great Depression and the failure of the American government under President Herbert Hoover to address it decisively. Also, the radical left in America openly opposed racial segregation when the two major political parties tacitly supported it. So in 1932, Hughes jumped at an invitation to work on "Black and White," a proposed Soviet Union–sponsored movie about American race relations. Hughes's friend Louise Thompson (Patterson), now a radical, had been charged with finding black performers and writers who would go to Moscow for the filming. On June 14, a band of twenty-two travelers, including Hughes and Thompson, sailed for Russia from New York to work on the project with the Soviet company Meschrabpom Film. After controversial delays, Soviet authorities postponed the project indefinitely. Hughes then decided to spend several more months in the USSR, including the "colored" republics in Central Asia.

TO NOËL SULLIVAN
[Telegram]

1932 JUN 14 PM 9 50*
NOEL SULLIVAN=
2323 HYDE ST SFRAN=

DEAR NOEL ARRIVED IN THE NICK OF TIME LATE LAST NIGHT DASHED ABOUT MADLY ALL DAY RECEIVED WESTON PROOFS† LIKE THEM IMMENSELY AM ON WAY TO EUROPA NOW SHALL SAIL WITH MY LAST PLEASANT AND UNHURRIED MEMORY OF AMERICA YOUR HOUSE YOU AND MY VISIT AT CARMEL SINCERELY=

LANGSTON.

* Hughes had been a guest at the San Francisco mansion of Noël Sullivan from May 15 to May 23, when he left for Portland and Seattle to continue his poetry tour. Returning to San Francisco, he traveled south with Sullivan to read in Carmel-by-the-Sea, a noted haven for writers and artists where Sullivan owned a cottage he called Ennesfree. There he met several of Sullivan's friends, including the writers Ella Winter, Lincoln Steffens, and Robinson Jeffers, and the photographer Edward Weston. On June 3, Hughes continued south to Los Angeles to end his poetry tour. The next day, he and his driver and manager W. Radcliffe Lucas, along with two men recruited for the Soviet film project, drove to New York City. The men arrived on the night of June 13 with only hours to spare before the departure of their ship, the *Europa*, for Russia.
† Edward Henry Weston (1886–1958), an influential American photographer, is famous for his studies of nudes, landscapes, and other natural forms. Weston had photographed Hughes two weeks earlier in California.

TO EZRA POUND   [ALS]

[On Norddeutscher Lloyd Bremen, D. "Europa" *stationery]*

June 17, 1932

Dear Ezra Pound,

My books, sent to you c/o <u>Indice</u>, came back, so I re-sent them directly to you. Also a Scottsboro booklet of mine, the proceeds of which go to the defense of the boys.

After a hectic all-winter lecture tour, I'm now bound for Moscow to work on a Soviet film of Negro life. A group of 22 of "my people" from the U.S.A. and probably others from the Paris and Berlin colonies. Will be there all summer.

Address:

c/o Meschrabpom Film,
Moscow, U.S.S.R.

Sincerely,
Langston Hughes

TO CARL VAN VECHTEN   [TLS]

Ashkhabad, Turkmenia,
Soviet Central Asia,
November 15, 1932.

Dear Carlo:

Probably you thought I never intended to write you, but I believe I did send you cables from Russia. At Moscow, cables were so cheap, I used to send a few almost every time I passed the office, but down here they can't be sent in English, you probably don't read Russian, and Turkmenian is out of the question . . . . . . I well remember what you said in prophecy about the picture. Amid great confusion, it was postponed until next year. But, at least nobody walked home. The four months contracts were paid in full, money reimbursed for expenses over, and tickets home supplied via Paris for those who wished. Besides two or three tours over the Soviet Union. Some have stayed in Moscow to work: radio, theatres, etc., and one as supervisor of the modernization of the postal service . . . . . . I'm doing a series of articles for IZVESTIA[*]

---

[*] *Izvestia* was a Russian daily newspaper (1917 to 1992) that served as the mouthpiece of the Soviet government. (Its counterpart, *Pravda*, was the official paper of the Communist

on the contrast between the darker peoples of the Soviet and the darkies at home, therefore my sojourn in this part of the world. It will be swell material for a book,* too, and I've written Blanche |Knopf| that I'll send her the manuscript by March. I'm going practically all over this part of Asia. Have already been in Bukhara and Samarkand, and shall probably go back to Samarkand in January to write up the book, as I liked it there, and have met some nice people. Last week in Bukhara I talked with one of the former Emir's three hundred wives. And got a little of the low-down on palace life. He had forty boys, too, and when he went away he took the boys and left the wives! This one is now cashier of a tea house. . . . . Have been out in the desert, with the nomads. . . . And next week, go for a month or so to Tashkent, the administrative center for these darker Republics. The contrasts here are amazing: camels and airplanes, modern schools for kids who live in yurts, herd-boys broadcasting nightly on reed pipes from a high-powered radio station. And brown, yellow, and white mingling from the tea houses to the highest Soviets. . . . . Letters from Prentiss |Taylor| and the printer inform me in no uncertain terms of the bankruptcy of THE GOLDEN STAIR PRESS† so if I get an advance on this Asiatic book it will have to go to pay that off. It was too bad the SCOTTSBORO books didn't reach me in time, as I could have sold out the edition the last month of my tour in California. I only got them when I had three engagements left. After FIRE and this, I will hardly venture into the publishing business again in life‡. . . . . The papers say Nora |Holt|'s gone to Shanghai. I want to come home in the spring via Siberia, and will get to Shanghai too if it's possible to get the dollars and the visa. Let me know if Nora will still be there. And maybe you'll come over. . . . . Word from Noël Sullivan says he might visit New York this month. Have you seen him?. . . . And what else is news back home? Down here I learn nothing of what's going on. My Russian doesn't penetrate the newspapers. . . . . Roses of the desert to Fania |Marinoff|, and happy holidays to you both. . . . . Write: c/o Meschrabpom Film, Moscow, USSR.

Sincerely,

Langston

Party.) Karl Radek (1885–1939), then its editor, hired Hughes to write a series of articles for the journal.

* Hughes intended to write "From Harlem to Samarkand," a book on the Soviet Union. He anticipated publishing a book that would be partly an autobiography and partly a treatise about life among the darker peoples of the Soviet Union.

† While in Moscow, Hughes received word that he and Prentiss Taylor owed their printer $162 for his work for the Golden Stair Press.

‡ The sole issue of *Fire!!: A Quarterly Devoted to the Younger Negro Artists*, edited by Wallace Thurman, was published in 1926. *Fire!!* sold poorly, leaving Thurman, Hughes, and other backers in financial distress. Several hundred copies were later destroyed in a house fire.

TO EZRA POUND   *[TLS]*

1st Dom Soviet,
Tashkent, Soviet Asia,
January 20, 1933.

Dear Ezra Pound:

Do you know this about Negro schools? That most of them are missionary schools (or philanthropic institutions) still highly religious, highly imitative of the "best" white models, and mostly controlled by white gentlemen who live in Boston and New York, and never heard of Benin.* The two best of the lot, Howard and Fisk, are trying desperately to become little Harvards. Fisk is becoming fashionable, and Howard is in Washington among the politicians who give it money, and the aristocratic Negro families who try to run it. And both have ministers for presidents. And both of them probably think Benin is somebody's back yard somewhere. Tuskegee is a huge trade school going dead. . . . . . Of course, there ought to <be> a chair of Africanology in a Negro university. But one can't ought it into being without a sensible place for it to be in, and somebody who knows something about the subject and loves it to head it . . . . . . Did I ever suggest that you write to Alain Locke about the matter. He's a professor at Howard Address: Howard University, Washington, D.C., brought the Theatre Arts Exhibition of African sculpture to America, and probably could exchange a much more informed opinion on the matter with you than I can. (But remember, he's an Oxford man, and a Ph. D.). . . . . Liked your letters and advice about my poems . . . . . . I've had a swell time in Middle Asia this winter: Samarkand, Bukhara, and the Turkmen desert, and a Beluchi kolhoz†. . . . . Please send your books for me to my publishers, Knopf, Inc., 730 Fifth Ave., N. Y. and I'll pick them up there in the spring. I'd like to have the ones you've promised.

Sincerely,
Langston Hughes

* Located in what is now Nigeria, the Benin empire dates to prehistoric times. The Ga peoples of Ghana, known for their bronze and brass sculptures, trace their ancestry to the ancient Kingdom of Benin.
† Usually spelled *kolkhoz,* the term refers to a collective farm of the former Soviet Union.

TO NOËL SULLIVAN   [TLS]

Meschrabpom Film,
Moscow, USSR,
January 31, 1933.

Dear Noël:

I'm afraid you probably think me dead, my silence indicating that I have departed this earth—but the truth is that there is somebody in this world at least a little worse than you are at writing letters. But I judge that you did receive my cables and an occasional card now and then from Asia. One thing that discouraged my writing down there is that the mails are terribly irregular, the trains and the camels being equally slow, and things get lost. . . . . I had a marvelous trip, and have just got back to Moscow;* about four months away. I have a great deal of interesting material for the book I want to do about the DARK PEOPLE OF THE SOVIETS (which I think I shall call it), and a grand collection of pictures. Arna Bontemps and I shall perhaps do a child's book about Samarkand, too. (He is coming to California in June, and I want to be there.). . . . . Perhaps you have seen Matt Crawford, and maybe he has told you something about our trip.† But after I left our group in Ashkhabad, little city in the Turkmenian desert, I was quite on my own, without an interpreter or anyone. But I got along fine, learned quite a little Russian, and even bits of the local Asiatic languages. Everyone was swell to me. The writers of Middle Asia saw that all avenues were open in exploring both the old and the new life there. I went with a Tekki poet to Merv, one of the world's oldest cities, and from there out into the desert for a visit with the once nomad Beluchis who have settled under Soviet guidance on the very edge of the desert where the last grasses of the oasis and the endless sands meet—the desert at their doors, so (perhaps) if they should get bored they can be off again. I spent some time on a native kolhoz, a Turkmen collective farm, where they killed a sheep for me, and played music almost all night. . . . . At Bukhara I interview|ed| an Emir's wife, one of <a> hundred that he used to have before the revolution ran him away and freed all the veiled women and girl brides. . . . . In Tashkent I

---

* Hughes returned to Moscow late in January 1933. In *I Wonder as I Wander* he recalls that "the train from Tashkent got to Moscow in the middle of the night, several hours late, on one of the coldest nights of the year, more than twenty below zero."
† Matt Crawford (1903–1996), a chiropractor, insurance clerk, and civil rights activist, and a longtime Berkeley, California, friend of Louise Thompson (Patterson), accompanied Thompson and Hughes to Russia.

fell in love with the Uzbek theatre, whose music is not unlike the Chinese, and whose leading dancer, Tamara Khanum, is a marvelous artist. She was grand to me, and sent for the oldest drummers and reed-blowers so that I could hear the folk music of the land. She did for me many of the subtle dance patterns that include movements of the eyes and fingers too delicate to be seen when performed on the stage. . . . . Unfortunately, I was ill for a month in Tashkent, I think from eating camel meat, as that was the only food to be had in some of the places I visited. I was put on a diet (but ask Ella Winter[*] how one finds a diet over here) so I lost a lot of pounds, but I'm getting them back now. . . . . I've been writing quite a little for the papers, and all of my poems are to be published in the Uzbek language (as well as in Russian) so I have a lot of rubles.[†] This is the only place I've ever made enough to live on from writing. Poets and writers in the Soviet Union are highly regarded and paid awfully well; as a class, I judge, the best cared for literary people in the world. And books sell <like> hot cakes. Usually ten days after a new book has appeared, not a copy can be found. And in spite of the paper shortage, they print large editions. Imagine in America, 10,000 copies of anybody's book of poems—as a first edition. And that is common here! And then come the translations into all the minorities' languages. . . . . I'm wondering how the Scottsboro benefit came off that you were helping with? And if you went to New York or not? And how you are? And if your winter has been interesting? I hope so. . . . . Do you want to go to Brazil with me after I come back and get my novel written? It has a population (I mean a Negro population) as large as America's, and nobody seems to know much about them. There ought to be |a| book! And I want to see the bay at Rio before I die. . . . . I plan now on coming home in May via the trans-Siberian and, if possible, Shanghai. Then across the Pacific right to the foot of your hill. Don't be surprised if I call you some day from quarantine to let you know that I've just come up out of the steerage, and am taking a few fumigations before landing, (which won't be much of a price for a peep at the Orient.). . . . . Will it be alright for me to come in June to Carmel and write

---

* Ella Winter (1898–1980), a socialist formerly married to the muckraking journalist Lincoln Steffens, started the Carmel chapter of the John Reed Club, an organization founded in 1929 by members of the *New Masses* staff as a center for radical writers and artists. The club was named in honor of John Reed (1887–1920), a journalist and the author of *Ten Days That Shook the World* (1919), a book based on his eyewitness account of Russia's October Revolution. After visiting the Soviet Union Winter published *Red Virtue: Human Relationships in the New Russia* (Harcourt Brace, 1933).
† Hughes made more money as a writer in the Soviet Union than he ever had in America. He received an advance of 6,000 rubles from the Uzbekistan State Publishing House for a book of his poems, and his series of articles for *Izvestia* earned him 2,000 rubles.

my novel? Which means that I will be accepting your generous invitation, if it still holds, for a corner of your cottage where one might set a typewriter, and be quiet for a while. My last two years have been continual movement: Haiti, then those 37,000 miles of lectures, and now all over the Soviet Union. I want to rest and create again. . . . . It will be good to see you once more. Our acquaintanceship was for such a short and hurried moment. And I liked you very much. I think, Noël, that life has given us the same loneliness. . . . . I was happy to find your Christmas card in the great stack of mail that was waiting here for me when I returned. After October, I had had nothing forwarded as some letters were lost, so I was months without mail. I appreciated that nice newsy letter in September, too. I hope Kenneth and Dot are very happy.* And that Rabbi Weinstein† has widened his range of activities in the East. He seemed like a splendid fellow. . . . . I haven't had a chance to look up Miss Wallenburg's friend yet, nor to use the letters which Ella Winter gave me. But I did meet Edward Weston's friend, Tina Modotti,‡ and liked her very much. She has asked me to come and see all her pictures. . . . . I liked some of the Weston photographs immensely, particularly 4, 9, and 14, and 1. What did you think of them? It was good of him to send me the proofs. I shall write him, but thought I'd see Tina Modotti first since I'm back so I'd have some news to tell him about her work here. . . . . I guess I've been photographed a million times in the USSR. I'm enclosing one of a little Turkmen kid and I at a kolhoz. There were adorable children there with silver medallions on their necks like Gypsies. . . . . Well, it seems that my passport runs out in a few weeks. I've had it for two years, so I shall have to go to Berlin to get it renewed, which I hate to do, as I don't want to take time out on my writing, and there is so much to do and see here in the short months that I have remaining. I intend to leave Moscow right after the May 1st celebrations, which it would be a shame not to see, since I missed the November ones. Then across to Vladivostok, then Tokio or Shanghai, and the big ocean. I ought to reach the

* Kenneth Spencer (1913–1964), a talented baritone born in Los Angeles, was trying to launch his professional performing career. Later in 1933, recommended by Noël Sullivan, he was cast successfully as Joe in a production of *Show Boat* that opened on October 30 in San Francisco. He reprised the role on Broadway in 1946. On April 25, 1932, Sullivan had written Hughes that Spencer and Dorothy Fisher had married but that the news was not to be made public. (Hughes had probably met them in 1932 during his stay with Sullivan.)
† Rabbi Jacob J. Weinstein (1902–1974) was fired in 1932 from his San Francisco synagogue, Sherith Israel, for his outspoken support of local longshoremen in their struggle for improved working conditions and unionization. Longshoremen on the Pacific Coast voted to strike in 1934.
‡ Tina Modotti (1896–1942), an Italian photographer, model, actress, and leftist, was an intimate friend of the Carmel-based photographer Edward Weston.

States in mid-June at that rate. . . . . Give my very best regards to Eulah* and
Charlie and Eddie and the others that are with you. And Ed Best.† And please,
to the charming Mrs. Erskine,‡ Mrs. Ball, and the Woods.§ I'm going to write
Ella Winter as soon as I look up her friends here. I've been glad to read about
her work for the Scottsboro boys and Tom Mooney.¶ Saw her picture here
meeting |Theodore| Dreiser as he came to California. Read that the meeting
was tremendous. . . . . Would love to have a letter from you, but don't worry if
you never get it written. One thing I understand deeply: how letters never get
answered. Anyway, I hope to see you in the spring. . . . . And until then

Sincerely,
Langston

TO PRENTISS TAYLOR [TLS]

March 5, 1933
Moscow

Dear Prentiss

We were fully two years paying for one issue of FIRE, the Negro quarterly we
started once. Everytime Aaron |Douglas|, Wallace Thurman, or I sold any-
thing, off the whole of it had to go to pay some debtor who stood like a wolf on
our heels. That was only for Art's sake that time. But just think, we are on the
rack for both Art and the Scottsboro boys now—even if the Scottsboro boys
never feel the effect of it. We are doubly noble, my dear Prentiss. But poor Mr.
Clark** is not interested in that, I know. And you have quite as much nobility
as I, and don't need to be told about it. So I haven't written, because I had no

---

* Eulah Pharr was Noël Sullivan's longtime housekeeper. Eddie, her husband, was Sullivan's butler.
† Ed Best was Noël Sullivan's secretary.
‡ Dorothy Erskine (1896–1982) was a San Francisco writer and social activist. She was
a member of the Northern California branch of the National Committee for the Defense
of Political Prisoners, as were Sullivan and several other local intellectuals and artists.
Hughes later joined the branch.
§ Charles Erskine Scott Wood (1852–1944) was a Pennsylvania-born poet and writer who
lived in California from 1925 until his death. His published work includes the satirical
Heavenly Discourse (Vanguard, 1927). He was living at this time with the poet Sara Bard
Field, who became his wife in 1938.
¶ Thomas J. Mooney (1892–1942), a leader of the California Federation of Labor, and his
associate Warren K. Billings (1893–1972) were tried and convicted on questionable evi-
dence in connection with a bombing that killed ten people in San Francisco in 1916. The
men served twenty-three years in California prisons before their release in 1939.
** William J. Clark was the printer of *Scottsboro, Limited*.

money to send you to send Clark to cut down the bill that sits like a wolf on our heels and which is howling louder than ever now that it has other wolves, hungered by the depression, to keep it company . . . I shall more than likely become a wolf myself when I return to America, what with the books not selling and the jobs to be had nowhere. I don't even know why I am coming back. I've never lived better than here, or sold more work for actual cash, even if it is not changeable in capitalistic lands. However, if only I can see Shanghai before War destroys the world, I won't mind coming back to starve (much). So I'm planning to leave in May for the Far East. If I get any further it will be a miracle. What with the banks closing (the waiter has just brought the morning paper with my breakfast and the reports are appalling), I think I'll become a coolie and let it go at that. . . .

That was a swell Christmas card you sent me. I like the cat and the Child particularly. And the caption was apt for these times. But now one would have to depart further than Egypt to get anywhere in the Depression . . . I saw a fellow recently here in the hotel who had just come from Egypt. He says the jails are full of people locked up for saying the government and the Depression are not good. And that because he came to Russia as a tourist last summer, on his return found his job gone, and the police took him to task. He's only a rather dumb young Oxford Englishman with no ideas of revolution, and that's what he got. . . . The repercussions of the Radio City failure rebounded way over here. A very blond young dancing girl from New Yawk showed up here in the hotel other day. She's looking the Moscow field over. Says nobody can get a job at home, and when you do they don't pay. Said Radio City was a great disappointment to all the ballet folks, etc, who thought they were hired for life. And what's happening here, of course, is that exports no longer bring in the proper sums. So most foreigners are not being rehired, and few machines are being bought, and the USSR is depending on itself more or less for the second Five Year Plan—with a resultant great displeasure in the foreign colony here, most of whom don't want to go home and face the Depression. Really, Moscow must be a paradise compared to New York or Chicago now. At least everybody has something to eat here, even if a few things are limited like milk, which, at the moment, goes only to kids, tourists and the invalids. You know, a few years back the kulaks (collective farm enemies) killed most of the cows. And a new cow does have to grow up to give milk. Gladys Bentley's solution[*] is

* Gladys Bentley (1907–1960) was a noted blues singer based for several years in New York City. When the Great Depression caused many Harlem clubs to close, she settled in at the gay-oriented Ubangi Club on 133rd Street.

only good for Harlem. Although the Muscovites would probably like her singing. They are crazy about jazz and Negro records.

Well, Prentiss, I did have a few dollars in the bank as you know in case of deposits from my publisher being forthcoming. But the paper says the N. Y. banks are closed, so I guess I haven't got that. Therefore, please ask Golden Stair Press not to apply anything to my credit there, should there suddenly be a rush on SCOTTSBORO LIMITED and the profits should outrun the bills. Rather, hold on to it and send it to Shanghai, because I might not be

Sylvia Chen in Uzbek dance costume, c. 1933

able to master a rickshaw before hunger gets me.

I've met a pretty Chinese dancer here, Sylvia Chen, whose old man was prime minister of China.* You remember the Chen whose wife was a Negro woman. Well, all the kids are here and have left the old man to his conservative ways and gone over to the Soviet government which is strong in China.—even if they do kill them by the hundreds. And what they are doing in Cuba is nobody's business. I am afraid to write my friends there for fear the Soviet postage stamp on the letter will mean jail for them. The terror is tremendous. . . . As to the Scottsboro booklet and its sale to radical groups, it seems we have Christ in there a couple of times and left-wingers can do nothing much about books that have Christ in them as Marx said religion was the opium of the masses so all its signs and symbols must be forgotten and if used at all in literature and propaganda, must be used to clearly show up the weakness and hypocrisy of the church. Never must mysticism or beauty be gotten into any religious motif when used as a proletarian weapon. See

---

* Sylvia "Si-lan" Chen (Leyda) (1905–1996), the mixed-race daughter of Eugene Chen, a Trinidad-born former foreign minister of China, was a modern dancer who introduced elements of Chinese dance to the West. After her marriage in 1935 to the American film historian Jay Leyda (1910–1988), whom she met in Moscow, Chen moved to the United States and worked as a choreographer in Hollywood. Later she and Leyda lived in New York, where he taught at New York University.

the forthcoming issue of International Literature and the long critique of my work there.* Or better still if you could see the new Gorky play† here (which is quite superb, by the way) you'd see how he shows up the priests and pilgrims of Old Russia as the gorgeous fakers that they were, and how the church is always linked body and soul to reaction, and submission to earthly exploitation and Tsarist greed. You see I am becoming clarified. Hey! Hey! I would like to see Harlem once before everybody starves to death. I get letters that make me shudder. What is going on at home anyway?

Sincerely,

Langston

TO BLANCHE KNOPF   [TLS]

Meschrabpom Film,
Moscow, USSR,
April 20, 1933.

Dear Blanche,

I was very happy to have your notes affirming the arrival of the material I sent you: my book of poems,‡ the short story, and the pictures. I shall send other pictures shortly. And I am mailing today under separate cover two more stories, since you were so kind as to say that you would take care of them until someone occurred to you who would handle them. Perhaps you might try these also on THE MERCURY or any other magazine you think wise. Some time ago, when I asked Arthur Spingarn about an agent, he suggested Brandt and Brandt, but I haven't their address. I expect to have a dozen or so short stories ready for publication in the next few months, aside from the sections from the Asia book that might be used as articles. A friend here suggests Liberman as an agent who is in touch with the liberal and left-wing publications that are most likely to print my stuff.§ But please turn them over to

---

* The communist journal *International Literature*, edited by Walt Carmon, was published six times a year in English, German, Russian, and French. Lydia Filatova's essay "Langston Hughes: American Writer" appeared in the first issue of 1933. That year, the journal also published three pieces by Hughes: the poem "Columbia" in the first issue of the year; a personal essay, "Negroes in Moscow," in the third; and the poem "Letter to the Academy" in the fourth. The poems are among the most radical Hughes ever published.

† Maxim Gorky wrote *Egor Bulychev* in 1931.

‡ In March, Hughes had sent the Knopfs and Van Vechten a collection of his radical poems entitled "Good Morning, Revolution."

§ Presumably Maxim Lieber, who became Hughes's literary agent (from 1933 to 1951). Born in Warsaw, Lieber (1897–1993) opened his agency on Fifth Avenue in 1930. Openly

whomever you think most capable of handling them, and I will let them handle all my magazine prose and plays (should there be any) from now on. . . . . SCRIBNERS wrote me a nice note recently rejecting a story MOTHER AND CHILD. They said it was excellently written and novel in theme, but "it would shock our good middle-class audience to death."* From another story that I sent to PAGANY,† I have had no news. I asked that both be returned to me c/o Louise Thompson, 409 Edgecombe, N.Y.C. as that was before I got your note that you would turn them over to someone for me. So they are there in care of Miss Thompson should an agent be found who will handle them—unless in the meantime she has managed to sell one of them herself.

I've lately been doing a series of sketches about American and Cuban Negro writers for the LITERARY GAZETTE here. And I've been asked to do a play for a swell and very modernistic kind of theatre, but probably can't get to work on it before I leave. I want to finish instead a draft of the Asia book and mail you—as the notes and all might get lost crossing two or three frontiers and a war zone in the Far East. I hope to be in China in early June, and in California by July 4, so I can shoot a few fire-crackers.

I'm anxious to know what your official readers think of my poems. Lots of them are being done into French and Spanish. Louis Aragon has done some rather nice translations for some of the Paris journals.‡

I met here the other night a friend of the Norwegian ambassador's who is also one of your authors—a Scandinavian fellow who wrote the THE SHIP SAILS ON which you published a couple of years ago. His name is Nodle something or other.§ I didn't get the rest because the party was too noisy, but I shall see him again as he wants to do some of my poems in his native language. The poets in Moscow all seem to delight in translating one another.

Marxist, he encouraged political radicalism in his writers, who over the years included Erskine Caldwell, Carson McCullers, John Cheever, Richard Wright, and Thomas Wolfe.
* *Scribner's* magazine, founded in 1887, was one of America's most prestigious popular magazines. The magazine rejected Hughes's "Mother and Child," a story about the reactions of blacks and whites when an upper-class white woman gives birth to a mulatto child. This story was later published in *The Ways of White Folks* (1934).
† Richard Johns founded the quarterly journal *Pagany* to promote the work of contemporary American writers. During its three-year (1930–1933) run, it published works by authors such as William Carlos Williams, Ezra Pound, Gertrude Stein, and e. e. cummings.
‡ Louis Aragon (1897–1982) was a French poet and surrealist as well as a prominent figure in the French Communist Party. He worked as an editor and also as director at *Ce Soir*, a communist daily evening newspaper published from 1937 to 1953.
§ Hughes refers to Nordahl Grieg (1902–1943), a poet and playwright from a prominent Norwegian family. Grieg died during World War II while fighting with British forces against the Nazis.

I've done translations lately from the French, Russian, and Chinese. (But the Chinese poet knew English—that's how that was done!)

Best wishes to you and greetings to Mr. Alfred A.

> Sincerely,
>
> Langston

<P.S. Your air mail came successfully and quicker. Thanks.>

TO CARL VAN VECHTEN   [TLS]

> Meschrabpom,
> Moscow, USSR,
> May 23, 1933

Dear Carlo,

Swell of you to write me so frankly about my poems.* I agree with you, of course, that many of the poems are not as lyrical as they might be—but even at that I like some of them as well as anything I ever did—which is merely my taste against yours, and means nothing, as everyone has a right to his own likings, I guess. . . . . About the Waldorf, I don't agree with you.† At the time that I wrote the poem it was one of the best American symbols of too much as against too little. I believe that you yourself told me that the dining room was so crowded that first week that folks couldn't get in to eat $10.00 dinners. And not many blocks away the bread lines I saw were so long that other folks couldn't reach the soup kitchens for a plate of free and watery soup. . . . . Blanche bases her note to me on your reactions. Certainly, I am (as usual) willing to make revisions in the book, omitting the least good poems, and perhaps putting in a few new pieces that I have on hand, but I would not like to change the general ensemble of the book. I think it would be amusing to publish a volume of such poems just now, risking the shame of the future (as you predict) for the impulse of the moment. And if Knopf's do not care

---

* On April 3, Van Vechten wrote Hughes regarding his manuscript "Good Morning, Revolution": "I am going to be frank with you and tell you that I don't like Good Morning, Revolution (except in spots) at all. . . . The revolutionary poems seem very weak to me: I mean very weak on the lyric side." He concluded: "I think in ten years, whatever the social outcome, you will be ashamed of these."

† Hughes's poem "Advertisement for the Waldorf-Astoria" is a bitterly anti-capitalist verse parody. Van Vechten singled out this poem in his letter of April 3: "Why attack the Waldorf? This hotel employs more people than it serves and is at present one of the cheapest places any one can go to who wants to go to a hotel." The poem was first published in New Masses (December 1931), and then reprinted by the International Workers Order in A New Song (1938), a pamphlet of radical poems by Hughes.

to do it, they have a perfect right to refuse. One must admit that their clientele hardly consists of workers and peasants, so I could understand how they might feel. . . . . . I seem to have a gift for writing unsa\<lable\> stuff. For years I wrote for the Negro magazines which paid nothing. Now I write for the proletarian journals which pay equally well! Lord have mercy!. . . . . I wish I could see Run Little Chillun*. . . . . The Georgian theatre is giving some stunning performances here these days—up from Tiflis for a month's stay. . . . . I'm leaving very shortly now, I reckon, for Vladivostok and whatever comes next, so don't write me here any more. . . . . I'll see you in the fall. Tell Fania |Marinoff| that if she'll just invite me to dinner, I've learned to eat fast by now. The Russians eat like a house afire (when they have anything) and I've been trying to keep up with them for fear of getting left. . . . . . The May Day Demonstration here was tremendous. Luckily I had a place on the Red Square. That moment when the military parade is over and the Square is cleared, a sea of workers bearing banners and slogans and emblems above their heads pours into the vast space before Stalin and Kalinin† and the other leaders— well, there is nothing else like it to be seen in the world. And from then on until darkness they pass. This has even the hundreds of tanks and soldiers and airplanes beat for impressiveness.

Bugles and banners to you,
Langston

TO NOËL SULLIVAN [*TLS*]

[On L.H. monogrammed stationery]

Trans-Siberian Express,
June 12, 1933.

Dear Noël,

At last I'm off. Moscow is a hard place to leave. There's always something else one should see or do. The non-professional Workers' Theatres Olympiad began |May| 26th.‡ And on the 1st the professional Theatre Festival (which

---

* Hughes's mother, Carrie Clark, had landed a small role in a production of Hall Johnson's musical play *Run, Little Chillun*.

† Joseph Stalin (1878?–1953) was the de facto leader of the USSR from 1929 until his death in 1953. Mikhail Ivanovich Kalinin (1875–1946), the only leader in high-level party circles from an authentic peasant background, served as the titular head of state of the USSR from 1938 to 1946.

‡ Hughes mistakenly identified the opening date of the Workers' Theatre Olympiad as "June 26th."

is to be an annual thing) opened. For that the Georgian Theatre came up from Tiflis, and all-star casts played at the other theatres. About two hundred theatre people from Europe and America came to Moscow, including quite a group from New York. I met several people who had seen RUN LITTLE CHILLUN and could tell me what my mother does in it. (Her first time on the stage.). . . . . Just a couple of days before I left, I had good news. The AMERI-CAN MERCURY will publish two of my new short stories soon.* They are the kind that are hard to sell, about inter-racial relationships at home. . . . . On the 17th I arrive Vladivostok. Sail on the 20th for Tokio. And from Yoko-hama on the 29th (N.Y.K. Line) for San Francisco. If I find that I can afford to go down to Shanghai for two weeks, I will. Then I will get home probably on the Taiyo Maru reaching San Francisco on August 9. I'll cable you from Tokio. . . . . If only the Chinese Eastern were not closed up by fighting, one could go directly from Moscow to Shanghai by rail, and very cheaply as I could have paid most of the mileage in rubles—and one'd get a glimpse of Japan on the way home anyhow. But I think in summer, it's not expensive so after all I may see China. Intourist in Moscow (the world's worst travel bureau) had no information or schedules of Oriental travel at all. I had to send to Berlin for all the sailing dates, so I have information only about one line. . . . . Anyway, I'll be seeing you soon. And it will be pleasant to renew our short but happy acquaintanceship. We didn't get to talk half enough last time. And now I have a lot more of interest to tell you about. . . . . I've taken the liberty of sending on by post several envelopes of manuscripts and pictures from Moscow, addressed to myself at your address—things that would be difficult to get through the customs in Japan as they confiscate most written material coming out of the Soviet Union. It's all material that I need for my book on Central Asia, so please keep it for me until I arrive. Also hold all mail that Knopf's might send on. (Royalties are due July 1st! Hurray! If there be any with the crisis on!). . . . . I'm bringing several dozen photographs with me which I trust the Japanese won't take. . . . . Please tell Ella Winter, if you see her, that I've sent on a lovely book for her that a friend asked me to bring, but I thought it safer to put it in the post. I trust she gets it O.K. . . . . . Will you be at Carmel this summer? I hope so, if I'm to work down there. I hope you've not been terribly depressed by the crisis, but from what one hears in Moscow, it sounds as if the whole world were falling to pieces. Let's hope it doesn't until we've lived a little while longer. There are so many interesting things yet to

---

* *The American Mercury* published two short stories by Hughes in the fall of 1933: "Cora Unashamed" (September) and "Poor Little Black Fellow" (November).

do. . . . . Remember me to all my friends within and without your house. I've the grandest memories of San Francisco. . . . . And you may expect my cables from point to point. . . . . Sincerely,

Langston

TO NOËL SULLIVAN   [TLS]
[On The Imperial Hotel of Tokyo *stationery*]

June 30, 1933.

Dear Noël,

Have had the grandest time imaginable in Japan. Visited Kyoto and Nara and then came to Tokyo where the proletarian writers and the members of Tsuki-jiza Theatre have shown me about. Seem to have seen just about everything important (for a short stay) and last night they made me an honorary member of the theatre. This is Japan's only modern theatre, doing O'Neill plays, Soviet plays, and modernistic Japanese pieces in a most exciting manner. And to go to the other extreme, at luncheon today I was guest of the Pan-Pacific Club centering in the House of Peers! So I met a few of the nobility. . . . . From here in yen a trip to Shanghai is very inexpensive, so I am sailing tomorrow. Will arrive San Francisco August 9 on the Taiyo Maru*—but to be definite, will wireless you from ship. Awfully anxious to see you again and tell you about my trip and the wonders of the proletarian world. Over this way life is awfully exciting. You may be killed, but you'll never be bored.

Sincerely,
Langston

---

* Around mid-July, Hughes sailed from Shanghai on the *Taiyo Maru,* bound for San Francisco via Kobe and Yokohama. In both cities, Japanese security officials questioned him about his dinner in Shanghai with Madame Sun Yat-Sen, the widow of the founder of the Chinese republic. With the *Taiyo Maru* scheduled to be in port for several days, Hughes decided to visit Tokyo, where he arrived by train on July 23. Police there interviewed him about his dealings with various writers and artists, searched his luggage, and kept him under surveillance until his departure on July 26.

With Noël Sullivan, c. 1932

Let America be America again.
Let it be the dream it used to be.
Let it be the pioneer on the plain
Seeking a home where he himself is free.

(America never was America to me.)
—"LET AMERICA BE AMERICA AGAIN," 1936

Arriving in San Francisco from Japan on August 9, 1933, Hughes
lived for a year in Carmel-by-the-Sea, California. Noël Sullivan
and Hughes had decided that Hughes would stay in Ennesfree, Sulli-

van's cottage there, along with Sullivan's three-year-old German shepherd, Greta. While in Carmel, Hughes focused on writing fiction, with the goal of producing one short story a week and, ultimately, a book of stories. Making friends among the many other writers, artists, and intellectuals in the village, he played an important role in the affairs of the Carmel chapter of the leftist John Reed Club. His stay coincided with one of the most controversial eras in modern California history, dominated by a bitter strike by longshoremen that reflected the deepening rift between radicals and conservatives across America in the middle of the Great Depression.

While he was there, Knopf published Hughes's short story collection *The Ways of White Folks* (1934). In late 1934, he received word that his father had died in Mexico. Hughes went to Mexico, where he spent six months. (His father had left him nothing.) During this time he translated the work of several Mexican fiction writers. Returning to the United States short of cash, he stayed for a while in Oberlin, Ohio, with his ailing mother, although he was often on the road trying to earn money from readings and lectures.

TO BLANCHE KNOPF   [*TLS*]

Carmel, California,
Box 1582,
November 6, 1933.

Dear Blanche,

I am sending you shortly, at the end of this week, in fact, as soon as copies are ready, ten of my black and white short stories which, with the five others I expect to finish by the end of the month, I hope you will consider as a book.*
Most of them are written from the Negro view-point concerning situations derived from conditions of inter-racial contacts with which we are all familiar, but which have seldom been used in fiction, if at all. The writers here at Carmel who have read them seem to feel that they would make an interesting and provocative collection. . . . . The new magazine ESQUIRE has bought

---

* Hughes refers to the manuscript of *The Ways of White Folks* (Knopf, 1934). On December 7, he sent twelve short stories to Blanche Knopf and Carl Van Vechten for their consideration. Knopf accepted the work for publication, with Van Vechten, who read the manuscript in one sitting, giving it a ringing endorsement.

one. And Edward O'Brien has written me for my life story. It seems he has selected <u>Cora Unashamed</u> from THE MERCURY*..... I'd appreciate knowing the opinion of your readers on them as a book.

The weather here at Carmel is great. It is still warm enough to swim. I don't think I'll be coming East this winter. I like it too well out this way. And I'm really getting some work done.

Sincerely,

Langston

TO COUNTEE CULLEN [TLS]

[On National Committee for the Defense of Political Prisoners stationery]

Carmel, California,

P.O. Box 1582,

November 19, 1933.

Dear Countee,

We are trying, out here, to work up an intensive campaign for Scottsboro Funds, and for interest in the general problems of the Negro in the South. The remoteness of this part of the world to all that is amazing. But aside from a series of meetings, concerts, etc., here on the coast, we have sent out an appeal from here to all those white writers like Julia Peterkin, |Eugene| O'Neill, etc. who have written so much about Negroes, to contribute to the Fund, and to send us a press statement about Scottsboro. The response so far has been most gratifying. Checks and swell statements have come from Paul Green, Carl Van Vechten, DuBose Heyward,† and others within the first week after the letters went out air-mail. We shall probably raise at least a thousand dollars for the defense..... Another plan (that really originated with our John Reed Club at Carmel) was that each person having famous artists or writers among their acquaintances, request said friends to donate a picture or original manuscript to an exhibition and sale-benefit <for> Scottsboro. This, too, has gotten underway very well. John Howard

---

* Hughes's short story "Home" was published in the May 1934 issue of *Esquire*. His story "Cora Unashamed," from the collection accepted by Knopf, first appeared in *The American Mercury* (September 1933). Edward J. O'Brien also included it in his anthology *The Best Short Stories of 1934* (Houghton Mifflin, 1934).
† DuBose Heyward (1885–1940), a noted white writer from South Carolina, was the author of a popular novel of black life, *Porgy* (1925). He and his wife Dorothy cowrote a stage version that later served as the basis of the opera *Porgy and Bess* (1935), with music by George Gershwin and libretto by Ira Gershwin and DuBose Heyward.

Lawson* and others are giving canvasses, Steffens offers part of the original draft of his autobiography,† etc. We hope to have this exhibition in a San Francisco gallery next month. (There are several wealthy collectors there—one of whom may buy all the manuscripts outright for his collection.). . . . . I took it upon myself to write to all the Negro writers and artists I knew asking for their contribution. (You probably have your letter by now.) But aside from sending us a manuscript, you could help us out greatly being in New York, if you would yourself personally ask the artists and writer friends you know to send what they will to me here, or to the Committee address above, as soon as possible. Get Aaron Douglas, Jimmy Allen to give a camera study,‡ Augusta Savage a small figure, etc, in Harlem.§ And your white writer-friends to give you manuscripts (or parts) of first drafts. Perhaps in some cases you could take them directly yourself and send them out to us. . . . . Only because of the great urgency for help in the Scottsboro Defense, and because I know how you feel about those nine boys, would I or our Committee group here, ask you to undertake this work in New York . . . . . . But we feel that not only will this exhibition and sale out here help financially, but it will also attract and interest a great many people in the case who have not heard of it this far West before . . . . . . With greetings to you,

Sincerely,
Langston

TO NOËL SULLIVAN   [ALS]

Christmas.

Dear Noël,

These stories are for you.¶ You helped me with them, have listened to many of them before they were even written, have read them all, have given me

---

* The leftist playwright John Howard Lawson (1894–1977) was perhaps best known for his plays *Roger Bloomer* (1923) and *Marching Song* (1937).

† *The Autobiography of Lincoln Steffens* was published in two volumes (Harcourt Brace, 1931). Steffens (1866–1936), a muckraking California-born journalist, held editorial positions at various magazines. Many of his articles were collected in volumes such as *The Shame of the Cities* (1904), *The Struggle for Self-Government* (1906), and *Upbuilders* (1909). After a visit to Russia in 1919, Steffens proclaimed (in a statement often misquoted): "I have been over into the future, and it works."

‡ Hughes refers to James L. Allen (see note for September 30, 1931).

§ Augusta Savage (1892–1962), who lived mainly in New York and contributed to the Harlem Renaissance, was an acclaimed sculptor. In 1924, her study of a black boy, *Gamin*, helped to gain her a fellowship from the Rosenwald Fund.

¶ As a Christmas gift in 1933, Hughes presented Sullivan with a copy of the manuscript of *The Ways of White Folks*. He also dedicated the book to Sullivan.

the music, and the shelter of your roof, and the truth of your friendship, and the time to work. You're a swell fellow. And having cast your bread upon the waters, it comes back to you (this time)—manuscript. My first drafts.

Happy Birthday!

Merry Christmas!

And a glorious New Year!

Langston

Carmel,
December 25, 1933

TO BLANCHE KNOPF   [TLS]

Box 1582
Carmel, Calif.
January 22, 1934

Blanche Knopf,
730 Fifth Avenue,
New York, N.Y.

Dear Blanche,

I posted to you yesterday four stories, BERRY, SOMETHING IN COMMON, IN ALL THE WORLD, and REJUVENATION THROUGH JOY. I don't know how you feel as to the length of the book. If all four are needed to make it a decent size, then use them. If only two more are enough, then kindly use BERRY and REJUVENATION THROUGH JOY.* The other two, we will save for a later collection,† as this group is only about half of those I have outlined to write this year.

In any case, please let my agent, Maxim Lieber, know which of these last stories are being included in the book, so he can regulate his magazine sales

---

* At Hughes's request, Blanche Knopf included both "Rejuvenation Through Joy" and "Berry" in *The Ways of White Folks* (1934). First published in *The Brooklyn Daily Eagle,* "Rejuvenation Through Joy" is the story of a confidence man. It was inspired by news of a notorious scam of the 1920s perpetrated in wealthy Westchester County, just outside New York City, by a religious charlatan known as the "Great Om." "Berry" tells the story of a black child, the orphaned son of house servants, who is reared uneasily by the privileged white family who had employed his parents.
† Although Hughes alluded to publishing another book of short stories with Knopf, this never happened. Nearly twenty years later, the company Henry Holt published his second collection of short fiction, *Laughing to Keep from Crying* (1952).

accordingly. Also, in regard to the story HOME, which he has sold to Esquire, and which it appears they cannot use before their May number (out in early April): It seems they are withholding payment of the story until they find out whether the publication of the book will scoop them on it. Since I very badly need the money from this sale, and since I have the excellent opportunity of selling other stories to Esquire (I suppose you saw the full page of letters in their present issue devoted to my first story) I hope the publication date of the book can be made not to conflict with the Esquire publication of HOME. Will you kindly have your office confer by phone with Lieber on this at once, as he has just air-mailed me about it.

I wrote Lieber about your wish to have THE MERCURY see the group of stories I have just sent you for the book, submitting them at the same time through him for magazine sale, since I have promised to let him handle all my magazine sales—and he has certainly done very well so far. So if THE MERCURY feels that it could use some of them before the book publishes them, I am writing him to that effect, and trust he will communicate with you.

Now as to details about THE WAYS OF WHITE FOLKS: Dedication to Noël Sullivan. . . . . Revised order of contents enclosed. If either of last two stories are not used, simply omit them and continue with the listed continuity. . . . . I trust you will attend to the formality of securing the copyrights from the magazines where the stories were first published. . . . . On a single page following the list of contents, I wish a quotation from BERRY:

"The ways of white folks,
I mean some white folks. . . ."

to set the tone of the book, and to indicate that I do not consider my portraits of white people in this book as a final and complete picture of the whole white race. The ones I portray are only "some white folks.". . . . . I am enclosing some notes as to my ideas about the book which may help your publicity staff in the preparation of blurbs, etc. I would like, if possible, to see the jacket blurb before it is printed, as we must be careful to offend neither Negroes or whites—on the blurb!. . . . I am glad you are bringing out the book this spring.

With best wishes to you,

Sincerely,
Langston

<Blurb notes coming later>

TO COUNTEE CULLEN [*TLS*]

Feb. 22, 1934.

Dear Countee:

Yesterday at an invitational preview of the Scottsboro manuscripts and pictures held for society and the press at Noël Sullivan's house in San Francisco, your poem was one of the first things to be sold. It brought $25. We have more than a hundred items from almost all the best writers from Robinson Jeffers to Julian Huxley. The public Sale opens Monday at the Western Women's Club.*

Sincerely,

Langston

TO BLANCHE KNOPF [*TLS*]

Box 1582,
Carmel,† Cal.,
June 5, 1934.

Dear Mrs. Knopf,

Thank you for sending A NEW SONG‡ down to |Maxim| Lieber.

I think it might be amusing for your publicity department to send a copy of my new book to John Gould Fletcher§ and also to Allen Tate,¶ as both of

---

* In Carmel, Hughes coordinated an auction to raise funds for the defense of the Scottsboro Boys. Cullen was one of many writers and artists who contributed manuscripts, books, and other items (see also the letter dated November 19, 1933). The event at the San Francisco Women's City Club, with the Hollywood star James Cagney as auctioneer, raised more than $1,400.

† As Hughes's year in Carmel under his agreement with Noël Sullivan was coming to an end, Sullivan made plans to renovate Ennesfree. On June 11, some friends threw Hughes a farewell party. Although he moved out of the cottage a few days later, he was still in Carmel in July.

‡ Hughes's poem "A New Song" was printed twice in 1933, first in *Opportunity* (January) and then in *The Crisis* (March). A version of the poem was published in *A New Song* (1938), a pamphlet of Hughes's radical poetry brought out by the International Workers Order.

§ In the 1920s and 1930s, the poet John Gould Fletcher (1886–1950) was a member of the Agrarians, a group of conservative Southern writers associated with Vanderbilt University in Nashville, Tennessee. Other members included John Crowe Ransom, Robert Penn Warren, and Allen Tate. The Agrarians' manifesto, *I'll Take My Stand* (1930), is a collection of essays that reject liberalism, modernism, and industrialization. Hughes's "new book" in question is *The Ways of White Folks*.

¶ Allen Tate (1899–1979), a poet and critic, was integral in developing *I'll Take My Stand*. In Nashville in 1932, Tate refused to attend a private party that was to include Hughes and James Weldon Johnson. The party had to be canceled. Tate stated in writing that while

them have been creating a lot of anti-Negro discussions this winter in the magazines and papers. Maybe my book might make them mad. Then they'd give it a good bad boost, and lots more people would read it, to see what it says about the white race! <Please!>

Also maybe this might interest you, I don't know: A very fine trainer of horses here, and riding master—a former jockey who has taught riding and polo all over the world from Paris to Melbourne to Shanghai—has written a book on riding and on training horses. Not being a writer, it probably needs a lot of going over—but I am sure the material is good, as he has often been employed to teach in Hollywood, Gloria Swanson, Chaplin, and others. And is a marvel at teaching children. If you'd be interested in that sort of book, you might write him: Elder Green, Green's Riding Stables, Pacific Grove, California. (Box 632.) He has just asked my advice on where to send it.

Sincerely,
Langston
Langston Hughes

TO SYLVIA CHEN (LEYDA)   [ALS]

Box 1582
Carmel, Cal.
July 7, 1934.

Darling kid,
You know what would happen if you came over here? I would take you and keep you forever, that's what would happen. And even if you didn't come over here and I ever found you anywhere else in the world—I'd keep you, too. So you see, I love you!

Swell to have your letter. But listen—were you any more serious than I was? And how did I know I was so much going to <u>miss</u> the hell out of you after you went South to dance or I came half a world away from you? But I do miss you—lots more than you miss me, I guess,—and I want you, Sylvia baby, more than anyone else in the world, believe it or not. I love you.

But to change the subject, (so you won't think I'm kidding) I've seen quite a little of the Soviet consul out here Galkovitch.* He's a grand little fellow. I

---

he would have been willing to meet them in the North, to do so in Nashville would have violated basic white Southern racial etiquette.

* Moissei Grigorievich Galkovich (1902–?), a Russian historian and diplomat, served as consul general of the Soviet Union in San Francisco from 1934 to 1935.

had dinner with him once down here at Ella Winter's (who knew you in Moscow), met the family at the opening consulate reception, and tonight have just come from a party for them at the seashore here.

That's great news about your success in Norway. Wish I could put you in touch with New York managers. If I were there, I'd hunt them up, but way out here one can't do much. See Oliver Sayler* when he comes over with the next American group in September for the theatre festival. He's done publicity for so many foreign attractions. He'd know the ropes about Broadway.

I'm hard at work on a play now. Intend sending it to Moscow, too. If it has any luck there, I'll be back over.

My book of stories is just out. I ordered one sent you a month ago. Trust you have it by now. Some of the reviews are excellent. Here's hoping it sells so I can take you out for supper when you arrive. (And don't eat so little.)

Please, dear kid, believe what I say about how much I like you. If you want me to say it over and <u>over</u> and more and <u>more,</u> just act like you don't believe it in the next letter you write me.

How's Yolande and Jack and Lucy and Shura and Walt and Rose?† I'm pretty awful at writing letters.

Two tons of love to you,

Write soon,
Langston

Wish I could kiss you! Do you?

---

* Oliver Martin Sayler (1887–1958) wrote numerous books and articles on the theater, including *Our American Theatre* (Brentano's, 1923) and *Inside the Moscow Art Theatre* (Brentano's, 1925).
† Yolande, Jack, Lucy, and Shura were Sylvia Chen (Leyda)'s siblings. Jack was also the son-in-law of Walt and Rose Carmon, with whom he and his wife shared an apartment in Moscow. In the winter of 1933, Hughes stayed for a month with the Carmons.

TO MAXIM LIEBER [TL]

Carmel, Cal.,
Box No. 1582,
August 8, 1934.

(San Francisco)*

Dear Maxim,

Our play is finished and a copy went off to you this morning. Its title at present is BLOOD ON THE FIELDS,† although I am sending a list of other suggestions as to its name. . . . . Ella Winter, when I last saw her ten days ago in Carmel, did not want her name used on the script—although it is copyrighted in our joint names. The Red Scare in Carmel and the vicious rumors put out concerning my associations with whites there and the fact that the Steffens home was branded as a nest of Reds and a meeting place for Negroes and Whites, etc. etc. prompted this move on her part. After all she does have to live there and send her kid to a school headed by a Legionnaire and get her milk from a dairyman who declared he was just waiting for the day when he could get behind a machine gun and drag all the members of the JRC |John Reed Club| out in Ocean Avenue and shoot 'em. And lots of good citizens visiting the City Council and urging them to do something about the Steffens. And one Jo Mora,‡ a sculptor, (And a banker's son-in-law) heading a Committee of 110 to do active duty against the 24 members of the JRC. And not a hall to meet in any more as the landlords are all threatened with destruction of property if they rent to us. And a great frothing at the mouth from the New Dealers when Steffy issued from his sickbed a statement to the press, saying among other things, "Let them come and get me. Let them send me to jail. I'd rather go there than to the White House. It's more honorable!". . . . . A good time was had by all. And if Ella Winter changes her mind about her name on

---

* The open support given by the Carmel chapter of the John Reed Club to the longshoremen's strike in San Francisco angered part of the larger Carmel community. Many residents viewed communist agitation as the source of the strike and some saw Hughes as a dangerous radical and an outsider. Warned of an imminent attack on him by vigilantes, he left Carmel on July 24 for San Francisco. He did not return until August 13.

† The play called "Blood on the Fields" (also known as "Harvest") focuses on the struggles of agricultural workers in California. It was never produced or published.

‡ Joseph Jacinto Mora (1876–1947), born in Uruguay but reared in Boston, was a writer, sculptor, photographer, muralist, painter, and illustrator. After Mora moved to California in 1903, the American West became his main subject.

the play, I'll let you know. Meanwhile, she has no objection to having the Theatre Union know she is co-author, and we are to share equally in any proceeds. She will also probably come East for rehearsals should anybody decide to do the play . . . . . . At the moment I cannot locate the Theatre Union's address. But please go ahead and submit the play to them, saying that we realize it is probably too long, and that we are perfectly amenable to suggestions as to cutting and revision, etc. If you think it wise to, have several copies made in play form, etc., do so, and charge to us. I'd be very pleased to have your reaction to it as a play, too, if you have a chance to read it yourself. . . . . If the Theatre Union or anyone else does the play, we have a huge scrap book of newspaper pictures and clippings covering the whole strike in the San Joaquin Valley last October, as well as many photographs and handbills, etc. that will be of use to the producer, and which we will send on when needed. Jennie, the heroine of the play, is of course, Caroline Decker*—and most of the happenings and situations in the play come directly from the things we ourselves saw in the Valley last fall, or from what the participants, both growers and strikers, told us. The play follows the strike almost exactly. We hope it is dramatic as well as historical and true. Having worked so intensely on it the last few weeks, I am too close to it to read it critically now. Let's hear what you think of it. And the Union. . . . . As to details, had Ella Winter and I better draw up a legal agreement out here on our half-and-half share in royalties? And should she join the Dramatist Guild, etc?

Send me the BALLAD OF ROOSEVELT.† I haven't got a copy. And I will send you another NEW PEOPLE‡ when I go back to Carmel next week . . . . . . Enclosed is a note from THE FORUM, so if you ever have anything. . . . . Now that the play is done, I'm going to finish my Soviet book, which means you'll be getting more articles shortly.

Sincerely,

---

* Caroline Decker was a secretary for the Canning and Agricultural Workers Industrial Union, which organized the Cotton Strike of 1933. When Pat Chambers, the union leader, was arrested, the twenty-year-old Decker stepped in to lead the strike of around eight thousand cotton pickers.
† Hughes's satirical blues poem "The Ballad of Roosevelt" appeared in *The New Republic* on November 14, 1934.
‡ Possibly an alternative title for the poem "Wait."

TO SYLVIA CHEN (LEYDA)

[On Postcard of Bronco Rider]

Reno[*]

Sept. 12.|1934|

Dear Sylvia,

This is where the West is wild, Indians and cowboys and all. Quick divorces, too. I've been up in the mountains, but am flying back to San Francisco tomorrow. Wish I could see you. Consider <u>me</u> the answer to your last letter. Will write soon.

L.

TO AMY SPINGARN   *[ALS]*

Carmel, Cal.,

Box No. 1582,

September 19, 1934.

Dear Mrs. Spingarn,

I've enjoyed both your letters so much, and have been meaning to write you for the longest while. I've had an interesting summer, and lately have been for the first time in the California mountains—at Echo Lake, and on to Tahoe, then down to Reno for a week. And I flew back—my first time in the air. This I really enjoyed, crossing the Sierras in 40 minutes—that it takes a train five hours to do—and coming straight into the sunset when the plane landed in the late afternoon at San Francisco. If I could afford it, I'd fly all the time from now on. . . . . On Saturday I lectured in San Francisco on my book of short stories—the first time I've ever spoken on my prose. I was very much interested in your reaction to the stories. But I'm sure you know I don't hate white people. And I greatly regret that some critics got that impression from the book. In the stories I wanted only to show the various forms, from the subtle to the violent, that race relations in this country very frequently take, and to indicate the difficulties that even the best of white people face under our present society in their friendships with Negroes. But I realize now that I should have included one or two stories in which there was no tragedy, just to

* On September 4, Hughes went to Reno, Nevada, to be out of the public eye in Carmel.

show that not always do inter-racial contacts stumble on seen or unforeseen snags. But I thought the little quotation from "Berry" at the beginning would indicate that I was not writing about all whites, anymore than I have ever been writing about all Negroes. I wonder how one can write a book that will not immediately be taken as a generalization of the whole race problem? Martha Gruening's* review in the New Republic is typical of several that I have received, in which she says that I "find white people either silly or cruel." In "Poor Little Black Fellow," "Little Dog," and "Home," I didn't mean to picture the main characters in that light. And certainly in the other stories, I didn't mean the whites to be taken as prototypes of their whole race. But, I suppose, my problem is to write more clearly in the future—and such criticisms make me realize that.

You must have had a marvelous time in Guatemala. Is Ruth Reeves† back yet? I've wanted to write her and thank her for the lovely drawing she sent me. Here are two snaps I took of Mr. |Noël| Sullivan that I thought she might like. Please give them to her, or send them, if you are writing.

Krishnamurti‡ is at Carmel now, and I have attended two interesting groups with whom he has held discussions. His talks are like clear running water—a great deal goes by that nobody seems to understand—but ever so often there is a glimpse of something beautiful and sound beneath—like a lovely and solid rock at the bottom of the stream. I am interested in hearing a further development of his ideas of non-acquisitiveness, which seems to be one of the bases of his way of life—but, so far, unexplained in terms of our physical world.

I went recently to a marvelous anti-war and fascism meeting at which Bevan of the British Labor Party spoke,§ and an exiled Jewish lawyer from Prussia. Such excitement and enthusiasm in an audience, I've never seen. . . . . The Upton Sinclair campaign¶ out here is exciting, too. I hope he wins. His

---

* Martha Gruening was a white writer who worked for the suffragist cause and also (from 1911 to 1914) as an official of the NAACP in its early years. "White Folks Are Silly," her review of Hughes's book of stories, appeared in The New Republic (September 5, 1934).
† Ruth Reeves (1892–1966) was a painter and textile designer. Her textile work has adorned the children's room of the Mount Vernon Public Library in New York, and also Radio City Music Hall at Rockefeller Center in Manhattan.
‡ Jiddu Krishnamurti (1895–1986) was an Indian mystic and spiritual teacher with a substantial following at one time in America.
§ Aneurin "Nye" Bevan (1897–1960), a leader of the British Labour Party, was first elected to Parliament in 1928. He made a tour of the United States in 1934 to raise money for the Relief Committee for Victims of German Fascism.
¶ Upton Sinclair (1878–1968), the novelist and social crusader, was nearly elected governor of California in 1934.

opponents are so terribly reactionary and intolerant. The police and vigilante brutality and intimidation in California these last few months is unbelievable. The Carmel paper even launched a long attack on me and The Woman's Home Companion because of my article on the end of the harems in Soviet Asia in the Sept. issue. . . . . In the new <u>Asia</u> (October) my piece on the Soviet Theatre in Asia has just appeared.* They will probably attack that, too.

I've several exciting writing projects set for myself this winter. And in the spring I want to begin the second part of "Not Without Laughter," developing it eventually into a trilogy. But I do not want to begin so sustained a piece of work without some financial security to allow me several uninterrupted months of work—so I think I shall apply shortly for a Guggenheim Fellowship. May I use your name? (It was largely through your kindness and the years at Lincoln, that "Not Without Laughter" was begun.) Although I've sold a dozen or more articles this year, my mother being unemployed (and for a while ill) and my kid brother still in high school, I've been able to save nothing as a reserve for future writing. So my first application to the Guggenheims. Wish me luck!

Please remember me to Mr. Spingarn and to the family. I'd love to hear about Hope's† experience with the theatre in Virginia.

All my best to you,

Sincerely,
Langston

TO SYLVIA CHEN (LEYDA)   [ALS]

October 18, 1934.
Box No. 1582,
Carmel, Cal.

Dearest Sylvia,

I got all your letters and was mighty glad to hear from you each time. Carmel was pretty exciting for a while (California has turned Hitler on us since the general strike was broken), but I am still about. I stayed away from Carmel about a month (not wishing to be tarred and feathered) but am back again

---

* Hughes's mildly titillating article "From an Emir's Harem" was based on his interview with a former wife of the emir of Bokhara. His essay "The Soviet Theatre in Central Asia" appeared in the October 1934 issue of *Asia*.
† Hope Spingarn (Malik) (1906–1988) was the eldest of Amy and Joel Spingarn's four children.

now, and have but lately written an article on our village terror for the New Masses*—so you can read all about it there. I have to stop the story to tell you how much I love you, and if the vigilantes (100% California Americans) had chased me all the way to Moscow and you, then everything would be O.K. As it is, I'm still half a world away from the sweetest little girl I have ever ever seen! I wish I could have come to the Writer's Conference, but I wanted to finish my book and play first. (Before I was so rudely interrupted by the Red Scare—and had to hide my manuscripts, as did other Carmel writers.) See just one of the articles they had in the papers about me. (Enclosed.) And they wrote even worse ones against Ella Winter (who met you once in Moscow) and others of our John Reed Club members. But the club meets right on, altho we can't any longer rent a public hall—but we put out a bulletin. All of which has interrupted me again from telling you I love you. And what else is important? Say, when are we due to meet again? Where will you be next spring? And suppose I came back to Moscow? Or are you still thinking maybe of touring our part of the world or something? How would you like to go to Brazil? So would I, if had the ¢ £ $, etc. Anyhow, we've got to pick out a meeting place. California and you are too far apart. So tell me what you think? Maybe I'll have some money by spring. I'm broke now. I'm jealous of all those other writers seeing you dance at the Conference! But I liked your picture. Send me another one. I can't get enough—of you—Lovin' You The Way I Do—do you know that song? Ethel Waters sings it on the records. (I've got a lot of new ones I'll try and bring you, if I ever get back.) I've sent you some dance programs and things recently. Did you get them—2 or three envelopes of stuff. I was sorry I missed seeing the Chinese dancer. She performed during all the Carmel excitement. . . . . Are you going to dance in the Dance Festival? When is it to be? And will you be Chinese-Japanese-Negro-Uzbek or Anti-Fascist? I don't care which, and we're too far apart to talk politics—as you put it. Who wants to talk anyhow. Will you kiss me next time or not? Heh? You better! What nationality would our baby be anyhow? Just so he or she is Anti-Fascist! (I got a long letter from Pat, of our group, and Vera.† Their baby is a year old and nearly walking—Ours would be dancing by this time, wouldn't it?) But

---

* In his essay "The Vigilantes Knock at My Door" Hughes attacked the right-wing political tactics that had victimized him. He also criticized four local blacks who opposed the local John Reed Club and the longshoremen's strike despite its goal of ending racial discrimination on the docks. The essay was never published.

† Lloyd Patterson was one of the group of twenty-two persons (including Hughes) who traveled to Moscow in 1933. Choosing to stay in the Soviet Union, Patterson married a Russian, Vera Ippolitovna Aralovna. Their son, James Lloydovitch Patterson, was born on July 17, 1933.

since when did you make up your mind that way? You hate to have Jack and Lucy ahead, I'll bet? Give them my regards, and send me back theirs. And be a good girl and a great dancer, and <u>Sylvia</u>. Don't be nobody else—cause I don't want nobody else—but you. Love and—kisses. XXXXXX These are the kisses XXXXXX Lang

TO NOËL SULLIVAN [TLS]

October 24 |1934|,
521 Elko Street, Reno, Nevada, U.S.A.*

Dear Noël:

Thank you so much for all your letters and for sending me so much mail. There was a nice note from Robin† saying that I might use his name for the |Guggenheim| fellowship, and that it was about to rain in Carmel. . . . . And I guess you saw Carl |Van Vechten|'s card saying that he was sending me photos of Bricktop‡ and two tap dancers, which you may open if you'd like to look at them. One is Louis Cole formerly of New York's basement night clubs, now of Paris, Biarritz, and the Cote d'Azur—whom Carl thinks is about the grandest in the world. . . . . My agent writes that the new NEW JERSEY magazine METROPOLIS published a story of mine, SPANISH BLOOD, in its first number last week and that ESQUIRE is considering DEATH IN HARLEM.§ He also says, "You are certainly sending me some grand stuff—I was bowled over by ON THE ROAD¶ and at the same time I cried Where in God's name can I sell it? It's too darned good." But I hope he does sell it. He says the MERCURY turned down the Vigilantes article, so he then sent it to the MASSES, all before my wire arrived, having decided to try on the MERCURY first himself. Checks, so far, are conspicuous by their absence, but there ought to be

* Returning to Reno in mid-October, Hughes remained there until November 15. Only Blanche Knopf and Noël Sullivan knew Hughes's address there.
† The poet Robinson Jeffers (1887–1962), who had lived in Carmel with his wife, Una, since 1914, was among Noël Sullivan's inner circle of friends.
‡ "Bricktop" was the stage name of the singer Ada Beatrice Queen Victoria Louise Virginia Smith (1894–1984), called Bricktop because of her red hair. In 1924 she was a regular performer at Le Grand Duc nightclub in Paris when Hughes worked in its kitchen.
§ Hughes's ballad "Death in Harlem" tells the story of Arabella Johnson, who shoots her lover's other woman. As Arabella heads to prison, her lover finds yet another woman. Seven major magazines rejected the work before *Literary America* bought it for a token fee for its June issue.
¶ Before his return to Reno, Hughes completed "On the Road" in Carmel. In late November, *Esquire* magazine paid Hughes $135 for this short story, which appeared in its January 1935 issue.

one in his next letter. . . . . It is certainly nice of you to send what you did for my mother,* and certainly right now it is a <u>great</u> help. Nevertheless, I hate to take it. There's no reason why you should take care of 90% of the troubles of the world. No wonder you never have any money for yourself anymore. The last letter from mama says that she intends to keep the house all winter now, and it seems that my brother is becoming famous in Oberlin as sort of Cab Calloway, conducting a jug band at the high school—a <u>jug band</u> being the kind of band that I think originated with the colored kids of New Orleans, in which they play jazz on washboards, jugs, combs, mouth organs, and tin cans, a terrific but rhythmical racket. . . . . I am having a grand time writing, I have again started the |Soviet| book over—for the third time. I didn't like what I wrote when I first got here, but now I think it is beginning to "sound like me." I think my real <u>métier</u> is protesting about something, so I now begin the first chapter by protesting about Paul Robeson's lawyer living in a hotel that doesn't want Negroes to use the front door, and how I go from that experience to have dinner with Louise Thompson |Patterson| in Harlem and get my first news of the picture they are going to make in Russia. So it gets off now with an emotional bang! that I trust Knopf's will feel "sounds like me." Since that is what they desire. . . . . I have also written two stories—one white one and one colored one. The colored one is about a professor who sells out his ideals for a big salary. And the one white one is about a man who writes a letter every day to his dead wife who died in childbirth taking their baby with her. And after twenty years, he gets an answer. It's called MAILBOX FOR THE DEAD.† (But don't tell anybody I'm writing <u>white</u> stories. They might think I was trying to pass!) I am going to put all these stories (the first drafts) in my suitcase, and when I get about a dozen, go over them and send them up to Roy‡ to copy for me. Revision takes so much time that I think I'll put that off and do nothing but straight writing for about a month—or until the book is done. Then revise everything at once. . . . . . It is grand sunny weather here, with snow on the mountains. . . . . Did you see the <u>Profiles</u> of Bill Robinson (Bojangles)§ the tap dancer, in the October 6 and 13th numbers of THE NEW YORKER? Very

---

* For a while, Noël Sullivan sent Hughes's mother $30 every month to help with her expenses.
† Hughes never published this story.
‡ Roy C. Blackburn (1912–2000) was an Oakland-born former student at the University of California in Berkeley who began working as Hughes's secretary in Carmel on January 8, 1934.
§ Bill "Bojangles" Robinson (1878–1949) was a successful African American tap dancer of the Harlem Renaissance and the Depression eras. He appeared on stage and screen, and is perhaps best known for his film performances with the child star Shirley Temple.

amusing, and I think worth your reading. Ask Marie* to lend them to you, as she usually gets the magazine every week. I'm sending you a clipping from there, too, called "Little Dog.". . . . . Tell me about STEVEDORE†. . . . . And give my best to Mario‡. . . . . It would be fine if you happen to have time to telephone or look up Arna Bontemps. His address is 10310 Wiegand Avenue, and the telephone number is under the name of P.B. Bontemps. Tell him I'm "in the mountains" and communing with the Muses, but will come down in a few weeks, and maybe we can work together.

Affectionately Yours,

Langston

TO NOËL SULLIVAN [TLS]

Dear Noël,

Please give the enclosed letter to Peter.§ You can read it, too, if you like. It's some good advice about writing our play. . . . . And if any other letters should come from the Theatre Union, please let Peter read them first before sending them on to me. . . . . Did you have a good time in the South?. . . . . And did Elsie¶ get home O.K.?. . . . . And are you still going to Mexico maybe for Christmas?. . . . . I think I will probably be here, the way the book is going, but it is going, so that is some consolation. . . . . Reno is still amusing, but they are going to close up the little colored club, as they are not making enough money to keep it going. It was a grand little tough place where you could hear marvelous blues. Now there will be nothing left but a couple of gambling joints for the Race to go to. But no doubt the Race will get along. . . . . Thanks for sending me the SPOKESMEN. I hadn't seen any colored news since I got here. . . . . The article about the dancer is in THEATRE ARTS for November with two nice pictures. . . . . It is autumn over here and all the trees are red and gold. The first American autumn I've seen for a long time. Almost every day I go climbing up the mountains to the North of us and you can look

---

* Probably Marie Short, a Carmel friend of Noël Sullivan. Her former husband, Douglas Short, was an attorney whom Hughes occasionally consulted.

† Paul Peters, a playwright and communist, and his coauthor, George Sklar (1908–1988), saw their play *Stevedore*, about blacks on the New Orleans docks, produced successfully by the Theatre Union in New York in 1934.

‡ Perhaps Mario Ramírez Calderón (1894–1939), an actor and director originally from Buenos Aires, who was a frequent guest of Noël Sullivan in Carmel.

§ Peter was the nickname of Ella Winter (the wife of Lincoln Steffens), with whom Hughes wrote *Blood on the Fields*.

¶ Elsie Arden (1882–1945), an actress and singer, was a close friend of Noël Sullivan.

down on the whole valley. The mountains are full of rabbits jumping up from behind the sage brush. Tina and Greta would have a grand time here running them down . . . . . . Did you see STEVEDORE, and was it well done? . . . . . THEATRE ARTS says Paul Green's new Negro play was marvelous in New York,* but failed as a box office success, and closed. . . . . I have sent |Maxim| Lieber and mama my address here, so they can write direct—but nobody else. There might be a letter occasionally from Knopf in a blue envelope that you might send on, and one from Sylvia |Chen Leyda| in Moscow, otherwise I can't think of anybody else I need to hear from, or that you need bother about forwarding, unless they are airmails, specials, or something of the sort. It is a great relief not to have a lot of mail on one's mind. <u>Out</u> of <u>sight</u> is <u>out</u> of <u>mind</u> is only too true in this case. That's one good reason for you to go to Mexico. Nobody would expect you to answer their letters, if you didn't get them. . . . . Love and greetings to Marie |Short|, Steffy |Lincoln Steffens|, Douglass,† the Jeffers, Pat, and Leslie Roos,‡ if you see her. . . . . Don't let the witches or the black cats bother Tina or Greta or Boz or Diana on Hallow'ene night. . . . . And write soon—but don't worry if you don't. I'll know you mean to! And that will be O.K. . . . . . . Have you gotten into the second volume of THE MAGIC MOUNTAIN?§ If the Guggenheims give me that Fellowship, I will write a second volume of NOT WITHOUT LAUGHTER, too. Authors ought to be ashamed of themselves, just writing and writing—but then I guess it's the system!!! . . . . . Will Upton Sinclair give us all a typewriter and a quiet place? What will he do about writers? And especially letter writers? If I thought he would help us any there, I would certainly vote for him.

Sincerely,

Langston

<My love to the Bests and their new little baby girl! Tell Peter to send me by you a copy of the new Carmel <u>Controversy.</u>>

October 29, 1934,

521 Elko Street,

Reno, Nevada.

---

* Paul Green's *Roll, Sweet Chariot* opened at the Cort Theatre in New York on October 2, 1934, but ran for only seven performances.
† Probably Douglas Short (see note for letter of October 24, 1934).
‡ Wealthy San Franciscans Leslie Roos and her husband, Leon Roos, were friends of Noël Sullivan.
§ The novel *The Magic Mountain* (1924) was written by Thomas Mann (1875–1955), the German author and Nobel laureate.

TO MAXIM LIEBER   [TL]

521 Elko Street,
Reno, Nevada,
"The Biggest Little City In The World,"
November 3, 1934.

Dear Maxim,

Your recent kind letter received—but just as checkless as it can be—and authors must eat! This particular author must also send money home to pay the rent of a family that strangely enough insists on not going on relief, having a son who is a "great" writer—although I am about to go on relief myself. Not wishing to rush you at all, but do you suppose you could maybe sell some of my Soviet articles to the colored papers, CHICAGO DEFENDER, DEBATE, anybody for seven or eight bucks so that I might with complacency greet my landlady, until TRAVEL, METROPOLIS, or Death In Harlem bring in a few dollars?

I have a half a dozen new stories all ready for you but the copying. Most of them, however, are not very "commercial" in theme, leaning mostly to the left, so they will probably end up in THE NEW MASSES or THE ANVIL.* Therefore, I have hit upon an idea. Tell me what you think of it: to do every week one story with sentiment, love, romance, and a happy ending, under a pen name; the race, the colored race, conspicuous by its absence, and no problems involved except the all-eternal problem of LOVE. Maybe we could even sell them once in a while to the movies. I have in my note book a number of themes that do not need color or Negroes to make them true, and that could work up into good American short stories about ladies and gentlemen. I have already put down a couple and find them easy and amusing to do, and probably salable. Would you be willing to handle them for me? Give me your opinion on the project?† And not tell anybody about it? Etc. Wallace Thurman, as you probably know, has made a fairly good living for years doing True Stories about people 20 shades lighter than himself, writing under various names. Since I must make a living by my pen—typewriter, to be exact—and since the

---

* *New Masses* (1926–48) and *The Anvil* (1933–35) were American literary magazines associated prominently with the far left.
† Hughes produced four of his proposed series of "white" stories while in Reno. Lieber tried to sell three under Hughes's name ("A Posthumous Tale," "Eyes Like a Gypsy," and "Hello Henry") and the fourth under a pseudonym, David Boatman, chosen by Hughes (it anticipates the title of his 1940 autobiography, *The Big Sea*). Each story was rejected several times.

market for Race and Russian stuff is distinctly limited, I see no reason why I should not weekly turn to LOVE, and Love in the best American Caucasian 100% slick paper fashion. Do you? I shall await your reaction, and advice.

I suppose you have received by now a story called BIG MEETING that I sent you last week.

Also I see that my article on Tamara Khanum has appeared in the THE-ATRE ARTS MONTHLY,* and I wonder if you would do me a very great favor in regard to it. Since I cannot buy the magazine out here, would you kindly ask them (or your office) to send a copy to Tamara Khanum herself so that she can see what I said about her. The address is:

TAMARA KHANUM, UZBEK MUSICAL THEATRE, TASHKENT, UZBEKISTAN, U.S.S.R.

marking the page number on the front so she'll know what it's all about, as she does not read English, but can get it translated there. Deduct the cost from your next check due me—if they charge you for it.

Sincerely,

TO NOËL SULLIVAN   [TLS]

November 5, 1934,
521 Elko Street,
Reno, Nevada.

Dear Noël,

Thank you so much for the package of mail you've sent me. . . . . Among the letters was one from Señorita Patiño in Mexico City advising me that my father is gravely ill there and requesting that I come at once. It seems that he has been in the sanitarium for twenty-two days (in his last letter he told me that he was going) and that he is getting steadily worse, paralysis of the intestines, and they fear that even before their letter reaches me, he may be gone.†

---

* Tamara Khanum, according to Hughes, was the first woman Uzbek dancer to perform in public. Hughes's article about her, "Tamara Khanum: Soviet Asia's Greatest Dancer," appeared in the November 1934 issue of *Theatre Arts Monthly*.
† Hughes's father died on October 22, the day Señorita Patiño sent her letter, from complications after surgery. Langston received the news of his father's death in a second letter from Mexico City, delivered to him on November 6.

Apparently, it is certain that he cannot get well. I have just wired for further information, as their letter was dated the 22nd of October, quite a long time ago. If there is in Carmel any communication from Mexico, perhaps you had better open it and wire or telephone me the contents. Of course, if my father is still living, I would like to go to him if he wishes it, and give him that evidence of friendship. On the other hand, if he is no longer here, I have no idea how important it might or might not be that I go there. In a recent letter he spoke of expecting a sum of money due in payment for a ranch, and that he might then fly up to Los Angeles for a trip. But I have no idea what other assets he might have, or what disposition he may have made of them, or what Mexican law in regard to inheritances may be, or whether I might not be stranded there forever in case I did go down there now. . . . . Of course, I am as broke as usual, having this morning only six dollars in the world. But I am airmailing Knopf's to see how my book royalties stand and what they could advance me in case I should have to go to Mexico. . . . . |Maxim| Lieber's letters report two articles sold but payment to be made on publication—TRAVEL and METROPOLIS, neither of which have appeared yet. . . . . And the New York Times would probably consider one of my articles on Samarkand if I would re-do it with more color and less statistics. So I wouldn't be so much worried about getting back. In case my father is no longer living, however, it may not be at all necessary that I go there, as surely he had legal advisors who would take charge of his estate—and it would be of concern to me only if he has so instructed them. If you see Douglas |Short| or anyone who might know, please ask them about Mexican inheritance laws, etc. in regard to foreigners. And I'll let you know what answer I receive <from the> wire. . . . . I guess you got my letter to Los Angeles, and also one more recently to Carmel with an enclosure for Peter |Ella Winter|. . . . . I've written seven short stories this week, and am about to revise and send them off. I thought I ought to give Lieber something to sell for me, so I could write the book with an occasional rent-check in view. Three of the stories are "white" stories. It will be interesting to see how they go. One is serious, the others are sort of smart and humorous—about mistaken love affairs in a New York setting. . . . . I worked all day long yesterday getting them ready to mail off. Still have three to revise. And am doing all my own typing myself!

Best of good wishes to you,

Langston

TO NOËL SULLIVAN   [ALS]

[On El Correo Aéreo llega primero stationery]

San Ildefonso 73,
Mexico*, D.F. Mex.,
December 14, 1934.

Querido Noël,

I arrived safely yesterday after a not-so-bad trip—except that I only got 3 chapters of Nijinsky read—and I meant to read it all! I don't seem to have done anything in the train except repack my baggage, and dine, and then go back and dine again. In Nogales where the Immigration held me over the weekend because my entrance permit did not state that I was colored, I had a fine time. The porter introduced me to two colored fellows who have a little ranch nearby, and on Sunday we (or rather they) roped three horses and we went riding into the hills. I had a big white horse that had the smoothest gallop you've ever seen—just like a rocking chair. The next day I was hardly sore at all. Afterwards, being colored, we had chicken to eat, and I went around and met a number of old colored soldiers, and two on the Mexican side, who had been generals in the Mexican revolution. (I must get their stories when I come back through.) On Monday, the Immigration compromised and put down "mestizo" on my permit—which apparently means mixed. And I had to put up in cash a $250 peso bond, about $75 dollars—so once again I returned to my natural state of being broke. But it is nice to know that that sum awaits me on my return to Nogales. Also held up at Nogales was Mr. S. E. Woodworth who is a near neighbor of yours. But he went on before I did.

Concerning affairs here, apparently my father left a will bequeathing everything to the three nice old maids who took care of him in his last years of semi-invalidism, which I think was pretty decent of him. But they, in turn, wish to divide four ways with me, which is again mighty nice of them, I think. So far as I can tell, the estate consists of not more than 8000 pesos, more than half in amounts still unpaid on property sales. Government tax is 21%. So,

* Learning of his father's death, Hughes decided to go to Mexico. On November 15, he went to San Francisco to obtain a visa, a process that took two weeks. He traveled on December 3 to Los Angeles, where he visited his uncle John Hughes and Arna Bontemps. Later that day he boarded a train to Mexico City.

por <u>fin</u>, I think I shall have just about enough to repay my Uncle for the trip,* and <u>quien sabe</u> how many weeks it will take to get that, things move so slowly here. The first thing we have to do is go to Toluca and find the original copy of the will. I am sure that will take days, if not years. Then the rest begins.

The three Patiños are still just the same, age, ear-rings, and all, as they were 25 years ago when I first saw them. They have already taken me to church three times—one very lovely benediction with music and hundreds of candles. They were delighted to know about you, and about your sister, <u>la Carmelita</u>, and they want to know how it is you have not gotten me to come into the church. . . . Now, they are spending all their time preparing gifts for <u>los pobres</u> at Christmas time, making little dresses for the children, and putting by packets of food. We are going to give all my father's clothes, too, to the poor. . . . . They are all three in heavy mourning for my father. (And as fate would have it, the train laid over two hours in Guadalajara where I intended to buy a black tie—but it was a Saint's Day and every store was closed—so I had to arrive without one.) All three of the sisters wept when they saw me—and in general it was very sad. But now the house is quite lively again, there are lots of birds and flowers, and they are darling old ladies who try to do everything they can to make it pleasant for me. Already they've introduced me to a young aspirant to the priest-hood, and a young guitar-player, an orphan of the streets, who is their god-child—so between the two, I am sure I shall meet some interesting <u>Mexicanos,</u> and won't be bored. . . . . The only thing is—they close, lock, and bar the door every night at nine, take their candles and retire—and nobody (save one of the Saints) need ask to get in or out! I see where I shall get plenty, plenty of sleep.

Your package of mail just came. Thanks so much. The maid says the mail man was very drunk, and pronounced Hughes, <u>Jesus</u>! and wanted her to sign that way for the package.

Why don't you come down and sing the Cesar Franck in one of these lovely cathedrals? Best to Marie |Short|, Peter, Eulah |Pharr|, Billie.†

Siempre,
Langston

---

* John Hughes, Langston's paternal uncle, lent him $100 to make the trip to Mexico. In addition, Knopf lent him $150 and Noël Sullivan added $50.
† Possibly Noël Sullivan's friend Billy Justema.

TO CARRIE CLARK   [*TLS*]

San Ildefonso 73,
Mexico City, Mexico,
January 10, 1935.

Dearest mama,

It was awfully sweet of you to send me your picture for Christmas and nothing could have made a nicer gift. The Patiños were delighted to see it, and want you to send them one, too. New Year's day I had dinner with Cholie and her daughter and son-in-law. (I think I told you they have a very cute little baby.) In the afternoon, I went to the boxing matches with her daughter's husband, who has a sporting goods store here.

I hope Gwyn |Clark| had a good time in Richmond. Too bad you did not go to Cleveland for Christmas, and I hope you got to go for New Year's. I received a lot of cards, and the Patiños gave me a white silk scarf and little purse for presents. And I went to one party that the people who live in the flat below had.

Not having any money, I have been staying at home and working most of the time. I have written three stories since I have been here. We went to Toluca and got the will legalized, but it will take a couple of months to get it probated and all, so I guess it will be about March before I get my part of the money. Since I have no expenses here (it will all come out of the estate) I think I had just as well stay here and wait for it to be settled. In the meantime, I am studying Spanish and gathering material for some stories about Mexico.

Oh, yes, I saw my father's German wife‡ and she has agreed not to fight the will. There is hardly enough to make it worth while.

I have your letters and the account. You did not say whether or not you received a check for forty dollars from my agent. (I have a letter from him saying that he sent it, as I hoped, in time for Christmas.) During December then I sent you

Money Order $20.00
Check 16.20
Cash (Gwyn) 5.00
Agent's check 40.00
                                                          $81.20

---

‡ Frau Bertha Klatte (formerly Schultz) was his father's ex-wife.

which I hoped would help you catch up a little. I trust you received all these amounts, and I wish that in the future you would acknowledge <u>each</u> check so that I will know if you have received it or not, because traveling around as I have been, sometimes a letter might get lost or something. You don't need to send me accounts or anything like that. I only want to be sure that nothing is lost in the mail. Gwyn didn't say if he received his five or not, nor did you let me know if the $40 came from Maxim Lieber—but I hope you all got both these sums O.K. . . . . I won't be able to send any more money until I sell another story, or get paid for one. Two are now sold but do not pay until they are published. Let's hope that will be soon. . . . . If there is any of my father's money left after expenses of my board and trip are taken out, you shall have it.

Did you see the fine article about Oberlin in the December CRISIS with quite a little about your father in it?* If not, be sure to look it up and read it. I guess I told you a story of mine was in the January ESQUIRE, and I have gotten several nice letters from people about it.

Lots of love to you,
Langston

<Write soon!>

TO NOËL SULLIVAN   [*TLS*]

San Ildefonso 73,
Mexico City, D. F.,
February 1, 1935.

Dear Noël,

Remembering last year and Robin and Una |Jeffers|'s picnic at the Big Sur and your party in the evening, I thought I would write you all a line to let you know what's happening to me here, now that my thirty-second year of life is beginning—I mean ending, and my thirty-third beginning. As amazing as it may sound, I get up now at six o'clock and go to gym, and sometimes to mass! So this morning I went to the gym, and when I got back the dear old ladies with whom I live had prepared two huge bowls full of <u>buñuelas</u>, a kind

---

* In her article "Will Prejudice Capture Oberlin?" (*The Crisis*, December 1934), Caroline Wasson Thomason recounts Charles Langston's central role in the celebrated Oberlin-Wellington Rescue case. In 1858, Langston and Simeon Bushnell, a white man, were convicted and jailed under the controversial Fugitive Slave Law for their prominent role in rescuing and hiding from slave-catchers an eighteen-year-old escaped slave from Kentucky named John Price. (Price fled to Canada.)

of gigantic pan cake fried to a crisp in a big skillet, and served especially on dias de fiesta. And real hot chocolate for breakfast. And for dinner (we dine at mid-day here) there were all sorts of amazing Mexican dishes, starting off with a delicious bean and herb soup into which one squeezes lots of lime juice; after that, what they call a dry soup of macaroni and tomatoes; then several kinds of fish, for today is Friday, and potatoes in patties, and a big mixture of green vegetables; then candied squash, a marvelous paste of zapote, and fruit. And with all, a bottle of old Rioja wine that they've had for years in some dark closet. So you can imagine how well filled I am. On my Saint's Day they assure me that there will be an even bigger dinner, but I haven't looked on the calendar yet to see when Saint Jaime comes. And if the dinner were any bigger, I don't know what I would do. . . . . Tonight I am going to the rosario (which I guess you would call vespers) to see the big procession they have on the first Friday of every month, when they carry the host under a canopy and most of the parishioners march with lighted candles. There is music and singing, and when they come out almost everyone stops to kiss the feet of an image of Christ near the door wounded and bleeding as He was the night He was taken in the Garden and beaten by the soldiers. The church is just across the street from us, and is one of the twenty-five still permitted a priest in the Federal District. Curiously enough, the Catholics and the Communists, among others, both participated in an anti-fascist mass meeting after the Coyoacán shootings.[*] (I wish we could achieve a similar united-front in America.) And the other day, El Hombre Libre, a Catholic paper, quoted almost a column of Lenin to prove the fake-Socialism of the present administration! It's an awfully interesting situation here.

For no good reason at all, I haven't been to call on Jose Mojica[†] again. Nor have I looked up my friend in the Cuban embassy. You know how the days just seem to pass by and nothing gets done—except eating and sleeping. Somehow, miraculously, that is achieved. Walter White's sister-in-law, too, I still must visit. But, withal, I've been having a swell peaceful time. And it's a great relief not to be known, or to have to go to literary teas, or make speeches, or read anybody's manuscripts, or worry about engagements ten days in advance. I'm having great fun with DON QUIXOTE. And belong to a hiking club of

---

[*] On December 30, 1934, an anti-Catholic paramilitary organization known as the Red Shirts invaded the Mexico City suburb of Coyoacán and shouted taunts outside a church during afternoon mass. When the Catholics rushed out in response, the Red Shirts shot into the crowd, killing five people. The Catholics captured a radical and beat him to death.
[†] José Mojica (1896–1974), an acclaimed Mexican tenor in the 1920s, became a popular actor in the 1930s in Hollywood and Mexican films. He later became a Franciscan monk.

fellows and girls called <u>Los</u> <u>Dragones</u> who make excursions to nearby mountains and deserts and out-of-the-way places. And go every Sunday to the bull fights, but have just discovered that the <u>novilleros</u> are much more astounding performances than the de luxe fights in the big ring. For at the <u>novilleros</u> the young and unknown fighters are out to make a name for themselves, and the stunts they pull off in front of the bull's horns are hair-raising. Butted, trampled, and gored Sunday after Sunday, thus they try to make a reputation that will bring them—if they live long enough—to the main ring, El Toreo, to South America, to Madrid, and to 20,000 pesos a week. Now they get 50 and have to pay their helpers from that. Sunday, a youngster called El Ajiado del Matadero had his trousers ripped wide open up the left leg on his first bull, only to get them sewed up behind the barrera and again ripped wide open by the second bull, on the other leg. This made him angry, and when he went to kill, he got too close and was tossed way up in the air, landing flat on his back. But with all this, he got up, shook the darkness out of his head, picked up his red cloth and went ahead with the kill. They gave him the ears and the tail when he finished, and the crowd carried him around the ring on numerous shoulders, ragged and bloody as he could be.

Nothing has happened yet with the estate, except that it is now in the <u>fiscal</u>, whatever section of the court that is where it is supposed to be. So I thought I might as well stay here and see what happens. My ticket is good for six months, and living here is awfully inexpensive. Anyway, I had just as well stay until March or April, as by that time they expect the bank account anyway to be released, and I can pay my uncle back for the trip. . . . . Knopf's are publishing this month Kisch's book on Soviet Asia,[*] so I think I'd just as well give up the idea of writing mine. Whatever material is still timely, I might do in the form of articles when I come back, and let the Friends |of the| Soviet Union[†] make a little booklet of the best of them, (as they have recently written me.). . . . . There are now almost enough short stories for another book. I'd like to do about a dozen more to have a little income for my mother, and then start work on my next novel, Guggenheim or no Guggenheim. . . . . My brother has had the flu lately and is still out of school, it seems. . . . . How about Rhys[‡] and his book? I hope it is finished by now?. . . . . Today I'm writ-

---

[*] In 1935, Knopf published *Changing Asia*, Rita Reil's translation of *Asien Gruendlich Veraendert* (1932) by the journalist Egon Erwin Kisch (1885–1948).
[†] Hughes's friend Louise Thompson (Patterson) helped to found the Harlem branch of the Friends of the Soviet Union, an international communist organization.
[‡] Albert Rhys Williams (1883–1962) was a journalist and labor organizer. Williams and his wife moved to Carmel, California, in 1932. In *The Soviets* (1937), Williams describes the idealistic fervor inspired by the communists at the expense of organized religion.

ing Una and Robin, too. . . . . Greetings to everybody else. And you'd better send on my mail, I guess. With DON QUIXOTE to finish, (3 volumes to go) I'll be here a while!. . . . .

<All my best to you, and write soon.>

Langston

<In the last mail there was a nice letter from Anna Cora Winchell[*] about my book. . . . . How are Tina and Greta?>

TO NOËL SULLIVAN   [TLS]

San Ildefonso 73,
Mexico, D.F.,
March 28, 1935.

Dear Noël,

Comme toujours, I have been meaning to write you for weeks, but now that I have good news, I have to tell you. I've just been notified that I am to receive a Guggenheim—$1500 for nine months—and I am sure yours and Robin's and Ben's letters helped a lot, and I want to thank you for them.[†] So I hope to begin work on the novel in the summer.

Lately I've been translating some Mexican short stories, but haven't got very much done. I know too many people, and have been going to too many parties and dinners. I was lunching in Las Caszuelas the other day with a bull fighter when I ran into Tirzah[‡] for the first time. She was with a gentleman and the place was awfully noisy so I didn't get much news of California, but I am going to look her up some day this week. She has taken an apartment here for a while.

Last week-end I went down to Cuautla, which is just over the mountains in Tierra Caliente. There are some fine warm sulphur springs there and lots of palm trees and sunshine. About five miles away in Huastepec, there is a big pool in the heart of the woods where nobody goes except Indians and where you can bathe as God made you in the same sulphur water as in town— without the city crowds. On Sunday there was an Indian rodeo with about a

---

* Anna Cora Winchell was the music and art editor of the *San Francisco Journal*.
† Robinson Jeffers, Noël Sullivan, and Ben Lehman wrote letters of recommendation for Hughes when he applied for a Guggenheim Fellowship. Benjamin H. Lehman (1889–1977), a friend of Noël Sullivan, was a professor of English at the University of California in Berkeley from 1920 to 1956.
‡ Possibly Tirzah Maris Gates, a friend of Noël Sullivan.

hundred horsemen and lots of bulls. Sunday night I went to a <u>cantina</u> and drank beer with a French photographer* and Mexican truck driver until a military man pulled out his pistol and threatened to shoot the orchestra if they didn't dedicate a piece to him. Then I thought it was time to go. Coming back in the bus on Monday morning, there were wrecks all along the road. I don't think the Latin-Americans are very good drivers.

The street cars went on strike yesterday, otherwise everything seems quiet here right now. The professional wrestlers say they are going on strike next week, too. There was to have been a railroad strike, too, but that seems to have blown over for the moment. The dear old ladies with whom I live say that things were much better in the days of Porfirio Diaz,† and that such goings on were never heard of then.

Of course, nothing has happened about my father's estate yet. That is nothing tangible. And, as I probably told you, my step mother has decided to contest the will, so it will probably go on for years now, although some efforts are being made to settle out of court. The conferences are so long drawn out and uninteresting that I usually cannot keep my eyes open. But every<one> else seems to take a few thousand pesos as seriously as if it were a billion. My only pain is that I'm ashamed to come back to California until I have enough to pay my uncle back for the trip. I have had a swell time—but I am sure my relatives expect something more<!>

Anyway, I think I shall stay here only about a month more. I want to finish translating a dozen Mexican and Cuban stories and articles that I think we ought to know about in the States. And if I get a check from |Maxim| Lieber, I hope to go for a week or so down to the coast where there are thousands of Mexican Negroes living, about whom very little has been written, even in Mexico. Once in a while you see one in the city here, perfectly jet black. My friend, Jose Antonio, of the Cuban Embassy,‡ is interested in making a study of them, too, for comparison with the Cuban Negroes, so he and his wife and I will perhaps all go down to the coast together.

Peter |Ella Winter| sent me a copy of the Pacific Weekly with Marie

---

* Henri Cartier-Bresson (1908–2004) became one of the most influential photographers of the twentieth century. The men shared living quarters for a while in Mexico.

† Porfirio Díaz (1830–1915), a dictator, served as president of Mexico from 1876 to 1880 and then from 1884 to 1911.

‡ José Antonio Fernández de Castro (1887–1951), a white Cuban journalist and writer with a notable interest in black culture, served as a diplomat to Mexico (1934–1944). In 1928, he became probably the first person to translate Hughes's work into Spanish. The two men met when Hughes visited Cuba in February 1930.

Welch's* poem in it. Evidently the feud with By Ford is still on, judging from the leading editorial.†

They have formed a marvelous committee in New York to get the poet, Jacques Roumain,‡ out of jail in Haiti: Joel Spingarn, Carlton Beals,§ and people like that are on it. At a party here the other night, I saw an American painter who had just come back from Haiti, and he says it is on the road to becoming another Cuba, another little island of terror.

This week I've been kept busy buying the New York papers to read about the riots in Harlem. Only a week or so ago I had a letter from a friend of mine there saying that people were awfully hard up. . . . . I had a note from Roy |Blackburn| saying that he had driven Roland Hayes down to Carmel. I hope you succeeded in getting the Scottsboro money from him. . . . . They are doing my play about the case over the government radio down here shortly, so they say, and afterwards in one of the portable theatres.

With best regards to all, and tell Marie |Short| I am going to write her soon. How is Eulah |Pharr| and where? And Colonel |Charles Erskine Scott| Wood? And the children at Santa Cruz? and Eddie |Pharr|? . . . . . I had a nice card from Matthias in N.Y.¶ . . . . . If you write soon, please send me Emily Joseph's address. I'd like to send her a card while I'm here. . . . . Pat Greta and Tina for me. And old Boz if he is still there.

Sincerely,

Langston

* Marie de Lisle Welch, a poet, had traveled with a group of liberal and radical sympathizers, including Hughes, to the agricultural town of Visalia in Tulare County, California. They went there in support of a strike by cotton pickers in the fall of 1933.

† Byington Ford (1890–1985), a developer, owned the Carmel Realty Company. In Hughes's article "The Vigilantes Knock at My Door," he writes that Ford formed a group to intimidate supporters of the cotton pickers' strike: Ford "began to make extremely patriotic speeches in the name of his one-hundred percent American Citizen's Protection Committee to sign pledges of loyalty to the government and the constitution and 'make this town one-hundred percent American.'" Hughes adds that as the "only Negro member" of the local John Reed Club, he "seemed to be singled out as especially worthy of attack." Lincoln Steffens, in his column in the *Pacific Weekly*, denounced Ford as a fascist.

‡ Jacques Roumain (1907–1944) was a Haitian poet, novelist, and communist arrested several times for his political activities, which included opposition to the ongoing U.S. military occupation of Haiti. He founded the Haitian Communist Party. After his death, at the behest of his widow Hughes and Mercer Cook translated and published his novel *Gouverneurs de la rosée* as *Masters of the Dew* (1947).

§ Carlton Beals (1893–1979) was an American journalist and author with a special interest in Latin America. He covered the protracted Sandino uprising in Nicaragua (1927–1933) for *The Nation*.

¶ Russell and Blanche Matthias owned a home in Carmel. He was president of a lumber company; she had worked in the 1920s as an art critic for the *Chicago Herald Examiner* and *The Chicago Evening Post*.

TO NOËL SULLIVAN   [ALS]

Santa Fe,*
August 31, 1935

Dear Noël,

I arrived Santa Fe last night just in time to miss seeing Myron[†] who left the same evening for the coast. Bynner is in New York, but Bob Hunt[‡] received me and altho he was just about to leave for a Fiesta party, he asked a number of folks, who weren't going to the party, over to meet me, including Ida Rauh and her son (Max Eastman's boy) and some other left-folks, including Frieda Lawrence's son-in-law, a most amusing Scotsman.[§] Mrs. Rauh told me that Mrs. |Mabel Dodge| Luhan was in Albuquerque and probably hadn't received my wire, but that she was motoring back today, and that she (Ida Rauh) was going to Taos with her to escape the Fiestas, and that I could perhaps come up with them. They would telephone me.

This morning, however, her son, young Eastman, and the Scotsman, came to tell me that Mabel had just passed through in an awfully bad humor, picked up Mrs. Rauh, and gone on, saying that she would call me from Taos. So far she hasn't called (5.P.M.). And the town is full of stories of how badly she has been receiving guests lately (Edna Ferber, for one;[¶] and more recently, Thomas Wolfe,[**] who it seems, never did get in the house (after having been especially invited) so from the outside, he flung all sorts of bad words at her through the bed-room window, enlivening the night and out Jaime-ing Jaime

* After six months in Mexico, Hughes returned in June 1935 to Los Angeles. He then spent nearly three months in California writing children's stories with Arna Bontemps and trying to break into the film industry as a writer. Macmillan turned down Hughes and Bontemps's "The Paste Board Bandit"; various publishers also refused their "Bon-Bon Buddy." Hughes then decided to rejoin his mother, who was now seriously ill, in Oberlin. En route, he visited Santa Fe.

† Myron Brinig (1896–1991) was one of the first notable Jewish American writers of his generation to write in English rather than in Yiddish.

‡ Witter Bynner (1881–1968), a poet also published by Knopf, moved in 1922 from the East to Santa Fe. He lived there with his partner, Robert Hunt. Bynner also became friends in Santa Fe with D. H. Lawrence and Frieda Lawrence and later wrote *Journey with Genius: Reflections and Reminiscences Concerning the D. H. Lawrences* (John Day, 1951).

§ Ida Rauh (1877–1970), actress, artist, and feminist, was married (1911–1922) to the writer Max Eastman, author and editor of *The Masses* magazine and its successor *The Liberator*. Rauh and Eastman helped to found the Provincetown Players.

¶ Edna Ferber (1885–1968) was a prominent novelist and playwright. Her novels include *Show Boat* (1926) and *Giant* (1952).

** Thomas Wolfe (1900–1938) of North Carolina wrote the acclaimed novel *Look Homeward, Angel* (1929) and the posthumously published *You Can't Go Home Again* (1940).

D'Angulo!* He came back to Santa Fe, feeling that America's greatest novelist had been outraged!|)|. . . . . I guess Mabel probably feels like you did after that hectic Bach week—that you hoped "never to have another guest."†. . . . . Jean Toomer, who lives just outside Santa Fe, was most evasive on the phone as to when I might run out to see him, or just when he would be in town, or just where or when, anywhere!‡. . . . . Bob Hunt came in, high as a kite in the early morning hours, but was very nice the few minutes I saw him around noon. He has now gone back to bed after saying how awful he feels and showing me his dark-brown tongue to prove it. . . . . So I have sort of come to the conclusion that most of the inhabitants of this region must be possessed of devils, or else the Kundalini§ isn't working right these days (the town is full of tourists from Texas who have America's position at San Diego beat a thousand miles for prejudice) so I've decided to take the evening train on East, and am at the bus station (to Lamy) now (so excuse this letter in pencil) because, anyhow, the floods are rising, trains are getting later and later, and all the Rain Gods know I don't want to have to stay here very much longer. (It was raining last night when I arrived. The day was sunny. But it's raining again, now that I'm leaving.) Certainly, that Thunder of the Rain-Gods part of my poem was right; concerning the rest of it about a house in Taos, I'm afraid I'll never know.¶ Me for no. 24, Kansas City, St Louis, and the East. . . . . This month's high spot was the trip to the Fair with you. To paraphrase Dr. Locke, "I had the Harmon award. What more do I want?". . . . . Look for a letter from farther down the road. The bus is off, the skies weep, and I am on my way.

Bien à toi and Elsie |Arden|, Langston

Some awfully amusing things to tell you about the Mexican maids at Bynner's next time I meet you.

---

* Jaime de Angulo (1877–1950) was an anthropologist as well as a novelist, linguist, and specialist on Native Americans in California.
† Founded that year, 1935, with Sullivan's enthusiastic support, the Carmel Bach Festival is an annual celebration of Johann Sebastian Bach.
‡ Jean Toomer (1894–1967) and his second wife, Marjorie Content, spent the summer of 1935 in Taos. In 1936, the couple moved to Doylestown, Pennsylvania, where Toomer eventually joined the Religious Society of Friends (the Quakers) and virtually withdrew from society. (See also the letter dated March 17, 1962.)
§ In 1935, Sri Swami Sivananda (1887–1963), an Indian physician turned Yoga master and spiritual teacher, published *Kundalini Yoga*. *Kundalini* is a supposedly dormant spiritual power coiled at the base of the spine that can be awakened through Yogic practices, leading to the attainment of the ideal state of Divine Union.
¶ Hughes's poem "A House in Taos" was published in *Palms* magazine in November 1926 (long before he first visited Taos).

In Madrid with Mikhail Koltzov, Ernest Hemingway, and Nicolás Guillén, 1937

Did you ever try livin'
On two-bits minus two?
I say did you ever try livin'
On two-bits minus two?
Why don't you try it, folks,
And see what it would do to you?
—"OUT OF WORK," 1940

In 1935 Hughes hurried to New York after learning to his surprise that his play *Mulatto* was about to open on Broadway. There he discovered that its producer, Martin Jones, a man he had never met, had changed the script in ways Hughes found distasteful and then had listed himself as its coauthor. After the play opened, Jones virtually refused to pay Hughes, who had to take legal action to get any royalties at all. Broke, he then returned to Ohio to be with his cancer-stricken mother. A Guggenheim Fellowship, starting in March 1936, provided them with some financial relief. Then, stirred by reports of dire political events in Spain, Hughes decided to go there as a war correspondent for a group of black newspapers. Entering besieged Madrid in August 1937, he remained in the city until November 19. He then visited other parts of Europe before heading for New York in January 1938. Later that year he visited Europe again to attend the International Association of Writers congress in Paris as an official American delegate. Also in 1938, Hughes's mother died. Broke yet again, he had to turn to Carl Van Vechten for a loan to put some money down with an undertaker to pay for her funeral. His radical spirit recharged by his adventure in Spain, that year he also formed a troupe in New York called the Harlem Suitcase Theatre, which successfully presented his radical play *Don't You Want to Be Free?* In addition, he published a pamphlet of leftist verse, *A New Song* (1938).

———————

TO NOËL SULLIVAN   [ALS]

634 St. Nicholas, Apt. 1D,
New York, N.Y.
October 28, 1935*

Dear Noël,

Ever since the opening, I've been trying to get a chance to send you these clippings. On the whole, the play took an awful beating from the critics (but mostly for the melodramatic things inserted by the producers, and to which I had objected during rehearsals, as they completely distorted the poetic moments of the play).† Anyhow, a few reviews were complimentary, and all

---

* Hughes reached Oberlin in early September and moved in with his mother and step-brother. Later that month, he went to New York City after his drama agent informed him that his play *Mulatto* was heading to Broadway. On his arrival, Hughes found the show in production with his friend Rose McClendon cast in the starring role of Cora. *Mulatto* opened on Broadway at the Vanderbilt Theatre on October 24, 1935.

† *Mulatto*, Hughes's drama of miscegenation and violence, had evolved from the play he began at the Hedgerow Theatre in 1930. The play had its debut at a summer theater in Dobbs Ferry, New York, in August 1935, produced by Martin Jones, about whom Hughes knew little or nothing. Jones brought the play to Broadway, but with melodramatic changes in the text to which Hughes strongly objected. Jones treated these objections, and Hughes himself, with disdain. The New York critics praised the performances, particularly Rose McClendon's, but (unaware of Jones's changes) were harsh on Hughes as a playwright.

the papers praised the cast and Rose McClendon. I didn't attend the opening,* but perhaps Elsie |Arden| has written you about it. Since, I've been very busy, as the directors are now trying to get back into the play some of my quality which they had previously taken out—so we're still rehearsing every day and changing. The manager promises to run it at least a month, hoping that it will catch on by that time. I hope so, because the very day of the opening I received a note from the Cleveland physician to whom I sent my mother for an examination, saying that what she really has is cancer, and that she must have an almost immediate operation. Since Ohio has no funds for the treatment of the needy sick (and the Oberlin City doctor who first examined mama told her, "you need radium treatments, but how are you going to pay for them,") the only thing to do, it seems, is to pay for the operation myself. All the clinics are overcrowded, and people must wait weeks for their turn, if it comes at all. So I hope the play runs a little while. Thanks for your wire, and all my affection, Lang

P.S. Harry Burleigh has made a beautiful setting for a poem of mine.† Have seen the Robesons. Paul still ill with flu, Essie's writing a book. They spoke affectionately of you.

TO MAXIM LIEBER   [TL]

212 S. Pleasant Street,
Oberlin, Ohio,‡
December 26, 1935.

Dear Maxim Lieber,
I wrote you yesterday from Cleveland saying that I'm glad you're going to help about MULATTO.§ Today I wrote Mr. Rumsey saying that you would

---

* Hughes decided to boycott the opening after he learned that Martin Jones had deliberately planned a "whites only" opening-night party that neither the author nor the star, Rose McClendon, could attend (white actors played all the other roles in the production).
† Henry "Harry" Thacker Burleigh (1866–1949), an African American composer, set to music Hughes's poem "Lovely Dark and Lonely One."
‡ Hughes had returned to Oberlin to care for his mother. On the day (October 24) *Mulatto* opened on Broadway, he learned that a doctor had diagnosed his mother as suffering from breast cancer.
§ John W. Rumsey of the American Play Company, Hughes's drama agent for the play, had reached an agreement with Martin Jones for Jones to produce *Mulatto* at the Vanderbilt Theatre. Rumsey had limited success in representing Hughes, not least of all because Jones was a hard bargainer with apparently no respect for Hughes's rights. Six weeks after

act as my personal representative during my absence from New York (which no doubt will be permanent, seeing as how I have no money to get back to Harlem with, let alone Broadway) and I told Mr. Rumsey that he could send all future statements of the play and monies due to your office, and that you would keep me informed as to what is going on, since you write me frequently in regard to other work of mine that you are handling.

I hope the above arrangement will be satisfactory to you also.

So far as I can recall, neither in my sane nor insane moments have I ever committed myself to the American Play Company as to the handling of any other works of mine saving MULATTO which went to their office long before I went to Russia, and was sent there at the suggestion of Mrs. Blanche Knopf. I am duly grateful to them for the present production, but I would be more grateful had they procured statements for me regularly and checks when due, and had not answered all my letters with absolute silence. (And probably what put me off them, too, was calling up the last day I was in New York and hearing Mr. Rumsey's voice telling his secretary at the other end of the wire that he was not in, and said secretary then blandly proceeding to lie to me . . .

. . . Sure, I know people have a right to be out when they're not "in," but they ought to be politely quiet about |it| and not shout half-way across the room, "Tell him I'm not in" when a hungry author's worried about when he might perhaps expect a few dollars from his first Broadway production. . . . . Before I left New York, Mr. Martin Jones also complained loudly to me about Mr. Rumsey's not having answered a letter he wrote him more than a week before regarding some new adjustment of division of royalties between him and I. And according to Mr. Jones, Mr. Rumsey seemed most uninterested in our mutual MULATTO—which may account to some small extent for Mr. Jones' reluctance in submitting statements, etc. God knows I don't know and don't care, just so I get my $88.50 due me this week.)

FUTURE BUSINESS: Regarding the play which I've just been working on with Arna Bontemps in Chicago: (Macmillan's are bringing out his BLACK THUNDER, a pre-civil war slave-revolt novel, next month.) Our play is based on a folk-belief in some parts of the South that when a "jackass hollers, a woman's love comes down!" The jackass being considered a sexual animal, and therefore capable of arousing sex in others. That theme, however, is secondary in the play and incidental to the comedy, the piece as a whole being a

---

the opening Jones had sent Hughes no royalties. Near Christmas, with the play still running, Jones finally sent a financial statement asserting that he owed Hughes a total of $88.50.

kind of tragi-comedy of plantation life, voo-doo, and love among the peasants of the Mississippi Delta, touching on their relations with whites, (a comic scene with the Klan), and the share-croppers' present misery. . . . . As a play, it is quite different from LITTLE HAM,* and (if any good at all) might be something that the Group or Guild might like. (Or perhaps the Theatre Union, although it's done from a left viewpoint, but not about class conscious people, and is treated more or less in comedy style, with folk stuff mixed in.). . . . . Arna Bontemps has committed himself to allowing his agent (who placed his novel for him) to handle this play. Said agent is John J. Trounstine, 819 Madison Avenue, New York, who is, so Arna says, agent for one or two other plays now on Broadway, including SQUARING THE CIRCLE. You perhaps know him, anyhow. The point is this: When the play is submitted to Mr. Trounstine (probably sometime next month) could I not write him that you will look after my part of the interest in the income of said play, namely 50% of the authors' royalties due me as collaborator with Arna Bontemps? Or should I request Arna to ask him if he would be willing to handle the play in collaboration with you? (Or would you want to have such an arrangement?) . . . . . . Kindly inform me what is usually done in the case of a collaboration in which each author has his own agent. Do the agents collaborate, also, in the placing of the finished product, or just what. This play will probably be called WHEN THE JACK HOLLERS,† so please let me know just what you'd like me to do or say to Mr. Bontemps and Mr. Trounstine, regarding you and I, since by all means I want you to safe-guard my part of the said JACK.

If you have a manual regarding the proper conduct of an author in respect to his agent under any and all circumstances, I would be delighted to receive it and follow its advice, so that the New Year will find us unperturbed regarding outside influences.

(Arna has only one more agent Leah Salisbury, who is handling his <u>St. Louis Woman</u>, the play that he and Countee Cullen did together. Should Mr. Bontemps take a notion to send WHEN THE JACK HOLLERS to Miss Salisbury, would the same procedure be in vogue as with Mr. Trounstine? Please cover all points in your answer.)

---

* Hughes's comedy *Little Ham* tells the story of Hamlet Hitchcock Jones, a four-foot-tall bootblack who enjoys the numbers gambling business. The Gilpin Players could offer Hughes only $50 for five performances, but their production in March 1936 was a hit with its audiences.

† Hughes and Bontemps wrote *When the Jack Hollers* in Chicago during the winter of 1935–1936. In April 1936, when the Gilpin Players staged the comedy as a follow-up to their production of *Little Ham*, the response this time was lukewarm.

Someday perhaps some one of my many plays (to come) might be a hit, then we will get our postage stamps back. (I'm behind quite a little postage on MULATTO already.)

Let the Jelliffes in Cleveland, the PWA,[*] the Shuberts,[†] or anybody you think wise do <u>Little</u> <u>Ham</u>. I leave it up to you—and them.

I wrote the PWA people through Rose McClendon before she got ill, saying that I would do (as they requested of me when I was in New York) a play for them at the rate of $25.00 a week which they offered for their Negro Theatre in Harlem. Said play to be about the trials and tribulations of the Negro intellectuals—or the "better classes" as represented by a family of that type. I have lots of notes and ideas for such a play. I've had no answer from them, probably due to Miss McClendon's serious illness. Perhaps the letter never reached Houseman.[‡] You might ask him.

In case you really think you'll be able to collect something from MULATTO or sell something of mine that you now have on hand sometime from which to repay yourself, I'd appreciate it immensely if you would immediately advance me Twenty Dollars, depositing said $20 today on my checkings account with the Dunbar National Bank, 2824 Eighth Avenue, New York—as I had to draw said account down to 33¢ in order to get away from Chicago, naively expecting the promised American Play Company check to be awaiting me in Oberlin on the 24th. It wasn't. The Dunbar Bank People might not like carrying an account of 33¢—and in the eventuality that I've misfigured and overdrawn by even a dime, they'd probably put me in jail, so I think, if you will, you'd better deposit something there for me, at once, if not sooner . . . . . . Would you also kindly check up on the report in yesterday's MIRROR (Dec. 25th) that MULATTO is to be done in Mexico City (Ben Washer, Empire Theatre Building, is <u>Mulatto's</u> publicity man.)? If it is to be done in Mexico, get my pesos! Or else I'll get mad, like Munoz did about SHOT INTO SPACE[§] and start writing Mr. Rumsey in Spanish! Caramba!. . . . . Please let me know airmail special if the money reaches the bank or not. Also if Mr. Ramsey has the $88 yet.

---

* The Public Works Administration was a government-run construction agency founded in 1933 as a major anti-Depression measure.
† The Shubert brothers, Sam (1875–1905), Lee (1872–1952), and Jacob (1880–1963), were highly successful theater owners and producers.
‡ John Houseman (1902–1988) was one of the most influential theater and film producers of the century in the United States as well as a respected actor. At this time, he and Rose McClendon headed the "Negro" units of the Federal Theatre Project.
§ "Shot into Space" by the Mexican journalist and novelist Rafael F. Muñoz (1899–1972) is one of the stories Hughes translated in 1935 and planned for his collection "Troubled Lands: Stories of Mexico and Cuba," which Lieber rejected outright.

TO NOËL SULLIVAN   [*TLS*]

c/o Arna Bontemps,
731 East 50th Place,
Chicago, Illinois,*
January 29, 1936,
(Until February 10)

Dear Noël,

It has been grand having your letters and cards and the holiday greetings, and I've been trying daily to write you—but these last six weeks, I seem to have been out-doing even myself as the world's worst letter writer. And in the face of things that seemed every day to just have to be attended to immediately— work to be finished, lectures to be given, people to be seen, relatives to be placated—that peace and calm which one likes to enjoy when writing to friends has been most completely lacking. I've thought about you every day, and that's as far as I've gotten toward writing. . . . . My life of late, creatively, has been entirely devoted to Drama—such as it is—and if you see Steffy |Lincoln Steffens| you might tell him that I'm determined to be a playwright in spite of all. To that end, I've turned out one comedy about the numbers in Harlem, LITTLE HAM, of which I think I wrote you. My agent has had it typed and is sending it around now in New York. Carl |Van Vechten| has read it and says it is "authentic Harlem folk-lore" and that it should be very funny if properly produced. Then just before Christmas I finished the first draft of a Southern comedy drama with Arna |Bontemps| about sharecroppers, conjure, and the Ku Klux Klan, all treated humorously, but having some social basis, and therefore a bit more serious than LITTLE HAM. In the meantime, I did a play about Angelo Herndon in one act† (in which Herndon doesn't appear except as a picture on a poster) which seems to have won the <u>New Theatre</u> award of $50, although I haven't gotten the money yet. And more recently, a one-act tragi-comedy of a wake in which the dead boy sits up to carry on the usual nightly family quarrel!‡ Why should I be so devoted to the Drama, I do

---

* Hughes left Chicago to spend Christmas 1935 with his mother in Oberlin, Ohio. He returned after the holidays to complete his play *When the Jack Hollers*.
† Hughes's militant one-act play *Angelo Herndon Jones* is based on the life of Angelo Herndon (1913–1997). A young black communist from Ohio, Herndon was sentenced to twenty years on a Georgia chain gang for allegedly inciting insurrection in connection with a march in 1932 in support of relief for black workers.
‡ Hughes's macabre little play *Soul Gone Home* is about a dead son, laid out just before his funeral, who suddenly sits up and chastises his mother in a bitter exchange.

not know, because <u>Mulatto</u> has been nothing but a trial and tribulation since its opening, and I'm having a terrible time trying to collect the royalties. My letter writing activities have been devoted to that end exclusively, and I've written enough for a book. Arthur Spingarn, my friend and attorney, Maxim Lieber, the agent whom we called in to help force the play-agent to get the contracted statements from the box office, and more recently the Dramatists Guild, to whom the whole story had to be related again, have kept me at the typewriter and running to the post office to get air mail stamps. No wonder the typewriter is all askew and won't hardly write anymore. The Drama has ruined it, as it has almost ruined me! <u>Mulatto</u> is still running, and apparently has good houses, but the producer still refuses to pay weekly royalties. And every week the Dramatists Guild swears they will close the show—and don't. Because apparently if they force the show to close, the management, being incorporated, very likely then couldn't be forced to pay a cent, as they could merely show a deficit and go merrily on their way producing shows anew under a new corporation name. Such are the tricks of Broadway. Formerly, my agents, The American Play Company, kept assuring me that a check would arrive by the next mail. And I naively kept waiting in Chicago for it to come, so I could go home for Christmas. Finally had to borrow the money from my cousin to go home, thinking maybe the check had been <sent> there (about $300 then due) but got <to> Oberlin Christmas Eve and no <u>Mulatto</u> money. So I had to borrow $25 from Carl by air to buy a few presents and Christmas things for the family, as we were all penniless. Then it was that I appealed to the Dramatists Guild to either collect royalties for me or close the show. I also asked Lieber to see what he could do. Finally I got $88.00 from the show about two weeks ago, the management swearing they couldn't and wouldn't pay any more as they weren't making expenses—the usual Broadway plaint to keep from meeting obligations. (Nobody would keep a show going three months and not be making something.) They owe me, according to box office statements, almost $400 up to mid-January, the last statement I received. But I'm not very hopeful about getting it now, and am writing the Guild to kindly force the production to close, since it's most embarrassing to have a play running that everyone thinks you are making money from and therefore should pay one's bills—and the money isn't coming in at all. I really never heard of the like!. . . . . That's why I've had to go ahead and book all the lectures I could, at all sorts of fees from car-fare up, when I finally realized that the play people had no intention of living up to their contract. So you can visualize my financial ups and downs. At the moment, I'm in Chicago where I've had one lecture and two more dated for early February. Meanwhile, I'm gathering my riot material* for the novel and am finding that most interesting, since there are all sorts of tragic and humorous personal experience stories to be found from folks who were in it. This week I'm going to see a girl whose father was killed in front of the family by raiding ruffians. Today I was at the Y and saw the bullet marks on the front of the building, still there, and heard tales of how both whites and Negroes were killed in that vicinity . . . . . . Chicago is still a savage and dangerous city. It's a kind of American Shanghai. And almost everybody seems to have been held up and robbed at least once. A few weeks ago Arna's two-room apartment was rifled while they were asleep, in both rooms. Luckily, he woke up as the robber was still in the closet, so most of the clothes were dropped on the way out . . . . . . 85% of the Negroes are on relief. And there are whole apartment houses packed with people who haven't paid rent for months, and the landlords letting the houses go to rack and ruin, so that they look like nothing you ever saw inside and out . . . . . . Kids rove the streets in bands at dusk snatching women's pocketbooks, so people are even afraid of children. . . . . And when you go to call on somebody, they never open the door until they have hollered out to ask who it is, and are sure they recognize you. . . . . I real<ly> never saw anything like Chicago!!!. . . . . I was to have read my poems at the colored Roosevelt High School in Gary, Indiana last week, but Mr. Wirt, principal of the Gary schools (that same Mr. Wirt who went to Washington a year or so ago to accuse the President and the New Dealers of Communism) made the school cancel the lecture, saying he felt the need of protecting the Race against such as I. However, the colored people were very upset about it, and the Negro ministers of the town got together and are presenting me under their auspices on February 10th in one of the big halls of the city. . . . . My mother is in Cleveland taking treatments at one of the clinics there. She was very much opposed to an operation, being prejudiced against operations in the first place, and feeling that in a clinic the students would "experiment" on one. It is a cancer of the breast and an operation would not be especially difficult or expensive, if she would have <it.> I haven't seen her doctors since she went back for an examination, and began taking those treatments, but she writes that they are equally as effective as an operation, so they tell her. They are some sort of electro-therapy and, through the clinic, cost $25 every 15 days. She has to remain in Cleveland for month or so, and is living at the colored YWCA there. So far, we've been unable to find a reasonable apartment or house to move to there—but I must get her moved from Oberlin

---

* Hughes interviewed people who recalled the infamous Chicago rioting of 1919, in which thirty-eight people died. He hoped to use this material in his proposed second novel about Sandy, the main character of *Not Without Laughter* (1930). He never finished the sequel.

before I go away on the Guggenheim. . . . . My brother left CCC camp* to take a job driving for a traveling salesman, but he only paid $12 a week, out of which my brother had to pay his own living expenses. And most of the small towns, of course (in Ohio, and Indiana) had no accommodations for Negroes anyway, and those that did wanted a dollar or a dollar and a half a night, so he found that he couldn't make enough to eat and sleep on, out of the salary the man was willing to pay, so he is again out of a job, and is trying to get on the PWA. . . . . If only the producer of MULATTO would pay my royalties, the economic problem would be temporarily solved, anyhow . . . . . . But I have come to the conclusion that Fate never intended for me to have a full pocket of anything but manuscripts, so the only thing I can do is to string along with the Left until maybe someday all us poor folks will get enough to eat, including rent, gas, light, and water—said bills being the bane of my life. Maybe, before I go to Spain, however, something can be extracted from MULATTO. (See enclosed letter from Lieber, where he is trying to collect.). . . . . The poem he speaks of at the beginning is a long one called LET AMERICA BE AMER-ICA AGAIN.† Esquire bought half of it!!. . . . . Please tell Mrs. |Blanche| Matthias that I'm going to present the letters she gave me while I'm in Chicago this time. It has been so cold lately, 15 to 20 below zero, that I haven't been going out much, except on the South side, my own neighborhood . . . . . . Marian Anderson‡ gave a most successful concert here Sunday night, almost packed even in this zero weather. I didn't go, but they say she received an ovation . . . . . . Did you see Paul and Essie |Robeson| while they were in California?. . . . . Arna's wife had a new little baby just before Christmas. Its name is Camille. I urged him to apply for a Rosenwald Fellowship to write children's books, and they were seemingly very impressed as they answered his letter by inviting us both to lunch the next day, and spending all the afternoon talking about the book-needs of the Southern Negro schools where reading knowledge is very poor, and 16 and 18 year-olds sometimes have a vocabulary of only third grade variety—so one of their needs is stories suitable for adolescents, but with a very simple vocabulary that they can understand. It seems that Arna has a very good chance for a Fellowship under them next year to write specifically for their needs. . . . . His novel BLACK THUNDER comes out today. . . . .

* The Civilian Conservation Corps (CCC) was established in 1933 as part of Roosevelt's New Deal. It signed up unemployed young men for an intensive six-month term in which they worked on environmental conservation projects such as reforestation, flood control, fire safety, and wildlife habitat protection.
† A part of Hughes's lengthy poem "Let America Be America Again" was published in Esquire (July 1936).
‡ Marian Anderson (1897–1993) was a world-famous African American contralto.

A colored girl here, Margaret Bonds (who has appeared as a pianist with the Chicago Symphony) has done some excellent settings for some of my poems.* One is of THE NEGRO SPEAKS OF RIVERS, quite different from the Hayes-Parham setting, but equally as beautiful, I think—which she has submitted to Marian Anderson. . . . . You can imagine how sorry I was to hear about poor little Boniface, and I know it must have saddened the holidays for you. If you get another little dog, and he is young enough, you must teach him to be car-broken—because even Carmel is dangerous in that respect. I shall never forget about little Chloe. The only good thing in both endings is that they were instantly killed, and so didn't suffer from pain and injury . . . . . . I know Greta is as darling as ever, and thank you so much for sending me the snap-shots of you and her. They really made me homesick for that backyard garden at Ennesfree. You can imagine the contrast between this bitter-cold, dirty, dangerous Chicago South Side and Carmelo Street near the clean Pacific. . . . . Thanks, too for the amusing cravat with its horses and riders. Remember the fun we had that day you and Bill and Roy and I went riding on Mr. Green's horses? . . . . . But to answer some of your questions: My aunt who died wasn't Aunt Toy† (she's busy with her own dress-making shop in New York and I stayed with her when I was there) but was my father's sister in Indianapolis |Sallie Garvin|. . . . . I'll be back in New York about February 20th, I think, when I hope to be somewhere near ready to sail. I certainly hope to see Elsie |Arden| then and will ask her to show me the Bassett-Pacific Weekly-Briffault correspondence‡. . . . . How terrible about Betty's sister! I am so sorry . . . . . . I have been trying my hardest to write Lillian Mae,§ but haven't. Have you been back to Los Angeles lately? How is she, and Mario |Ramírez Calderón|, and Nora |Holt|? Etta Moten,¶ I hear, will be on here next week. Louise Beavers** was here

---

* Margaret Allison Richardson Bonds (1913–1972) was an African American composer, pianist, and musical director. A devoted admirer of Hughes and his work, she set to music several of his poems, including "The Negro Speaks of Rivers."
† Toy and Emerson Harper, both of whom would survive Hughes, became his surrogate family in New York City. Ethel Dudley Brown "Toy" Harper, a friend of Hughes's mother from their Kansas days, probably knew Hughes as a baby. An expert seamstress, she was living in Harlem with her husband, Emerson, a musician, when Hughes came to New York in 1921 to attend Columbia University.
‡ Ella Winter and Lincoln Steffens edited the magazine *Pacific Weekly* in the 1930s. Given the date of the letter, this reference probably has to do with Steffens defending Stalin and Robert Briffault (a British novelist) objecting.
§ Lillian Mae Ehrman was a Carmel friend of Hughes who also had a home in Beverly Hills. Her brother-in-law Ivan Kahn was an executive at Paramount Pictures.
¶ Etta Moten Barnett (1902–2004) was an African American singer and actress.
** Louise Beavers (1902–1962) had a memorable career in Hollywood. Although racial discrimination forced her to play maids and other servants mainly, fans and critics admired her acting, especially in *Imitation of Life* (1934).

la<st> week and I also saw her in Cleveland. She seemed delighted to be leaving for the coast the other day away from this terrifically cold weather. . . . . People are wearing ear-muffs! And lots of folks have frozen ears and frost bitten toes and fingers. I believe it's really worse than Russia was the year I was there. When I go out, I put almost all the sweaters you gave me on. They come in handy!. . . . . About the bank account at Carmel—it's down to $3 dollars and few cents. I was hoping my play would have given me enough to see my mother safely through the winter and spring, but so far it hasn't done so. I'm afraid now it won't, although the Dramatists Guild will probably give <us> the moral satisfaction of forcing it to close. So if you could add something to the Carmel account, as you so generously offer to do, it would be a great help until I can be sure that something else will turn up to keep things going. While I've been writing this letter a wire comes from New York saying that MERMEL IS INTERESTED COLUMBIA DEFINITELY IMMEDIATE <production> STAGE SCREEN COCKO STOP WHEN COULD SCRIPT BE READY STOP DO YOU APPROVE ELLINGTON MUSIC PLEASE WIRE, which is concerning the musical play which I told you I once wrote for Robeson with Kai Gynt three or four years ago, but which now needs further revision.* So maybe something will happen from that. But one can never be sure of the theatre, and I do not know what arrangements have been made with <Duke> Ellington. I suggested that they show him the libretto when I was in New York, but this wire is the first I've heard since November. Anyway, maybe something will come of some of the things I have in Lieber's hands now. And once on my Fellowship, all else that I make can go in the bank for mother's expenses. . . . . I only hope that I can write something beautiful enough to be worthy of the help you've given me. And I know you don't want to be embarrassed by gratitude, so we won't mention that. . . . . The books which you ordered are here and I'll get them posted this week to Roland |Hayes|, Ruth Reeves, etc. They came out here while I was still in Ohio, as I didn't get back to Chicago as soon as I had expected, since I stopped to take a couple of small lectures, being broke. One turned out to be quite pleasant—the librarians of Cleveland had me to open the first of their series of authors evenings, and I've never had a more appreciative audience. . . . . Lij Tasfaye Zaphiro, young Ethiopian first secretary of the Legation in London, was here Sunday for a series of talks.†

---

* The Swedish actress and writer Kaj Gynt collaborated with Hughes on a musical they called "Cock o' the World." The musical was never produced.

† Lij Tasfaye Zaphiro visited America to raise money for Ethiopian aid during the Second Italo-Ethiopian War (1935–1936). Although he claimed to be first secretary to the Ethiopian Legation in London, his credibility was later called into question.

He is very charming and intelligent, and looks like he is only about 18 or 20 years old. (He won't answer people who ask him how old he is, since he says there's so much else of importance to ask about his country.) Anyway, the amusing thing about his visit was that the city of Chicago gave him a police escort of about a dozen enormous colored plainclothes men in cut-away coats and high hats, and perhaps twenty uniformed cops, that went with him everywhere he went, even to dinners and private parties during the two days he was here. They claimed that was to protect him from the Italians, but I think it was really to watch him as to where he went and what he said, as two detectives even slept in the same room with him at his hotel. He is light (about Glenn's wife's color) but two downtown hotels refused to house him, although at one reservations had already been made, so he had to come to the South side to sleep. He says he will be coming to the coast, so I hope you'll meet him. He has much of interest to say about the war and European diplomacy. He was educated at Cambridge and in Switzerland, I believe he said.

I must stop and mail this off. A half dozen people chose to call in the writing of it, and the typewriter seems to have decided just not to write straight anymore, but anyway you'll know that I'm thinking of you and that I wish I had my own private plane so I could fly out there for the week-end tomorrow and see you. . . . . Very best regards to all our friends at Carmel, and write when you can,

Affectionately,
Langston

<P.S. Needn't return any of the enclosures!>

TO BLANCHE KNOPF   [ALS]

2245 East 80th Street
Cleveland
March 27, 1936

Dear Blanche,
The enclosed clipping of my play now running out here might be of use to your publicity dept. It seems to be a local hit, S.R.O.

You know what you really ought to do? Publish "Little Ham" with illustrations by Corvarrubias, and an amusing instructive foreword on the numbers by some well-known racketeer, and a post-script by the police commissioner! No kidding! Or would you rather be the producer?

I'm sick abed with grippe. And mother is in the hospital, so I'm having a time.

Sincerely,

Langston

TO NOËL SULLIVAN   [TLS]

2256 E. 86th Street,
Cleveland, Ohio,
February 9, 1937.

Dear Noël,

I was of course delighted with your messages and with your gifts of Sara's book at Christmas* and the very lovely cigarette case from Paris which came later. It made me resolve not to resolve to stop smoking again—for a while, since I never stopped anyway. . . . . It seems ages since I've written you. Christmas was very pleasant this year, with a nice tree and plenty to eat—in contrast to 1935 at Oberlin—all being due to MULATTO which came through, at the insistence of the Dramatists Guild, with several weeks back royalties just before the holidays . . . . . . Then when it was about to be banned in Chicago, they wired for me to come over and help cut out the bad words, which I was happy to do. I saw Glen Boles† again, who asked about you, and was sorry to have missed you on the coast. . . . . Arna |Bontemps| and I started a new comedy that he is to do a first draft of. His new child's book is due out next month, SAD FACED BOY, of which the Rosenwalds are buying more than a thousand copies right away for their Southern libraries. . . . . Back in Cleveland, I spent most of January finishing up TROUBLED ISLAND and getting a start on the libretto for Still.‡ I hope to have it done this month, if I can, as he says he has a great many musical ideas already down and wishes to work on it at once. Later in the spring after I go East, I hope to come out there for a few weeks and work directly with him, arriving about the first of April. Will you be in California at that time?. . . . . I want to stay a month or so. . . . . This summer I have a job!!

---

* In 1936, Sara Bard Field (1882–1974) published her second collection of poetry, *Darkling Plain*, with Random House. She was living in California, and would marry the radical civil liberties advocate and lawyer Charles Erskine Scott Wood (1852–1944) in 1938.

† Glen Boles (1913–2009), an actor, appeared in the Broadway production of Hughes's *Mulatto*.

‡ Hughes refers to his drama *Troubled Island* and to the libretto of his opera of the same name (first staged in 1949) that he wrote for the composer William Grant Still. Both tell the story of Jean-Jacques Dessalines and the Haitian revolution.

To direct a tour to Europe and the Soviet Union for eight weeks, sailing on July 3rd and returning August 31st for Edutravel, Inc.* It is to study the minority races of the USSR, spending a week in Moscow, and the remainder of a month in the Caucasus, along the Black Sea, and in the Ukraine, ending at Kiev. I'm trying to arrange to leave via Vienna and Switzerland to Paris, rather than through Germany. We go into Russia by Soviet boat from London, which will <be> nice for me, as I've never seen London. It's to be a mixed group. The only thing that worries me is how I'll ever get up at nine in the morning to lead my people sight-seeing! One portion of the tour includes a trip on horse-back to the Tsei Glacier, and it seems that I've heard one always visits glaciers at sunrise! Is that true?. . . . . Thanks for the birthday wire.

The day after my birthday both my mother and I took to our beds with colds, and today is the first day we've been out since. I suppose we had a mild form of the flu that's been going around this winter. The weather has been so unusual, mostly rain, rain, rain, and far too warm for Cleveland, that there has been much illness. The undertakers report a boom year, and Mr. Wills, the man you met the evening you visited at my cousin's house, has bought a gorgeous new auto hearse with chimes and organ music in it that plays as it rolls along! I never saw the like before anywhere! And I am sure it must cost a lot to be buried from it.

Mason Robertson† has recently arrived in town to work on a local colored paper here, and brought much news of Dot, Charlie, and Eulah |Pharr|, that I was happy to have. He is living next door to us, so we see him often.

Has Rhys |Albert Rhys Williams| at last finished his book on Russia, or is he doing it all over again? And how are Marie and Douglas |Short|?

The name of the young Mexican whom I think you'd like to know, if he is still in Berkeley, is Andres Henestrosa,‡ who was stopping at International House. He's a real Oaxaca Indian, although he doesn't look Indian at all, and has a Guggenheim to study in this country. He did a most beautiful folk-book called MEN WHOM THE DANCE SCATTERED, and is a friend of many friends of mine in Mexico. (I haven't written to him yet, and am afraid he isn't in Berkeley any longer, but if I can find his letter I will try to write him tonight.)

While I was ill in bed I read a book on playwrighting, but it seemed to be instead all about the <u>conscious</u> <u>will</u>, and quite a lot about <u>free</u> <u>will</u> which I think you would have enjoyed. It seems that for the purposes of playwright-

---

* This Edutravel tour never took place.
† Mason Robertson (1890–1964) may have worked at the *Call & Post* in Cleveland.
‡ Andrés Henestrosa (1906–2008) was a Mexican writer, historian, and political leader. His book *Men Whom the Dance Scattered* was published in 1929.

ing one must consider the will free whether it is or not, as it seems that the struggle of the conscious will against the necessities of a fixed environment is what makes a drama. Finally the author admits, however, that the will is only relatively free, and maybe not that, but the character must think it is, or else there'd be no tragedy. Nor comedy either!

Mama sends her very best wishes to you. And here's hoping to see you in April if nothing thwarts my conscious will.

Sincerely,
Langston

TO SYLVIA CHEN (LEYDA)   [TLS]

March 4, 1937.

Dear Sylvia,

Welcome to America! It will be swell to see you again, and to meet your new husband.* I'll be in New York by the 10th for a few days, and will give you a ring. I suppose you've seen the Carmons |Walt and Rose| and the Ellises† by now. I haven't yet, since they've been back, as it's been a long time since I've been East. I'm a playwright these days. Are you still a dancer?

Sincerely,
Langston

TO CARRIE CLARK   [TLS]

American Express,
11 rue Scribe,
Paris, France,
December 28, 1937.

Dearest Mama,

I was glad to find all of your letters here when I arrived, and happy to have so much news of home. I got here just before Christmas, and expect to sail for New York shortly after New Year's. I would love to go to London for a few days

---

* In 1935, Sylvia Chen had married the American film historian Jay Leyda, whom she had met in Moscow. In September 1936, Chen finally told Hughes about her marriage.

† Fred Ellis (1889–1965) was a political cartoonist and illustrator. He left the United States in 1930 to work in Berlin and Moscow, and returned in 1936. The Ellises threw a farewell party for Hughes before he left the Soviet Union in 1933.

first, but don't think I will have enough money. . . . . I'm so pleased to know that you are feeling better, and hope that you had a nice Christmas. I wrote you early in December from Madrid,* and sent you an order on my bank to let you have what money there was on the account there, since I didn't know how much there might be, and I wanted you to have enough for a pleasant holiday season. I also wrote the bank to that effect. If as you say, there was two hundred dollars or so, put it on your account (in case mine is closed out) and use it as need be for the household expenses. But just in case something happened that that letter wasn't received, here is a blank check enclosed that you can fill out for the amount you need now. (Sometimes in Spain the trains are stopped for days on account of military movements and the mail piles up so that I guess some of it is never delivered. Several cards I wrote to friends in Paris, I discover, never reached them. And perhaps that happened with some of my letters and cards to you and Kit |Gwyn Clark| and others at home—as I wrote at least a card to Julia, the Lanes, Bessie and Charlie and everybody.)

Better write me to New York, c/o Knopf, 501 Madison Avenue, and mark: Please Hold Pending Arrival. So they won't send it over here. Keep all my mail at home for me until I know where I will be. I may have some lectures to give before I'll be able to get out to Cleveland.

Yes, the fellow received the stories all right here in Paris. And thanks so much for sending them. They are going to make a book of them here.†

Paris is sort of cold, but not so bad. I am fine, and had a wonderful time in Spain. They say |Paul| Robeson is going down next month. . . . . Marian Anderson gave a concert here just before I got back, and packed the Grand Opera House. Big pictures of her all over Paris.

As soon as I know when I'm sailing, I'll let you know. Lots of love and my best to Bessie and Charlie and Kit |Gwyn Clark|.

Langston

---

* Hughes served for three months as a foreign correspondent in Madrid for the *Baltimore Afro-American* and other newspapers during the Spanish Civil War (1936–1939). Sailing to Paris on June 30, 1937, he stayed there for several weeks visiting with friends. On July 24, he began his journey to Madrid with the poet Nicolás Guillén (they had met in Cuba), who was reporting on the conflict for a radical Cuban journal.

† Georges Adam wrote for the Paris newspaper *Ce Soir*. He translated and published short stories from Hughes's collection *The Ways of White Folks*.

TO MARIE SHORT   [ALS]

[On Cunard White Star, R·M·S "Berengaria" stationery]

c/o Knopf, Inc., 501 Madison Ave.

New York.

January 15, 1938

Dear Marie,

Homeward bound* again—and still without having seen London! My fourth
time in Europe, too. I was going to England this time, but in Paris my francs
went on the wings of the morning (too soon) and the best I could do was get
to the boat train and sail on home. I've been asleep for three days, so now
I thought I would wake up and write you a letter. . . . . I think you would
love Madrid, too. I didn't want to leave. Nobody does that lives there. That
is why the government has never succeeded in evacuating the city. It's still
about a million people—and at least half of them ought to be gone. No rail-
roads, and therefore almost no food. No coal at all, so no heat. No tobacco,
and shells falling anywhere any time they choose. Trenches, barricades, and
battle lines half-way around the town. All the war you'll ever want to hear:
artillery, mines, air-bombs. And yet, streets full of people. Theatres, movies full. Schools running. New schools for children and soldiers. Schools in
the trenches for the illiterate. Concerts. Lectures. Fiestas. Dancing. Cocktails
in cafes where shells shake the glasses. Famous international visitors from
every where: princes, diplomats, congressmen, writers. (Dorothy Parker† was
among the most charming of all, and made a fine radio speech.) I saw quite a
little of Hemingway, and liked him.‡ I lost a lot of pounds (not enough to eat)
but I never felt better in my life. The Madrid folks are wonderful. Every other
city now, I'm sure, will seem flat by comparison. I'm afraid there's nothing

---

* Leaving Madrid near the middle of November 1937, Hughes reached Paris in December.
He stayed there for about one month before returning to Cleveland by way of New York
City.
† Dorothy Parker (1893–1967), a writer noted also for her scathing wit in conversation,
was a member of a Manhattan literary coterie known as the Algonquin Round Table (so-
called after their meeting place, the Algonquin Hotel). In her will, Parker left her entire
estate to the NAACP.
‡ The novelist Ernest Hemingway (1899–1961) served as a foreign correspondent covering the Spanish Civil War for the North America Newspaper Alliance. Between 1937 and
1938 he spent eight months in Spain.

left for me except to start a theatre and produce plays. That will be equal to anybody's battle front!

Salud, Marie!

Langston

P.S. I am sending you a book for New Year's. Drawings of Spain.

P.S. I wrote you, didn't I, that Rhys |Albert Rhys Williams| was on the boat with me going over? I never did see Connie. I think she is like London! In Paris I lived in an Ethiopian Hotel! Barcelona is awful!

TO FRANKLIN FOLSOM   [TL]

COPY <Given Yale> COPY

% American Express
11 rue Scribe
Paris, France*
August 16, 1938

Mr. Franklin Folsom,†
League of American Writers
381 Fourth Avenue
New York, N. Y.

Dear Franklin Folsom:
I received your cable today, and by the time this reaches you, you will of course have had my answer which I shall send in the morning. But this is by way of certification. Dreiser was to have sailed on the Cunard White Star Liner, Laco-

---

* On July 18, Hughes arrived in Paris as an official delegate of the League of American Writers (he was a vice president of the league) to the Congress for Peace Action and Against Bombing of Open Cities. A major part of his responsibility was to keep an eye on the notoriously erratic novelist Theodore Dreiser, who was a heavy drinker. The most famous American writer at the gathering, Dreiser obstinately refused to join the league although he was sympathetic to its goals. After the conference, Hughes made his first trip to Great Britain. He returned to New York City on September 18 aboard the French liner *De Grasse*, in time to keep the lecture commitments to which he alludes in this letter.
† From 1937 to 1942, Franklin Folsom (1907–1995) was executive secretary of the antifascist League of American Writers, an association of left-wing writers, journalists, and literary critics. The league actively supported the Spanish Republic against the fascist forces of rebellion during the Spanish Civil War.

nia, on August 13th from Liverpool, reaching New York August 22nd. But on July 29th he left for Spain, and since then we in Paris have had no news of him except through the papers in early August. On his return to France, he was to have sent me a wire, also M. Fouquet of the Maison de la Culture, so that we could meet him in Paris. The newspapermen also wished to see him on his return. We had no wires to date, so, a few days ago, becoming worried about him, we begin to try to find out where he is. His hotel here in Paris claims he has never returned to claim his baggage there. But a wire to Barcelona brought the answer that he left Spain August 2nd. And Perpignan reports that he departed for Paris August 5th. But so far, we have been able to find no one who has seen him in Paris, and the hotel says they still have his belongings, so today it developed into a major mystery as to his whereabouts, with the Spanish Embassy, the Writers Association, and Aragon's associates on CE SOIR all trying to trace him, so far with no results, except that it does seem sure he did leave Spain, and did take a train from the border to Paris. But the strange thing is that for the last ten days his hotel, the Lutetia, has answered all inquiries by saying that Mr. Dreiser has never come back to claim his belongings there. And certainly, if he did pass through Paris, neither the Association des Ecrivains nor myself knew of it, and he had promised to let us know. His ticket on the Laconia was purchased through Cook's before he left for Spain, but they are not so far able to give us any information as to whether he sailed or not. So please, by all means, let us know here in Paris whether he has arrived safely in New York, or no, since for the last few days here we have been considerably mystified and concerned about him. But perhaps by the time this reaches you, we will have been able to check on it directly with the steamship line, but they will have to cable to Liverpool for the list.

As to myself, it is very difficult to get space on any boat returning before the end of September as this is the rush season, but I have the possibility of a place on a small steamer sailing from Antwerp on the 10th, which would put me in New York the 20th. I hope to make it as I have four lectures in New England beginning the 22nd.

Aragon and all the officials of the Writers here are on vacation the whole month of August and out of town, but before they left I got full information on the Maisons de Culture for us, which I will bring back. But to visit any of them outside of Paris is impossible since they are all closed in the summer, and the Paris one might as well be, since there is practically no activity there.

The Writers office said they were sending you reports on the Peace Congress, etc., and Dreiser said that he had mailed you his speech, so I sent only the newspaper clippings, particularly the Paris Herald Tribune where, due to

Dreiser's presence, the Congress got much more space than that usually conservative sheet gives to such things. The speeches of the one-day Writers Congress held following the one on Peace are to appear shortly in booklet form, so you will receive them all, probably in French. I have a copy of Dreiser's there, but since it was taken down in shorthand by a French steno whose grasp of English was not perfect, I did not send it to you. However Dreiser promised to revise it en route to Spain and forward you a copy. It was quite an interesting review of American literature and its economic background from the early days up to now. In case my own speech was not already sent you (can't check because everyone left on vacation right after the Congress) I'm making a copy now to send you.

The English delegates, including Rosamond Lehmann, Rex Warner, and Spender, and C. Day-Lewis,* gave a luncheon for Dreiser and me in the garden of the Circle des Nations while they were here, but unfortunately Dreiser was working on his speech that day and was unable to attend.

The Peace Congress itself was rather dull with too many speeches and in too many languages that were hard to hear and to which nobody paid any attention anyway, so far as I could tell. As you know, the Congress ranged from right wing religious groups to as far left as the French Socialists would permit it to go, which wasn't so far. Pasionaria received a tremendous ovation from the delegates, but the presidium refused to allow her to speak, which almost broke up the meeting, with various people grabbing for the microphone, for and against, the British M. P. Ellen Wilkinson being forcibly removed from the platform, and the whole thing adjourned until people got their tempers back, and the stage was cleared. The following night, Pasionaria spoke at our Writers meeting and was magnificent.†

About next June's Congress in Mexico, Aragon had heard nothing, but has written them a letter to find out, and believes it will be held there, and does not feel that we in New York should take the lead until we know. However, he feels that a post-meeting in New York would be good, following the Mexican one, like the Madrid-Paris meetings of last year. He feels that the Paris office could secure the funds for a few European writers to attend, perhaps five or six, I gather, but the other world sections would have to contribute to a fund

* The British delegates were the novelist Rosamond Lehmann (1901–1990), the classicist Rex Warner (1905–1986), and the poets Stephen Spender (1909–1995) and Cecil Day-Lewis (1904–1972).
† Isidora Dolores Ibárruri Gómez (1895–1989), a political activist known as La Pasionaria ("The Passionflower"), was a charismatic leader of the Spanish Republic during the Spanish Civil War. Her autobiography, *They Shall Not Pass: The Autobiography of La Pasionaria*, was published in 1976.

for the others. He thinks at least thirty distinguished foreign writers should be invited, transportation paid—which is about the only way to get most of them there. And of course there would be their board and keep in New York to think of. So if we intend having them, we'll have to start raising funds at once, I should think, and pretty big funds at that, for no doubt the burden of their New York entertainment would fall on us.

Dreiser's presence in Paris was a great help to the American group, and of great interest to the French. He acquitted himself well, and I am glad he was chosen as a delegate. I hope he is safely aboard the Laconia, but we shall be uneasy here until we find out.*

Greetings to you,

Sincerely,
Langston Hughes

TO DOROTHY PETERSON   [TLS]

Paris,
August 30,
1938.

Dear Dorothy,†

Your letters were swell! You're one of the world's best correspondents—and the only one who sent me any news of the HARLEM SUITCASE THEATRE,‡ all summer long. Also of the progression of FUENTE OVEJUNA§ which must be hard to translate as I read it on the boat again, and understood about every fifth word. It's too much like Shakespeare. I guess you never did send that first

---

* Dreiser left Spain for London without stopping to claim his baggage in Paris and apparently without telling anyone of this change in plans.
† Dorothy Peterson (1897–1978), a teacher and lover of the arts from a prominent African American family, was an old friend of Hughes from the glory years of the Harlem Renaissance. One of the patrons of *Fire!!* in 1926, she served as technical director of Hughes's Harlem Suitcase Theatre in 1938.
‡ Politically recharged by his three months in Madrid, on his return home Hughes founded the Harlem Suitcase Theatre as a "people's theater." In February 1938, he leased a space and began rehearsing his new, agitprop play, *Don't You Want to Be Free?* Opening on April 21, the production was a hit. It ran for 135 performances. However, the Suitcase Theatre never staged any of the plays mentioned in this letter. Without his presence, the company foundered. He resigned as executive director on July 14, 1939.
§ *Fuente Ovejuna*, a verse play, was written by the Spanish dramatist and poet Lope de Vega (1562–1635) in 1619. It concerns an uprising in 1476 in the town of Fuente Obejuna. Hughes and Dorothy Peterson, who was fluent in Spanish, collaborated on a translation of the drama.

act, deciding probably that you'd wait until I get back, which is just as well. By excellent good fortune, I met the man who worked with Garcia Lorca during the days of his traveling theatre when they did <u>Fuente Ovejuna</u> in a modernized version in the villages of Spain, and he indicated to me how they cut the play, leaving out all the king business, and doing it in ordinary present day clothes of village folk. They staged it on a truck, with only suggested sets, but excellent lighting, he said, for dawns, sunsets, a fire, etc. So that is something for us to worry about. I hope our campaign for funds is making some headways so we can get a few more lights and a decent switchboard with a dimmer that functions well. . . . . Meanwhile, I've written a little one-act Blues opera* (shades of Tate and innumerable $7.00-$7.0-$7-$!) but I can't help it! A theatre, especially a cullud one, has to have music. It's a labor subject, sharecroppers, all in song, and ought to be amusing. . . . . Have also started a long play about love on the FRONT PORCH, which is probably what it will be called.† But it's drama, not a comedy, unfortunately, since things don't turn out so well for the lovers. . . . . And besides that, have translated Lorca's BODAS DE SANGRE,‡ a beautiful thing done here last season by a left theatre group with much success. I'm afraid it's too hard for us, without sets, but maybe some other group in New York will like it. So you see, Paris has agreed with me! No money, but lots of work! And at last I got to the Bois de Boulogne! Which I've been planning to see for years, every time I come to Paris. So this time I went, in spite of all—and found it looks about like Central Park! Also saw <u>Dieux du Stade</u>, the Olympic film with all the Negro runners in it. Pretty nice. See it if it is in New York. Other than that mostly colored tourists (here by the dozens—Geraldyne,§ Pickens,¶ Countee |Cullen|, etc.) and in between dieting to make

---

* Hughes started writing *De Organizer* while in Paris on this trip, then began working on the music with the jazz pianist and composer James P. Johnson (1894–1955) on his return to New York. After a successful performance by the International Ladies' Garment Workers' Union, Hughes sent the script to the CBS network. Rejecting the project, a CBS representative said that the network thought it would be "too controversial to give an emotional treatment on an essentially dramatic show."

† Hughes's three-act play *Front Porch* tells the story of the Harpers, a black family living in a nominally integrated but mainly white neighborhood. In September, Hughes promised the play to the Gilpin Players at Karamu House. Staged in November, *Front Porch* failed to entertain either its audience or the critics.

‡ Hughes's translations of *Bodas de Sangre* (known in English as *Blood Wedding*) and *Yerma* by the Spanish dramatist and poet Federico García Lorca (1898–1936) eventually would be published in 1994 by the Theatre Communications Group, New York.

§ Possibly Geraldyn Dismond, who wrote society columns for the *Amsterdam News* and the *Inter-State Tattler*.

¶ William Pickens (1881–1954), a skilled linguist and educator, was an active leader in the NAACP. He published two volumes of autobiography.

my francs stretch. I decided not to go to Spain, since |Theodore| Dreiser went, and more recently Pickens. And Madrid is very difficult to achieve at this moment. So it'll be London instead, for a couple of days before sailing on the 10th on the DeGrasse to reach New York |on| the 18th or 19th. So I'll be seeing you. . . . . Mighty nice news, that about Sidney!* Tell him Salud!. . . . Also so glad Leigh got CHIP WOMAN'S FORTUNE under way.† It ought to be very amusing. We'll open with it and what else? Has the committee met yet? You-all better meet and get some money together that won't be rent either!!. . . . . Also a little discipline! Make Rita behave herself!‡ And start Waring singing!§ We'll need him in the OPERA! IN fact, I wrote it for him, tell him!

Salud, until—

Langston

* Dr. Jerome "Sidney" Peterson (1903–1987), Dorothy's brother, earned his medical degree from Columbia University. He worked with the New York City Department of Health and the World Health Organization.

† *Chip Woman's Fortune* was written by Willis Richardson (1889–1977), a playwright and pioneer of the black theater movement who lived and worked mainly in Washington, D.C. The director and actor Leigh Whipper (1876–1975) apparently planned a revival of the play.

‡ Probably Rita Romilly (1900–1984), a veteran dancer, actress, and acting teacher (of Paul Robeson, among others). A newspaper announcement on June 24, 1939, about the new season of the Harlem Suitcase Theatre mentions that Romilly would co-teach an intensive theater workshop course for actors.

§ The poet William Waring Cuney (1906–1976) was an old friend of Hughes, and a fellow student at Lincoln University. His poems include the often anthologized "No Images" (1924) and also "The Death Bed," published in 1926 in *Fire!!* In 1930, the men collaborated on the anthology *Four Lincoln University Poets* (Lincoln University, 1930). Cuney also acted with the Harlem Suitcase Theatre.

PART III

I Do Not Need Freedom
When I'm Dead

1939 to 1949

With the Bontemps family, July 1939

My old mule,
He's got a grin on his face.
He's been a mule so long
He's forgot about his race.

I'm like that old mule—
Black—and don't give a damn!
You got to take me
Like I am.
—"ME AND THE MULE," 1942

In January 1939, Hughes went to Los Angeles to work on a film project, *Way Down South*. Although this job brought him some sorely
needed cash, the humiliating way in which whites in Hollywood rou-
tinely treated him and other blacks wounded him deeply. In addition,
after the movie opened in cinemas in July, many liberals attacked *Way
Down South*—and Hughes—as endorsing shabby stereotypes about

blacks in the South. On the defensive, he retreated to Noël Sullivan's Hollow Hills Farm in Carmel Valley. There he worked mainly on an autobiography, *The Big Sea*, which Knopf published in 1940. On its appearance, however, followers of the popular evangelist Aimee Semple McPherson loudly picketed a Pasadena hotel just before he was to publicize the book at a major luncheon there. The picketers focused on his poem "Goodbye Christ," which denounces McPherson by name as a charlatan. The organizers canceled the talk. As negative publicity about the poem and about his political and religious views in general began to spread, Hughes holed up at Hollow Hills Farm. He lived there quietly until well into the following year, 1941.

TO NOËL SULLIVAN   [ALS]

(Chicago, Ill.)*
66 St. Nicholas Pl.
New York, N.Y.
May 27, 1939.

Dear Noël,

For the past month I've been in seclusion in Chicago writing a book—the autobiography. I have 250 pages done—a little less than half—so I'm afraid it's going to |be| about the size of "Gone with the Wind!"† I'm not yet quite up to that first trip to California and the departure for Russia. I'm leaving for New York tomorrow for a month, then back to California. In the late summer, if you'd like it, I'd love to come to Hollow Hills and revise and complete the second draft there—with your help and consultation, particularly on the Carmel portions which I want to meet your approval.‡ So far I've had a very amusing time writing it, and I hope it will make good reading to others. There |is| lots to tell!

---

* Finding Hollywood disturbingly hostile to blacks, Hughes completed his work on the screenplay for *Way Down South* and left Los Angeles. In early April, he joined Arna Bontemps on a lecture tour, then returned with him to Chicago, where Bontemps lived.
† Margaret Mitchell's best-selling novel, *Gone with the Wind*, was published in 1936. The film version appeared in 1939.
‡ Sullivan had relocated from San Francisco to rural Carmel Valley, inland from Carmel-by-the-Sea. He settled in a spread he called Hollow Hills Farm. As with his Carmel cottage, Ennesfree, he took the name from a poem by the Irish writer William Butler Yeats.

My very best to Lee,* Marie |Short|, the Jeffers, and Eulah |Pharr|. . . . . In what a rush I left Los Angeles! Worked at the studio until train time, and had lectures in Kansas City 2 days later.

Affectionately,

Langston

Read Arna Bontemps' new novel, "<u>Drums at Dusk</u>."

TO BLANCHE KNOPF [*TLS*]
[On Hollow Hills Farm (Carmel Valley), Jamesburg Route,
Monterey, California *stationery]*

September 4, 1939

Mrs. Alfred A. Knopf,
501 Madison Avenue,
New York, New York.

Dear Blanche,

I have settled down in a charming little Mexican house on the side of a hill above the pear orchard here on this beautiful farm in the Carmel Valley—to finish my book. The house is entirely my own for work, and as remote and quiet a place as one would want to find, so I shall not be interrupted. I am sorry the manuscript is not ready to send you now, as I had hoped it would be, but it is going along splendidly and is two-thirds finished, so a month more of steady work should get it done. However, my difficulty at the moment is this: having turned down all lectures for this fall and put aside everything else in order to get the book done, my sources of income have temporarily ceased— and I find myself with an eviction warning from my New York landlord if I do not come through with the August rent. Which is bad enough, but not quite as bad being unable to employ a typist to assist me in the preparation of a final draft—some five hundred pages—which I shall shortly have ready to have recopied. So, much as I dislike to do it at this stage of the game, I am writing to ask you if it would be possible to now allow me an advance of $200.00 on the book, at the moment tentatively entitled THE BIG SEA and which, barring an act of God, will be ready for you in October.

* A young Canadian, Leander "Lee" Crowe (1905–1989) was a close friend of Noël Sullivan. Crowe, who lived at Hollow Hills Farm, wrote short stories and poems and published his column "The Crowe's Nest" in *The Carmel Pine Cone.*

I hope you had a pleasant trip to the coast. I'm sorry I didn't get out in time to look you up. I was held up in New York doing some special song material for Marianne Oswald with Vernon Duke and Herbert Kingsley.*

My best regards to Alfred,

Sincerely,

Langston

Langston Hughes

P.S. I shall, of course, be willing to do further revision on book should you have suggestions, or find it too long, after you have read it. . . . . The above address good until Nov.

TO ROY WILKINS

[*TLS*]

<u><COPY></u>

<To Roy Wilkins,

Crisis,

Sept. 20, 1939>

DEAR ROY,†

I hate to be a professional quarreler, but what you guys on THE CRISIS do to poetry is a sin and a shame. You stick it off in far corners in a column next to the ads, and put it in small type that makes it harder than it naturally is to read, and you thus hurt the poets' souls. Poets like to be published in good spots, with lots of nice-looking margin around them that attracts the eye so somebody will look at what they have to say, otherwise they're likely not to get looked at at all. . . . . . . But maybe you've reformed your make-up somewhat in your last two issues which I haven't seen being here on a farm in the Carmel Valley finishing a book in which I shall write quite a little about the CRISIS. Perhaps portions of the book will interest you, and I shall probably send you some parts of it, in case you might like to select portions for publications. . . . . The enclosed poems you may return to me here in case you do not care for

---

* Born in France, Marianne Oswald (1901–1985) was the stage name of Sarah Alice Bloch, who gained fame singing in Berlin cabarets but fled to Paris in the early 1930s because of rising anti-Semitism. During World War II she lived in the United States. Vernon Duke (1903–1969) and Herbert Kingsley (1882–1961) were composers.
† In 1934, Roy Wilkins (1901–1981) replaced W. E. B. Du Bois as editor of *The Crisis*, the monthly magazine of the NAACP. Wilkins became executive director of the NAACP in 1964.

them. When I have others that I think you might like, I'll send them on . . .
. . . With best regards, <as ever,>

Sincerely,
Langston Hughes

TO ARTHUR SPINGARN   [*TLS*]

[On Hollow Hills Farm, (Carmel Valley) Jamesburg Route,
Monterey, California *stationery]*

January 20, 1940

Dear Arthur Spingarn,
Russell Jelliffe is at the Buckingham Hotel in New York this week on behalf of the Gilpin Players of Cleveland who, as you probably know, have recently lost their theatre through fire, and who are in need of immediate assistance in order to continue their activities, and to sustain them in their campaign for funds to build a new theatre.* Mr. Jelliffe has asked me to write a few of my friends about the Gilpins. I think you already know my high regard for them. I feel that they can become the Negro Abbey Theatre. And certainly they are the ONLY permanent Negro theatre in America, and the ONLY place where Negro playwrights of talent can be sure of a chance to see their scripts tried out (and thus learn to write better in terms of living theatre). They are the ONLY colored group having (over a period of 16 years) a regular and consecutive producing program. And now that the Federal Theatre† is gone, we need the Gilpins more than ever. The enlarged plans that they are hoping to carry through, including as they do the training of Negroes in every branch of the theatre, and the establishment of Fellowships for playwrights, etc., seem to me most important. The Jelliffes themselves have a fine free attitude about the scripts used, ranging from the religious to the radical, comedy to tragedy, folk plays to farce, and for 16 years they have fought against both the intoler-

---

* Karamu House, the Gilpin Players' theater, was destroyed by fire in 1939. In 1949, it was rebuilt and expanded to include two theaters, exhibition space, and dance and visual arts studios through the support of the Cleveland philanthropist Leonard C. Hanna, Jr. (1889–1957), and the Rockefeller Foundation.

† The Federal Theatre Project, part of the Works Projects Administration of President Roosevelt's New Deal, ran from 1935 to 1939. A unit of the Federal Theatre was located in Harlem. Hughes worked later with Clarence Muse, the director of the Negro Unit of the Federal Theatre Project in Los Angeles, on *St. Louis Woman,* a musical version of the play by Arna Bontemps and Countee Cullen based on Bontemps's novel *God Sends Sunday* (1931).

ance of many whites and the bigotry and ignorance of many Negroes in the Cleveland community who wanted to limit in one way or another the scope of players and their plays. But in spite of all (and a bank crash that robbed them of a laboriously built up fund) and in spite of the present fire, they've kept on producing. And I hope they will now find help to grow and enlarge because I think they have proven their worth and their potential (and actual) power as a force in American theatre. What they need, of course, is large sums of money to rebuild and create for themselves a center and workshop. Perhaps you can aid them in making Foundation contacts that will be helpful in this respect.

I've been working very hard here for the past six months on my autobiographical travelogue |The Big Sea| which Knopf has accepted and which is now just about done. I've also done a number of new poems and a few stories, California being most conducive to writing for me somehow. I guess it is the sunshine—and the quiet here in the country.

Please give my best to your wife and to Mrs. Amy |Spingarn|. I hope to see you all again soon as I must come East for lectures in mid-February.

Sincerely,

Langston

Langston Hughes

TO BLANCHE KNOPF   [TLS]

Hollow Hills Farm,

Monterey, California,

February 8, 1940.

Mrs. Blanche Knopf,
501 Madison Avenue,
New York, New York.

Dear Blanche,
THE BIG SEA has been sent off to you again Monday by express from San Francisco, complete except for two short chapters to be inserted when I get to New York shortly, as the material to complete them is there.

I went over the book carefully, cutting and polishing in the light of yours, Carl |Van Vechten|'s, and Ben Lehman's comments and criticisms. It has been shortened some 50 pages, and I think thereby improved.

The portion which you liked the least has been cut one third, about thirty five pages out of a hundred in the Harlem Renaissance section. Carl, as you know, felt that most of that material was important historically and had not been written before. But I have tried to speed it up, and make it more personal, and more readable. I hope I have succeeded. . . . . My own feeling about that section is this: That it was the background against which I moved and developed as a writer, and from which much of the material of my stories and poems came. Also the people to whom the most space is devoted there, Carl Van Vechten, Wallace Thurman, Zora Hurston, Rev. Becton[*] were people who were certainly very much a part of that era, their names known to thousands of folks. And since, I believe, a large part of the sale of my books is to readers who sort of specialize in Negro literature and backgrounds, and to schools and colleges, sociology classes, etc., it would seem to me that <that> material would be of interest. And to Negro readers as well, who would certainly give me a razzing if I wrote only about sailors, Paris night clubs, etc., and didn't put something "cultural" in the book—although the material is not there for that reason, but because it was a part of my life. And the fault lies in the writing if I have failed to make it live. But I hope that in the revision I have bettered it. . . . . Many of the superfluous names have been cut, as have the excerpts from reviews of my early poems, and the <portions of the> WALDORF ASTORIA, and the chapter PATRON AND FRIEND, as you suggested. Most of the abstractions have been cut, too. So I hope you will find the whole thing somewhat better. Certainly, I have greatly appreciated yours and Carl's help and advice.

One other observation regarding some of the material in the book and some of the names mentioned that are widely known to Negro readers (and I suppose to students of Negro life and literature): I have a large Negro reading and lecture public (as witness my annual lecture tours largely to Negro schools, clubs, etc.). For instance one could not write about life in Negro Washington without including the names I mention therein and who are nationally known to most colored people and who are very much a part of the literary and social life of colored Washington—which is, as I point out, a segregated life. I mention this so that you won't think they're being included as a "courtesy gesture," they being as much a part of Negro life as Dorothy Parker would be if a white writer were writing of literary life in New York. I give you this as an example because, although I hope most of my book will <be> interesting to the general public regardless of color, some small portions

---

* A controversial figure, Rev. George Wilson Becton (1890–1933) held profitable revivals regularly at the Salem Methodist Episcopal Church in Harlem (where Countee Cullen's father had once been pastor). In *The Big Sea*, Hughes characterized Becton as "a charlatan if ever there was one."

of it may have vital meaning only to my own people. But that, it seems to me, would only add to the final integrity and truth of the work as a whole. And I am trying to write a truthful and honest book.*

A few minor details:

Do you think there should be an appendix of names and places?

Do you think there should be dates beneath the sub-titles of each section indicating the period covered therein, as for instance:

I. TWENTY-ONE
(1902-1923)

Do you think it will be possible (as you ask<ed> me to bring to your mind later) to get out shortly after the appearance of the regular edition, a cheaper edition (perhaps paper bound even) that might be sold exclusively by myself at lectures limited, if you wish, to Negro organizations and audiences—since many places where I speak have no bookshops in town anyhow, and most colored people cannot buy the more expensive books—but will buy them if they fall within their price range and are brought <u>directly to</u> them, as I do when I lecture. For several years past now, as you know, I've taken all my royalties in books anyhow—and probably will continue to purchase a great many of my own books to sell at lectures as long as I continue to lecture—which I guess will be a long time, as it certainly helps to sustain life.

Thanks for returning the manuscript of the poems. And for my copy of the Stevens contract.†

I'll be in New York, I think, around the 25th or 28th at the latest. Kindly ask Miss Rubin to send all mail for me from now on to me at 634 St. Nicholas Avenue, c/o Harper, Apt. 1-D, New York, as I leave the coast day after tomorrow.

I plan to return to the coast in the early summer and write the second volume of the autobiography,‡ and I hope a new novel. (But you have heard about that novel for a long while now haven't you?) Well, all things get done in time! And it's surely coming up.

With my best to you,

Sincerely,

Langston

Langston Hughes

* The Harlem Renaissance section of *The Big Sea* would come to be seen as an invaluable source of firsthand information on the period.
† On January 30, 1940, Blanche Knopf sent Hughes a contract signed by George D. Stephens and a representative of Knopf for a screenplay based on Hughes's story "Rejuvenation Through Joy," from *The Ways of White Folks* (1934). Nothing came of the project.
‡ The second volume, *I Wonder as I Wander*, was published by Rinehart in 1956 after Blanche Knopf declined Hughes's proposal for the book.

TO RICHARD WRIGHT   [ALS]

[On Telluride Association, Ithaca, New York *stationery]*

On tour,[*]
Cornell College,
February 29, 1940

Dear Dick,[†]

I've been reading "Native Son" on the train. It is a tremendous performance! A really good book which sets a new standard for Negro writers from now on. Congratulations and my very best wishes for a great critical and sales success. Judging from the "New Yorker's" early review, you're bound to have both.

I wonder what Chicago critics (and the colored ones) will say about it? It will be fun to see.

Hastily, but
Sincerely,
Langston

P.S. I've been ballyhooing the book at all my lectures. Several folks want to book you to speak (naturally) but I told them I didn't think you were engageable right now—but to write c/o Harper's.

---

[*] On February 10, Hughes left Hollow Hills Farm to begin a poetry reading tour, with his first stop in Downingtown, Pennsylvania. He then went on to New York, Kentucky, Ohio, Tennessee, West Virginia, Illinois, and Michigan. On May 8, Hughes gave his last lecture and ended his journey in Chicago, where he stayed with Arna and Alberta Bontemps.

[†] Richard Wright (1908–1960) was born outside Natchez, Mississippi. His mother was a schoolteacher, and his father was a sharecropper. He moved to Chicago in 1927 and then to New York in 1937 to run the Harlem Bureau of the communist *Daily Worker.* Wright's first novel, *Native Son* (Harper & Brothers, 1940), was a best-seller after the Book-of-the-Month Club chose it as a main offering. Set in Chicago, it tells of a young black man sentenced to death after killing two women. Also chosen by the club, Wright's autobiography, *Black Boy* (Harper & Brothers, 1945), was another best-seller. He thus became the most acclaimed and financially successful black writer in the United States.

TO MAXIM LIEBER   *[TL]*

Hollow Hills Farm,
Monterey, California,
December 17, 1940.
(Written at Los Angeles)*

Dear Maxim,

Not dead. Nor down with flu—as is half Los Angeles. But merely entangled in that unprofitable thing known as the show business—going out to Hollywood or Beverly Hills or Hollywood every morning and not getting back to the hotel until 12 or 1 or 2 o'clock at night—since those remote districts are from where I live just about like going from Harlem to Philadelphia—and in this charming democracy of ours there seems to be no place for Negroes to live in Hollywood even if they do work out there occasionally. . . . . I have been intending to write you for ages and let you know how the revue is coming along, so here goes:

1. Henry Blankfort† is (or should be) now in New York arranging to open MEET THE PEOPLE there Christmas. Address, c/o The William Morris offices. Do get in touch with him and straighten out our business.

2. We have enough material for two or three revues, both sketches and music, which we have been cutting, changing, and editing for the past six weeks. It is now only a matter of finally making up the collective mind as to just what stays in, what comes out, and how strong the social note be emphasized. It is apparently very difficult for a collective mind to make itself up. Some days it is very socially minded and most of the non-social or mildly social skits are removed from the script. A couple of days later it is somewhat more commercial and leans toward more nearly pure entertainment so the love songs go back in and the

---

* In November, Hughes went to Los Angeles to work on a "Negro Revue" with Donald Ogden Stewart (1894–1980) for the leftist Hollywood Theatre Alliance (HTA). He was the only black writer creating material for the review. Although he disliked the work, he stayed on because he needed money and hoped to write a hit song. In mid-December, Hughes quietly left Los Angeles to return to Carmel. Two weeks passed before the HTA noticed his absence. The HTA asked him to return to the project, but Hughes remained in Carmel.
† The screenwriter Henry Blankfort (1904–1993) was director of the Hollywood Theatre Alliance. Blankfort cowrote and served as stage manager for the HTA's Broadway production of the labor revue *Meet the People,* which opened that year in December. In the 1950s he would be blacklisted for alleged communist affiliations.

lynching numbers come out. Last night a very important audition of the material was held for about 150 writers and theatre people in Hollywood and the general opinion was that the show was too heavy, too much on the social side and not enough Negro geniality and humor for a revue that would be box-office—so today I presume we'll swing back to entertainment. (Much of the more entertaining stuff was not done last night as the current revue committee is very socially minded and tends to insist on putting content into every last love lyric.) So

3. While the collective mind is being made up, I have decided to return to Carmel this week-end for the holidays and remain there until the general line is settled and they want to start rehearsals when, if they need me, I'll come back, providing they vote a continuation of the $25.00 per week expense money advanced on royalties—which after this week will be down to the last $25 of the two hundred voted anyhow—and it would all have to come before their board again.

4. Personally and confidentially (to you) I do not enjoy this collective way of writing very much as I feel that when too many people are involved in the preparation of scripts, the material loses whatever individual flavor and distinction it might otherwise possess. That is probably what was the matter with ZERO HOUR.* After everybody got their paragraph in, it was simply a depersonalized un-human editorial, well-meant but with none of the blood of life or the passion of mankind in it. I do not think plays, or even skits can be written by eight or ten people with various ways of feeling and looking at things.

5. DO YOU? Kindly answer me that as it worries me and I would like to have yours and Minna's† opinion on it.

6. Unfortunately, I am the only Negro writer (or Negro) on the active writing end of the committee (although William Grant Still |is| on the musical end) and it is no easy job convincing good and clever white writers that excellent and funny as much of their work is, merely putting a thing in dialect doesn't give it a Negro or Bert Williams flavor. And that some of our material has just no feeling for a Negro or of Negroes even if it will be done by Negro actors. Since no colored writers were available here on the coast, that couldn't be helped, however, and from a social viewpoint some really excellent stuff has been gath-

---

* The melodrama *The Zero Hour* (1939) tells the story of a young aspiring actress, the producer who mentors and then weds her, and the circumstances leading to his suicide.
† Minna Zelinka (c. 1909–2011) worked for Maxim Lieber's agency. She became his third wife in 1945.

ered together. My problem has been to guide and get it into the racial groove and keep it from having that distant and editorialized feeling heretofore mentioned. I think we have now enough material certainly for a show which would ring true.

7. As to the music, there is agreement that two or three more really hot bang up memorable tunes would be a help, but that the music, as a whole (so the group last night apparently felt) is O.K. So if you would be so kind as to call Jimmy |James P.| Johnson, Margaret Bonds, and perhaps W. C. Handy and see if they have any fresh tunes not done in shows or on the air which Henry Blankfort could hear while he is in New York or which they would care to send directly to CHARLES LEONARD,* HOLLYWOOD THEATRE ALLIANCE, LOS ANGELES. If the tune is good, the lyrics can always be changed here on the spot to suit production ideas.

8. I have done about 15 or 20 sketches and lyrics since I've been here and am having them all typed up to send you. Three or four of them are apparently certain to be in the show, especially GOING MAD WITH A DIME† which everybody seems to love and which gets a big hand and lots of favorable comment at each audition or each new committee reading. The other numbers of mine go in and come out and go in again every other day or so according to who happens to be judging material at the time. SO:

9. SINCE I LEARN THAT A SIMILAR NEGRO REVUE IS IN PREPARATION FOR THE NEW NEGRO PLAYWRIGHTS GROUP AT THE LINCOLN THEATRE following the closing of BIG WHITE FOG‡ we

---

* Charles Leonard, born Chaim Leb Eppelboim (1900–1986), a successful screenwriter, was a member of the radical wing of the Hollywood Theatre Alliance. He was blacklisted after he was named as a communist in testimony heard by the Senate Permanent Subcommittee on Investigations of the Committee on Government Operations, the official title of the controversial unit that Senator Joseph McCarthy (1908–1957) chaired from 1953 to 1954.

† Hughes's sketch "Going Mad with a Dime" (or "Mad Scene from Woolworth's") is about a woman who goes to a dime store with only ten cents. In 1941, a song based on this sketch was briefly included by Duke Ellington (1899–1974) in his musical revue *Jump for Joy* (see letter dated November 8, 1941). This song was not a hit, and Ellington cut it from the revue after Hughes and Leonard approached him about royalties.

‡ In May 1940 Abram Hill (1910–1986) formed the Negro Playwrights Company with Hughes, Richard Wright, Ralph Ellison, and Ted (Theodore) Ward (1902–1983), among others. Their first and only production was Ted Ward's *Big White Fog* at the Lincoln Theater in Harlem in 1941. Ward wrote the play with support from the Federal Theatre Project in 1938.

might sell them whatever stuff is not used here, and when the script reaches you, kindly submit it to them.

10. With all this on my mind out here, it just wasn't possible to work out anything for Moe Gale,* as the kind of outline he would want and need with two or three really good samples would take two or three weeks of thought and preparation on my part—which I will devote to it as soon as I get back to Carmel and settled after the holidays.

11. So far I haven't seen any sort of contract with Hollywood Theatre Alliance, unless you consider the letter you have one. I have signed nothing here (nor will I sign anything) except the checks for $25.00 weekly I've received which I have to sign on the back to cash and which (by the way) do not fully cover my living and transportation here, so I've spent here as well the income from book sales and a couple of local speaking engagements applied to living expenses while working on their revue. I have received so far six checks, $150.00 all told, and owe you commission for same which, had I been able to get two minutes ahead of the hotel bill, would have been sent you. But that being, so it seems, out of the question—since the bill presents itself regularly every Saturday even before the check arrives—would you kindly deduct said amount due you from whatever comes in on the New York end. If nothing comes in, I'll send it to |you| myself the next time the Lord sends me a small amount of cash and I am safely at Carmel with no overhead and nothing but my art to worry about—which is a matter of soul, not material.

Charles Leonard, in charge of the show for HTA, is a swell fellow to work with, and I've enjoyed my experiences here very much. I do not suppose it is up to me to puzzle out how a Future Works Committee, a New Negro Theatre Board, a HTA Executive Board, a Negro Revue Committee, and Mr. Blankfort and Mr. Leonard can ever all of them and all at once agree on any one sketch or song or production idea, let alone on the 25 or 30 needed to make a show. That is why I think, now that there is certainly enough good stuff on hand to argue about from

* Moe Gale, born Moses Galewski (1899–1964), a producer and talent agent, invited Hughes to develop a radio series based on *Little Ham,* his comedy about the numbers racket. Gale had opened the famous Savoy Ballroom in Harlem, a nightclub where whites and blacks mingled. On March 12, 1941, Hughes would send Lieber and Gale an outline for sixty-five episodes of "Hamlet Jones." Hughes stood to make as much as $400 a week if Gale found a major sponsor. However, Hughes was once again disappointed; no such sponsor came forward.

now to doom's day, I had just as well betake myself off to the comfort and security of Hollow Hills Farm until said above collective mind is made up, as I cannot afford to stay around here indefinitely for $25.00 a week with no time or leisure for other and more lucrative (artistically at least) work which I have in mind to do this winter. DO YOU AGREE WITH ME? And if and whenever the show is set for rehearsals, if they wish me to come back and help further then, I'd be happy to do so. Or am quite willing to re-write and help edit skits and lyrics by mail if anything comes up that they need for me to assist on.

12. WHAT KIND OF AGREEMENT ARE WE GETTING FOR all this work?[*] Better get Henry Blankfort to sign it while he is in New York. The revue is being produced by the HTA and they therefore must sign all papers as it is they who will raise the money, etc., and the New Negro Theatre is merely an assisting group artistically—but are broker than HTA, so be sure contracts are with Hollywood Theatre Alliance.

13. Had a long talk with Paul Robeson a few weeks ago. He liked the revue material we read him very much, is willing to be in the show here for a couple of weeks if desired to help out the project. But HTA would rather (if show is hit here) interest him in appearing in a New York company. . . . . If only they'd hurry and get it on before somebody else beats them to it with a Negro social revue—since the idea is now in the air.

14. From the genial efficiency of your office, I judge that you and Minna put your collective heads together and produce a single thought—but now what would you-all say is the ratio of two plus multiplied by x-y over black z divided by liberal q plus left a over the necessary b of the unified zip desired for a revue?

15. I await your answer for clarification.

Sincerely, your humble client,
Langston Hughes

---

[*] As sketch director, Hughes was to be paid a royalty of one half of one percent of the gross, plus separate payments for original material. He received a weekly advance of $25 against these future royalties.

TO MAXIM LIEBER   *[TL]*

Hollow Hills Farm,
Monterey, California,
December 30, 1940.

Dear Maxim,

A few days ago I sent you a copy of the words and music of AMERICA'S YOUNG BLACK JOE,* and also the revised versions of the ballads that went to you sometime ago. I trust you have received them O.K. I am trying my best to get my desk cleared by New Year's so I can plunge into the serialization of LITTLE HAM immediately thereafter.

Here is something I wish you could do for me, or advise me about. In its issue of December 21st, very prominently placed, (and no doubt as a result of Aimee's doings)† THE SATURDAY EVENING POST published without my permission, and certainly in violation of copyright, an old poem of mine entitled, GOODBYE CHRIST,‡ which I had withdrawn from circulation years ago. As a result, I have issued the enclosed statement which I would like for the editors of the POST to see and publish, entirely or in part, particularly the last paragraph, if that be possible.§ What do you think? And would you be in a position to call it to their attention for me? I certainly do not choose to have Aimee and her sound trucks picketing all the lectures which I give from now on. Nor do my various sponsors.

---

* Hughes wrote "America's Young Black Joe" for the "Negro Revue" project of the Hollywood Theatre Alliance. The song was for a skit about the heavyweight boxing champion Joe Louis (1914–1981).

† Aimee Semple McPherson (1890–1944) was a notorious California evangelist who founded the International Church of the Foursquare Gospel. On November 15, 1940, when Hughes visited Pasadena to appear at a literary luncheon and promote his new book, *The Big Sea*, members of her church loudly protested and passed out leaflets near the site of the event. The leaflets, which included the text of "Goodbye Christ," denounced Hughes as a communist. The luncheon was canceled.

‡ Hughes's radical poem "Goodbye Christ" attacks the gross commercial exploitation of religion by certain leading evangelists. The poem was first published, without Hughes's permission, in *Negro Worker* (November/December 1932). It was also included in Nancy Cunard's anthology *Negro* (Wishart & Co.: London, 1934). The leaflet from Aimee Semple McPherson's demonstration that included the text of "Goodbye Christ" was reprinted in *The Saturday Evening Post* (December 21, 1940), again without Hughes's permission (the magazine is named in the poem).

§ Hughes also sent his statement to the Rosenwald Fund, Knopf, and the Associated Negro Press, among others. In it, he described himself as "having left the terrain of the 'radical at twenty' to approach the 'conservative at forty.'"

Also would you be so good as to get from ESQUIRE the copyright to SEVEN MOMENTS OF LOVE, and from the NEW YORKER, to HEY-HEY BLUES, poems which Blanche Knopf wishes to include in my new book—sending same direct to her?*

I have almost a dozen short stories outlined which I shall send you in due time. And I also want to get off to you copies of all my revue material. Did Henry Blankfort get in touch with you, or you with him, in New York? How did MEET THE PEOPLE fare at the hands of the Broadway critics?† If it flops I see no cullud show in Hollywood. After Moe Gale, no more show business for me—only literature. Would you not advise so, dear Maxim?

Happy New Year to you and Minna! And peace!

Sincerely,

Langston Hughes

TO DOROTHY PETERSON   [ALS]

[On Hollow Hills Farm, (Carmel Valley) Jamesburg Route,
Monterey, California *stationery]*

Peninsula Hospital,
Carmel, California,
January 25, 1941.

Dear Dorothy,

Being ill for the past two weeks here in the hospital—an arthritis-sciatica pain in one leg that won't let me put foot to the floor as yet‡—I have thought of you often and wished I could see you. I keep thinking of the grand times we've had, our adventures in Conn., in the theatre with a big T, and at your delicious board with the poor dog always without the window. Tell Nicky these weeks in the hospital I sympathize with him more than ever. (In fact, if you are spiritual (can't spell it), you must have heard me barking at your window—all the way from coast to coast! I seem to see Brooklyn—380—a lot these days.). . . . .

---

* Hughes's forthcoming book of poems was *Shakespeare in Harlem* (Knopf, 1942).
† *Meet the People* was a satirical labor stage revue that played in San Francisco, Chicago, and New York. The Broadway production opened on December 25, 1940, and ran for 160 performances. The 1944 film took its title from the stage revue but lacked its pointed political message.
‡ Hughes had claimed to be suffering from flulike symptoms for some weeks. When his illness worsened, he entered the Peninsula Community Hospital nearby on January 14. Hughes wrote to friends that he was ill with sciatica or arthritis, but hospital records show that he was diagnosed as suffering from gonorrhea. Following his release from the hospital on February 1 (his thirty-ninth birthday) he returned to Hollow Hills Farm.

I've really been ill since New Years—flu, worry, complications: revue, theatre, Aimee |Semple McPherson|, broke, whatnot, my doom suddenly come upon me! Anyhow, I loved your letter, which I had been waiting for a long time. And I do wish I could go to Puerto Rico this summer! Well, maybe! Spring might bring a bonanza. . . . . I hear the Playwrights |Negro Playwrights Company| are $10,000 (Ten!! Thousand!!!) in the hole! They have beat the Suitcase all hollow for debts! Also for committees that wrangle till dawn, I hear! Dear Dorothy, the next theatre <u>we</u> have will be in our own backyard. Nobody running it but us! <u>Nobody!</u>. . . . . The Los Angeles revue moves on. They phoned and wired me to come back to work, but by now evidently realize I am laid low. I'll have some material in it, tho, no doubt. My "Mad Scene from Woolworth's" they seem to love. Also "Hollywood Mammy". . . . Well more next time. Write soon. Love, Langston

TO ARTHUR SPINGARN   [ALS]

[On Hollow Hills Farm, (Carmel Valley) Jamesburg Route,
Monterey, California *stationery]*

Peninsula Hospital,
Carmel, California,
January 30, 1941.

Dear Arthur Spingarn,

Thank you so much for your note. In it you said you had just come from the hospital. Strangely enough, the next day I went to the hospital—where I have been until now—flat on my back until this week when I have been getting up a little every day! I expect to go home, back to the farm tomorrow. New Year's Day I took the flu. Being worried about my work in Los Angeles on a show, and little bills that needed to be met the first of the year, I guess I got up too soon. Anyway, an attack of acute arthritis laid me low so I could hardly move for 2 weeks—so here I am. But delighted to be leaving this week—altho I guess I'll be two or three weeks really getting back to myself. And will stay here in the country.

Let us do no more about the poem.* Knopf's lawyer took it up, but decided to let it all drop, except to publicize my statement.

---

* Hughes had sought legal advice regarding a possible lawsuit against *The Saturday Evening Post* for its unauthorized publication of his radical poem "Goodbye Christ" on December 21, 1940. An attorney for Knopf advised against pursuing a lawsuit, and Hughes dropped the idea.

In May I shall have a new book of poems, "Shakespeare In Harlem," on the folk and lighter side.

This June will be <u>twenty</u> years since my "Negro Speaks of Rivers" appeared in the <u>Crisis</u>. I want to do something very special for the "The Crisis"—a poem or article, for that issue. It is really 20 years of my creative career since that was my first published poem. My best to you and your wife.

Sincerely, Langston

TO RICHARD WRIGHT   [TLS]

[On Hollow Hills Farm, (Carmel Valley) Jamesburg Route,
Monterey, California stationery]

February 15, 1941.

Dear Dick,

Delighted with the fact that the Spingarn Medal* goes to you this year! Your statement to the press in acceptance was very well said indeed . . . . . . I've meant to thank you for a long time for sending me HOW BIGGER WAS BORN,† but before the holidays was head over heels in the HTA Negro revue in Los Angeles, writing and re-writing songs and sketches, my own and dozens of others, as they expected to go into rehearsal the first of the year, but (as is usual in show business, left, right, colored, or white, amateur or professional) various hitches developed. I came here for the holidays, got ill with the flu and general disgustedness, got up too soon and had a relapse, went to the hospital and so am just now up and about a bit, but still house-bound. . . . . I was sorry to learn of the downfall of the Playwrights |Negro Playwrights Company|. It takes a terrific amount of money to run a theatre, even an amateur one, let alone professional—and cullud have got no money. This system is hardly designed to let us get much either. So for a real Negro Theatre, looks like we will have to wait until!. . . . . Me I am going back to words on paper and not on the stage. But I wish Ted |Ward| and the rest of you playwrights well. May your dramatization of your book be a wow—as it should be if done well. I hope I'll be East to see it. . . . . Federal Music Project's combined white and

* Joel Spingarn, then chairman of the NAACP, created the Spingarn Medal in 1914. Since then, the NAACP has awarded this gold medal annually (with the exception of 1938) to a distinguished African American. Wright received the award in 1941.
† Wright had given Hughes a copy of "How 'Bigger' Was Born; the Story of <i>Native Son</i>" (Harper & Brothers, 1940), a pamphlet based on his lecture on March 12, 1940, at Columbia University. Subsequent editions of <i>Native Son</i> included this essay.

color units are doing mine and Still's opera, TROUBLED ISLAND, about the Haitian slave revolts, in Los Angeles in April, chorus of a hundred, orchestra of seventy, Still himself conducting.* With all those voices, they ought to sing up a breeze.

Best to you,

Sincerely,
Langston

TO MAXIM LIEBER   [TL]

Hollow Hills Farm,
Monterey, California,
April 23, 1941.

Dear Maxim,

Metabolism intact. Merely success deferred. None of my material is committed to anybody since we have no contract with HTA and they never made up their minds what they wanted to use of mine or made any arrangements with you or I about using it. And as you can see from the enclosed letter, it looks like they'll just about never have a show now, at least, not a professional one, if any. So from that standpoint, I think we can feel quite free to peddle the stuff elsewhere. As to the few sketches in which Charlie Leonard is involved, I have just written him asking him to permit you to offer them for sale, and I am sure he will be willing to do so. However, there |are| only one or two such sketches, the main ones being YOUNG BLACK JOE which Leonard sometime ago gave me permission to peddle elsewhere as HTA turned it down during their last committee change. So that one is clear. He has an interest in the sketch part <u>only</u> of MAD SCENE FROM WOOLWORTH'S, the lyric and the song being mine with music by Elliot Carpenter.† And I gather he is as anxious as I am to dispose of that material now. In case you would care to write him for confirmation yourself, his address is: Charles Leonard, 326 North Kilkea, Los Angeles, California.

Now, as to MOE GALE and the radio business.‡ I would be delighted to

---

* By 1941, the Federal Music Project (1935–1939) had been restructured as the WPA Music program (1939–1943). The WPA funding was discontinued, and this production of *Troubled Island* did not occur. The opera was not staged until 1949.
† Elliot Carpenter (1894–1982) was an American composer, lyricist, and music arranger.
‡ By June Hughes would learn that Gale could not find a major sponsor for the serialization of *Little Ham*.

come East, of course, if an advance comes forth sufficient to cover the trip. Otherwise, I am pleased to collaborate as best I can from here. You know and I know it is folly to ride any horse too hard until you get the bit in his mouth. The bit is $$$$$, so you have been telling me lo these many years. I begin to believe you. In fact, I go farther: I do believe you. (And I know from experience that $ is the only thing that buys a train ticket.)

Re WHAT THE NEGRO WANTS,* I recall that you used to write me every time I sent you a story that nobody would publish nary a one of them but THE NEW MASSES. And it turned out that they never saw one to publish because YOU always sold them elsewhere. So?

Next time I go to China Town I will send you a Chinese puzzle and you will see how delightful and simple they are to work compared to getting me into show business.

The government, thank God, helps out farmers, but nobody cares about playwrights. From now on I write dramatic monologues and deliver them myself under my own direction. Since you have never seen a show of mine, I will come down and give one in your office.

Metabolism intact, Jack.

Sincerely, as ever,
KINDLY RETURN ENCLOSURE.

TO ALFRED AND BLANCHE KNOPF [ALS]

Dear Alfred and Blanche,
This June marks for me twenty years of publication†—largely thanks to you as my publishers. With my continued gratitude and affection, as ever,

Sincerely,
Langston

Hollow Hills, May 17, 1941.

* In his essay "What the Negro Wants," Hughes identified seven things that Negroes wanted: the chance to earn a decent living; decent housing; equal educational opportunities; participation in government; fairness under the law; common courtesy; and social equality—the end of Jim Crow. Louis Adamic (1899–1951) published the essay in his new magazine *Common Ground*, which was devoted to questions about multiracial and immigrant cultures. It appeared in the Autumn 1941 issue.
† Hughes dated his career as a writer from the appearance of "The Negro Speaks of Rivers" in *The Crisis* in June 1921.

TO CARL VAN VECHTEN [*TLS*]

Hollow Hills Farm,
Monterey, California,
June 21 |22|, 1941.

Dear Carlo,

We had a very pleasant visit yesterday from Henry Miller* at luncheon. He
drove up from Hollywood with Mr. and Mrs. Gilbert Neiman.† It turned out
that Mr. Neiman has translated for NEW DIRECTIONS the same play that I
did, Lorca's BLOOD WEDDING. Henry is going to see the Jeffers today. He
says he is tired of his trip and thinking of giving it up and living out here in
California which he likes a great deal. . . . . Noël and I are delighted to hear
that Fania is arriving and we very much hope she will pay the Carmel Valley
a visit. I shall write her a note today. . . . . Judith Anderson‡ is appearing at the
Del Monte summer theatre in FAMILY PORTRAIT.§ And on the week-end of
the 4th in the Forest Theatre in Carmel in Jeffers' TOWER BEYOND TRAG-
EDY.¶ I have to read it today and do a publicity piece for the PINE CONE.** I
never was much for such long poems, so I thought I would write a few letters
first. . . . . I am so sorry to hear about Elmer Imes.†† It seems that my brother
|Gwyn Clark| is in the hospital on Welfare Island‡‡ with what he says is pleu-

---

* The American writer Henry Miller (1891–1980) is most famous for his sexually explicit
novels *Tropic of Cancer* (1934) and *Tropic of Capricorn* (1939), published in Paris where
Miller had been living. He spent three years touring the United States, gathering material
for his nonfiction book *The Air-Conditioned Nightmare* (1945). During this trip Miller met
Hughes and first saw the scenic Big Sur region (which starts about twenty-five miles south
of Carmel). He would later settle there.
† Gilbert and Margaret Neiman were friends of Henry Miller who moved to Big Sur in
1945 and lived next door to Miller at Anderson Creek. New Directions published Neiman's
translation of *Blood Wedding* in 1939. Hughes translated *Blood Wedding* in 1938, but his
version would not be published until 1994, after his death (see also letter dated August
30, 1938).
‡ Judith Anderson (1897–1992) was an Australian stage and screen actress who enjoyed
success on Broadway and in Hollywood from the 1930s through the 1950s. Anderson was
married to Noël Sullivan's Berkeley friend Ben Lehman from 1937 to 1939.
§ The 1939 Broadway production of the drama *Family Portrait* (1939) by Lenore Coffee and
William Joyce Cowen starred Judith Anderson.
¶ Based on Aeschylus's *Oresteia*, Robinson Jeffers's poetic drama *Tower Beyond Tragedy*
was staged in Carmel with Judith Anderson as Clytemnestra.
** Founded in 1915, *The Carmel Pine Cone* is a local weekly newspaper.
†† Once married to Nella Larsen, Elmer Imes (1883–1941), a research scientist, was one
of the first African Americans to earn a Ph.D. in physics. He died from throat cancer on
September 11, 1941.
‡‡ Welfare Island, in the East River of New York City, has been known as Roosevelt Island
since 1973.

risy. . . . . Tuesday I am going up to San Francisco to see CABIN IN THE SKY* and CITIZEN CANE.† Certainly I agree with you about Ethel Waters, and hope to do ballads about her and Mrs. Bethune, too. That you liked the BAL-LAD OF BOOKER T.‡ and the article makes me very happy. . . . . Of course I will sign all the things you have unsigned when I come East in a month or so. What a wonderful title you have given the Yale collection and what a great compliment to Jim Johnson!§ I know it will furnish the basis for a collection that will grow and grow. And it must have many items in it that are unique of their kind. . . . . Did I tell you I had a card from Nora Holt who expects to go East soon to spend the summer with a niece in Washington, D.C.?. . . . . And when last I saw Mrs. Blanchard¶ she was thinking of going to Michigan again . . . . . . When is Barthe** coming out? And has Dorothy |Peterson| sailed for Puerto Rico yet?. . . . . She won't answer letters!. . . . . Well, I have just heard Churchill's speech from London.†† And I do declare! All of which will no doubt make the Communist Party change its line again. Strange bedfellows! But it's more like Ringling's flying trapezes. Will Muriel go all out for Britain now and she and Noël make their ideological peace?‡‡ Will the Red Cross start

---

* The all-black musical *Cabin in the Sky* by Lynn Root (book), John La Touche (lyrics), and Vernon Duke (music) opened on Broadway in 1940, and then went on a tour that ended in Los Angeles in 1941. A film version directed by Vincente Minnelli and starring Ethel Waters, Eddie "Rochester" Anderson, and Lena Horne was released in 1943.
† The masterpiece *Citizen Kane* (1941) was the first feature film directed by Orson Welles (1915–1985), who also produced it, starred in it, and cowrote the screenplay.
‡ Hughes's "Ballad of Booker T." (about Booker T. Washington) was published in *Southern Frontier* (July 1941) and *Common Sense Historical Review* (May 1953).
§ In 1941, Carl Van Vechten founded the James Weldon Johnson Memorial Collection of Negro Arts and Letters at Yale University (it opened formally in 1950). Johnson, one of Van Vechten's dearest friends, died in 1938 when a train struck his car near his summer home in Maine. Hughes agreed at once to donate all of his papers, including his correspondence, to the JWJ Collection at Yale. Over the years until his death, he regularly sent batches of material to Yale.
¶ Van Vechten's cousin Mary Blanchard (Mrs. Frederic Mason Blanchard) was then living in Carmel.
** Richmond Barthé (1901–1989) was a well-known African American sculptor. The Whitney Museum of American Art bought his sculptures *Blackberry Woman* (1932) and *African Dancer* (1933).
†† Presumably Hughes refers to the June 22, 1941, radio address by Winston Churchill about the German invasion of the Soviet Union, in which Churchill said that "[t]he Russian danger therefore is our danger and the danger of the United States, just as the cause of any Russian fighting for his hearth and home is the cause of free men and free people in every quarter of the globe."
‡‡ The poet Muriel Rukeyser (1913–1980) had met Sullivan a number of times in the San Francisco area. Sullivan was not sympathetic to the radical left, and in a letter to Ella Winter he strongly criticized Rukeyser after he heard that she had written in favor of the Soviet invasion of Finland.

sponsoring Sacks For The Soviets as well as Bundles for Britain? I'm glad I'm
a lyric poet. It might be interesting to search for new rhymes for moon and
June as the old ones have been worn out . . . . . . I hear the lunch bell, so,

Sincerely,

Langston

TO PAUL ROBESON [TL]

Hollow Hills Farm,
Monterey, California,
September 18, 1941.
(Clark Hotel, L. A.)*

Dear Paul,

Charles Leonard and I have just had quite a conference with Harold Clur-
man, producer at Columbia, and John Marc, head of the story department|,|
who have expressed interest in doing a picture with you as star. Leonard and
I worked out several ideas for such a picture, but the one which seems to all
of us most entertaining and most "commercial", built around a series of situations which could in no sense affront even the Solid South is, briefly, this:

> The story of a great Negro singer (yourself, renamed) who wearies of
> the hub-bub of public life, and the trials and tribulations of an eccen-
> tric manager, gets a chance to return to the simple life when his best
> friend of childhood days, a Pullman porter, takes ill, is afraid if he
> misses his run he will lose his job, and so the singer (who greatly
> resembles the porter) agrees to substitute for him on the train. The
> main body of the picture would take place on the train, the complica-
> tions of a porter's life on a crack express, the assortment of passen-
> gers (a la Grand Hotel), the children traveling alone for whom the
> porter cares, who get lost and wander into town at one of the stations,
> the porter's chase through the city to gather them up, the beautiful
> Negro maid traveling with a wealthy family with whom he falls in love,
> the Pullman Porters' Quartette who, amazed at his fine voice, take

---

* After visiting Phoenix in August, Hughes returned the following month to Los Angeles
to try yet again to break into the highly segregated Hollywood screen industry. Failing
again, he retreated to Carmel.

up a collection to further his musical education, etc., etc. ending in the star's manager himself getting on the train, and the attempt to hide from him who he really is. . . . . The whole, of course, to be tied together with a sound plot providing natural opportunities for song, and possibly ending with the appearance of the "porter" as himself, the singer, in the Hollywood Bowl.

This is, as you see, an idea at the moment, not a story. An idea based on the old "masquerade" theme with all the light and humorous implications it implies. In discussing this, Mr. Clurman felt that it might be better to not start as we had planned with the singer already famous, but to start instead at an early stage of his career, and build him up from there—keeping, however, the Pullman porter angle—which all concerned felt would be an acceptable and "natural" situation which the American public would accept and which lends itself to a mixed cast picture—not <u>all-Negro</u>—as the studios are wary of the latter.

Now, the studio likes the above embryo idea. As a first step before any of us go further with it, they wish to know whether or not you approve of it in general. And specifically, if so, which of the two ways of developing it seems best to you:

1. The famous singer pretending to be a porter.
2. The unknown singer as a porter working up.

In other words, do you like the general idea? Which form? A note from you on this would help Clurman to make up his mind, and to give us the go-ahead signal to develop a definite story based on the above material. Would you be so kind as to write or wire Charles Leonard, Columbia Studios, Sunset and Gower, Hollywood, at once. (Or to his home address during the weekend: 326 North Kilkea, Los Angeles, California.)

I'd love to work on a picture with you.*

Sincerely,
Langston Hughes

---

* Eslanda "Essie" Robeson responded on October 6 that "Paul was nervous of the rags to riches idea" and wondered if the hero could not be a worker. She continued, "What Paul really wants . . . is an American picture not built around him, . . . like, say *Grapes of Wrath*." Nothing came of the film project.

TO CARL VAN VECHTEN   [*TLS*]

Dear Carlo,

Thanks for your delightfully long letter and all the nice compliments and advice. I agree with you about the second part of The Big Sea. Only I don't want it to get so weighty that it weighs me down, too.*

|Richmond| Barthé left Los Angeles Thursday for Chicago. We enjoyed his visit greatly here. But I didn't report it in more detail because nobody got cut, and it was just a pleasant quiet time, with some dinner parties, and teas, and cocktails. And Ethel Waters came by one Sunday morning for breakfast with Archie† and a car full and Noël |Sullivan| took them all to call on Mrs. Blanchard.

It was too bad Eulah and I didn't get around to having our colored party while Barthé was here. (Eulah Pharr is Noël's housekeeper, and a very charming person who's been with him for twelve years or more.) But we had it Thursday, cocktails 3 - 6, except that it lasted from 3 to 3 in the morning—and nobody made a move to go home before midnight, and then didn't go. The joint jumped. We had about 50. And played plenty Lil Green.‡ Everybody was dressed down, and most proper in a gay manner, and nobody got too high or anything, except one girl got mad when she heard her soldier boy intended to take another girl home, so she simply pulled all the wires out of his car so it wouldn't budge—which left him and six other members of Uncle Sam's citizen army stranded out here in the country, and they had to be taken back to Fort Ord in our station wagon just in time to hear "reverie" blow in the morning.

Your paragraph on the art of illustration was most interesting. And I am sure the Kauffer drawings are charming.§ But still, if they come out with <u>NO</u> hair on their heads—after all the millions that have been spent with Madame

---

* Van Vechten had advised Hughes in his letter of November 4 that "the second volume of your life will have to be more weighty than the first. It should, I think, seriously discuss the plight of the Negro (and the hopes) in modern America."
† Probably Archie Savage (1914–2003), an African American dancer who had appeared with Ethel Waters in the touring production of the musical *Cabin in the Sky*. In 1944, he was convicted of stealing from Ethel Waters.
‡ Lil Green (1919–1954) was an African American blues singer and songwriter.
§ Blanche Knopf had selected E. McKnight Kauffer (1890–1954) to illustrate *Shakespeare in Harlem*. Her choice distressed Hughes because the black people in Kauffer's ten sample sketches all had unstraightened or "nappy" hair, which was then unfashionable in the community.

Hughes objected to E. Kauffer McKnight's sketches used by Knopf to illustrate *Shakespeare in Harlem*. These illustrations by McKnight appear, respectively, opposite the poems "50-50," "Shakespeare in Harlem," and "Southern Mammy Sings."

Walker and Mr. Murray[*]—my Negro public—whom I respect and like—will not be appreciative. I wrote as much to Blanche |Knopf| when I first saw the samples. Harlem just isn't nappy headed any more—except for the first ten minutes after the hair is washed. Following that the sheen equals Valentino's and the page boy bobs are as long as Lana Turner's.[†] And colored folks don't want no stuff out of an illustrator on that score. Even Lil Green has finger waves. And if some of the ladies in SHAKESPEARE IN HARLEM don't have them, too, I will catch hell—in spite of whatever "strictly, personal illumination emanates from the painter." Do you get me?

I'm sure Henrietta Bruce Sharon is white.[‡] But since I couldn't swear it, I've asked Arna |Bontemps| to let you know. (But she draws heads and feet as if she were.)

Duke's I GOT IT BAD is good. But unfortunately the words aren't mine. They're by Paul Webster, the white chap who wrote most of the show.[§]

* Madame C. J. Walker developed a line of hair-care products aimed mainly at black women. Murray's Pomade was popular among black men.
† Rudolph Valentino (1895–1926) and Lana Turner (1921–1995) were Hollywood stars.
‡ Henrietta Bruce Sharon illustrated Arna Bontemps's anthology *Golden Slippers* (1941). She was indeed white, as Hughes surmises in his letter.
§ Duke Ellington's show *Jump for Joy* grew from the "Negro Revue" Hughes had worked on for the Hollywood Theatre Alliance. Opening on July 10, 1941, in Los Angeles at the Mayan Theater, *Jump for Joy* ran for 122 performances. The hit song "I Got It Bad (and That Ain't Good)," with music by Ellington and lyrics by Paul Webster (1907–1984), originated in this revue.

No, Mamie Smith* didn't get her throat cut. She just lost her contract.

Why, I will tell you when I see you. (Leaving space at the bottom of this here letter for annotation.)

I am now on my way to hear Lotte Lehman sing.†

Ere I lay me down in questa tomba obscura I shall try to find all your letters for Yale, but they are in so many various files, boxes, suitcases, and trunks stored from here to yonder that I shall start here to finding recent ones tomorrow.

To whom are you giving your Mary Bell's?‡

The blues seem to be coming back in a big way. Every club out here now has a blues singer as a part of the floor show. And Joe Turner§ was the hit of the recent Duke show, pulling it out of polite prettiness.

Did I tell you I did a libretto of THE ST LOUIS BLUES for Katherine Dunham, a danceable story woven around the song?¶ Hope she uses it. But she rather thinks she ought to do Latin American things—Cuba, Brazil, etc. Easier to sell to concert managers and Hollywood.

So,

Sincerely,

Langston

< November 8, 1941>

---

* On August 10, 1920, Mamie Smith (1883–1946) became the first black vocalist to record a blues song. Her recording, "Crazy Blues," is said to have sold 75,000 copies within a month.

† Fleeing the Nazis, the German opera singer Lotte Lehmann (1888–1976) immigrated to the United States in 1938. She sang at the San Francisco Opera and at the Metropolitan Opera until 1945. Her last public recital was in 1951.

‡ Hughes refers to letters between the African American artist Mary Bell (1873–1941) and Carl Van Vechten. The letters are in the James Weldon Johnson Memorial Collection in the Beinecke Library at Yale University.

§ The great blues shouter Big Joe Turner (1911–1985) went to Hollywood in 1941 as a performer in Duke Ellington's *Jump for Joy* revue.

¶ Katherine Dunham (1909–2006), a noted dancer and choreographer, blended traditional ballet and modern dance techniques with African and Caribbean styles. Dunham founded the Negro Dance Group in Chicago in 1937, then moved her company to New York City in 1939. Hughes's first draft of the libretto for "St. Louis Blues" is dated September 10, 1941. He outlined four potential ballet scenarios for Dunham.

With his Aunt Ethel Dudley "Toy" Harper,
1944. Photograph by Marion Palfi

You say I O.K.ed
LONG DISTANCE?
O.K.ed it when?
My Goodness, Central,
That was *then*!
—"MADAM AND THE PHONE BILL," 1949

In 1941, Hughes finally settled down in Harlem. Moving in with
Emerson and Toy Harper, he would live with them for the rest of his
life. First he shared their cramped apartment at 634 St. Nicholas Avenue, and later they lived together at 20 East 127th Street. In the early
1940s, he created two of his most memorable characters. Starting in

1943, the genial Jesse B. Semple, or "Simple," became a stellar feature in his column for *The Chicago Defender* (and later in his column for the *New York Post*). Around the same time, Alberta K. Johnson, or "Madam," showed up in a number of poems. World War II and the civil rights struggle shaped much of Hughes's work in this period. He strongly advocated what was called the "Double V" strategy—victory over Hitler abroad and victory over Jim Crow at home. *Jim Crow's Last Stand*, a pamphlet that contains many of his poems about race and the war, was published in 1943.

TO NOËL SULLIVAN   [*TLS*]

Bill of Rights Day,
December 15, 1941,
Chicago, Illinois.*

Dear Noël,

As usual there is so much I would like to write you about and, as usual, time is flying, flying, and I have got to leave the Rosenwald office where I have been working and go home and pack to take off for New York as my thirty-day ticket is up tomorrow. Really, how time flies!

Your letter came and I was deeply distressed to learn the sad news of your sister's illness. She is a sweet and lovable person whose simple, kind enthusiasm about the little things of life made me warm to her immediately. From the tone of your letter, I am terribly afraid her illness may be the same that took my mother away.† Knowing its inevitable end, the only thing one can do is try to make the final months as comfortable and friendly as possible. And keep loneliness and fear as far away as those things can be kept. Certainly faced with that final limit on time—time that most of us misuse so carelessly and so badly—I can understand the shortcomings that you feel in

---

* Practically broke, Hughes reached Chicago on November 20. Friends there came to his aid. Arna Bontemps arranged for him to stay at no charge at the Good Shepherd Community Center, while Arna's wife, Alberta, offered to feed him. The Rosenwald Fund, from which Hughes had received a $1,500 fellowship in June to work on a series of plays about black heroes, lent him an office at its headquarters. Hughes was there when the Japanese attacked Pearl Harbor and the United States went to war. He left Chicago on December 16 to stay with the Harpers in New York before returning to Chicago in mid-February 1942. He remained there until late April.
† Hughes's mother died of cancer.

yourself—although I have found you always the most thoughtful person in all the world to those whom you love. To say what your friendship has meant to me would take more pages than I have ever written in any of my books. The way you stood by me last winter in my various and varied vicissitudes makes me believe in you like the early Christians must have believed in that rock on which the church was founded. (What I am really trying to say is that I know you have within you the strength and love and power to make the coming weeks for your sister full of warmth and affection that will bear her up through days that might, without you, be too full of helplessness and pain.)

My trip East was a pleasant one, and the little surprise of the candy and the book in my bag helped to make it so! That little book was useful in preparing a broadcast which Arna |Bontemps| and I did for Columbia—or rather the portion of a special Bill of Rights SALUTE TO FREEDOM program aired locally here yesterday on which the Governor of Illinois spoke, the Ballad For Americans was sung, and Canada Lee of NATIVE SON* did our portion—a short sketch of contributions of Negroes to American life based largely on the lives of W. C. Handy and George Washington Carver,† both sons of slaves, who came up—thanks to the positive side of American democracy—to positions of eminence and usefulness in our commonwealth. They point the way toward ever greater fulfillment of the American dream. Ending with my poem, "I'm making a road . . . . . ." done with very stirring background music. It was quite a thrilling broadcast with many soldiers and sailors in the audience.

Jake Weinstein was there, too. The Caytons (my hosts) and I had dinner with them,‡ and spoke much of you. I read my poems to a group of young folks from his temple for which they sent me a check for $35.00 and a most beautiful letter. Miss Carr§ of Hull House (who succeeded Jane Addams) was there, and invited me to come and live at Hull House and write whenever I

---

* The actor Canada Lee, born Lionel Cornelius Canegata (1907–1952), had starred as Bigger Thomas in Orson Welles's Broadway staging of *Native Son*. During Hughes's stay in Chicago, Hughes and Bontemps collaborated on a special "Bill of Rights Salute to Freedom" show. Lee read their script on black achievement to an audience that included soldiers, sailors, and the governor of Illinois.
† The agricultural scientist George Washington Carver (c. 1864–1943) of Tuskegee Institute created hundreds of food products from peanuts, sweet potatoes, and other native Southern plants. He was widely recognized for his contributions to the economy of the region.
‡ That December, Hughes spoke against racism to a youth group in Chicago from the KAM Temple of Rabbi Jacob Weinstein, whom he had met previously in California. A sociologist, Horace R. Cayton, Jr. (1903–1970), and his wife, Irma, ran the Good Shepherd Community Center in Chicago, known as "the world's largest Negro settlement house."
§ Charlotte E. Carr (1890–1956) was the director of Hull House from 1937 to 1943, during which time she encouraged the organization to address the needs of African Americans.

might wish. She is an amazingly vital and amusing Irish woman—a physically bigger edition of Una |Jeffers|.

I hope things came out all right with Lee |Crowe|. Did they? He had so looked forward to these holidays with his parents.

How much I am regretting not being in California these days. The papers here have much about the blackouts and alarms there. But perhaps New York will be equally exciting and live. I will let you know. We were all certainly shocked here last Sunday by the Japanese attack. But Chicago life still goes on just about the same. Except that around the corner from the Community House where I'm staying the police closed up a Japanese restaurant the night war was announced—but it has since reopened. It was a mistake—the owner being not Japanese—but Chinese!. . . . . Has there been many mix-ups of the sort on the coast? I imagine so. They say all the Orientals here on the University of Chicago campus have been asked to wear buttons identifying their nationality so that the Siamese and others be not taken for the enemy. The American born Japs wear American flags. . . . . What is happening to poor Ota?* Let me know.

And how is Eulah |Pharr|? I hope better.

BE SURE AND READ in this month's POETRY (December) a review of Jeffers' book by Stanley Kunitz under the title, "The Day Is A Poem."† It says very clearly some of the things we had been thinking and worrying about, and is a clearer analysis of his work than any of us arrived at, I believe.

Marius' letter!‡ Well, I guess he won't be getting out now! Not right away.

I'm sending you under separate cover, along with some clippings and things, a copy of a letter from George Ficke§ in exchange.

Thanks a lot for the snap shots from |Richmond| Barthé. A young Negro photographer here has just taken some excellent pictures of me (if a bit surrealiste). I'm sending you copies.

I'm glad Tony is back helping you. My mail has piled up like a mountain since I've been here. I've been devoting my days to creation, however, working at the Rosenwald Fund where they have qui<et> and delightful rooms to work in. Arna |Bontemps|'s office is just down the hall. He sends his best to you.

I saw a most amusing dog-stocking for the Christmas tree for Joel and

---

* Possibly a Japanese American employed by Noël Sullivan.

† In his book *Be Angry at the Sun* (1941), Robinson Jeffers argued against American involvement in World War II.

‡ Apparently a reference to a Selective Service letter received by someone Hughes and Sullivan knew.

§ George Ficke, a pianist, was a friend of Noël Sullivan and a member of the Carmel community.

Greta and the puppies so I sent it on out to them then and there. I trust it's reached the farm by now. How I hated to leave Hollow Hills! And I hope it will not be too long before I may return. And remember, if ever you need me let me know, and I'll be there! My plans now call for my return to Chicago for a program in February and the try-out of the first of my Fellowship playlets which I have almost finished while here this time.* The Chicago papers (even Hearst) have interviewed me and been most cordial in their write-ups so I have offers for more lectures here after the New Year. My book |Shakespeare in Harlem| comes out Feb. 16 and CBS is arranging a broadcast from here then, too. I'll let you know the day and hour. Over OF MEN AND BOOKS where I appeared before, the Northwestern University program.†

But until further notice, write me c/o my aunt, MRS. TOY HARPER, 634 St. Nicholas Avenue, New York. And ask Eulah to forward mail there. And would you be so good (since I neglected to do it) |as to| write for me on the enclosed post card the addresses I wanted for Christmas and mail it back. (This so you won't have that "I must write a letter" feeling, too.) But when you do have a chance to write, tell me all the news. <E>specially about the blackouts. (Better disconnect the little lighthouse lest some unwitting guest turn it on!)

My love to Marie |Short|. And the Jeffers.

Affectionately,

Langston

TO MAXIM LIEBER   [TL]

634 St. Nicholas Avenue,

New York, New York,

January 27, 1942.

Dear Maxim,

Mr. William Alexander of the Office of Civilian Defense, who flew over from Washington the other day to see me and bought me a whiskey sour and flew

---

* As part of his Rosenwald Fund fellowship project, Hughes wrote *The Sun Do Move*, a play based on one of the most storied sermons in the black religious tradition. The play tells the story of Rock, a slave who is sold away from his wife and son. The Skyloft Players, a drama group Hughes founded in 1941 at the Good Shepherd Community Center, launched *The Sun Do Move* before an enthusiastic house on April 24, 1942. The play ran twice a week through May.

† Northwestern University in Evanston, Illinois, hosted a weekly radio program called *Of Men and Books*, which was broadcast nationally by CBS.

right back, said that the government had no money with which to pay writers for scripts for the program "KEEP 'EM ROLLING"* and that all talent and writing services were being donated. So I said that was all very well to ask Mr. Norman Corwin† who makes a couple of thousand or so a week or more to donate a script—but that Negro writers made no such sums from radio, nor seldom if ever had commercial bids—though they wrote like Bernard Shaw, and that it would take a week out of my life to do what he requested; and that furthermore Negroes were never asked to write anything except when a segregated all-Negro program was coming up. Anyhow, I agreed to do it—since he thought it would help win the war—and God knows we better win it before Hitler gets over here to aid in the lynchings! So I posted him Saturday an eight page script called BROTHERS written to his and Mr. Bernard Schoenfeld's specifications to suit the actors they have in mind—Rex Ingram and Canada Lee—and designed to aid in building civilian morale by presenting (and solving in favor of national unity) some of the problems troubling the minds of Negroes today in relation to the war, ending up with a strong argument as to why we must all get together and beat the pants off Hitler. I hope they will like it.‡

I also sent them a copy of mine and Margaret Bonds' song, THE NEGRO SPEAKS OF RIVERS, which is most suitable to a Lincoln Birthday program. Tomorrow I am seeing Eric Bernays§ regarding a recording of this song along with our AMERICA'S YOUNG BLACK JOE on the other side. And Robins about publishing it.

I am anxious to know who is in charge of the "KEEP 'EM ROLLING" program here in New York, so that I might confer with them regarding these things.

---

* *Keep 'Em Rolling* was a radio series organized by the Office of Civilian Defense to boost public morale. Hughes agreed to write a script for a program celebrating the birthday of President Lincoln. Following guidelines from the screenwriter Bernard Schoenfeld (1907–1990?), Hughes wrote an eight-page script called "Brothers," with parts intended for actors Rex Ingram and Canada Lee. "Brothers" tells the story of a black soldier returning home from duty in a convoy.
† Norman Corwin (1910–2011) was a highly successful writer and director of radio drama during the 1930s and 1940s.
‡ In "Brothers," Hughes wrote boldly about racial segregation and explicitly applied the much discussed "Four Freedoms" recently identified by President Roosevelt to the issue. The Office of Civilian Defense rejected "Brothers" as being too controversial for airing.
§ Eric Bernays (1894–1949) owned a midtown Manhattan record store and an independent record label, Keynote. As the business manager of *The New Masses*, he had played a key role in organizing a successful show on black music called "From Spirituals to Swing" at Carnegie Hall a few years earlier. Also involved in left-wing politics, he produced *Talking Union*, a recording by the Almanac Singers in 1941.

Also is there any chance of getting a PAYING script to do—since the government seems to think I write well enough to help build civilian morale? Lemme know.

Best to you, Max,

Sincerely,

Langston Hughes

TO NOËL SULLIVAN [TLS]

Yaddo,*

Saratoga Springs, N. Y.,

August 5, 1942.

Dear Noël,

Here I am at Yaddo, the old Trask-Peabody seven-hundred acre estate with rose gardens, rock gardens, fountains, statues, two lakes, and a couple of dozen studios scattered about in the woods. But only ONE dog on the whole place—a little cocker spaniel named Brownie.

My studio is way way back in the woods and so surrounded by trees and vines that you can't see anything inside even in the morning without turning on the lights. Someone must've told them I like to work at night so I think they must be trying to provide the atmosphere. There is a rule that nobody can visit anybody else's studio—in fact, not even walk down their path—so there is plenty of peace and quiet. (I hope not too much for creative well-being.) But at least—and at last—I'm getting a letter or two written!

I found Nathaniel Dett† here and he spoke of once having stopped at your place, but regretted not having met you at the time. There are none others of the Race. But a most beautiful Chinese girl, a Miss Kuo,‡ arrived this morning. Besides Dett only one person I've met before is here, a Polish refugee writer I'd known in Madrid slightly, but whose name I can't spell. Carson

---

* Yaddo is an artists' colony in Saratoga Springs, New York, founded in 1900 by the financier Spencer Trask (1844–1909) and his wife, Katrina Trask (1853–1922), a poet. Hughes, Yaddo's first black writer, arrived on August 4 and stayed for three and a half months.

† The black musicologist R. Nathaniel Dett (1882–1943) was director of music at Hampton Institute in Virginia from 1913 to 1931. He led its renowned choir on tours of the United States and Europe.

‡ Helena G. C. Kuo (1911–1999) was a Chinese journalist and writer who had moved to the United States in 1939. She published her first book, *Peach Path* (London: Methuen), in 1940.

McCullers is here.* And Kenneth Fearing.† And Leonard Ehrlich who wrote the novel about John Brown, GOD'S ANGRY MAN.‡ But most of the others are names unknown to me—a young poet from Denver who used to play in a college jazz band and so enlivens the very stately music room every night by beating it out on the grand piano; a couple of handsome Mediterranean-looking boys who paint Picasso-like pictures with the eye at one corner of the canvas and the mouth at the other upside down; a lady short-story writer; a Czech composer; a couple of literary essayists; and a few husbands and wives. Everybody is most congenial and it looks as though it is going to be fun. I'm here for six weeks, until September 10, so I'll write you more later.

New York has made me mighty near as thin |as| Ramon§—who, by the way, is in New York, but I didn't see him. The last few days there were most hectic, what with the MARCH OF TIME¶ using my song on their program and the publicity, interviews, and excitement on the part of the publishers who are rushing to get the music out and orchestrations made. Since Kenneth Spencer introduced the number, I think his picture is going to be on it. (He's leaving for SHOW BOAT in St. Louis this week, then on to the coast for CABIN IN THE SKY in the films.)** The colored army band in Harlem is making a 70 piece orchestration to play in parades, the Treasury Star Parade†† has made a transcription for the air, and this Saturday it will be sung at the big Navy Relief Program. So it looks like FREEDOM ROAD might just maybe catch on—and make my fare back to the coast for me. (HOPE SO.)

Another song my Aunt and Uncle and I wrote, THAT EAGLE,‡‡ I think

---

* The Southern writer Carson McCullers (1917–1967) became Hughes's best friend at Yaddo. Her acclaimed first book *The Heart Is a Lonely Hunter* appeared from Houghton Mifflin in 1940.

† The American writer Kenneth Fearing (1902–1961) published several collections of poetry including *Angel Arms* (1929) and *Afternoon of a Pawnbroker* (1943), as well as seven novels.

‡ Leonard Ehrlich (1905–1984) was the author of *God's Angry Man* (Simon & Schuster, 1932), about the radical abolitionist John Brown.

§ Hughes met the actor Ramón Novarro (1899–1968) in San Francisco in May 1932 when the two men were houseguests of Noël Sullivan.

¶ *The March of Time* was a radio series broadcast on CBS from 1931 to 1945. When Hughes's song "Freedom Road" aired, he took part in the broadcast and endorsed the war.

** Kenneth Spencer first performed the song "Freedom Road" during a program at Café Society in New York. He played a supporting role in the film *Cabin in the Sky* (1943) and a leading role in the acclaimed 1946 Broadway revival of *Show Boat*.

†† *The Treasury Star Parade* was the U.S. Treasury Department's thrice-weekly radio program that promoted the sale of war bonds. Hughes's song "Freedom Road," cowritten with his "uncle" Emerson Harper, had also aired on this program.

‡‡ Hughes collaborated with Toy and Emerson Harper on the song "That Eagle of the U.S.A." It was first performed by the African American actor Rosetta LeNoire (1911–2002) at the Stage Door Canteen in New York.

will be in the new Stage Door Canteen show—where I am now a bus boy every Sunday night. The Canteen is really a wonderful place—what the USO Centers <u>ought</u> to be. Fania |Marinoff| and others on the board have insisted that there be no color line—and there isn't. Soldiers and sailors of all the United Nations—black and white—come and eat and dance and get along fine—not even a fight so far in all the months they've been running. Jane, Walter White's daughter, Dorothy Peterson, and others act as hostesses—Blanche Dunn, too.

Give my best to Lee |Crowe| and tell him to write me once in a blue moon. And to Marie |Short| my love—and a letter <u>soon</u>. (Now that I have peace and quiet once again.) After song-writing, it's wonderful! . . . . . . Affectionately,

Langston

<P. S.—(over)>

P.S. I didn't know I was to be on the MARCH OF TIME program until the morning of the broadcast—and it being Thursday I wasn't sure you'd be at the Farm, so sent a wire to either you or Eulah |Pharr| so she could phone you in town in case you'd have liked to listen in. . . . . Is there a Bach Festival this summer, or has the War affected that, as it has so much in the East?. . . . By the way, lightning struck the Stadium shell the other day and tore it up. Fortunately, it was a couple of hours before a concert, so only one person was hurt. Have you had any news directly from Roland?[*] I very much hope he will no longer live in Georgia. The papers have centered so much interest on him recently—and I hear one wealthy Boston white lady flew down to see the family after the incident—and a number of reporters, I think, went. So I'm afraid the local residents will not be pleased with all that and—sub-normal as they <are>—further physical harm might result.

The position of Negro troops training in the South—many Northern boys who have never been used to such severe and irrational Jim Crow—is very dangerous, so soldiers returning on furloughs say. It seems the lower Southern elements resent colored boys in uniform and so go out of their way often to be rude and unpleasant. This added to the Jim Crow cars and lack of service in diners send the Negro boys back North much madder at the South than they should be at Hitler. Some of the Negro papers are requesting

---

[*] In an incident widely reported, a white clerk had beaten the internationally known concert singer Roland Hayes during a dispute in a shoe store in Georgia. Hughes wrote a poem, "Roland Hayes Beaten," about the episode.

a removal of all colored training units from the South. But it seems to me that would be bad, too, in that it would be an admission on the part of the Government and our War Department that they cannot protect our soldiers in certain parts of our own country. On the other hand, should a major racial clash suddenly break out somewhere down there, look how bad that would be for morale and international relations, too. Just one more complexity to worry about in this troubled world, isn't it?

Did you see Pegler's column on the Negro a few of weeks ago?*

Two or three magazines have asked me for articles on ourselves and the war, but so far the song, FREEDOM ROAD, is the best I could do. We all want to beat Hitler and we all want to march down Freedom Road. But that road will <u>have</u> to run past Roland's farm, too. Else it won't really be going anywhere—for anybody.

L.

TO ARNA BONTEMPS   [TLS]

Yaddo,

Sunday.

Arna, ole man,

Your review in the HERALD TRIBUNE is <u>swell</u>! Everybody up here has read it. . . . . Did I tell you THE SEVENTH CROSS is a |Maxim| Lieber book?† Half the authors up here this summer were his, including |Carson| McCullers, who don't get on with him,,,,,Leonard Ehrlich got his call for a physical. Those who've read parts of his new novel say it is swell. He's been working on it for years, and says he just needs two more months. That's what he said when I first came two months ago, but he still needs two <u>more</u> now. (Which I understand so well.). . . . . Zell Ingram writes from Camp way down in West Texas where he has been sent to train to fight Paratroopers..And a dismal prairie it must be, too. My next door neighbor in New York and college mate was sent to Mississippi. Soon as I get my call I'm going to write all the commanders and boards there |who| are howling about the <u>lack</u> of respect for the uniform in

---

* James Westbrook Pegler (1894–1969) was an influential columnist in the 1930s and early 1940s. His syndicated article "The White Press Is Fair to Negroes" appeared in many papers across the country in mid-June.

† *The Seventh Cross* is a novel by the German author Anna Seghers (1900–1983). An English translation by James Galton was published in 1942.

the South—and that I don't approve! Thought I would just howl about general army segregation on the first paper, and take up segments <i>n later communications. Also probably do a couple of articles in between. . . . . COMMON GROUND took my article on WHAT TO DO ABOUT THE SOUTH. Seems like most of the next issue is devoted to the subject. . . . . According to this poem enclosed, Jim Crow is on his last legs. But I neglect to say those legs are STRONG. Well, you can't put everything in a poem! That is why I also write prose books once in a while. I would be writing one now if I did not stop so often to write poems and songs and letters, etc. . . . . Say, can I get a Chicago lecture around November 20-21? I have one in St. Louis just preceding. But need a couple more out that way to make it really pay. HELP ME!. . . . . . Your friend and admirer,

L. Hughes

IMPORTANT P. S. (Kindly read)
Never did hear from Bush at Good Shepherd |Community Center| about the play, but with my questionnaire and all, and everybody going in the army making a play very hard to cast, probably better not consider our trying to stage (or at least my trying to stage) ST. LOUIS WOMAN this fall in Chicago.*
It would need a lot of people, besides Harvey isn't around to help on the technical end. Heard from him at some Mo. camp way down by Arkansas. Dismal, too, from all I could gather, but I imagine Hitler would put us (all) in sorrier camps than that if he ever got over here. And (all) the guards would be crackers!

---

* The Skyloft Players did not perform *St. Louis Woman*.

TO MARIE SHORT   [*TLS*]

634 St. Nicholas Avenue,
New York, New York,*
November 15, 1942.

Dear Marie,

Looks like if I keep waiting for a chance to write you a <u>long</u> letter, I'll never write any, but I think of you often, and the kids, and wish I could see you-all. In fact, I had expected to come on out that way following my lecture tour this fall—which <is> beginning this coming week in St. Louis—but the draft board says I have to report for induction in January. They gave me a sixty-day deferment since the tour was already mostly booked when I was classified 1-A a couple of weeks ago. Otherwise, I would have been called this past Wednesday. They're working fast these days, trying to clear out their files, I guess, for the 18 year olds. Almost all my friends are in already, or on the verge of going.

I had a delightful summer at Yaddo, but didn't get very far on my book. Wrote a lot of poems, though, and several new songs, and various articles. Did I remember you to say once you'd read Carson McCullers' books? She's still at Yaddo, and is a swell kid, very southern with a drawl, but strange and interesting, and I think a swell writer. Kenneth Fearing was my next door neighbor and a nice guy, too.

They have a wonderful cook at Yaddo, a Hungarian countess or something, I believe, anyway a charming and cultured lady who can cook like two French chefs. When I left, she said, "So, you are going back to Kentucky?" Which amused me no end. It seems that in Buda Pesh she'd always connected colored folks with the song, My Old Kentucky Home! Poor lady, she has not heard from her children since Hitler took over her country.

When I see you I will tell you some very funny stories about Yaddo.

Haven't had a chance to see Elsie |Arden| or Connie here in New York. Had just a week to see the draft board, finish two songs for a picture (I hope) and pack up and get off. Had to do all my booking and letter writing myself this year as everybody that type<s> a line in the East is employed in Washington.

Tell Noël |Sullivan| about my draft status, will you? And that I will write him soon since I won't be able to come on out there as I'd hoped in time for

---

* After Yaddo, Hughes went back to New York City. On November 18, he left on a lecture tour, which included several engagements before military audiences. He returned in early December when summoned by the draft board.

that Thanksgiving or Christmas turkey. But maybe they will send me to Fort Ord. That would be fun!. . . . . The papers say Saroyan[*] is there. I ran into him one night last summer at Cafe Society.[†]

Tell Kraig and Erik those cards they sent me last Christmas were adorable and I've still got them and look at them every so often. Ask Kraig how she likes "MR. FIVE BY FIVE". I do.[‡]

I've written a song you will boo! To be moaned and crooned—MY HEART IS A LONE RANGER with music by Irving Landau of Radio City Music Hall. But I hope Bing Crosby will moan and croon it. You'll like THAT EAGLE, though, the song I had in the Canteen Show, a folk style number about how that mighty bird spreads his wings over you and me.

Tell Bill and John hello when you write.

I felt lousy and sad when I started to write this letter, but writing to you and thinking of you makes me feel better, because I think you are just about one of the swellest persons in the world.

Tell Lee |Crowe| Hy! Tell him Jimmy Daniels is in the army, Tampa, Florida.

See by the papers where the Roland Hayes biography is out.[§] Well reviewed.

Had a very nice letter from Sis about her new baby. Haven't had a chance to answer it yet.

Here's a V for Victory! Let's hurry up and win this here war!

Sincerely,

Langston

---

[*] William Saroyan (1908–1981), a prolific American playwright and fiction writer, was born in Fresno, California, the setting of many of his stories.
[†] Café Society was a New York nightclub opened by Barney Josephson at Sheridan Square in Greenwich Village in 1938 to highlight African American performers. A second club, which became known as Café Society Uptown, was founded in 1940 on Fifty-eighth Street.
[‡] Erik and Kraig were Marie Short's two youngest children. "Mr. Five by Five" was a popular song in 1942 written by Don Raye and Gene de Paul. The inspiration came from Jimmy Rushing, a featured vocalist with Count Basie's orchestra from 1935 to 1948. Rushing was said to be "five foot tall and five foot wide."
[§] MacKinley Helm's biography, *Angel Mo' and Her Son, Roland Hayes,* was published by Little, Brown in 1942.

TO CARL VAN DOREN   [TL]
COPY—<u>NOT</u> FOR PUBLICATION

<Also sent to Arna |Bontemps|
Walter |White|
Yale>
634 St. Nicholas Avenue,
New York, New York,
March 18, 1943.

Mr. Carl Van Doren,*
Red Cross War Fund,
Authors' Division,
41 Central Park West,
New York, New York.

Dear Carl Van Doren,
I have your letter of March 12 in regard to the Red Cross War Fund. As a fellow author I am sure you will understand what I am going to say. When we write, putting down on paper our truest and our best thoughts, we write out of the heart, don't we? Well, I know in my mind that the American Red Cross is a vital and important institution, but in my heart, every time I think about it, I have a sinking feeling.

You know, of course, that I am a Negro. Perhaps you have read in my book, THE BIG SEA, about the summer of 1927 that I spent in the deep South, the summer of the great Mississippi flood. I shall never forget the disgraceful treatment on the part of the Red Cross of the Negro flood refugees in Mississippi which I have described in my book. For further light on this, read William Alexander Percy's LANTERNS ON THE LEVEE† where additional unpleasant facts come through, even from the pen of a dyed in the wool Southerner, as was Mr. Percy.

---

* Carl Van Doren (1885–1950) was editor of *Century* magazine. In 1939 he won the Pulitzer Prize for his biography *Benjamin Franklin*. On March 12, in his role as chairman of the Authors' Division of the Red Cross War Fund, he sent a form letter addressed to "Dear Fellow Author" asking Hughes for a donation. (Apparently, Van Doren did not reply to Hughes's indignant letter.)
† William Alexander Percy (1885–1942) wrote *Lanterns on the Levee: Recollections of a Planter's Son* (Knopf, 1942).

Of course, you know about the outrageous segregation of Negro blood and Negro blood donors in the present Red Cross blood bank set-up. Even the Hearst JOURNAL-AMERICAN in last Sunday's issue devoted a full page to showing how there is no scientific basis at all for distinguishing between bloods of any race and that it could make no possible difference to a wounded soldier whose blood was poured into his veins.*

You probably know further how the Red Cross has carried Dixie patterns of segregation abroad in its setting up of Jim Crow Red Cross Clubs for Negro troops in lands where segregation has hitherto not been the rule. Hitler could hardly desire more. General Douglas MacArthur may be right when he says, "The Red Cross never fails a soldier." Certainly it has failed thirteen million Negroes on the home front, and its racial policies are a blow in the face to American Negro morale.

Sincerely yours,
Langston Hughes

TO ARNA BONTEMPS [TLS]

4/17/43

Dear Arna,

Fate has overtaken me with a heavy foot again. I added up my bank book the other day and found out I had mighty near minus zero. And then when the income tax man told that, not being married and having no dependents, I would have to pay $126.00 tax, I mighty nigh fainted. However, I recovered enough to go home and figure that thing all up again, percentages and all by myself, and got it down to a more sensible figure. But still one that left me ruined and broke in both spirit and finance. So I reckon I can't buy any show tickets for us in advance. And I also reckon I'd better write myself half a hundred lecture letters AT ONCE and prepare to hit the road heavy this spring. (Always something to keep a writer from writing!) Chicago was cancelled. Said they'<d> recently had Horace.† (One Negro a season being enough, I guess. See how the color line hits the lecture business!) But I had already booked Wayne University at Detroit, so have to come out that way anyhow now. Know of any contacts in Evanston or round abouts?

---

* Hughes's poem "Red Cross" also addresses the question of racially segregated blood. It reads: "The Angel of Mercy's / Got her wings in the mud, / And all because of / Negro blood."
† Presumably the sociologist Horace Cayton.

Did you hear the Muni broadcast?* I didn't, at least not very well, being right there in the studio. Sound and singers being on different mikes, you couldn't tell how it sounded as a whole. But it got some good notices in the press next day, so I guess it was O.K. Muni, I thought, read it beautifully.

Did I tell you <u>ALL</u> my plays, a whole suitcase full, disappeared out of the basement? No use for poor folks to try to keep anything! Well, they are all up at Yale, anyhow, for posterity to worry about producing. Personally, I don't much care. And certainly I've written my last free bit of entertainment. Turned down two chances to do free scripts since the broadcasts. Folk know what I can do now. If they want ME to write for them, dig up some dough. Nobody else connected with radio or theatre works for nothing. Why should they expect the author to do so? Huh? The technicians don't, nor the directors, nor the studio executives. I WON'T NEITHER. Hell with 'em!

One more free lecture appearance in the offing—and that is ALL there. With Rackham Holt at a Carver Memorial on April 6th at Columbia University.† You'll probably be here at that time.

Did I tell you |I| met Wendell Willkie at Walter's the other night?‡ Swell guy.

Sincerely,

Lang

<Saw Saroyan's "Human Comedy" last night and like it very much.>

<Call up and see if Lou's baby is here yet.§ Tell her my brother's wife (no. 2) is also expectant. Send them both your pamphlet, please!>

---

* On March 15, 1943, accompanied by the gospel singing of the Golden Gate Quartet, the veteran actor Paul Muni (1895–1967) read Hughes's long poem "Freedom's Plow" over the national NBC Blue Network.
† Rackham Holt was the pen name of Margaret Saunders Holt (1899–1963), who wrote *George Washington Carver: An American Biography* (Doubleday, Doran, 1943).
‡ Wendell Willkie (1892–1944) was the Republican Party candidate for president in 1940. He had attended a gathering at the home of Walter White of the NAACP.
§ "Lou" is Hughes's long-time friend Louise Thompson Patterson, the wife of William L. Patterson.

TO COUNTEE CULLEN   [*TLS*]

Yaddo,
Saratoga Springs,
New York,
July 23, 1943.

Dear Countee,

I am back at Yaddo for the summer. Came to the city for the week-end, dropped by the Y but Claude |McKay| was out, and failed to get by your house, so maybe we can make a few plans about our proposed book by mail*—advance details, at any rate, and then when I'm next in town, around mid-August, if you and Claude are there, we can get together for discussion.

I brought up with me all my poems—several hundred—and will make a selection of hitherto unpublished in book form ones for our volume. If you all think wise, I'll stick to lyric and poetic kind of poetry and exclude the folk forms this time. The two don't mix very well, and blues and such would probably throw the whole book out of key.

My proposal is this: That each of us submit our poems to the other two for elimination. In other words, you and I would look over Claude's selection and suggest which ones are not up to his best standards, and which we would advise including. Claude and I would do the same for yours. And you and Claude would act as jury on mine. Then from the lot left intact, we <each> would arrange a sequence for a section of a book. How does that strike you?

I suppose the book would be in three sections, perhaps alphabetical in order:

COUNTEE CULLEN
LANGSTON HUGHES
CLAUDE MCKAY

Next thing is to think of a good title. You and Claude start thinking.

As I remember, Claude had some very beautiful sonnets he once sent back from Europe to |Alain| Locke that I've never seen in print anywhere. I hope he still has them on hand. Ask him. And if convenient, kindly show him this

---

* The proposed volume by these three aging lions of the Harlem Renaissance, Hughes, Cullen, and McKay, was to be (Hughes wrote) "a kind of reaffirmation that we are still here and strong and nobody has surpassed us." But McKay died, and the volume never appeared.

letter and get his reactions to these proposals. If you like the two man jury idea, I could post my poetry down to you anytime, and you two could initial the ones that you like best and think should be in the volume, then while I'm up here where it is quiet and there's time for work, if you'd send them back, I could make a sequence arrangement for the book and bring it down around the 15th when I come. We could then meet and possibly tentatively put the book together. Let me know?

There's a pleasant group here this summer: Agnes Smedley,* Margaret Walker,† Rebecca Pitts,‡ Karin Michaëlis,§ and seven others.

Best regard to your wife. As ever,

Sincerely,

Langston

TO KATHERINE SEYMOUR   [TL]

Yaddo,

Saratoga Springs,

New York,

July 29, 1943.

Miss Katherine Seymour,

Writers' War Board,

122 East 42nd Street,

New York City, N. Y.

Dear Miss Seymour,

I am very sorry to have been so long in answering your letter. I phoned you last Wednesday in New York, but you had not come in. On my return to Yaddo, I

---

* The radical author and journalist Agnes Smedley (1892–1950), known for her sympathetic accounts of the Chinese Revolution, wrote the semiautobiographical novel *Daughter of Earth* (1929).

† Later known as Margaret Walker Alexander, Margaret Walker (1915–1998) first met Hughes while she was in high school. Her best-known works are *Jubilee*, her 1966 novel about slavery in America, and her pamphlet of verse *For My People*, which was chosen for publication in the Yale Series of Younger Poets in 1942.

‡ Rebecca E. Pitts (1905–1983) was an educator, activist, and editor, as well as author of the posthumously published *Brief Authority: Fragments of One Woman's Testament* (Vantage Press, 1985).

§ Karin Michaëlis (1872–1950), a Danish novelist and short story writer, was the author of a series of children's books. Her most famous novel was translated as *The Dangerous Age: Letters and Fragments from a Woman's Diary* (London: John Lane, 1912).

found myself with a couple of urgent deadlines to meet, and still have a week or so of rush writing to do to catch up. Just today have I been able to give a little quiet thought to the problems of the UNITY AT HOME—VICTORY ABROAD broadcasts of which both you and Mayor LaGuardia have written me.

As I see it (from a Negro viewpoint) there would be two general ways of approaching the material:

1. That of positive achievement, such as the several recent broadcasts on the life of Dr. Carver were; such as those concerning Negro war heroes like Dorie Miller* might be.
2. Or the problem approach setting forth the difficulties of the Jim Crow military set-up, segregation in war industries, etc., and what people of good will might do about it.

Radio has been in the past fairly receptive to the first approach but has (at least in my experience) insistently censored out any real dramatic approach to the actual problems of the Negro people. In that regard it has been almost as bad as Hollywood. Radio commentators have been allowed considerable leeway, but not the dramatic script writer. And certainly Negroes have not liked most of the "handkerchief head" sketches in which Ethel Waters and other colored stars have been featured.

Just as soon as I can complete a promised article, now due, for an anthology of contemporary Negro opinion about to go to press, I will prepare two or three synopses and send you.† Should the Board like any of them, I'd be happy to work them out in more detail. For the musical programs, I have a number of songs (for which I've done the lyrics) that might be of use—like FREEDOM ROAD which was on the MARCH OF TIME and the TREASURY STAR PARADE. But there are others, new ones, never on the air, and I shall secure them for you. I will write you again soon.

Sincerely yours,

---

* Doris "Dorie" Miller (1919–1943), a black cook on the USS *West Virginia*, was awarded the Navy Cross (then the third highest honor for valor awarded by the Navy) for his actions during the Japanese attack on Pearl Harbor in December 1941. After helping to move his mortally wounded captain to a safer location, Miller manned a machine gun despite a lack of combat training and fired for several minutes at attacking planes. The *West Virginia* sank but Miller survived to become, in the black press especially, a prime symbol of the absurdity of segregation in the U.S. armed forces. In December 1943 he was killed in action on a ship in the Pacific.
† In August, Hughes sent Seymour a draft of *In the Service of My Country*, a radio script for use in her broadcast. It aired on September 8 over WNYC. A companion piece, "Private Jim Crow," was never used.

TO ARNA BONTEMPS   [*TLS*]

<8/5/43>

Dear Arna,

There is nothing like farewells to bring forth parties and dinners. If you and Alberta were in New York I would give one for you myself . . . . . . You know I am sorry I missed the riots.* It has always been my fate never to be in one. I think I will go down to New York this weekend maybe though and survey the damage. The better class Negroes are all mad at the low class ones for disturbing their peace. I gather the mob was most uncouth—and Sugar Hill is shamed!†

Thanks for all the interesting clippings. There's an article of mine in the current Canadian magazine THE NEW WORLD with a big picture spread of colored celebs.

Rain, rain, rain here at Yaddo. I got to read poetry to the kids on vacation here tonight. Agnes Smedley "organized" it. She's been working out classes and programs for them. She didn't use up all her energy in China.

I am so sorry to hear about Horace |Cayton|'s mother. I hadn't heard before.

You got a good point about the train column.‡ What do you think of this one enclosed?

I reckon I lost my watch in the riots. I left it at Herbert's opposite the Theresa to be cleaned—and they tell me the place was cleaned out!

Lots of Harlem glamour girls up here vacationing say they had their fur coats in "storage" (nee pawn shops) for the summer. And they were all cleaned out, too. So they reckon they will be cold next winter. I expect that is one of the reasons Sugar Hill is so mad. Laundries and pawn shops looted, they suffered almost as much as the white folks.

I do not know why that tickles me, and I am sorry in my soul.

---

* On August 1, 1943, a riot broke out in Harlem after a black soldier was charged with attacking a white policeman who was arresting a black woman named Margie Polite in a hotel. Rumors spread that the police had killed a black soldier who was trying to protect his mother. *The New York Times* reported that five persons were killed and about five hundred injured during the disturbances. Several hundred were arrested and property damage was estimated at $5 million. Hughes's sardonic poem "The Ballad of Margie Polite" was inspired by the incident that started the riot.
† Sugar Hill is a traditionally upper-income section of Harlem that includes Edgecombe Avenue, where individuals such as Walter White, James Weldon Johnson, and W. E. B. Du Bois lived at one time or another.
‡ On August 3, 1943, Bontemps had written to Hughes offering suggestions to improve Hughes's column "On Missing a Train."

Dear sweet POPO! I will certainly need that $35.00.

NEW DAY A-COMIN' says Mr. Roi Ottley. NEW NIGHT would probably be better.* (How sweetly optimistic is the cullud race!)

Kappo Phelan, cousin of Noël Sullivan's, is here. She writes NEW YORKER style stories and humorous poetry. Morton Zabel[†] arrives today.

I've picked out all my lyrics for the Cullen-McKay-Hughes book they've proposed. Nothing of race, just beauty. Has not that been known to soothe the savage beast? (Did I tell you, Claude is in Harlem Hospital—stroke?) Lang

WRITERS DINE OUT:

Carson McCullers and I were entertained at dinner Sunday by Mr. Jimmy Elliott, leading colored barman here. He had champagne and chicken for us. Good, too!

TO RAYFORD LOGAN   [TL]

634 St. Nicholas Avenue,
New York, 30, New York,
December 21, 1943.

Dear Rayford,[‡]

Naturally, I do not agree with Mr. Couch in regard to your book, or my own article therein, at all! I am appalled at the fact that the head of a distinguished university press can hold an attitude like that expressed in his comment regarding the Roland Hayes incident:[§] "Mr. Hayes with his background ought to have been amused (and careful not to show it) at the prejudices of the salesman, troubled over the label put on his race, and careful to do exactly what the blackest Negro entering the shop might have been expected to do."

---

* In his book *New World A-Coming: Inside Black America* (1943), the journalist Roi Ottley (1906–1960) discussed the history, problems, and hopes of African Americans.

† Morton Dauwen Zabel (1901–1964), a scholar of English and European literature, was associate editor of *Poetry* magazine from 1928 to 1936, and editor from 1936 to 1937.

‡ The Howard University historian Rayford W. Logan (1897–1982) edited *What the Negro Wants* (1944), a book of fourteen essays by prominent blacks about race relations in the contemporary United States. Hughes contributed "My America" to the volume. Other essayists included Mary McLeod Bethune, A. Philip Randolph, and W. E. B. Du Bois. All opposed segregation. At first a supporter of the project, W. T. Couch of the University of North Carolina Press balked (at times in questionable language) at publishing the book after he read the essays. On December 21 Hughes wrote to Couch: "We, too, are citizens, soldiers, human beings—and we certainly don't like Jim Crow cars! Would you?"

§ See Hughes's letter of August 5, 1942, to Noël Sullivan.

I am afraid the southern intellectuals are in a pretty sorry boat. Certainly they are crowding Hitler for elbow room.

I do not know whether you want to release this correspondence to the press, but if you do, I could make use of portions of it in my Chicago Defender column.* Kindly let me know.

Certainly I trust you will find another publisher for the book.† And soon! Happy New Year to you!

Sincerely yours,
Langston Hughes

TO BLANCHE KNOPF [TL]

June 28, 1944.

Mrs. Blanche Knopf,
Alfred A. Knopf, Inc.,
501 Madison Avenue,
New York City.

Dear Blanche,

Thank you for your letter of June 22nd. I am, of course, happy that my first five books will be back on the old basis without any payment from me. I am accordingly signing a copy of Mr. Lesser's letter dated June 21st reinstating my contracts for THE WEARY BLUES, FINE CLOTHES TO THE JEW, NOT WITHOUT LAUGHTER, THE WAYS OF WHITE FOLKS, and THE DREAM KEEPER as of May 1, 1944, which I enclose with this letter. It is my understanding now that all rights in the above property are my sole and absolute property, subject, of course, to the reinstated contracts.

It seems to me this will make things much simpler should I ever have a Selected or Collected Poems, a complete collection of my short stories, or continue NOT WITHOUT LAUGHTER into a trilogy.

At any rate, it worried me—as I signed Mr. Lesser's letter when I was in the hospital under sulfa drugs—which make a person dopey anyhow—and his letter had come in response to a totally different request—which was an advance on royalties to be earned, since the BIG SEA had just appeared, and

---

* Hughes's column *From Here to Yonder* first appeared in *The Chicago Defender* in November 1942. In 1943, he introduced the character Jesse B. Semple, or "Simple," a comic, urban black Everyman who became for many readers the best feature of the column.

† Couch published Logan's book in 1944 but provided a reactionary preface to the volume.

I believe (or rather know, according to the date on galley proofs) SHAKE-SPEARE IN HARLEM had already gone to the printers.*

I posted to you the other day a list of the eight blues from our books as set to music by Herbert Kingsley, which Decca Records proposes to record and publish as songs. I also sent the list to Mr. William Downer at Decca, asking him to get in touch with you. As a member of ASCAP and SPA my song contracts must conform with their regulations. Decca's has taken twelve songs in all, four not in my books.

Again with my thanks to you, and all good wishes,

Sincerely yours,
Langston Hughes

TO ALAN GREEN [TL]

July 1, 1944

Mr. Alan Green
Writers' War Board
122 East 42 Street
New York, 17, N. Y.

My dear Mr. Green:

Concerning "JUMP LIVELY JEFF", I think the reason most Negro readers would not like the book is because it seems to perpetuate almost all of the old stereotypes that have been used for many years to caricature the Negro people.†

The first two words of the first chapter are enough to make Negroes dislike it; naming a little colored boy after a rebel general, Jefferson Davis. Then comes persimmons and very shortly thereafter watermelon, and then an old Aunt Car'line. This particular fruit, and many varieties of Aunties have been used lo these many years to make Negroes a funny picture race. Then you

---

* In February 1941, Hughes had received a letter from Joseph C. Lesser, a Knopf employee, in response to his request for a loan of $400. Lesser proposed that instead of lending Hughes $400, Knopf would pay him the same sum "in lieu of all future royalties" from his five books with the firm. With sales of these books weak, and Hughes in dire need of cash, he agreed to the terms but with misgivings. Later, advised by his lawyer, Arthur Spingarn, he approached Knopf about recovering his copyrights. Although he offered to buy back his rights, Knopf returned them without charge.
† The Missouri writer Ada Claire Darby (1884–1953), author of *Jump Lively, Jeff* (1942), was known in the 1930s and 1940s for her historical novels for younger readers.

turn a few more pages and lo and behold there is a Mammy. Most Negroes nowadays loathe Mammy.

Since all of the conversation is in very broad dialect, and most Negro youngsters now who have been to school speak the same kind of English as other children, they naturally do not like slavery-time comic, antiquated dialect. These young people wish that books were written about colored children which would make them somewhere near the normal American pattern.

I do not have time at the moment to read this book for the story as I am about to go to St. Louis, Chicago and Detroit, to act as Emcee for the American Negro Music Festivals in those cities. Perhaps the story may be a good one, but from a modern American Negro viewpoint there are so many unfortunate surface nuisances, so many comic strip names like Abslinoun, and so many pappys' and mammys' and aunties', plus the dialect that one only has to glance through the book to see why Colored people to-day would not like it. It would seem to me the kind of book that would encourage perfectly nice little white children to mistakenly address a perfectly nice little Colored child in broad dialect, under the impression that that is the language Colored people speak now.

I am sorry that I cannot read the book carefully nor comment on its plot or story value at this time, but I think that someone could see by simply glancing through it, why it would hardly be a book to offer American Negro children. I personally am not a children's author or a literary critic. The leading <Negro> writer of children's book is Mr. Arna Bontemps, Librarian, Fisk University, Nashville, 8, Tennessee. Perhaps Mr. Bontemps could give Miss Darby a much more comprehensive criticism than I. I am returning the book to you, herewith.

Sincerely yours,
Langston Hughes

L
HUGHES
d
e
h

TO ARNA BONTEMPS   [TLS]

[On Langston Hughes, 634 St. Nicholas Avenue, New York 30, New York stationery]

December 8, 1944

Dear Arna,

Too bad you-all aren't here this week-end—Loren and Juanita* are, also Jose Antonio Fernandez de Castro and his wife of Havana (THE authority on Negro literature down there) just back from an air-plane trip around the world in Cuban diplomatic service, also Mrs. Browning of STORY MAGAZINE, and Charley Leonard of Hollywood—so I am having a cocktail party Sunday for all and sundry. Dorothy |Peterson| is also going ahead with her buffet supper tomorrow night. But no doubt things will be jumping equally but differently when you do arrive! I've sold some of your theatre tickets to Ralph Ellison and Fanny.† But will try to get you some more.

I've been head over heels in things to do—opera libretto to revise, some urgent articles to get done, etc. etc. so haven't been able to rummage through all my stuff to look for that statement for Crates, but will send him copies of all the wonderful letters that came in from the various high schools I've been lately, several in response to a troubled principal in Bridgeport who wrote everyone after the Sokolsky attack to see what I had said, also had the FBI in attendance, who evidently gave me a clearance, as his assembly was held.‡ The whole business made me a bit sore at folks who strain at a gnat and daily swallow all the camels of discrimination we have to put up with year in and year out. My personal feeling is TO HELL WITH THEM! I do not care whether they like me or my poems or not. They certain<ly> do us as a race very little good—Christian though they may be.

Your article on the two Harlems is very very good indeed! I think it is just about your most beautiful and effective piece of writing and, if widely

---

* Loren Miller (1903–1967), an attorney and civil rights activist from Los Angeles, had traveled with Hughes to the Soviet Union as part of the *Black and White* film group in 1932; Juanita was his wife.

† Befriended by Hughes in 1936 on moving to New York City, the Oklahoma-born Ralph Waldo Ellison (1913–1994) committed himself in 1937 to writing. In 1953, he won the National Book Award for his novel *Invisible Man* (1952). Ellison married Fanny McConnell in 1946. Hughes had known her since at least 1938, when she directed a Chicago staging of *Don't You Want to Be Free?*

‡ George Sokolsky (1893–1962) was a conservative syndicated columnist for the *New York Sun* and other papers. In his October 23, 1944, column, he attacked Hughes for his allegedly communist views.

read, should provoke a lot of discussion. I just about bet it will choke all these people with moral fishbones stuck in their throats!

Harlem writers have been invited to a press conference with Sec. of State Stettinius tonight.* Shall go see what it is all about.

Congratulations on the show contract! Hope it comes off and makes a big hit so you make some BIG money. . . . . Barney Josephson sent for me again to work on the proposed Cafe Society Revue. Says they definitely will start on it after New Year's with money up and all. Seems Oscar Hammerstein II is interested.

So, I leave you now to consider the stack of mail on top of mail piled on the bed. I cannot take my rest until I unpile some of it.

Sincerely, Langston

TO MAGGIE TREADWELL   [TL]

January 11, 1945

Dear Miss Treadwell:

Thanks very much indeed for the very nice poem which you wrote about me and which you were so kind to send me. You must forgive me for not answering your letters more often but I have been almost continuously out of town on lecture trips until the holidays, and tomorrow I leave for Boston, then shortly to the Middle West and South, to be away for several weeks. So you see how difficult it is for me to keep up with my mail.

I send you my very good wishes for a happy and successful New Year, and may you continue to write.

Sincerely yours,
Langston Hughes

Miss Maggie Treadwell
1014 Lombard Street
Wilmington, Delaware

P.S. This letter was dictated January 7, 1945. Meanwhile, your other letter came. Certainly, I am greatly complimented by your high regard for me. But,

---

* Edward Reilly Stettinius, Jr. (1900–1949), was secretary of state from December 1, 1944, to June 27, 1945. In 1945, he attended the Yalta Conference with President Roosevelt. Later he served as chairman of the United States delegation to the conference in San Francisco that led to the founding of the United Nations.

look here! You mustn't have too much affection for persons you don't know! It is hard enough to work out a smooth romance with someone you are near, let alone somebody away off. . . . . You know, I receive dozens of letters like yours. I suppose everyone in public life does. I think I explained to you once that it is not physically possible to keep up a correspondence with one-tenth of the people who write, as the mail box is full of mail every day, and to answer them all regularly would mean doing nothing else in life but writing letters—which is not possible for a writer who also must earn a living. So you will understand if I do not answer your letters. At this time of year I am on the road lecturing most of the time, anyhow, and often do not see my mail for weeks. In a few days I head for Illinois, Michigan, then Alabama, and Georgia. . . . . Best wishes to you,

L. H.

TO MERCER COOK   [TL]

March 16, 1945

Dear Mercer:[*]

I shall be very much interested in receiving Jacques Roumain's new book and, if we can find a publisher for it before hand, I would be happy to assist in the translation, providing you will do the rough draft, as you say you will. When I receive my copy I think I shall allow the Knopf office to read it and see if they would be interested in it. Unfortunately, I understand from publishers that Latin American books have not sold very well here, and that now most of the publishing houses are averse to accepting new ones. I know some of the Latin American writers that I have met here in New York, and who are quite famous in their own country, complain bitterly about not being |able| to get their work published here. Some years ago when I translated some thirty short stories by Mexican writers, I was able to place only three.

One of the larger publishing houses asked me the other day if I would be willing to do another children's book for them about Haiti. In case I were to do that, and in case we are able to secure a publisher for Jacques' novel, it

---

[*] Mercer Cook (1903–1987) was a Howard University professor of French and, in the 1960s, U.S. ambassador to the African republics of Niger, Senegal, and Gambia. Cook was teaching at the University of Haiti in 1944, the year Jacques Roumain died. When he approached Hughes with an invitation from Roumain's widow to translate into English his posthumously published novel *Gouverneurs de la Rosée*, Hughes agreed to do so after Cook offered to provide him with a first draft. The firm of Reynal and Hitchcock published their translation, *Masters of the Dew*, in 1947.

might not be a bad idea if I were to come down to Haiti for a couple of months this summer, particularly since I would like to write about present day Haiti in the children's book, and about other phases of Haitian life than that of the peasantry. If I were to come down, we could complete the translation of the novel then. In any case, I would not be able to even start on it before summer, as I am leaving New York again in a couple of weeks for an eight-weeks tour of Louisiana and Texas and will not be back in New York again until June.

I have been out of town so much this winter that I have not even had a chance to work on the poem which I started in honor of Jacques Roumain.* When I do have a chance to finish it, I shall send it to you for possible translation and publication in Haiti. I ran into your mother a few weeks ago on 125th Street and she looked fine. She "balled" me out for not having answered your letters, for which I do not blame her, but I am sure you know, if you have ever been on a lecture tour, that it is hard to find time to even wash your face let alone write letters, particularly when you are lecturing for colored people. Our race seems to have a special fondness for lecturers. Certainly they entertain us lavishly and feed us well, but they do not leave time for combing the hair.

With very best wishes to you, I am

Sincerely yours,
Langston Hughes

Dr. Mercer Cook
United States Embassy
Port au Prince, Haiti

TO NOËL SULLIVAN   [TLS]

[*On* Langston Hughes, 634 Nicholas Avenue, New York 30, New York *stationery*]

June 26, 1945.

Dear Noël,

Maybe it is because I got up at six this morning and went to mass at Our Lady of Lourdes—or maybe it is just because I got an early start—that I find myself writing some long delayed letters to friends I have been thinking of a long time. I don't believe I ever wrote you how much I enjoyed the several lovely little Christmas cards that accompanied my present. And my birthday gift must

---

* The actor Canada Lee read Hughes's "Poem for Jacques Roumain" at a memorial for Roumain in New York in May 1945.

have been blessed because it has been fuller than any purse I have ever had up to date. I carried it with me on my recent long tour of the South—from which I have just returned. And since this has been the best tour I have had in years, I find myself at long last able to pay off some of the—in fact just about ALL of the little debts that accumulated during my mother's illness—or my own in California. (By the way, did I tell you that I offered to buy back the book rights I sold Knopf that time for Four Hundred Dollars, but they gave them back to me? Arthur Spingarn showed me the kind of legal-like letter to write.). . . . . You remember you lent me $150.00 when I was in the hospital? Well, a mere check doesn't mean a thing, and I can't begin to repay you for that or the million other wonderful and helpful things you've done for me, but anyhow, here that <u>one</u> particular check is, with all my gratitude. Certainly it was a great help to me at the time. . . . . I really had a very pleasant tour with travel much better this winter than last, and trains not as crowded. I made most of my reservations in New York before I left, and didn't have any real inconveniences at all. I flew from New Orleans out to Texas—San Antonio, and on up to Dallas. I found school kids going to classes by plane out there. A few years more and I expect they will be as common as cars. . . . . Pullman and diner car service is better for colored people than before, but still far from ideal. The Supreme Court decision caused thousands of new colored voters to register, or seek to register, and some communities resorted to rather childishly amusing run-a-rounds, such as hiding the registration books, or locking the door when Negroes came!* One town in Alabama registered two hundred colored voters, but after that simply told the others to go on back home, that enough had signed up for one year! And they didn't intend to let any more vote this time!. . . . . . Democracy comes hard to the South, but it slowly, slowly seems to be coming. Texas, which is half Western, half Southern, probably will have lots of brawls along with the birth pains, as both the Negroes and the white folks are mean down there. . . . . Well, I am trying to get my agency to book me through to the Coast in the fall so I can spend a part of the winter with you-all on the farm. (Mississippi has me for Negro History Week already, and a Mormon University in Utah in January, so the pattern isn't straightened out yet, but somehow I hope and intend to get to California, and back to my little house again.). . . . . Give my love to Lee |Crowe|, and Marie |Short|, and all. I

---

* The U.S. Supreme Court decision *Smith v. Allwright* (1944) overthrew a Texas state law that in effect allowed the state Democratic Party to bar blacks from primary elections.

shall write Marie tomorrow. . . . . Enjoyed that card from you and Edna. Did you get to the San Francisco Conference?* It's good they chose your city.

Affectionately,

Langston

TO ARNA BONTEMPS   [*TLS*]

[*On* Langston Hughes, 634 St. Nicholas Avenue, New York 30, New York *stationery*]

November 14, 1945.

Dear Arna,

I never was so glad to get back to New York before in my life! The Middle West raw, cold, and prejudiced, trains crowded and smokey and travel the worst I've seen it so far, soldiers going home and mad, and an air like pre-cyclone weather in Kansas used to feel with open and under-cover gusts of fascism blowing through forlorn streets in towns where desperate little groups of interracial Negroes and whites are struggling to keep things half way decent. . . . . Charles S. |Johnson|† was at the Grand as usual (he ought to buy the joint) but seemed |as sleepy and tired as I was, although we had a good visit. . . . . Me, I caught a bad cold mid way the tour, and only pulled through because I know the old routine by heart. Cold seemed to disappear the minute I got back to Penn Station!. . . . . Your HERALD TRIBUNE piece looked swell. . . . . Horace |Cayton| was in New York so I didn't see him. . . . . Had dinner with the NEGRO DIGEST Johnsons‡ who have a big Packard, FINE apartment in house they have bought, over-crowded office so they're looking for a new and better one, business booming!. . . . . Got a ten dollar raise from my paper. Under threat of retiring altogether. They want you and Mrs. Bethune. . . . . Thanks for TOMORROW.§ Reckon I forgot to tell you

---

* The United Nations Conference on International Organization (UNCIO) convened in San Francisco from April 25 to June 26, 1945. At the closing session, delegates from fifty countries signed the charter for the United Nations.
† In Chicago, Hughes had met Charles S. Johnson, a professor at Fisk and codirector of the Julius Rosenwald Fund race relations program.
‡ John H. Johnson (1918–2005) began publishing the magazine *Negro Digest* in 1942. The periodical, modeled on the nationally popular *Reader's Digest,* continued until 1951. In 1945, his company started the even more successful *Ebony* magazine.
§ *Tomorrow* published a section of *They Seek a City,* a 1945 volume by Arna Bontemps and leftist writer Jack Conroy (1899–1990) on black migration to Chicago. It was partially funded by the Illinois Writers' Project. The men also collaborated on a juvenile book, *The Fast-Sooner Hound* (1942). Conroy's semi-autobiographical novel about the son of a

Marion* gave me a copy just before I left. . . . Did you EVER get your records? They swear they were finally sent!. . . . . I wish I had known w<h>ere Paul |Bontemps| was since I was nearby in Massillon. (Got your letter after I got back here yesterday.) I certainly would have called him. . . . . I guess PHYLON is using the piece as they had wired DEFENDER for permission to reprint some column or other with it. . . . . Do you not recall that Simple did go to Chicago once and spoke of how dark the bars are there?. . . . . Stop spelling Dr. Du Bois with an e, BOISE it is not! Did you see all the mistakes in name-spelling in Ben Richardson's note preceding his piece on me in his new book?† How can cullud be so careless?. . . . . A darling old lady of eighty tottered up to me at the Oak Park 20th Century Women's Club and told me all about how her family had been active in the Underground Railway in Ohio in the old days, and how she remembered one slave they had saved at risk of their lives by holding off the slavers with rifles. "But," she said, "don't you know, he wasn't worth saving! He had the nicest little wife, and he just beat her all the time!". . . . . Which probably is what helped to give me the cold. I never had thought before that escaped slaves were other than heroic and noble! Had you?. . . . . . Had a nice note from Marion in Ocala, Florida—Zora |Neale Hurston|'s country . . . . . . YOU are telling me about the theatre!?!?. . . . HUH?. . . . . I have bought two fine suits with the STREET SCENE check and intend to see some fine shows, and it do not worry my mind!‡ I have wished Mr. Stokowski§ well on his South American honeymoon, and the American Negro Theatre which was to have opened with my JOY TO MY SOUL but have now put it last for spring, do not worry my mind neither.¶ Cullud, white, ama-

---

coal miner growing up during the Depression, *The Disinherited* (1933), received critical acclaim.

* In 1940, photographer Marion Palfi (1907–1978) emigrated from Europe to the United States and settled in New York City, where she met Hughes in the course of developing an interest as a photographer in civil rights issues. In 1946, she received a grant from the Rosenwald Fund to spend three years documenting the impact of Jim Crow laws and other forms of racial discrimination on everyday people in the South.

† Ben Richardson's *Great American Negroes* (1945).

‡ Hughes received advance money to work as the lyricist on *Street Scene*, an opera based on Elmer Rice's Pulitzer Prize–winning drama of the same name (1929). With a libretto by Rice (1892–1967); song lyrics by Hughes and, eventually, Rice; and music by the German-born composer Kurt Weill (1900–1950), the opera opened on Broadway in January 1947. The production was a critical and commercial success.

§ Leopold Stokowski (1882–1977), a renowned conductor, declared his interest in staging *Troubled Island*, Hughes's opera with William Grant Still, if $30,000 could be raised to fund the project. Only $2,000 was raised.

¶ Hughes's *Joy to My Soul: A Farce Comedy in Three Acts* was first presented by the Gilpin Players of Karamu House, Cleveland, on April 1, 1937.

teur, professional—all same—nothing ever as is swore will be! SKYLOFT in Chi split in two groups—each with big posters out all over town about their coming season. Bob Lucas won their contest with a very good war play in one act that I helped judge. . . . . Front of Theresa is all scorched like top of Empire State Building. Beautiful lady who jumped out window nude was well known matron from up Yonkers way in bed with playboy when their mat<t>ress caught on fire. They say she could have escaped in hall but couldn't find her clothes, so she jumped to her death instead. Too much modesty does not make sense in cases of emergency like that! ◄——► The playboy just walked on down the hall as he was!. . . . I gave THEY SEEK A CITY a plug in several of my talks when I speak of urban conditions and trials and tribulations. . . . . Josh White* is using my CRAZY HAT song at Cafe Society. Golden Gates† plan to record it soon, I hear . . . . . . You had better stop reviewing all those books and get down to your WORK. (I am just mad because I can't even read anything, let alone review it.) I had to turn down doing a piece for the Christmas issue CHICAGO SUN. . . . . I am getting a new said-to-be-very-good secretary (half day every day till I go to Coast in January) starting this week— fellow who is studying for MA at NYU. . . . . My agreement for Atlanta next fall, half year, came through at rate I told you. . . . . I find a whole basket of full of books here on my return—including <u>two</u> of Horace's big volumes which look most imposing.‡ . . . . . . CARMEN and ANNA both are making a mint of money in Chicago, so the road is not a bad idea for both your shows long about now.§ Another road company of ANNA as well as a London one are said to be casting. Looks like all actors will work for a while, which is good. . . . . Now if Negro playwrights can just get started!. . . . . Give my best to Alberta and tell her maybe I will get by that way sometime during the winter. I'm booked for Mississippi in mid-February. I don't know yet which college that Decem-

* Josh White (1914–1969) was an African American gospel, folk, and blues singer, a songwriter, and a political activist. His fame grew in the 1930s, when he was said to be a close friend of President Roosevelt.
† The Golden Gate Quartet, an African American gospel singing group, had accompanied actor Paul Muni in the March 15, 1943, NBC radio broadcast of Hughes's *Freedom Plow*.
‡ St. Clair Drake and Horace R. Cayton, Jr.'s *Black Metropolis: A Study of Negro Life in a Northern City* (about Chicago) was originally published in 1945 in two volumes.
§ The musical *Carmen Jones*, a modernization by Oscar Hammerstein II (1895–1960) of Georges Bizet's opera *Carmen* for an African American cast, was first staged on Broadway in 1943. *Anna Lucasta* by Philip Yordan (1914–2003), also written for an all-black cast, was produced on Broadway in 1944. Both were important vehicles at that time for black performers.

ber War Bond rally will take Mark Van Doren and I to.* Wish it would be yours.

Sincerely,
Langston

TO MAXIM LIEBER   [TL]

November 24, 1945

Dear Max:

I have your note regarding the introduction to the Whitman book.† I am sending someone to the library today to look up the necessary additional material for me, and will try to add this to the introduction on Monday, and send it to you. God forbid that I should ever attempt such a job again since it is so much easier and simpler to make up things out of my own head!

The Negro Digest Publishing Company of Chicago has just written me that they wish to publish my "Simple Minded Friend" columns in a paper bound book to sell for 50¢. I personally like this idea very much and will type and arrange the columns for them shortly. The Editor writes: "We are definitely interested in publishing your 'Simple' stories in a pocket-book size, and can meet you with your percentage allowed in such cases. Please send us copies of the 'Simple' stories and have your agent send us the necessary contract and blanks to be signed."

Could you attend to this matter for me and see if we can get an advance of $100 from them? The Chicago Defender, where these columns first appeared, has only the rights to weekly newspaper publication, and no control over my other rights. The Negro Digest wishes to have the book illustrated by Ollie Harrington.‡

Sincerely yours,

Mr. Maxim Lieber
489 Fifth Avenue
New York 22, New York

---

* The poet Mark Van Doren (1894–1972) served on the executive board of the leftist Independent Citizens Committee of the Arts, Sciences, and Professions.
† Hughes wrote the introduction, "The Ceaseless Rings of Walt Whitman," for *I Hear the People Singing: Selected Poems of Walt Whitman* (International Publishers, 1946).
‡ Oliver Harrington (1912–1995) was a well-known black cartoonist and political satirist. His most popular cartoon character was Bootsie, whom Harrington described as "a jolly, rather well-fed but soulful character." Nothing came of the plan mentioned here.

With Gwendolyn Brooks, Hall Branch
Library, Chicago, 1949

But someday somebody'll
Stand up and talk about me,
And write about me—
Black and beautiful—
And sing about me,
And put on plays about me!
I reckon it'll be
Me myself!
Yes, it'll be me.

—"NOTE ON COMMERCIAL THEATRE," 1940

In the years after World War II, Hughes continued to seek acclaim—as well as money—with an outpouring of work in various forms. The most successful of these endeavors was the opera *Street Scene* created with Elmer Rice and Kurt Weill. The opera was indeed a hit with the critics and, to some extent, at the box office (although Hughes had to fight to get his fair share of the profits). Moving with Toy and Emerson Harper from their St. Nicholas Avenue apartment, he bought a three-story brownstone on East 127th Street. This success led to work on other operas, including a revived project about Haitian history with the black composer William Grant Still, *Troubled Island*, and others undertaken with another German-born musician, Jan Meyerowitz. None of these matched the success of *Street Scene*. Hughes endured other setbacks. In 1947 critics dismissed his book of purely "lyrical" poems, *Fields of Wonder*, and in 1949 they were almost as cool to his collection *One-Way Ticket*, in which he explored more familiar themes. More than ever, he depended on the lecture circuit and his newspaper column to cover his basic expenses—but moving around the country made him an easy target for his right-wing opponents.

TO NOËL SULLIVAN   *[TLS]*

[On Langston Hughes, 634 St. Nicholas Avenue, New York 30, New York *stationery]*

July 22, 1946

Dear Noël,

It was very good of you to let me know about the loss of darling Mrs. Blanchard. I phoned Carlo |Van Vechten| and Nora |Holt| right away. I read your wire to Carl as it contained more information than he had had. He said he had written you. She would have been 87 this week.

Me, I am up to my neck with that show |*Street Scene*|. We are trying to get a complete rehearsal script by the end of this month—Elmer Rice, Kurt Weill,* Charles Friedman (the director who did CARMEN JONES) and myself working together almost every day all day. I had just come from Stamford yesterday when I found your wire. Some of the music is really beautiful and it looks as though it will be quite a show. It is costing $180,000! (Imagine!) Richard

----

* Kurt Julian Weill (1900–1950), a German composer who emigrated to the United States in 1935, is perhaps best known for his collaborations with Bertolt Brecht (1898–1956), which include *The Threepenny Opera* (1928).

Manning has the tenor juvenile lead, and someone named Stoska of the Civic Opera is signed for the mother. They've found no Rose as yet?* Do you know a beautiful young soprano who can sing and also act? If so, let me know. They may send the director to the Coast looking for someone.

I wrote a note to your friend in SONG OF NORWAY† and spoke to Lina Abarbanell‡ of the Dwight Deere Wiman office about him. She's casting director—in case you're writing Ross or anyone else you know who might be interested. The baritone part is about the only important one besides the female lead that is not yet cast. Rehearsals are scheduled for end of October, and a Philadelphia opening at the end of November, New York Christmas week.

I am looking for Aunt Toy |Harper| back tomorrow. She is a bad letter writer, so I have to hear details of her trip up the Coast, but I was happy to have your letter telling me she was there, and I know she loved it. It was wonderful of you to invite her, and please thank Lee |Crowe| for me for being so nice to her. How did she and Marie |Short| make out? They both have something of the same energy.

Well, I must write my column. This time—THE FAULTS OF THE SOVIET UNION. (See what you have driven me to!!!) And I will give the house a midnight dusting—so Mrs. Harper will think I am a good housekeeper. So, more next time,

Affectionately,
Langston

---

* Anne Jeffreys was cast as Rose Maurrant in *Street Scene*, and Polyna Stoska performed the role of her mother, Anna. Richard Manning appeared in the three-week run of *Street Scene* in Philadelphia that opened on December 16, 1946, but left the cast prior to the Broadway opening on January 9, 1947. The veteran performer Brian Sullivan replaced Manning.
† *Song of Norway*, an operetta with music by the noted composer Edvard Grieg (1843–1907), was produced on Broadway from 1944 to 1946.
‡ Lina Abarbanell (1879–1963), a German-born opera singer and recitalist, immigrated to the United States in 1905. Beginning in 1934, she worked as a casting director and producer.

TO MAXIM LIEBER   [TL]

September 20, 1947
Mr. Maxim Lieber,
489 Fifth Avenue,
New York City.

Dear Max,

The information which I got from ASCAP (Mrs. Rosenberg's office there) is that co-credit on the score of the STREET SCENE folio would definitely reduce my own ASCAP rating (and therefore income) from any future use of the music. In other words, by giving Elmer |Rice| equal co-credit with myself, I would be sharing with him all the performing rights (air, television, night clubs, etc.) that ASCAP controls on the STREET SCENE music.* This might amount in the long run to considerable money (so no wonder Elmer wants such credit at this late date) especially should the score ever be played as much as parts of PORGY AND BESS or VICTOR HERBERT'S† TUNES are.

One of the original inducements put forward to me by Kurt Weill and Elmer Rice to justify my having only 2% of the show while they each had 4%, was that all the record and sheet music income would be equally divided with me and Kurt, and that also I would have my ASCAP rights. In my conversation with Kurt Weill at luncheon yesterday, he agreed that such statements were made to me in the first conferences about the show. Kurt further said that in his opinion it would not be fair for Elmer now to cut in on my ASCAP rating by demanding co-credit on the <full> score, and he said that he would say as much to Elmer on Monday when they meet at the Playwrights. Weill also said that in his opinion, rather than a preface note to the score, it would be better to give Elmer credit for each of the seven numbers I've agreed to by a footnote to each number—since Kurt says an "Opera" score never has credits interspersed throughout at the top of the numbers—which is what I proposed since the score is divided up anyhow into numbered Scenes and Songs. However, the footnote is O.K. by me.

* The American Society of Composers, Authors and Publishers (ASCAP) is a membership organization that manages royalties and licenses for the performances of copyrighted musical works. Hughes contacted them while defending his interests in Street Scene against Elmer Rice's claims and what he saw as yet another unfair attempt (as with Mulatto on Broadway in 1935, for example) to deprive him of money owed to him. Eventually he turned over the dispute to his lawyer, Arthur Spingarn.
† Victor Herbert (1859–1924), an Irish-born American composer, was a founder of ASCAP.

But I repeat, in answer to your letter of September, <u>CERTAINLY</u> we stick by our guns. The three points are:

CO-CREDITS: 7 numbers to Elmer denoted by footnotes on score as
    Weill suggests and Dr. Sirmay[*] agrees would be best.
FOLIO: Same royalty arrangement as on show.
RECORDS: $^1/_3$ of lyric royalties to Elmer.

We sign no rider for the folio or anything else until ALL points are cleared up once and for all. Since they are very anxious to get the folio to the printer action should be forthcoming this week. Please tell Dr. Sirmay that the proofs are not O.K.ed by me until I see ALL title pages and give my O.K. Yesterday when I was in his office, they had already written in Elmer Rice's name as co-author of the lyrics—which Dr. Sirmay erased in my presence and Weill's since I told him I had never agreed to this, and certainly would not O.K. <it> on the proofs. Looks kinder like to me they would pull a fast one, if they could, just as the co-credits were already on the records before I was told about <it>— which I do not believe Chappell or anyone else had a right to do, did they?

I pointed out to Weill and Dr. Sirmay yesterday that on at least four occasions (and Weill corroborated me on this because he was present each time) I had tried to settle the matter with Elmer as to the numbers on which he would have a co-credit—once at his home in the country, once at the Algonquin in the room where we were working, and twice during rehearsals, particularly the day you came to rehearsal at my request for that purpose. Each time Elmer was too tired to talk any more, or else he had to make a train back to the country. So, as I told Dr. Sirmay, it is certainly not my fault that this co-credit business was not settled before now. And that, now as then, it's still up to Elmer.

I have read and corrected proofs of the folio through page 238, with the exception of the title pages. I await proofs of those, and of the pages on which the footnotes will be inserted. These I must see for my final O.K. without which this folio should not go to press.

Re Meyerowitz and MULATTO.[†] I talked to him on the phone last night. It is agreeable to him that you handle the show, his share as well as mine, and he would like to come in and talk to you, so I suggested that he phone you and make an appointment. Hold the collaboration agreements until you see him and he can sign them in your office.

[*] Dr. Albert Sirmay (1880–1967) was a Hungarian composer and Broadway music editor.
[†] Jan Meyerowitz (1913–1998) worked with Hughes on the operas *The Barrier* (1950), based on Hughes's *Mulatto*, and *Esther* (1957), as well as other musical projects.

*

Weill asked me for a list of the numbers on which I agree Elmer has co-credit and says he will do his best to get him to accept them, as seven would certainly be enough to apply for ASCAP, so I am sending him the enclosed list since he and Dr. Sirmay wish to get all straight Monday so the printing can go forward. <See below>

Sincerely,

*

P.S. On second thought, I am NOT sending any list to Weill. The whole business should go through you, and I put nothing on paper until you secure the rider to the Chappell contract. I enclose the list for you to pass on to Elmer, and Kurt if you see fit . . . . . . By the way, Kurt said I should NOT allow Elmer more than ⅓ of record royalties because, if granted more, he would demand more on folio credits. In other words 50% on records would justify his demand for full 50% co-credit on folio.

TO JACOB LAWRENCE   [TL]

September 25, 1947

Dear Jacob Lawrence:*
Under separate cover I am sending you a carbon of the manuscript of the new book of poems which I have just submitted to Alfred A. Knopf.† I have written Mrs. Blanche Knopf, who is my editor there, about your work and have said that I would very much like to have them consider you in connection with the book. Of course, I myself can make no commitments in this regard. But I send you these poems so that you might further make up your own mind as to whether you would perhaps like to illustrate them in case my publishers come to a decision.

Zell |Ingram| called up the other day and said that he was planning on

---

* Jacob Lawrence (1917–2000) would emerge as one of the most honored American painters and illustrators of the twentieth century, with examples of his work now in the permanent collections of institutions such as the Museum of Modern Art and the Metropolitan Museum of Art in New York.
† Tired of the work of white artists (chosen by Knopf and other major publishers) who depicted scenes from black culture insensitively, Hughes sought the services of Jacob Lawrence for *One-Way Ticket* (1949). Knopf reluctantly gave in to Hughes's unusual pressure but declined to pay for the illustrations. Hughes then sent Lawrence $600.

Hughes chose the African American artist Jacob Lawrence to illustrate *One-Way Ticket* (1949). These illustrations by Lawrence appear, respectively, with the poems "One-Way Ticket" and "Too Blue."

coming over to see you and invited me to come with him. Unfortunately, however, I am unable to do so this week since I am terrifically rushed in order to get away this week-end for a few weeks in Cuba, since I have not had any vacation this year. But I hope I shall have the pleasure of meeting you when I come back in November.

This book of poems would not be scheduled before next summer or the fall of 1948, as I have just had a new book of poems a few months ago,[*] so a decision about it may not be made for several weeks. However, because I do wish an illustrated book, and I realize that an artist must have plenty of time to develop his own conception, I have submitted the manuscript well ahead of time.

All my good wishes to you,

Sincerely,

Mr. Jacob Lawrence
385 Decatur Street
Brooklyn
New York

[*] Knopf published Hughes's *Fields of Wonder* in 1947.

TO JESSIE PARKHURST GUZMAN   *[TLS]*
                                    COPY

December 2, 1947

Miss Jessie Parkhurst Guzman
NEGRO YEAR BOOK
Department of Records and Research
Tuskegee Institute, Alabama

My dear Miss Guzman:

On my return from a midwestern lecture tour today I was happy to find awaiting me a copy of the new NEGRO YEAR BOOK. In glancing through it, it
seems to me a most useful and well edited publication, and I am delighted to
see it back in print and up-to-date again.

There is, however, one error in the material relating to myself that I would
like to see corrected immediately. On page 280, 2nd column, 2nd paragraph,
last sentence, there is this statement:

> "Among those to desert the Communist Party . . . are A. Philip Ran-
> dolph . . . Angelo Herndon . . . Langston Hughes and Richard Wright,
> eminent writers."

The implication here is that I was once a member of the Communist
Party. Since I am sure you wish your statements to be accurate, the fact is that
I have never been a member of the Communist Party, therefore I could hardly
"desert the Communist Party." For years I have stated this fact in my public
lectures, and several times in printed form, particularly following the picketing of one of my public appearances by Aimee Semple McPherson in California about ten years ago, and more recently in the enclosed articles from THE
CHICAGO DEFENDER and PHYLON. Should you doubt my word, however, a
couple of years ago the principal of a high school in Bridgeport, Connecticut,
faced with the protests of a few reactionary parents who wished me barred
from the assembly (probably since I was the first Negro speaker ever to appear
there) contacted the F. B. I. as to my political affiliations, and the F.B.I. gave
complete clearance, to the satisfaction of the principal and the school board.
So you might check my statement with the same source, if you so desire.

Since the NEGRO YEAR BOOK is not a newspaper or magazine, but a
permanent book of reference that will be used by students and library readers

for years to come, I would appreciate the removal of my name <u>at once</u> from the above mentioned paragraph, or else the immediate insertion of correction on an <u>errata</u> page.*

Very truly yours,

SIGNED

Langston Hughes

Enclosures:

    DEFENDER, 9/13/47

    PHYLON, Vol. VIII, 3

    CONCERNING "GOODBYE CHRIST"

TO G. B. WINSTON   [TL]

February 18, 1948

Mr. G. B. Winston,

Urban League,

Springfield, Illinois.

Dear Mr. Winston,

So many wires and communications have come to New York from Springfield concerning my scheduled appearance there that so much bother about such a mild and simple talk as I usually give hardly seems worth all that trouble and commotion to me. If I were a loud speaking gentleman—like Adam Powell[†]—delivering some world-shaking message, or a politician running for office, it would throw a different light on the matter. But all this worriation over a poet![‡] What's going on out there? Seriously, however, it would be quite O.K. by me if the engagement were cancelled[§] as certainly I would wish to be

---

* In January 1948, Guzman sent Hughes a copy of the slip inserted in *Negro Year Book, 1947*, in response to his complaint. The insert reads in part: "Page 280, 2nd column, 2nd paragraph, 3rd sentence. Both Mr. Langston Hughes and Mr. A. Philip Randolph state that they have never been members of the Communist Party; for this reason, not having been members, they could hardly have deserted the party."

† Adam Clayton Powell, Jr. (1908–1972), became the representative for the 18th Congressional District of New York, including Harlem, in January 1945. Famously outspoken, he served in Congress for more than twenty years.

‡ J. Edgar Hoover, director of the FBI, sent documents to the National Urban League after it asked for information about whether Hughes was a communist.

§ When the engagement was canceled, Hughes warned Winston, the executive director of the Springfield Urban League, on March 3: "I hope . . . that the colored people of the community realize what a dangerous precedent is being set, and that after a while they may not be able to have even William Pickens, Mary McLeod Bethune, or the venerable Dr. DuBois address them either (since these with dozens of other Negro personages have been on

the last person to embarrass the Urban League from when<ce> came my first literary prize, before whose branches I have so often appeared, and for which I have a high regard.

The carbon of my letter to Mr. Osby which I have sent you explains clearly how I feel about the matter. I also dictated a wire to the Colston Leigh office[*] over the phone today to Miss Marjorie Dickinson. Please tell Miss Dickinson I do not have her address so cannot write her directly, but I am enclosing the enclosed list of a few of my various engagements in recent years for her as she wished to know at what churches or before what religious groups I have appeared. You might also pass on to her copies of letters from various high schools which I am sending you under separate cover. (I would appreciate it if you would return these to me.) Perhaps also you might inform her that during the war I appeared at a great many army camps, at chapel services on military posts from Fort Eustis and Camp Kilmer on the East Coast to Fort Huachuca in the West, and also read my poems for a great many USO programs. Within the past three years I have appeared under the direct auspices of religious groups ranging from Catholic to Mormon, and Jewish to Baptist.

I am just back from a Negro History Week tour of the South as far down as Florida, and leave tomorrow for State College at Dover, Delaware, Penna. State Teachers College at Lock Haven, and other campuses. So I must make this note brief as it is 2 A.M. now and I must get up at 6 to catch a train for an early assembly at Dover. I am sorry I was not in New York when you were.

Good wishes to you,

Sincerely,

recent "red" lists). It is, therefore, pretty important to stand up for the traditional American right of freedom of speech and press—if we want any of that right to be left to us at all."
* The W. Colston Leigh Bureau booked Hughes's lectures for many years.

TO NOËL SULLIVAN   [ALS]

[On Clark Hotel, 1820-24 South Central Avenue, Corner of Washington Blvd.
and Central Ave., Los Angeles 21, California, Prospect 5357 *stationery]*

April 10, 1948

Dear Noël,

Father Dunn† (thanks to you) has seats for the Ivan Johnsons‡ and I on Saturday (in answer to my wire to him after box office said "all sold out for the entire run").

How I wish you had been with me last night—you'd have had a wonderful laugh—as I did—at Arthur Koestler's Philharmonic lecture.§ I'm sitting in the 12th row center when in the middle of his talk where he shows how the Russians have betrayed the Negroes and the Jews, I suddenly hear, "That great Negro poet whom I met in Soviet Asia, a Party member as I was then, but <u>who is now dead</u>, was broke and hungry there, etc. . . . . |"| (The story of the movie as distorted by the Hearst press.) <We traveled all over Soviet Asia together. He's an old time friend.>

Well, if you had seen his face when I went backstage—not dead at all—you would have been chuckling yet! ——➤ < Folks are still getting me mixed with |Countee| Cullen!> Koestler and I had a good laugh ourselves once he got himself together, and I spent a couple of hours with him in Beverly Hills this afternoon. He's speaking Tuesday in San Francisco at Scottish Rite—in case you'd like to hear the USSR really <u>laid low</u>! But reason I am writing you is, he'll be stopping in Carmel Friday and Saturday on the way up, and I asked him to give you a ring, as you probably know "Darkness at Noon" and some of his other books. <You'd be interested in his analysis of Europe now.> He also hopes to meet Robin |Jeffers|. He's a brilliant guy and more anti-Russian

---

† Father George H. Dunne (1906–1998), an influential Jesuit priest and scholar, was a leading crusader for civil rights. In a 1945 article in the Catholic magazine *Commonweal* he sparked controversy when he called racial segregation a "sin."

‡ Ivan J. Johnson (1902–?) became the first African American Assistant United States Attorney in Los Angeles in 1937. (Cullen had died in 1946.)

§ Arthur Koestler (1905–1983) was a Hungarian-born novelist, journalist, and essayist. In 1931, he joined the Communist Party but left it seven years later when he immigrated to the U.K. Koestler soon became an outspoken opponent of communism. He contributed an essay to the widely noted volume *The God That Failed: A Confession* (Harper, 1949), in which he and five other prominent writers, including Richard Wright, discuss their disillusionment with communism.

than Col. McCormick.* Also anti-Wallace, and anti-P.M.† (and he had me not only Red—but dead!)

I hear Ethel Waters is staying at the Fairmont, where I'll be on Tuesday, too.

Affectionately,
Langston

TO HORACE BOND   [TL]

Interlude in travel,
April 30, 1948

Dear Horace,‡

Thank you so much for sending me a copy of your answer to Rev. Strock.§ It reached me here on this lovely farm in the Carmel Valley (Catholic friends of mine) where I am resting a few days after feudin' and a-fightin' with the Gerald L. K. Smith-minded all across the country. I have written a brief answer to their censorship in a forthcoming Defender column,¶ but expect to do a more comprehensive piece on my adventures when I get back to New York in June.

I have just sent you an envelope of material, and the same to Rev. Strock. Should you get any more such inquiries, certainly you can state categorically

---

* Robert Rutherford McCormick (1880–1955), a colonel in World War I, was owner and editor of the *Chicago Tribune* as well as a staunch individualist and isolationist whose criticism of British imperialism, socialism, and communism were often included in the news columns of his paper.

† Henry A. Wallace (1888–1965) was the candidate of the Progressive Party in the 1948 U.S. presidential election. A former U.S. vice president (1941–1945), he based his campaign on issues such as an end to racial segregation, the need for universal health coverage, and cooperation with the Soviet Union. He won only 2.4 percent of the popular vote in the election won by Harry S. Truman. Ralph Ingersoll (1900–1985) published *PM*, a leftist daily newspaper, from 1940 to 1948.

‡ Horace Mann Bond (1904–1972) was the eighth president and the first African American president of Lincoln University, Hughes's alma mater. He held the position from 1945 to 1957.

§ On April 19, 1948, Reverend Henry B. Strock of the First Presbyterian Church of Lancaster, Pennsylvania, wrote to Bond asking for "the truth of the report that he [Hughes] is aggressively engaged in Communist activities in our country." Bond defended Hughes's record, and forwarded both Strock's letter and his own response to Hughes. Hughes then wrote to Strock directly.

¶ Hughes's essay "A Thorn in Their Side" appeared in *The Chicago Defender* on May 15, 1948. In it he charged "Gerald L. K. Smith, the Klan and others who think like them" with intimidating sponsors and potential sponsors of his lectures by falsely branding him as a communist.

that I am not now and have never been a member of the Communist Party. (And I haven't the least idea when or where the 8th Convention was held nor had I anything to do with it.) All I can say for Senator Hawkes is that he is an unmitigated liar.* My months in Russia were spent as a writer and journalist and my articles appeared in such respectable publications as THE WOMAN'S HOME COMPANION, ASIA, and TRAVEL.

An atheist or a good party-liner would hardly have permitted the publication of a group of religious poems, FEET O' JESUS, in my book, THE DREAM KEEPER, that appeared the very year I was in the Soviet Union; or the publication of a song based on the same poem, AT THE FEET OF JESUS, in 1947. (Music by Hall Johnson.) The Senator is a dope!

By the way, before I left New York in February, I ordered sent your Library as a gift two complete sets of my books—as I ran into a student in Harlem who said every time he tried to get a copy of my novel, it was out! I hope they arrived O.K.

Perhaps I will see you at the Rosenwald Dinner in Chicago May 28th. Hope so.

Sincerely,

TO CARL SANDBURG   [TL]

20 East 127th Street,
New York 35, New York,
August 2, 1948.

Mr. Carl Sandburg,
Flat Rock,
North Carolina.

Dear Carl Sandburg,
Arna Bontemps and I have prepared for Doubleday and Company a comprehensive anthology called THE POETRY OF THE NEGRO, containing not only the Negro poets of the United States, but a Caribbean section as well, and a section of tributary poems on Negro themes by non-Negro poets from Blake

---

* In a bizarre charge, Senator Albert W. Hawkes (1878–1971) of New Jersey had recently denounced Hughes in a church in Montclair, New Jersey. According to Hawkes: "I was amazed to see a Communist [Langston Hughes] stand up in the pulpit and to hear him . . . berate the United States, tear it down for 55 minutes, and eulogize Russia."

to Whitman up to the present time. In this latter section we are delighted to include two lovely poems of yours, JAZZ FANTASIA and MAMMY HUMS. The publishers will be writing shortly (if you or your publishers have not already heard) for the proper permissions.

There is, however, something that requires your own personal permission. (As a poet myself I hesitate to ask it of you, but the reasons I shall give will explain why.) The publishers expect THE POETRY OF THE NEGRO to have wide use in schools and colleges. Nowadays some school boards absolutely refuse to O.K. the use of books or songs that contain the word "nigger", and the Negro schools of the South will often refuse to put such books on their shelves. (I have run into that with some of my own work.) You are my favorite contemporary American poet and, I repeat, that I am very loath to ask this. But would you permit Mr. Bontemps and I to delete the word "nigger" from the 7th line of your poem, MAMMY HUMS? The line would then read thus:

Head, heels, and fingers rocked to the mammy humming of it,
to the mile-off steamboat landing whistle of it.

And would you be so kind as to air-mail me your answer in the enclosed envelope, since we are about ready to go to press?*

I still remember with great pleasure our meeting at Lincoln University some years ago.†

All my good wishes to you, as ever,

Sincerely yours,
Langston Hughes

---

* Sandburg approved the request. The amended line appears in *The Poetry of the Negro, 1746–1949* (1949).
† On May 18, 1943, Hughes and Sandburg received honorary doctorates from Lincoln University. As commencement speaker, Sandburg reportedly held forth for three hours and fifteen minutes.

TO BENJAMIN J. DAVIS, JR.   *[TL]*

20 East 127th Street,
New York 35, New York,
November 9, 1948.

Benjamin J. Davis, Jr.,*
200 West 135th Street,
New York 30, New York.

Dear Ben,

Yours just came as I am about to leave on a Southern lecture tour for Omega Achievement Week and Book Week to be gone until near the end of the month. This week-end will find me in South Carolina, doing the colleges there. I'm packing right now to depart tomorrow.

I'd be delighted to talk with you when I come back. But never having been much of a political theoretician, I doubt if I would or could be of much use in the trial, my feelings being more emotional than scientific. And never having been inside a court room, I reckon lawyers could tangle me up right good if they choose. Also the Hearst papers and the TRIBUNE have been hammering at me tooth and nail for the past two years, so I should think persons "above the struggle", so to speak, would be of more help to you-all than I could be, belonging according to the Hearst press and the Thomas Committee to "89 subversive organizations!" Myself! And trying to get ready to sue somebody. But, anyhow, on my return, I'll drop by your office.

Sincerely, though hastily,
Langston Hughes

---

* A graduate of Harvard College and a lawyer, Benjamin J. Davis (1903–1964) joined the Communist Party following his legal defense of Angelo Herndon in 1933. He later (1943) won election as a New York City councilman. In his letter, Davis asked Hughes to testify as a noncommunist on Marxist theory at the Manhattan trial of twelve communists, including Davis, accused of advocating the overthrow of the U.S. government.

TO ZELL INGRAM   [TL]

March 29 |probably 19 or 20|

1949

Dear Zell:

As I reckon you know, I am "writer in residence" at the University of Chicago Laboratory School for the spring quarter,* but had to fly back for a couple of days this week for rehearsals of my opera, TROUBLED ISLAND. I am returning to Chicago tonight. I tried to get you on the phone a couple of times to tell you that Nicolas Guillen is in town at the Hotel Governor Clinton, 31st Street at 7th Avenue, Room 420 (Phone PE.6-3400). He would like to see you while you are here.

But the main problem is that the Negro (Cuban though he be) wants to remain in New York for the duration of his immigration permission, which will be about two weeks more. Like most colored, he has very little money. If Aunt Toy |Harper|'s nephew had not just arrived from California, we could put him up here for ten days or so, but at the moment all of our space is filled. If you would like to have a distinguished Cuban house guest, amiable and with a sense of humor, just get in touch with Nicolas.

If he should move from the hotel, a letter or wire addressed to him: Cultural and Scientific Conference for World Peace, Hotel Waldorf-Astoria, 49 West 44th Street, would reach him.

I will be flying back to town next Thursday, March 31, for the opening of TROUBLED ISLAND at City Center. My first and only opera to date. It looks good in rehearsal and the opening bids fair to be quite an occasion. At least a large number of high notes will be made.

All good wishes.

Sincerely,

Langston Hughes

Mr. Zell Ingram
253 W. 114th Street, Apt. 2
New York, N. Y.

LH:HHS

---

* On March 1, 1949, Hughes began a three-month residence as "Visiting Lecturer on Poetry" at the Laboratory Schools of the University of Chicago. The Lab School, well known for its innovative curriculum, enrolls pupils from kindergarten through high school.

TO MELVIN B. TOLSON   [TL]

June 18, 1949

Mr. Melvin B. Tolson
Langston University
Langston, Oklahoma

Dear Tolson:
I like your poem, AFRICAN CHINA, immensely. In fact, I think it is one of
the best things of yours that I have seen, and if it is a portent of your new style,
more power to you! I am indeed happy to accept it for publication in the late
Fall issue of VOICES.*

There is only one thing that worries me about it and that is the false rhyme
at the very end:

> their elders' orches<u>trina</u>
> in the street they never made,
> the dusky children say, "African <u>china</u>!"

Besides, nobody knows what an <u>orchestrina</u> is (that is, nobody of the
Race). Would you be willing to do something about this? Perhaps change it to
something of this nature:

> in accents Carolina
> on this street they never made,
> these dusky children taunt,
> "African <u>China</u>!"

If you like this ending I make, I make you a free present of it all for noth-
ing. The poem is too good to be throw|ing| out an unsure rhyme at its close.
So let me know about it.†

I look forward to seeing you this summer, so don't disappoint me like you

* Harold Vinal (1891–1965) was founder and editor of *Voices*, a poetry journal. In February 1949, inviting Hughes to edit a special African American number, he observed that
"with so many fine poets among your race this strikes me as being a fine thing to do."
Hughes's special number appeared as the Winter 1950 issue.
† On October 15, 1949, Tolson wrote to Hughes: "PS. That change in the poem is Okay by
me." "African China" appeared in *Voices* with Hughes's revisions.

did last time when you missed my party at which I served rattlesnake meat especially in your honor, since you come from the Southwest. The Harlemites ate it all up before I could bat an eye, so I reckon I will have to stock an even larger supply the next time I am expecting you.

I am just back from four months of being a poet-in-residence at the University of Chicago, which was delightful but tiring. . . . . How do you like my new character, Old Ghost, in the <u>Chicago Defender</u>?* He can go anywhere and haunt anybody. (And will haunt you if you don't fix up this poem!). . . . All good wishes to you.

Sincerely,

TO MAXIM LIEBER   [TL]

August 29, 1949

Mr. Maxim Lieber,
253 West 101 Street,
New York 25, N. Y.

Dear Maxim,
I have delivered today to Miss Maria Leiper† at Simon & Schuster the completed manuscript of "LISTEN FLUENTLY", the SIMPLE book, due, according to contract on September 1. As you will see from the carbon of my letter to her, enclosed, I am of course willing to make further revisions should they seem desirable after they have given the new version a reading.

We must get for Simon & Schuster transfer of copyrights from the sources where the material first appeared. Would you attend to that since you know just what to ask, and how? 99½% of the material is from:

THE CHICAGO DEFENDER,
3435 Indiana Avenue,
Chicago 16, Illinois.

---

* Hughes featured the character "Old Ghost" in his *Defender* columns from June to August 1949. This African American ghost, able and willing to say anything to anyone, allowed Hughes to speak his mind on racial issues with relative freedom.
† Notably enthusiastic about Hughes's work, Maria Leiper was his editor at Simon & Schuster. The book was published in 1950 as *Simple Speaks His Mind*.

Address the Managing Director, Mr. Charles Browning there. It might be wise to get clearance on <u>all</u> Simple columns used there. The chapter "Down Under in Harlem" is from the NEW REPUBLIC. And a small portion of another chapter is from "Simple and The Rosenwald Fund" which appeared in PHYLON, Atlanta University, Atlanta, Georgia, Vol IX, NO. 3, 1948.

I am sending you by messenger today a carbon of "LISTEN FLUENTLY" in case you'd like to glance at it, your own self, and I'd love to have Minna see it. But tell her if it seems too long, NOT to read it all. Wait for the cut version— in print.

Since the movies seem to be going in for Negro themes right now—why not MR. SIMPLE as a character for Rochester* or one of their other cullud comedians? Maybe you could sell it to them, then we could pay our phone bill ALL next year.

Thanks a lot for that Doubleday report on THE POETRY OF THE NEGRO with nary a dime.† It's all so familiar, I did not bat an eye nor turn a hair.

Mon cher ami, adieu,

Sincerely,

---

* Eddie "Rochester" Anderson (1905–1977) was an African American comic actor whose films include *The Green Pastures* (1936), *Cabin in the Sky* (1943), and *Brewster's Millions* (1945). He was nationally beloved for his portrayal of Rochester, a Pullman car porter turned butler and chauffeur, on the Jack Benny comedy radio show.
† Although *The Poetry of the Negro, 1746–1949* (1949) sold well, Doubleday reported that because of the high cost of permissions to republish so many poems, it owed no royalties as yet to the editors.

PART IV

The Rumble of a Dream Deferred

1950 to 1960

With Frank Reeves before Senator McCarthy's subcommittee,
March 1953

What happens to a dream deferred?
Does it dry up
like a raisin in the sun?
Or fester like a sore—
And then run?
—"HARLEM [2]," 1951

The early 1950s challenged Hughes. The brownstone row house
he owned and shared with Toy and Emerson Harper at 20 East
127th Street became his castle. He often left town for lectures and
other commitments, and spent part of the summer of 1950 in bucolic
Greenwood Lake, New York, but loved to get back to "nice noisy Harlem." In 1950 he published *Simple Speaks His Mind*, a comic triumph
culled from his *Defender* columns that featured his black urban Everyman, "Jesse B. Semple," or Simple. In 1951 came *Montage of a Dream
Deferred*, a memorable book-length "poem on contemporary Harlem"

that dramatized both the community's dignity and humanity, on the one hand, and also its decline mainly in the face of racism, on the other. The short story collection *Laughing to Keep from Crying* appeared in 1952.

However, Hughes kept writing despite harassment that reached its apex, or nadir, in 1953. That year, Senator Joseph McCarthy forced him to testify before McCarthy's infamous subcommittee on "un-American" activities (although even the FBI asserted that Hughes had never been a communist). Without naming any of his former leftist associates—much less denouncing them, as some witnesses had done—Hughes again renounced his radical past. He declared that a "complete reorientation of my thinking and emotional feelings occurred roughly four or five years ago." Disturbed by this experience, and under constant pressure to find money despite living frugally, he let few offers of contracts for new works slip by. He became, or so he joked ruefully, "a literary sharecropper."

TO NOËL SULLIVAN [*TLS*]

[*On 20 East 127th Street, New York 35, N.Y. stationery*]

Sunday, September 3, 1950

Dear Noël,

I was delighted to return from Woodstock the other day to find Eulah |Pharr| here. And we have been enjoying stories of her wonderful trip ever since. (I am envious and jealous!) Unfortunately she and Aunt Toy |Harper| both have had terrible colds all week long and neither of them left the house until last night to have dinner with Nate and Cliff White* at Nate's house. Fortunately she is better now, Eulah, but was too poorly to see anything more of New York during her stay. . . . . As she will tell you, I have been head over heels with shows this summer—three!—and have been out of town most of the summer with one composer or another. THE BARRIER now seems to be all set, revisions and new opening all done, and Lawrence Tibbett is deep in rehearsals of his role and is quite good, they tell me, but I won't be likely to hear him until general rehearsals start on September 11 as I've got to go back up in

* Nathaniel V. White, an aspiring writer, was Hughes's secretary from 1945 to 1951. They had met in 1944 at Noël Sullivan's Hollow Hills Farm. Nate's brother Cliff (1922–1998) was a professional guitarist.

the country again tomorrow.* The show in progress of being written at the moment is sort of light opera musical in nature, commissioned by one of the Pennsylvania music societies, to be laid in that state, but otherwise no restrictions as to subject matter. We've decided to make it today, a love story set in the Western coal fields with the accent on folk music of the region. Elie Siegmeister is doing the score† . . . . . . The other musical that took me to Ogunquit, Maine, for a summer try-out is just plain musical comedy, and came off rather nicely up there, so much so that Mike Todd has taken an option on it but, as usual, wants the book entirely redone‡—which doesn't affect my part, the lyrics, as yet—nor, I hope, for some months to come—as I've had much too many things on my hands all at once. One show is enough! But three—all clamoring for attention in the same summer. Well, they caused me to completely forget a radio interview a month ago that had been arranged for my SIMPLE book. I didn't remember it until three hours after the program was over! So you see what show business does to one! . . . . . . Otherwise I've been O.K. except that I've been BROKE—all these shows being long term projects that don't pay off until they open—except small monthly option payments that can't cover the cost of keeping up with them from Maine to Michigan. (We had a delightful week there at the University with THE BARRIER.) But now they tell me there is already more than Fifty Thousand advance theatre party sales for THE BARRIER, and that we will probably do five weeks on the road before coming to New York—opening in Washington on the 25th of September, then Baltimore, Boston, and perhaps Philadelphia, depending on when the New York theatre they want will be available in the fall.

I was so sorry to find your note about Joel on my return to the city. Eulah and I had spoken about him when she came through en route to Europe and she had said then that he was getting older and frailer and that she hoped nothing would happen to him while she was away. Certainly I shall miss him

---

* The baritone Lawrence Tibbett (1896–1960), a star of the Metropolitan Opera and motion pictures, was cast on Broadway as the white father in *The Barrier*, Hughes's opera with the composer Jan Meyerowitz based on his 1935 play *Mulatto*.

† When the American composer Elie Siegmeister (1909–1991) was commissioned by the American Opera Company of Philadelphia and the Pennsylvania Federation of Music Clubs to create an opera set in Pennsylvania, he asked Hughes to write the libretto. For the opera, called "The Wizard of Altoona," Siegmeister drew on the folk music of western Pennsylvania. The work was never finished.

‡ Hughes's musical play set in the Depression, *Just Around the Corner,* had a summer try-out at the Ogunquit Playhouse in Maine starting on July 29, 1950. The work featured the lives of three young men in Greenwich Village, with a book by Abby Mann and Bernard Drew, music by Joe Sherman, and lyrics by Hughes. The producer Mike Todd (1909–1958), who was in town with another play, optioned *Just Around the Corner.* However, the project died after he insisted on a new book.

when I come back to the Farm—as I did Greta the last time.* That was a most beautiful tribute you wrote to him, and that he lived so long with us all is at least a blessing.

Toy has had her ups and downs this year, since she has so much energy that when she is well, she works herself down again—being in love with this big house and always doing things to improve it. The lawn has given us the most trouble. We've had it re-sodded and sown each summer—still it doesn't grow well. And this summer when it grew too well—ask Eulah to tell you what happened! It is amusing, but it also took most of the grass away!

Well, I wish I were flying out tonight with Eulah. If these shows get all set by the end of the year, maybe I can come out in the winter for a while to see you all again. And if, (as I hope) you do go to Rome, please say hello to us—if only for a minute on the way, and try to spend a few days—or as long as you'd wish—with us on the way back . . . . . . Arna |Bontemps| and his three daughters—in their teens—are expected today—we'd hoped before Eulah left—for a day or two before school opens.

All my best to Lee |Crowe|, Kappy,† Marie |Short|, and Una and Robin |Jeffers| when you see them. And I've loved your letters (and oh, yes, thanks so much for the Peyton book!)‡ and forgive me for writing so infrequently, but every time I get ready to set pen to paper a composer calls on the phone or else a producer. I never had such a year! But things seem to be clearing up a bit now. . . . . I think of you often. . . . . . . Affectionately,

Langston

TO JESSIE FAUSET [TL]

October 14
1 9 5 0

Dear Jessie:

Since I did not see you the other night at the Schomburg celebration at the library, I am dropping you this note to assure you that I am delighted to sponsor your application to the Whitney Foundation for an OPPORTUNITY FEL-

---

* Joel was Noël Sullivan's pet dachshund. Greta was the German shepherd who had kept Hughes company during his stay in Carmel in the early 1930s.
† Probably Kappo Phelan, a cousin of Noël Sullivan who published short stories and poetry and had been a fellow with Hughes at the Yaddo writers' colony in 1943.
‡ Thomas Roy Peyton's *Quest for Dignity: An Autobiography of a Negro Doctor* appeared in 1950.

LOWSHIP, and certainly I will give you a hearty send-off.* I wish you the best of luck. (But in talking with Bob Weaver† not long ago concerning some of the applicants I endorsed last year, whom he and I both thought worthy but who were unsuccessful in receiving fellowships, Bob told me that the Foundation leans strongly towards the younger and less well recognized people—which explains why most of those who received the first fellowships were in this category.)

I agree with you about the very great value which the themes of your books should be to Hollywood, especially since the films have opened up to Negro subject-matter in recent months. I have never been able to have any luck with my own books in Hollywood, even though my agent has a good representative out there, so I have no expert advice to offer you other than, to tap Hollywood at all, judging by what white writers tell me, takes much more than individual effort, and one of the top-notch agents is needed. My agent has even tried some of the foreign film companies but without success. But if you get an agent to handle your books for films, perhaps the Italian or French companies might be interested. Certainly I think they would be worth a try.

Of course, I have read all of your novels and have referred to them often in my lectures and in print as being most important contributions to the record of American Negro life.‡ Unfortunately, I am in no position to collaborate with you on turning them into scripts, since I am some six months behind now on two contracts of my own—one for a play and one for a book, having been greatly delayed in my commitments this year by my two shows, THE BARRIER and JUST AROUND THE CORNER, both of which have had try-out productions but have not yet gotten to Broadway, and both of which have required a great deal of changing and reworking. THE BARRIER is now in rehearsal again to open for a pre-Broadway run on October 17 at the Flatbush Theater, to be followed by the Windsor in the Bronx. There is nothing like the theater to take up a great deal of one's time and, with another show under way, due to be finished this fall insofar as the libretto is concerned, besides the two above commitments that I mentioned, I do not see my way clear before next

---

* John Hay Whitney (1904–1982), a philanthropist, created a foundation in 1946 to fund educational and community projects for minority ethnic groups. The John Hay Whitney Opportunity Fellowships were awarded to deserving individuals from these groups.

† Dr. Robert C. Weaver (1907–1997), a Harvard-educated economist and urban housing expert, directed the fellowship program of the John Hay Whitney Foundation from 1949 to 1955. President Johnson appointed him as the first secretary of the new Department of Housing and Urban Development in 1966, making Weaver also the first African American to serve in a presidential cabinet.

‡ Fauset published four novels: *There Is Confusion* (1924); *Plum Bun* (1928); *The Chinaberry Tree* (1931); and *Comedy, American Style* (1933).

summer before taking up anything new. At that time I would like to be free to begin the second volume of my autobiography.* It seems just about impossible for me to keep up with my own work, let alone attempting anything else. But you know my great admiration for you and I hope that you succeed with your projects. With very best wishes, as ever.

Sincerely,

Langston Hughes

TO BLANCHE KNOPF   [TL]

November 30, 1950

Mrs. Blanche Knopf,
Alfred A. Knopf, Inc.,
501 Madison Avenue,
New York 22, New York.

Dear Blanche,

In accordance with our previous conversations, your last letters to me, and our mutual desire I am submitting to you the manuscript of my selected poems, PRELUDE TO OUR AGE, The Selected Poems of Langston Hughes.†

It contains the best poems from my various books, including those most popular and most widely known, judging from reprintings, anthologies, translations, and lecture response—such as THE NEGRO SPEAKS OF RIVERS, I, TOO, FREEDOM TRAIN, and the MADAM TO YOU series, as well as the widely used radio poem, FREEDOM'S PLOW, twice performed on a national hook-up by Paul Muni.

There are poems from FINE CLOTHES TO THE JEW long out of print and so unavailable to the general public, and from the privately printed DEAR LOVELY DEATH and other booklets which never had a wide circulation and

---

* Hughes began writing his second volume of autobiography, *I Wonder as I Wander* (Rinehart, 1956), on July 17, 1954. The volume covers his life from 1931 through New Year's Day 1938. Earlier, on November 10, 1949, Blanche Knopf had rejected Hughes's proposal for the work: "The Autobiography sounds to me in reading the outline pretty weighted and I don't feel in fairness to you, and certainly in fairness to ourselves, much as I regret having to say this to you, that we should make any commitment for it until you have written some of it so that we can read it. If this means you feel that you should take it elsewhere, I think I will have to free you to do it with great regret."

† Citing its large stock of unsold books of Hughes's poetry, for years Knopf resisted his pitches for a volume of this kind. Finally, in late 1957, the firm gave in. In 1959 it published *Selected Poems of Langston Hughes.* (See letter of November 30, 1957.)

that have become collectors' items. It also contains a careful selection of my best blues, and the largest group of Negro humorous poems since Paul Laurence Dunbar,* as well as lyrics and ballads.

As you know, my first book, THE WEARY BLUES, appeared in 1926 so next year, 1951, will round off a quarter of a century of my publishing with you. PRELUDE TO OUR AGE contains 224 poems, a careful selection of my work over a 25 year period. When the next 25 years roll around, perhaps we will bring out a COLLECTED POEMS. Now, however, I think a SELECTED POEMS would be in order. At my programs, people have been asking for several years now where they can get their favorite poems of mine all in one volume. I have tried to assemble those poems here.

The book contains a number of poems never before published in book form, and about a dozen not heretofore published anywhere. (I will not submit these to magazines, but hold them unpublished until the book appears, which will give it added freshness and value.) It does not contain all of the poems from any one volume of my other books—so each of them would still be essential to libraries or collectors wishing my complete works.

I believe we agreed that this book should have a Preface. Since my work is used a great deal by schools and colleges, the Preface should contain enough biographical and background material to be of value to students, as well as being a kind of overall summary of and commentary on my poetry. Since last talking with you, I have given quite a good deal of thought as to whom might write such a Preface. Perhaps Arna Bontemps might be a good choice as he has written interestingly about poetry, is himself a poet and anthologist, critic and well known writer, and also being a historian, could relate my work to the times and the people from which it comes. Carl Van Vechten might be another choice; Louis Untermeyer,[†] Ridgely Torrence, Robert Morss Lovett,[‡]

---

* Paul Laurence Dunbar (1872–1906), the son of former slaves, was the first African American poet to gain a national reputation. Dunbar published his first volume of poetry, *Oak and Ivy*, in 1893. His third volume, *Lyrics of Lowly Life* (1896), with a preface by the eminent editor, critic, and novelist William Dean Howells, made him widely known.

† Louis Untermeyer (1885–1977) was perhaps best known for his anthologies of poetry, which he began publishing in the 1920s. He served as Poet Laureate Consultant in Poetry at the Library of Congress from 1961 to 1963.

‡ Robert Morss Lovett (1870–1956) was editor of *The New Republic* from 1921 to 1940. After the federal government fired him in 1943 from his job as government secretary of the Virgin Islands over his alleged communist associations, the U.S. Congress passed a bill barring him from the federal payroll. In 1946, the Supreme Court overturned this action (*United States v. Lovett*).

or perhaps Carl Sandburg. Or maybe Ralph Bunche,* if we seek someone outside the literary field. In any case, it should be someone who could either do a
good interpretative and literary evaluation, or else a penetrating social one<,>
relating the poetry to the problems of our times in relation to democracy and
the Negro people and showing how even the blues have deeply social roots.

Perhaps you might think of other possibilities to write a Preface. Please let
me know whom you might think suitable. (For whomever is chosen, I have a
good carbon of the manuscript I can let him have, so you won't need to send
out your copy.)

Since a large number of my poems have been set to music and are sung by
Marian Anderson, Lawrence Tibbett, Todd Duncan,† Roland Hayes, and others, I thought it might be interesting to both readers and musicians to include
a list of those poems which have been published in sheet music available to
singers, so I have done this at the back of the book.

All of the poems in PRELUDE TO OUR AGE either come from Knopf
books, are new poems, or else I hold the copyright on them myself except
for nine poems—four of them recently in magazines requiring simply the
transfer of copyright; and five of them in the forthcoming Henry Holt book,
MONTAGE OF A DREAM DEFERRED.‡ So there will be but little securing of
permissions or copyrights to do.

I am, of course, open to suggestions as to revisions or rearrangement
of the poems in PRELUDE. I hope the book can be published in the fall of
1951—in time for Christmas sales next year—and my annual autumn Book
Week lecture tour. (I've just gotten back from college appearances in Maryland, Virginia, and North Carolina. And in February, Negro History Week, I
go to the Deep South—Fisk, Dillard, and other colleges. But this season I can
only be out of town for a couple of weeks at a time, having another show on
my hands to finish. However, next fall I shall probably do a much longer tour
such as I usually do every other season—probably<,> in the autumn of '51<,>
through the Southwest to the Coast again.)

* Dr. Ralph Bunche (1904–1971) was a Harvard-educated political scientist and diplomat.
For his work as a mediator with the United Nations in Palestine, he won the Spingarn
Medal of the NAACP in 1949 and the Nobel Peace Prize in 1950.
† The baritone Todd Duncan (1903–1993) originated the role of Porgy in George Gersh-
win's *Porgy and Bess* (1935) and later became the first African American singer to join the
New York City Opera.
‡ *Montage of a Dream Deferred* (Henry Holt, 1951) is a book-length poem in six parts.
Hughes designed each part to be autonomous, yet unified them by repeated invocations
of the motif of the dream (of justice) deferred and by employing rhythms drawn from the
relatively new bebop jazz. Knopf had declined this book, as well as his second volume of
autobiography.

I await your comments on the above ideas and the manuscript I am submitting to you.

It was nice to read about the appreciation the Latin Americans have for what you have done for their literature here. Certainly you deserve it.

My continued good wishes to you, as ever,

Sincerely yours,

Langston Hughes

P.S. The letters after many poems in the manuscript indicate the books from which they came. For example TWB indicates THE WEARY BLUES. This for editorial use and identification only.

TO W. E. B. DU BOIS   [ALS]
[Draft of a telegram]

WESTERN UNION

To Dr. W.E.B. Du Bois Feb. 23 1951[*]
Essex House, 160 Central Park South
Testimonial Dinner
New York, N.Y.

YOUR BOOK DARK WATER[†] GREATLY INFLUENCED MY YOUTH. I GREW UP ON YOUR EDITORIALS. AS EDITOR OF THE CRISIS YOU PUBLISHED MY FIRST POEM. IN GRATITUDE ON YOUR EIGHTY THIRD BIRTHDAY I SALUTE YOU AS ONE OF AMERICA'S GREAT MEN AND THE DEAN OF NEGRO WRITERS AND SCHOLARS.

Langston Hughes

Morgan College

* Du Bois's eighty-third birthday found him recently indicted by the United States for allegedly operating as an unregistered agent of a foreign government because of his work at the Peace Information Center, an organization with ties to the Soviet Union. A judge would summarily dismiss the case against Du Bois and his five colleagues on November 13, 1952. Many people chose not to attend this dinner (on Du Bois's birthday in 1951) because of his indictment, but Hughes's greeting was read to the audience. (Hughes himself was then visiting Morgan College in Baltimore, Maryland.) In his newspaper column Hughes also defended Du Bois. He declared: "The Accusers' Names Nobody Will Remember, But History Records Du Bois." However, Hughes later appeared to bow to political pressure when he omitted Du Bois from his book *Famous American Negroes* (1954).
† *Darkwater: Voices from Within the Veil* (1920), by W. E. B. Du Bois, is a collection of essays, poems, and short fiction about race, gender, and politics.

TO MAXIM LIEBER   [TL]
<u>SIMPLY HEAVENLY</u>

April 16, 1951

Mr. Maxim Lieber,
253 West 101st Street,
New York, New York.

Dear Maxim,

So busy with those two auditions last week I couldn't get around to mail. And not having Nate |White|'s assistance (he's resigned) has caused letters to pile mountain high.

But, as you can see from the enclosed carbon, I would be happy to make a personal appearance along with the SIMPLE show next fall in Newark.* You may also O.K. this, if you wish, and are writing the lady again.

Did your representative in London say he would send us an air check on the BBC broadcasts of SIMPLE? I hope so, at my expense, of course.

I've got Mr. Battle piled up here in front of me to work on tonight—a new and more adventuresome beginning—so I hope—about the numbers.† But there will be no making an Ethel Waters out of this respectable pillar of the community—not at this late date in his comfortable old age. He is on too many Y. M. C. A. boards, etc. to tell ALL.

<">Simple,<"> however, has no such qualms. In the new novel—and NOVEL it will be—he relates his love life from A-B-C to J-O-Y-C-E as you will note in the pages I am sending you this week for submission to Maria Leiper.‡ I have assembled 20 chapters (100 and some odd pages) as the first draft of the opening section of the book, with a synopsis of the remainder. Since Simple

---

* After the successful publication of *Simple Speaks His Mind* in 1950, and taking a cue from Alice Childress (see below), Hughes began planning a musical based on Simple called *Simply Heavenly*. It was first performed in 1957.

† In 1911, Samuel Jesse Battle (1883–1966) became the first black policeman in New York City. After a long career, he retired as a parole commissioner. Around 1950, a Hollywood screenwriter proposed a movie about Battle's life if a biography were published first. Signing a contract that would assure him of a share of revenue earned by the book and the film, Hughes accepted $1,500 from Battle and began working on a biography called "Battle of Harlem." Various publishers, including Simon & Schuster, Henry Holt, and John Day, rejected Hughes's manuscript as inadequate. It was never published.

‡ Simon & Schuster published Hughes's second edited collection of Simple newspaper columns, *Simple Takes a Wife* (1953).

will probably continue indefinitely as a character in the DEFENDER, you can offer Simon and Schuster an option on the third volume, as well, which will concern his married life with Joyce. Then we will have a trilogy: THE SAGA OF SIMPLE, eventually. I like S. & S. as publishers, so wouldn't mind being tied up with them for an option or so, in case they take this novel. Anyway, I shall continue the Simple stories in the paper, writing them more with an eye toward a consecutive plot line in the future. This particular manuscript, I could promise to deliver completed by January 15, 1951 |1952|. (I would say January 1, but that's a holiday!)*

The ASP seems to be presenting "Just A Little Simple" in Philadelphia.† I saw a bill announcing it when I was over there last week with |Elie| Siegmeister.

Best to Minna, and to you, as ever,

Sincerely,

TO INA STEELE [TL]

April 21, 1951

Dear Ina,‡

I guess you'll think I'm the worst invitation-turner-downer ever—but I am under oath not to leave town again (except for my last two lectures of the season next week-end) until I get the man's book done, having been away so much this winter. It was due last January1st!!! Now he's after me, my agent's after me, and the publishers—and I have long since spent the advance!§ Now, I am nothing but a literary sharecropper, and can't go any place, as much as I would like to see the Eastern Sho' in May, and especially attend the "Q" dance with you and Youra. I've been working until daybreak the past ten days trying to get out from under. But still have stacks of notes, albums, clippings, and a tape recorder full of what he told that I haven't even listened to again. The

* Hughes delivered the manuscript on September 26, 1952.
† Alice Childress (1916?–1994), an African American actress and playwright, adapted a portion of *Simple Speaks His Mind* as a one-act play called *Just a Little Simple*. It was first produced in September 1950 at the Club Baron Theatre in New York.
‡ Hughes met Ina Steele (then Ina Qualls) and her twin sister, Youra, two young academics at Texas College in Tyler, Texas, on April 1, 1932, during his poetry reading tour of the South. He corresponded with both sisters for the next three decades. (See also Hughes's letter of April 9, 1963.)
§ The advance was for Samuel Jesse Battle's biography.

next time I do anybody's life it will be my own. No one else's a-tall! Besides what Negro can compete with Ethel Waters—and still live? I even had to turn down a chance to see GUYS AND DOLLS the other day—some rich folks had tickets. But I did go to the Press Club Dinner last night and saw Sweet[*] there taking pictures for OUR WORLD[†] and he asked to be remembered to you. Added to current excess of work, my secretary |Nate White| resigned to become a writer himself, and my in-a-pinch assistants (man and wife) went to Japan to teach last month—so all I do now is put the morning's mail in a drawer and hide it. (Two drawers are full so I'm moving my sox over.) This year I thought Easter was Christmas, my DEFENDER fans were so kind: a box of oranges from Florida, twelve cartons of cigarettes from Ohio, a box of fudge from an invalid in Illinois, maple syrup from Vermont, two ties, and a table cloth from a crazy lady in Mississippi who writes me all her troubles every day nearly. (As nearly as I can gather she has some sort of persecution complex, but writes very sane and sometimes charming poetries.) So tonight I'm trying to acknowledge those nice gifts—late. Since Youra reviewed SIMPLE so beautifully, maybe she'd like to see what England is saying about it—excerpts enclosed. When she goes through to Texas, why don't you come as far as Harlem and we'll all have a drink at the Theresa, huh? Or the Shalimar—or from the corner store. (In Montgomery only one licker store is open to cullud. In Harlem there's one per block!) . . . . . . Well, I will close,

Regretfully,

---

* Moneta J. Sleet, Jr. (1926–1996), whom Hughes incorrectly names "Sweet," was a photojournalist whose work in part documents the civil rights movement. In 1950, he was a reporter for the *Amsterdam News* when *Our World* hired him as a staff photographer. Five years later, Sleet became a photographer for *Ebony* magazine. He received a Pulitzer Prize for a photograph, printed first in *Ebony*, of Coretta Scott King at Martin Luther King, Jr.'s, funeral in 1968.

† Founded by the lawyer and activist John P. Davis (1905–1973) in 1946, *Our World* was a nationally distributed magazine written for an African American audience. In circulation for eleven years, the publication addressed topics such as history, politics, and entertainment.

TO ERA BELL THOMPSON   [TL]

June 20, 1951

Miss Era Bell Thompson,*
NEGRO DIGEST,
1820 South Michigan Avenue,
Chicago 16, Illinois.

Dear Era Bell,

Just a quick note to tell you I'll do my best to do a piece for you on the theme of DO BIG NEGROES KEEP LITTLE NEGROES DOWN.† But I don't quite see it as all one-sided—some do, and some don't. Therefore, shouldn't we put in the positive elements as well. Just recently I've come across a couple of examples of fine generosity on the part of professional Negroes to the less well-off. And my dentist, for example, (as his way, no doubt, of being a patron of the arts) never sends me a bill. (Dentistry being as high as it is, I couldn't pay him anyhow.)

I hope I'll see you if you come to town.

Sincerely,
Langston Hughes

* Era Bell Thompson (1906–1986) became the editor of *Negro Digest* in 1947 and associate editor of *Ebony* magazine that same year. At *Ebony*, she held several other major positions until her retirement. She published an autobiography, *American Daughter*, in 1946.
† Hughes's article "Do Big Negroes Keep Little Negroes Down?" appeared in the November 1951 issue of *Negro Digest*.

TO MAXIM LIEBER   [*TL*]

December 7, 1951

Mr. Maxim Lieber
Apartado 235
Cuernavaca, Morelos
Mexico*

Dear Max,

It is so nice to hear from you at last and to know that you are settled in so beautiful a place. I've justly recently gotten back from a lecture tour of the Carolinas as far down as Savannah, and I find your letters awaiting me. Thanks for them, and the Chappelle statement.

I am writing the Dramatists' Guild to follow through in collecting on THE BARRIER.

The Harold Ober Office is negotiating the new Henry Holt contract,[†] and will handle my future books, including the Battle book which is almost done. Leah Salisbury[‡] is handling my plays including the Siegmeister musical on which we are still working |"The Wizard of Altoona"|.

Everybody was certainly sorry to see you go out of business and we all hope that you will be quite well again soon. Minna was very sweet about taking care of things and she certainly had a big job closing down both the office and the house. Please give her and the children my love and let me hear from you when you have time. If you see Willard Motley there give him my regards.[§]

All good wishes to you,

Sincerely yours,
LANGSTON HUGHES

---

* Implicated in the infamous Alger Hiss spying affair, Lieber was publicly identified as a communist operative and fled the United States for Mexico. Minna Lieber, his wife, helped Hughes transfer his account to Ivan von Auw, Jr., of the Harold Ober Agency of New York City, which also listed among its clients writers such as J. D. Salinger and Agatha Christie.
† Henry Holt published *Laughing to Keep from Crying*, a volume of short stories by Hughes, in 1952.
‡ Leah Salisbury, Hughes's drama agent, dropped him as a client in 1952 after her repeated clashes with his collaborator Jan Meyerowitz.
§ Willard Motley (1909–1965), who began as a writer for *The Chicago Defender*, published his first novel, the best-seller *Knock on Any Door*, in 1947. In 1951, he emigrated from Chicago, his place of birth, to Mexico, where he wrote his last four novels.

TO ELMER RICE [TL]

February 6, 1952.

Mr. Elmer Rice, Chairman,
Committee on Blacklisting,
Authors' League of America,
6 East 39th Street,
New York 16, New York.

Dear Elmer,
Here are my answers to the questionnaire re the FCC and blacklisting in TV and radio:*

1. The publication of my name in RED CHANNELS has not affected my employment in TV or radio. Being colored I received no offers of employment in these before RED CHANNELS appeared, and have had none since—so it hasn't affected me at all.
2. Answered above.
3. Negro writers, being black, have always been blacklisted in radio and TV. Only once in a blue moon are any colored writers given an opportunity to do a script and then, usually, with no regularity, and no credits. Like Hollywood, Negroes just simply are not employed in the writing fields in the American entertainment industry.
4. My personal experience has been that in my 25 years of writing, I have not been asked to do more than four or five commercial one-shot scripts. These were performed on major national hook-ups, but produced for me no immediate additional jobs or requests. One script for BBC was done around the world with an all-star cast. No American stations offered me work. My agents stated flatly, "It is just about impossible to sell a Negro writer to Hollywood or radio, and they use Negro subject matter very rarely." Even the "Negro" shows like "Amos and

---

* On November 15, 1951, Elmer Rice (who had worked with Hughes on *Street Scene*) resigned in protest as a member of a group of playwrights because its commercial sponsor, the Celanese Corporation, began to investigate the political beliefs and activities of certain actors. After Rice spoke out on the matter, the Authors' League of America sent questionnaires to fifty authors identified as subversive in the controversial pamphlet *Red Channels: The Report of Communist Influence in Radio and Television*. (In June 1950, *Red Channels* had published the names of 151 persons, including Hughes, allegedly linked to communism.)

Andy" and "Beulah" are written largely by white writers—the better to preserve the stereotypes, I imagine.

During the war I did a number of requested scripts for the Writers' War Board, used throughout the country. Most of the white writers serving this committee also got any number of paying jobs to do patriotic scripts. Not one chance to do a commercial script was offered me.

My one period of work in radio covering several weeks was a few summers ago scripting the NBC show, "Swing Time at The Savoy", a Negro variety revue. This was achieved at the insistence of the N.A.A.C.P. that objected to the stereotypes in the audition scripts written by white writers. NBC had <at> that time had not one Negro writer on its staff—which would have saved them making the mistakes the N.A.A.C.P. objected to and which were offensive to the general Negro public. As far as I know, Negro writers are, however, "blacklisted" at NBC. I know of none working there regularly.

Richard Durham in Chicago and Bob Lucas and Woody Bovell in New York are excellent radio writers but, being Negroes, they work with great irregularity—not due to being red but due to being colored.

5. No point in my appearing—the color bars everyone knows have been with us since radio began, before TV was born, and long ere that.

I'd like to add, however, my personal gratitude to you and the committee for your very fine stand in relation to the freedom to work—for those writers who are white enough to work (when not red-baited) and I hope as well for those writers who have been blacklisted from birth.

And to you for your personal stand, Elmer, my very great admiration.

Sincerely yours,
Langston Hughes

TO L. B. SMITH   [TL]

March 9, 1952.

Mrs. L. B. Smith,
966 East Terrell,
Fort Worth 6, Texas.

Dear Mrs. Smith,

I'm just back in New York from my month long tour—arriving home in time for the heaviest snowfall of the season!

I was certainly sorry you were forced to cancel your program.* It seems that Pres. Clement of Atlanta University had the same trouble in Houston, and Pres. Mays of Morehouse not so long ago in Indiana, Lillian Smith in Savannah and Pearl Buck in Washington when both were to speak for Negro sponsors. It looks as if reactionary whites are out to destroy interracial good will in so far as audiences and speakers go, especially in the South. It would, of course, be much better from our viewpoint if they would use their energies attacking the evils of segregation, instead of the reversing the process and attacking Negro and white leaders and writers who are opposed to it. I hope they at least made you a donation large enough to get the kids a drinking fountain. I have thought that usually those making the loudest outcry are those who do |the| least for colored people, and the kind of "democracy" they claim to be protecting is the kind that keeps the FOR WHITE signs up all along the line, and not just in the South.

I wrote the publishers that the books would be returned directly to them, and I trust that you have been so kind as to see that they went back.

I was sorry not to have seen the Barnwells again. Please give them my best regards.

Again I regret all the inconvenience caused you by the forced cancellation, and I hope it will not happen again concerning future speakers in your city. If it continues, after a while we won't be able to listen to anyone other than the disc-jockies because almost every Negro speaker we have has been under

* Lucile B. Smith, the president of the Business and Professional Women's Club of Fort Worth, Texas, had invited Hughes to help raise funds for a local black school. The club had to cancel the program. Prominent writers such as Pearl Buck and Lillian Smith, as well as the presidents of Atlanta University and Morehouse College, ran into similar trouble with their own interracial efforts.

such attack recently in one place or another—even such distinguished leaders as Mrs. Bethune and Dr. Tobias.*

My thanks to you for taking care of the return of the books, and all my good wishes ever,

Sincerely yours,
Langston Hughes

TO INA STEELE   [TL]

April 17, 1952

Dear Ina,

I was hoping they'd forget that way last fall I'd accepted a May date for a program for an interracial group at Cornell (non-profit—but last year they had Roger Baldwin† and the year before that Mrs. Roosevelt—so cullud could hardly turn them down—I didn't) and now they've just written that it's all announced and they're expecting me for a dinner and a program and then a day of classes. So I'll be way upstate in New York and can't come to the Omega dance—AGAIN.‡ Which I really do regret, especially if you WON't never no more invite me! This Ithaca business is my last public appearance of the season but one, Brooklyn, June 1 for a cullud church. Then I retire to the country for another summer of book writing and composers, still having that biography to finish and the show of last season.§ After which I'd like to retire for GOOD, these past two years having been about the most contracted and committed years of my whole life! Nothing but a literary sharecropper! I do not intend again to work on anybody's books or shows but my black own! If them!. . . . . I missed the Marquand pieces, but if they're as good as your letters, I'll have to borrow the New Yorkers from a roomer downstairs and read them!¶ You are a good writer your own self. . . . . Ellison is my protégé!

---

* Channing H. Tobias (1882–1961), a cleric, joined the YMCA in 1905 and worked toward improving interracial relations. Retiring in 1946, he became director of the Phelps-Stokes Fund, an institution dedicated to the cause of African and African American education. The same year, President Truman appointed him to the Civil Rights Committee. Tobias won the Spingarn Medal of the NAACP in 1948.

† Roger Baldwin (1884–1981) was one of the founders of the American Civil Liberties Union (ACLU) in 1920.

‡ See Hughes's previous letter to Steele dated April 21, 1951.

§ In early May 1952, Hughes borrowed a cottage in Greenwood Lake to work on the biography "Battle of Harlem." He completed his sixth and final draft of the book in Harlem on August 9.

¶ In 1938, the novelist John P. Marquand (1893–1960) won a Pulitzer Prize for *The Late*

Dick Wright and I (me first because I introduced him to Dick) started him off writing—and look at him now. Wonderful reviews!* He and his wife just wrote me a swell letter sharing their new good fortune (in spirit). I expect he'll make some money, too!.... So sorry I can't come to that dance, see all those Q, Youra |Qualls|, AND YOU! Thanks immensely anyhow!

Regretfully,

TO RICHARD MORFORD   [TL]

May 27, 1952

Mr. Richard Morford,†
Executive Director,
National Council of
American-Soviet Friendship, Inc.,
114 East 32nd Street,
New York 16, New York.

Dear Mr. Morford,

Regretfully I must resign from membership in the National Council of American-Soviet Friendship. I was under the impression that my membership had long since lapsed, but I note on the April 23 Report that my name is still carried on the Membership List.

A major portion of my income is derived from lecturing in the Negro schools and colleges of the South. As you no doubt know, many of these institutions are now being forced by state boards or local politicians to screen their speakers according to the highly controversial Attorney General's list.‡ As I am sure you know, too, Negro speakers do not have the vast area of white women's clubs (with their teas and other social aspects) from which to secure engagements. So our fees must come almost entirely from Negro institutions. Most

---

George Apley (1937). The March 29 and April 15, 1952, issues of *The New Yorker* ran a profile of Marquand entitled "There Is No Place."

* That month, Random House published Ralph Ellison's novel *Invisible Man* (1952).

† A Presbyterian minister, Richard Morford (1903–1986) served as executive director of the National Council of American-Soviet Friendship from 1945 until 1981. The Friends of the Soviet Union, which Hughes supported in the 1930s, evolved in 1941 into the National Council on Soviet Relations and later into the National Council of American-Soviet Friendship.

‡ The Attorney General's List of Subversive Organizations, first published in 1947, was originally compiled as part of President Truman's attempt early in the cold war to determine the loyalty of federal employees.

Negro college heads are certainly not in sympathy with censorship or black-listing, but seemingly must at this period submit to it in order to maintain their already decreasing grants. And some colleges now ask speakers to indicate on signing of contracts that they do not belong to "listed" organizations.

I would, therefore, appreciate your removing my name from the membership list of the National Council.

Very sincerely yours,
Langston Hughes

TO CLAUDE BARNETT [TL]

March 28, 1953

Mr. Claude Barnett,*
Associated Negro Press,
3507 South Parkway,
Chicago 15, Ill.

Dear Claude,

Just in case your reporter present at my appearance last Thursday before the McCarthy Permanent Committee on Senate Investigations† did not send you any of the actual testimony verbatim, here is the entire latter portion of the proceedings as taken from the radio transcription of the hearings.

Not given in this is when, in the earlier portion of my questioning, I was asked about a chapter in my book, SIMPLE SPEAKS HIS MIND called "When a Man Sees Red" as to when and why it was written. I replied that in my opinion the chapter indicated clearly that Americans had freedom of press, speech, and publication, and the right of which we are all proud to freely criticize any branch of our government or any elected persons. And that this

---

* Claude Barnett (1889–1967), a Tuskegee Institute graduate, founded the Associated Negro Press (ANP), a news agency that operated from 1919 to 1964. Hughes sent a transcript of his Senate testimony to approximately 155 journalists, educators, publishers, and friends.

† Hughes was subpoenaed on Saturday, March 21, 1953, to appear the following Monday before Senator Joseph McCarthy's Senate Permanent Subcommittee on Investigations of the Committee on Government Operations in Washington, D.C. When Hughes asked for a one-week extension to prepare for the meeting, the committee gave him twenty-four hours. Unlike some witnesses who appeared before McCarthy's committee, Hughes declined to plead the Fifth Amendment. He instead answered all questions in a compromise worked out in private with McCarthy's staff.

chapter was written just after, and grew out of, an incident that occurred in the Un-American Committee when a member of the Committee called a Negro witness a name which I could not repeat on the air (the hearing being televised) but which comes under the heading of "playing the dozens" to Harlemites, namely talking badly about someone's mother. This incident greatly shocked Negro citizens and others of good will. And many translated it into terms of unfairness toward members of our race. So, in his imagined satire on the Un-American Committee the fictional character, Simple, was simply voicing his criticism which reflected a general community feeling.* After this answer, the McCarthy Committee did not pursue the subject further.

In general the entire hearing in relation to me mostly concerned my very early poems of the Scottsboro and Depression period when some of my work which never appeared in any of my books, but did appear in magazines and pamphlets, used leftist phraseology and in some cases reflected left ideas, particularly when such ideas coincided with the Negro desire for freedom from segregation, lynching, poverty, and Jim Crowisms—which I frankly admitted and explained to the Committee. I also stated clearly and unequivocally under oath in both the closed and open televised hearing that I am not now and have never been a member of the Communist Party, which I welcomed as an opportunity to get this on record. The hearing ended, as you can see from the enclosed transcript, with my being commended for my frankness and, although it was thought my early works should not be in the State Department's overseas libraries, such works might be replaced with my later and more recent works and books. In other words I was exonerated of any Communistic influences today.

Since some of |my| work has (to my pleasure and delight—and I hope to that of readers, |as| well) been syndicated through ANP, although this was never in any way brought up in Washington, I wanted you to have this resume of the hearing. With all good wishes,

Sincerely,

---

* In "When a Man Sees Red" Simple reveals what he might say if called before the House Committee on Un-American Activities:"I would say, 'Your Honery, I wish to inform you that I was born in America, I live in America, and long as I have been black, I been an American. . . . How come you don't have any Negroes on your Un-American Committee?' And old Chairman Georgia [referring to Chairman John Stephens Wood (1889–1968), Representative from Georgia] would say, 'Because that is un-American.'" Simple's words appear in the chapter "Something to Lean On" in *Simple Speaks His Mind* (1950).

TO FRANK D. REEVES   [TL]

Sunday, March 29, 1953

Mr. Frank D. Reeves,*
1901 11th Street, N. W.,
Washington, D. C.

Dear Frank,

No words—and certainly no money (even were it a million dollars) could in
any sense express to you my gratitude or from me repay you for what you
have done for me in a time of emergency. Without your able help and kind,
considerate, patient, and wise counsel, I would have been a lost ball in the
high weeds or, to mix metaphors, a dead duck among the cherry blossoms!
This note, or any letter that I might write, could only be a most inadequate
expression of thanks and my indebtedness to you. And I do not feel that in
any way this small check means anything in that regard. But I did want you to
have this immediately—which is all the weekend affords—as a token, at least,
of my deepest and sincerest sense of obligation to you for your sacrifice and
generosity in terms of both your time and talent, your willingness to help me,
and your personal kindness in doing so. Certainly you acted way "beyond the
call of duty" personally and professionally, and I am deeply grateful. There is
no way for me to repay you.

The hospitality of your home made me much more comfortable than I
would have been at the Statler or any other hotel, and the constant nearness of
your counsel made me feel more secure than I could have possibly been had
I stayed with other friends. And among the many pleasant memories I shall
retain of your home is your mother's apple sauce and your adorable puppy!

The phone calls which I personally made on your home phone and listed
in my pocket note book were two to New York, one March 24: 60¢, and one
March 25: 5.23; and on March 25 one call to Chicago: 2.65—totaling 8.48.
With the addition of 25% tax, this sum is $10.60.

Kindly add this amount to the total telephone charges for which I am
responsible that we may have run up, and whatever other expenses my stay

---

* Frank D. Reeves (1916–1973) of the NAACP served as Hughes's attorney at his McCarthy hearing. In New York, his colleagues in the NAACP Arthur Spingarn and Lloyd K.
Garrison of New York City also helped Hughes to prepare for the hearing.

in Washington might have involved, and I will send you a check as soon as possible.

Friday evening I had cocktails with Lloyd Garrison[*] and dinner with Walter White. Mr. Garrison went with me to Walter's and both heard the playback of the later portion of the open hearing which I had taken off on my tape recorder from the air Thursday midnight—a copy of which I'll have typed out and send you tomorrow. I gave them a detailed account of what went on, and am to see Lloyd Garrison within a few days regarding your follow-up suggestions and a few that I've thought of, too. I'll let you know the results of that conference.

I left my raincoat in your closet, so please put it in a manila envelope or parcel and post it to me. Thanks! And my very best regards to your wife, and office staff. At your convenience I await your financial statement. And surely hope that it will not be too long before we meet again under less pressing circumstances. I shall phone Mrs. Reeves whenever she's back in Manhattan. Meanwhile

Sincerely yours,

TO FRANK D. REEVES   *[TL]*

April 8, 1953

Mr. Frank D. Reeves,
1901 11th Street, N. W.,
Washington, D. C.

Dear Frank,
I've had a talk both with Lloyd Garrison and with Arthur Spingarn and have told them how helpful you were to me—and that without your logic and advice the TV show might not have come off nearly so well![†]

1. All agree with us about resigning from the one remaining questionable organization to which I may still belong. That I'm doing.

---

* Lloyd K. Garrison (1897–1991), a great-grandson of the abolitionist William Lloyd Garrison (1805–1897), was an NAACP official and a senior partner in the New York law firm Paul, Weiss, Rifkind, Wharton, & Garrison. He counseled others who testified before McCarthy's subcommittee.
† Hughes's appearance before McCarthy and his subcommittee was televised nationally.

2. Re Cohn or Schine's* suggestion regarding the FBI. Arthur Spingarn feels that especially since the FBI has interviewed me on two or three occasions concerning folks who've worked for me or given my name as reference in applying for government jobs (which they got), if the FBI wished to interview me, they would come or send for me. Therefore I shouldn't bother them. He quoted an old French proverb: "The man who excuses himself, accuses himself". Lloyd Garrison seems to agree with him, but suggests that, if you think wise (and I) you might send the FBI a copy of the transcript of my testimony for their files with a brief covering note, since Cohn told us Hoover once used "Goodbye, Christ" in a speech, and perhaps should therefore be advised that this no longer represents my views in any way. Please let me know your opinion on this, and I'll be guided thereby.

3. Lloyd Garrison feels that we might also draw up a brief statement using portions of the transcript of the open hearing to send the American Legion (or give directly) to some of the high officials of intelligence and goodwill who might pass the word down to the red-baiters in their Indianapolis office who've been sending out mimeographed material a la Red Channels on a number of writers and artists, to correct their material on me, at least to the extent that it conform with my sworn testimony. I think I have friends who can personally contact top officials. In any case, such a brief statement would be good for publishers to have in case of future charges, should they come up. Do you agree? All of my publishers are pleased with the outcome of the hearings, have backed me up beautifully, and are going ahead with their publishing plans in relation to my work. But it would do no harm to have a brief resume and interpretation of my testimony on tap, if needed, and I'll draw one up (getting your and Garrison's O.K before giving anyone copies) as soon as I get the transcript.

4. So: Would you get for me a couple of copies of my portion of the testimony in full, please, and send it on as soon as it is ready, letting me know the cost? (I agree with you, unless I was mentioned later in the hearing, we don't need it all.) If it is quite costly, perhaps one copy would do, and I could have it typed for Garrison, Spingarn, and Walter

---

* Roy Cohn (1927–1986) was Joseph McCarthy's chief counsel. G. David Schine (1927–1996) was a consultant to the subcommittee. Cohn's attempt to interfere with Schine's military posting would help to bring down McCarthy in the controversial Army-McCarthy hearings.

White. Use your own judgment on this. If it doesn't cost too much, get copies for all of us.

5. I gather from Garrison and Spingarn that the NAACP may (or is—not quite clear) assuming expenses for the hearings. (I have in the past done some radio scripts and mass meeting continuities, etc. for the Association without charge, waiving payment when offered. And am, of course, deeply grateful to them should they return the courtesy in this way.)* But in no sense do I want you to "be out of pocket". And, as I told you in my last letter, I do not feel that I could ever really repay you personally for your round-the-clock attention to my problems while in Washington. So that's out of the question. But anyhow, when you have a chance, please let me know exactly about the financial end of it all, and I'll certainly assume the obligation should it be one that I cannot meet in full now.

I think that's all the business. Trust you got the AMSTERDAM NEWS clippings I sent you. Theirs was the best coverage. Dozens of letters have come in from the Coast and all around of folks who saw the TV screening of the hearing. Several women want to know who "that fine looking fellow" was sitting with me! So I judge we both must have televised well!

Did you, by any chance, come across my raincoat in your closet? If not, don't worry. If so, maybe your wife could bring it along when she returns to town and I'll phone her and pick it up. It's the kind that doesn't take up any room in a bag.

If phoning is easier for you than answering letters, my number is Le. 4-2952 (private, so don't give out, please) and usually after two in the afternoon on until midnight is best to reach me. Reverse charges.

Should you drive your wife back, or be coming to New York soon, hope I'll have the pleasure of offering you a drink, and having you and your wife—and the Indian princess from Georgia—around to my place.

My new book, SIMPLE TAKES A WIFE, is almost ready, so you'll be getting a copy soon. It just missed being a Book of the Month Club selection—was a runner up until the last three choices, so the publishers tell me!

---

* Noting all the work Hughes had done free of charge for the organization over the years, the NAACP paid his expenses for the hearing.

Continued good wishes to you, and hoping to hear from you at your convenience,

Sincerely yours,
Langston Hughes

TO JAMES BALDWIN [TL]

July 25, 1953

Dear Mr. Baldwin,*

Just a note to send you some extra copies of reviews I've cut out for you. Sure you've seen them all, but extra copies, I've discovered, never hurt to have to give away or something. I'm very happy your book has been getting such good write-ups.† It and "Simple" was reviewed together a couple of times, but my clippings bureau only sends one copy, so no extras on those. We both came out mutually O.K.

What I liked best in your book was the story about the sad boy who killed himself. That's the part I read over twice lately. It's beautiful!

If you go to Geneva look up a very good friend of mine (and lots of other writers) who has just flown over there for the summer with her brother who is head of UN Health organization there. (They're coulored. *I put the u in the wrong place: coloured, I mean.) She is:

Miss Dorothy Peterson,
c/o Dr. Sidney Peterson,
6 Chemin des Crets de Champel,
Geneva, Switzerland.

And did you ever meet Nancy Cunard in France? Should. Lemme know if you go there. She is unique in this world.

---

* James Baldwin (1924–1987) was born and grew up in Harlem. He published his first article in 1946, and within two years had established himself as an essayist. In 1948, he received a Rosenwald Fellowship. He then moved to Paris, where he wrote the novel *Go Tell It on the Mountain* (1953).

† Knopf published Baldwin's first novel, *Go Tell It on the Mountain*, in 1953. Hughes didn't like the book. Reading it before its publication, he wrote to Arna Bontemps that "Baldwin over-writes and over-poeticizes in images way over the heads of the folks supposedly thinking them—often beautiful writing in itself—but frequently out of character" and that the book was a "low-down story in a velvet bag—and a Knopf binding" (Hughes to Bontemps, February 18, 1953). Nevertheless, he sent Knopf a note or blurb endorsing the novel.

If you want to die, be disturbed, maladjusted, neurotic, and psychotic, disappointed, and disjointed, just write plays! Go ahead!

Sincerely,

*Man, after reading
your piece in "Per-
spectives" I didn't
expect you to write
such a colored book
—without the u.*

TO RAY DUREM   [TL]

February 27, 1954

Dear Mr. Durem,†

I can hardly believe my eyes! Getting some good poetry in the mail! I receive at least a hundred or so envelopes of poetry a year from folks I don't know, and most of it is bad, illiterate, or dull. Some is conventionally good, or fairly good in spots. Once in a great while there is one good poem mixed in with several mediocre ones. And once in a blue moon a Gwendolyn Brooks turns up!‡

I don't believe I've gotten quite so interesting a collection of poems out of the blue as yours are since Gwendolyn Brooks sent me her early work ten or twelve years ago. Usually I glance at the first page or two of writing that comes in the mail, and put it away in a drawer with all the other unread manuscripts to await a time when I can struggle with it. But yours I read all

---

* James Baldwin and fellow African American writer Richard T. Gibson's "Two Protests Against Protest" in *Perspectives USA* (Winter 1953) argued, among other things, that "the young writer might do well to impress upon himself that he is the contemporary of Eliot, Valéry, Pound, Rilke and Auden and not merely Langston Hughes." On March 7, 1953, in response to this slight, Hughes wrote to Baldwin: "I agree that the more fences young writers jump over, the better. What a bore if they kept on repeating the old! More power to you!"

† The American poet Ramón "Ray" Durem (1915–1963) joined the Communist Party in 1931. In March 1937, he went to Spain to fight for the antifascist cause in the Civil War. Durem's militant poetry, which appeared in various newspapers, literary journals, and anthologies, anticipated elements of the Black Power movement. Hughes would include Durem's poem "Award" in his anthology *New Negro Poets: USA* (1964).

‡ When Gwendolyn Brooks (1917–2000) was sixteen and living in Chicago, she met Hughes for the first time. He read her poems and encouraged her to keep writing. Brooks received Guggenheim Fellowships in 1946 and 1947. In 1950, when she won the Pulitzer Prize for Poetry for *Annie Allen* (Harper, 1949), she became the first African American to receive this prize in any category.

the way through as soon as I opened the envelope. And most of the poems I like very much, particularly those humorously satirical ones like "Some of my best friends. . . ." and the ". . . . punch in the mouth" one, etc. I wish we'd had these a few years ago when Arna Bontemps and I were preparing our anthology, THE POETRY OF THE NEGRO, which seems to be serving as the source for most of the anthologies of Negro poetry that have been coming out abroad in the last three years—Germany, Sweden, Japan, and China. Certainly you would have been included therein.

There've been already two recent good anthologies of American Negro poetry in German. A third anthology of world-Negro poetry is about to go to press in Frankfurt in a couple of weeks. I've just had a letter from the man asking for help on last minute details, and wanting a few more poems from cullud poets who haven't answered him. So (since time is pressing) I am taking the liberty of sending him a half dozen or so of your poems (copies enclosed) in the hope that he might have space left to include some of your work. If this is O.K. by you, drop him an airmail note granting him permission to use them, and giving him some biographical notes on yourself— place and date of birth, etc., and work, publications, etc. (Send me a copy, too, please.) His name and address are on front of your poems.

If I were you, I'd try these same poems (plus others) on PHYLON, Atlanta University, Atlanta, Georgia; and on THE CRISIS, 20 West 40th Street, New York, N. Y. Also on some of the little magazines like EXPERIMENT in Seattle, and THE PARIS REVIEW, c/o of Peter Matthiessen,* 2 Columbus Circle, New York 19, N. Y. (Their U. S. office); and maybe also on POETRY in Chicago— altho at the moment they don't go for "race" poetry very much, or anything social.

I'm about to take off for a month's lecture trip to Middle West and Deep South, but will probably have more ideas re publication later, when I'm not so rushed trying to finish up odds and ends myself and get out of town. This is just to tell you I really like your work very much. (If the poems had titles, I'd list more I like especially.) Will so do next time I write. At the moment, hastily, but sincerely,

---

* In 1953, the American author Peter Matthiessen (1927–2014) cofounded the literary magazine *The Paris Review* with Harold L. Humes (1926–1992) and George Plimpton (1927–2003).

TO NNAMDI AZIKIWE   [TL]

May 28, 1954

The Honorable Nnamdi Azikiwe*
British Consul General
350 Fifth Avenue
New York, New York

Dear Zik,

I was certainly delighted to receive both of your letters and look forward to seeing you during your visit to the U.S.A. I have had many wonderful letters from readers of your papers in Nigeria who have seen my poems therein, perhaps a hundred or more during the last two years, and many of them speak of you and your leadership in glowing terms.

My home address is as above, and my telephone number is: ATwater 9-6559. But I rather expect you will be too busy to have much time for personal friends, and so I will say only that if you do find yourself with an hour leisure when you just wished to sit down and talk and have a drink, I would, of course, be most happy to receive you here at my home. Failing that, however, I shall surely see you at Lincoln during the Commencement period and our centennial celebration. I suppose you know that one of your poems is included in the LINCOLN UNIVERSITY POETS: Centennial Anthology, which I helped to edit.† And we have a copy of the book for you.

Welcome again to America and my continued good wishes to you, as ever.

Sincerely yours,
Langston Hughes

---

* Benjamin Nnamdi "Zik" Azikiwe (1904–1996), an alumnus of Lincoln University (where he met Hughes), was a leader in the Nigerian nationalist movement. In 1937, Azikiwe founded a newspaper in Lagos, the *West African Pilot*. Within a decade, he was running six newspapers throughout Nigeria. When Nigeria became independent from Britain in 1960, Azikiwe was named the country's first governor-general.
† *Lincoln University Poets: Centennial Anthology, 1854–1954*, coedited by Lincoln alumni Waring Cuney, Langston Hughes, and Bruce McM. Wright (1917–2005), appeared in 1954. The volume includes Azikiwe's poem "To Lincoln."

TO PETER ABRAHAMS   [TL]

May 30, 1954

Mr. Peter Abrahams,
37 Jessel Drive,
Loughton, Essex,
England.

Dear Peter,

Knopf sent me your book to read and I think it's wonderful!* (As you can
see from the statement I sent in.) Where you lived as a kid sounds about
like 18th and Vine in Kansas City where I lived! I hope you'll continue it on
with London and all. I am hoping to spend this summer writing the second
part of my autobiography—have a contract for it. Lots to put in it which I
hope will be as readable as THE BIG SEA. (By the way, error in spelling in
your English sheets—it's Sterling Brown†—with an e not an i.) That business about your first going to school—and the market lady—and the Bantu
center—and school teaching at the Cape—and the dung hunting—and the
kaffir boy and the African kings—is wonderful! And the old preacher! And
the humor of that prayer! But it's all wonderful! Great! I love that book! So
alive and immediate and real and moving! From your pictures you don't look
like you can write like that. But who does—in a picture! I don't think authors
ought to have pictures on books. I try to keep mine off, but not much luck.
Anyhow, I'll be doing a column about TELL FREEDOM in my paper I write
for when it comes out . . . . . . I met Alan Paton‡ last week at a big colored party
for him, Ralph Bunche and all there. He spoke most effectively. . . . . Thanks
a lot for those addresses of African writers. I'd already written several folks in
South Africa, Liberia, Gold Coast, etc., and to my college mate, Ben Azikiwe
whom I'll see here next week, so hope to be getting quite a few stories soon.
Have a few already. Have a publisher interested, so kindly send me your sto-

* Peter Abrahams (b. 1919) is a South African novelist whose autobiography *Tell Freedom:
Memories of Africa* (Knopf, 1954) recounts at one point how Hughes's work inspired him.
Hughes had just read the galleys of Abrahams's book.
† Sterling Brown (1901–1989) was an influential poet, critic, and teacher who served for
some forty years as a professor at Howard University. In his poetry, he built upon Hughes's
pioneering use of the blues, as in Brown's collection *Southern Road* (1932). He also pub-
lished landmark essays on race and American literature.
‡ Alan Paton (1903–1988), one of South Africa's leading humanists, was the author of the
novel *Cry, the Beloved Country* (1948). Hughes met Paton at a party given by his friends
Henry and Molly Moon.

ries, too, <u>soon</u>, if you can. Knopf won't mind you being anthologized.* Good publicity for your books, as anthologies go in lots of libraries and schools that a book may not, unless it's a classic, or something similar. If your short stories are anywhere as near as good as that autobiography, they ought to be great. LEMME SEE! . . . . I'm glad to hear DRUM is planning an anthology (which I didn't know) and will be happy to collaborate with them in any way they wish, sharing my material with them or/and vice versa, or working with them, or however they desire—the main thing being to get an anthology published here, too, in the U.S.A.—so please tell Sampson that for me. And I shall write the same to Nxumalo.† Usual American custom is to allot a set sum for anthology payments, and pro rata a flat sum to each of the contributors, depending on the number and amount of each person's work. Example: from the recent ESQUIRE anthology I received a payment of $75.00 for my story used therein‡ . . . . . . I'm delighted, of course, that AFRICA is running parts of "Simple". They're welcome to use it all, if they wish, from both books. And I'd be happy to see them use the BIG SEA or other work of mine, too, providing it's OKed through my agent or publishers, since I'm not free to grant the rights myself. . . . . About going to South Africa, naturally, I'm pleased no end to be invited. But can't even think about going for a year or two—I'm tied up with a play in the works for next season, and three book contracts (the autobiography being one, a rather big job) and none of them even started in the writing—so I have about 15 months of steady work ahead of me. But if I see my way clear a year or so from now, I might take my friends there in Johannesburg up on it. I want to go to that bioscope you went to!! But right now I'm a literary sharecropper tied to a publisher's plantation. . . . . I met a man at the Paton party who knows you, Daniels of the U.N., and told me quite a bit about you that I reckon will be in your memoires No. II. . . . . I know how hard it is to write letters—and books, too, so you don't have to answer right back this year—JUST SEND THE STORIES. With gratitude, as ever

Sincerely,

---

* In March 1955, Hughes sent two anthologies to publishers for consideration. The first collected fifty-four short stories by twenty-eight authors from seven African countries. The second, intended for a teenage audience, was called "Big Ghost and Little Ghost." The publishers rejected both manuscripts. Hughes's efforts to sponsor literary works by African authors culminated in his publication of *An African Treasury: Articles / Essays / Stories / Poems by Black Africans* (Crown, 1960).
† Henry W. Nxumalo (1917–1957) was assistant editor of *Drum: Africa's Leading Magazine.* Hughes would serve as a judge for short story competitions organized by *Drum.*
‡ "Seven Moments of Love," which Hughes called "an un-sonnet sequence in Blues," was published in the May 1940 issue of *Esquire.* The piece later appeared in *The Girls from Esquire* (Random House, 1952), an anthology of material about women from the magazine.

TO NANCY CUNARD   [*TLS*]

[*On* Langston Hughes, 20 East 127th Street, New York 35, N.Y. *stationery*]

June 2, 1954

Miss Nancy Cunard,
Lamothe-Fénelon,
Lot, France.

Dear Nancy,

It's always nice to get a letter from you—being one of my favorite folks in the world! And to know that you'll have a book coming out soon is great news indeed.* I certainly hope there'll be an American edition.

Surely, I'm delighted you're calling "Famous American Negroes" to the attention of Secker and Warburg.† It being a juvenile, agents and publishers here make no effort to sell foreign rights, so anything you do would be most appreciated. I've another little book for young folks coming up next fall, "THE FIRST BOOK OF JAZZ", a brief history and appreciation and explanation of jazz, that I think might interest publishers abroad, too.‡ I'm just finishing up the record lists, and it will be going to press in a month or so. Columbia Records may bring out an album of jazz for children, too, to accompany it.

I've had several letters from Bridson recently, who is hoping maybe to get "The Barrier" done on BBC.§ The Dutch broadcast received a lot of attention there and was, I though<t>, quite well done. (They sent me a tape of it that wouldn't play at any speed the machines use in this country—so it took TWO days to retape it here at a speed at which one could play it! The U. N. ought to internationalize the speed of tape recorders!) Just this week some of the music was played on WABC here.

When you go to the P.E.N.¶ if you see our American delegate, John Putnam, introduce yourself. I believe I was the first cullud member of the New

---

* In 1954 in London, Secker & Warburg published Nancy Cunard's *Grand Man: Memories of Norman Douglas.* Douglas was the author of the once widely admired novel *South Wind* (1917).
† *Famous American Negroes*, Hughes's collection of biographical essays for children, was published by Dodd, Mead in 1954.
‡ Hughes's *The First Book of Jazz* (Franklin Watts, 1955) appeared to excellent reviews. It was apparently the first book about jazz written for children.
§ Douglas Geoffrey Bridson (1910–1980) was an interviewer and producer for the British Broadcasting Corporation.
¶ PEN (Poets, Playwrights, Editors, Essayists, Novelists) is an international writers' association founded in 1921.

York P.E.N.—during the war days when a wave of democracy swept over our hitherto lily white institutions—said wave being one I hope to describe in my next autobiography which I intend to start writing this summer.

At the moment I've been having some correspondence with Peter Abrahams in London (whose TELL FREEDOM I've just read in proofs and like immensely) who had promised to send me some short stories of his for an anthology of African short stories I hope to edit (if enough material can be gotten together that's good) for a publisher here. Do you know any African writers of color writing in English other than Abrahams whose names and addresses you could send me <u>soon</u>? If so, needn't take time to write a letter, just jot down the addresses and <u>air-mail</u> them to me, as I'm already assembling material and have some very good stories from South Africa. <u>Help</u>, <u>Please</u>, m'am!

And if you go to Africa, let me know. I get lots of fan letters from all-over there, a few of which are from really interesting-sounding people whose names I'd like to give you, especially in Nigeria. And a good friend of mine, Griff Davis, the photographer and his wife are in Monrovia, who used to live here in our house.*

You've probably read that William Pickens died at sea on the Mauretania last month.† And two wonderful old-time comedians, Dusty Fletcher and Hamtree Harrington died, too, recently‡. . . . . And your book NEGRO is quoted at $50.00 in the University Place Bookshop catalogue. (Mine I see right now in my bookcase, thank God!)

Continued good wishes ever,

Langston

I'm sending the carbon of this to Lloyd's |Bank| in case.

---

* Griffith Jerome Davis (1923–1993), a photographer, was a student of Hughes in 1947 when he was a visiting professor of creative writing at Atlanta University. Davis started working for *Ebony* magazine that same year. In 1948, when he enrolled at Columbia University in its Graduate School of Journalism, he boarded with Hughes and the Harpers while he earned his master's degree.

† Yale-educated William Pickens (1881–1954), field secretary of the NAACP in the 1920s and author of the autobiographies *The Heir of Slaves* (1911) and *Busting Bonds* (1923), died during a pleasure cruise with his wife aboard the RMS *Mauretania*.

‡ Dusty Fletcher (c. 1900–1954) and Hamtree Harrington (1889–1956) were popular African American vaudeville performers. They collaborated on a short musical film called *Rufus Jones for President* (1933), which also featured Ethel Waters and a young Sammy Davis, Jr. (1925–1990).

Portrait by Henri Cartier-Bresson, c. 1957

There are words like *Liberty*
That almost make me cry.
If you had known what I know
You would know why.
—"WORDS LIKE FREEDOM," 1967*

In the second half of the 1950s, Hughes's major focus in his writings was probably on the civil rights movement in the United States and the independence struggle in Africa. He frequently linked the two subjects. The second volume of his autobiography, *I Wonder as I Wander*, appeared in 1956 and *The Langston Hughes Reader* was published in 1958. Still the self-described "literary sharecropper," he signed con-

* This poem was originally published as "Refugee in America" (1943).

tracts for—and delivered—a number of other works. These include *Famous Negro Heroes of America* (1958) and *The First Book of the West Indies* (1956) for younger readers, as well as (coedited with Arna Bontemps) *The Book of Negro Folklore* (1958). He also published another volume of Simple stories.

TO ARNA BONTEMPS   *[TLS]*

[On Langston Hughes, 20 East 127th Street, New York 35, N.Y. *stationery]*

July 17, 1954

Dear Arna,

Well, since my autobiography is due at the publishers the day after Labor Day and I haven't written a word of it yet, I thought this quiet Sunday afternoon I would get started. So I sat down and wrote three chapters some 30 pages. Between 4 P. M. and now, about 3 A.M. Which isn't bad. I hope it reads as easily as it writes. If I can keep this up, I'll have 330 pages in a month—which is with narrow margins, so that would be 400—which is just about a book.

I meant to sort out all the stuff in the basement, take notes, etc., and work from them. But if I wait to get around to doing that, it is liable to be Doomsday, and I'll never get a book done. So I think I will just write it from memory like I did THE BIG SEA. Then, if I have time, and it needs it, I can check through the basement stuff and see if I've forgotten anything important—in which case I can put <it> in Volume III, the next one. I can remember enough without notes to fill an encyclopedia.

If publishers want a really documented book, they ought to advance some documented money—enough to do nothing else for two or three years. I refuses to sharecrop long for short rations! Doubleday's royalty report was the ONLY one this year that had a check along with it. All the rest sent me BILLS with their reports asking ME to kindly remit to them—for books I had purchased. Sharecropper for true. Anyhow, I did get to the Bahamas for a few days. Don't reckon I'll ever get anywhere else. Kindly remember me in your prayers. (I wish somebody would remember me in a will.)

Hope your book is about done. You've been writing as long as Ralph |Ellison|!

Sincerely yours truly,

Lang

TO CHUBA NWEKE [TL]

July 25, 1954

Dear son Chuba,*

Since you've adopted me—and thus become my one and only son (and I'm very happy that you have), you will have to send me a photograph (just a Kodak snapshot will do, it needn't be an expensive one) so that I can see how you look. Certainly I am very proud and flattered to be taken as a father by so ambitious a boy as yourself, already working on a novel, and only fifteen years old! Are your father and mother living? How many brothers and sisters do you have? Are you continuing in school, or working? What do you intend to do in life?

Of course, I will read your novel for you. But I cannot guarantee to rewrite it (being awfully busy myself) or to do anything about publication as that is very difficult. But I would be happy to see it, and to give you my comments on it, in the hope that they might be helpful to you. So send it on over here to me. But I hope you have made a carbon copy, so you will have one in case it gets lost. In typing, always make a copy or two of your work, so as to be able to always keep one.

Meanwhile, I am sending you two of my books, one of poems and the other a story. But the boats are slow, as you know, so it will be about six weeks, I'm afraid, before the books reach you, although they were mailed yesterday. But let me know when they arrive, and if you'd like others, I will send them to you. Meanwhile, send me your picture, and write again soon.

With all my love and good wishes to my Nigerian son,

Sincerely,
Langston Hughes

* Chuba Nweke, a young man from Funtua, Nigeria, wrote to Hughes after reading one of his poems in Azikiwe's newspaper West African Pilot. The two exchanged letters for some months.

TO MARIA LEIPER   *[TL]*

COPY sent to ROY de CARAVA

January 4, 1954 |1955|

Miss Maria Leiper,
Simon & Schuster,
630 Fifth Avenue,
New York 20, N. Y.

Dear Maria,

We've had so many books about how bad life is, that it would seem to me to
do no harm to have one along about <u>now</u> affirming its value. So that is what
I'm trying to do with those beautiful photographs by Roy de Carava.* You'll
have about a half ton of pictures along with a minimum of text sometime next

Hughes wrote a brief story to accompany photographs by Roy DeCarava in their book
The Sweet Flypaper of Life.

* Roy DeCarava (1919–2009), hailed later as a major African American photographer,
won a Guggenheim Fellowship in 1952 to develop a pictorial study of Harlem. His project
resulted in more than two thousand photographs. Deeply impressed when he saw some,
Hughes sought in vain to find a publisher for the work until he tried Simon & Schuster as
a "long shot." Richard Simon (1899–1960), as a condition for accepting the book, asked
Hughes to write a little story to go along with a selection of the pictures. In 1955, his firm
published *The Sweet Flypaper of Life* to probably the best reviews of Hughes's career.

week, so don't try to lift it yourself. Just turn it over, picture by picture, and see if it comes alive.

I'm sending you a copy of my "Jazz" book, too[*]—just for fun.

Sincerely,

Langston Hughes

TO CARL VAN VECHTEN   [TL]

April 3, 1955

Mr. Carl Van Vechten,
146 Central Park West,
New York 23, N.Y.

Dear Carlo,

Curiously enough, I was just on the verge of writing you a note when the postman brought that charmingly written little book about you yesterday[†]—so I stopped to read it, and find it delightfully warm and real and to be no bigger than it is, a pretty thorough coverage of your life, ways, and activities. And certainly your personality comes through. (Incidentally, I love Saul's picture of you—which I'd never seen before; and that beautiful one of you and Fania |Marinoff|.) And, naturally, I am DE-lighted to be referred to and quoted therein! (Who wouldn't be?) Thanks so very much for sending me a copy so far in advance of publication.

What I was about to write you about yesterday was (and is) to ask you if by any chance you've got a spare hundred lying around loose anywhere you could lend me for a month. Brokeness suddenly descended upon me unawares and my stenographer's last check bounced. Turned out I was $1.48 short! (And I thought I was $87.00 ahead of that—but I'd neglected to make a deduct on my book.) So I was shocked! I don't mind being broke myself, but typists live more hand to mouth than authors, and I don't want to get more than a week or two behind with her—since I've just recently been fortunate enough to find her, she's reliable and very good, and I've a mountain of manuscripts in final draft stage to get typed up and turned in this month: FAMOUS NEGRO MUSIC MAKERS (a juvenile) due at Dodd, Mead's on the

---

[*] Hughes's *The First Book of Jazz* (Franklin Watts, 1955).
[†] Edward Lueders's biography *Carl Van Vechten and the Twenties* (University of New Mexico Press, 1955).

15th,* and the second volume of my autobiography (in which you figure again) due at Rinehart's early in May—on both of which I'll collect remaining advances due on delivery of manuscripts of almost a thousand bucks. But right now I don't have a thousand pennies—having awakened this week-end for the first time in a long time "cold in hand." (And the Harpers have had some enormous plumbing and heating bills this winter—old pipes bursting, etc.,—and neither have been too well, either. Fortunately, nothing intended for Yale is under any pipes, and lately I've almost completed the basement sorting—four BIG boxes of letters alone from you, Walter |White|, Du Bois, Zora |Neale Hurston|, Arna |Bontemps|, etc., mostly already filed under each name. But I want to list and sort them into years before boxing for shipment.)†

Anyhow, if you're broke, too, don't worry about it. But if you aren't, and want to help ART and the RACE through the rainy month of April, I'll send it back to you when the sun shines in May and ASCAP and publishers pay off.‡ What really broke me has been Africa—I've received almost two hundred manuscripts from there in answer to my letters for short stories to Azikiwe's paper, DRUM, AFRICA, and the BANTU NEWS, as well as various writers. From which I garnered 56 that I think are good, some excellent—Nigeria, Gold Coast, Kenya, South Africa, etc., for an Anthology of stories by African Negro writers—fiction, not folk, contemporary, which Simon and Schuster are now considering. But what a mountain of typing I had to pay for, and air-mail postage for the past six months. But, aside from the manuscripts (some in long hand) I've gotten some fascinating letters, and think I've discovered two really talented writers in Cape Town, youngsters, one 23, one 24, the former I believe as talented as Peter Abrahams (TELL FREEDOM, etc.) who helped me on this project I started last year.*

Thanks again for C.V.V. AND THE 20s, and tulips and jonquils to you,

Langston

*Amos Tutuola (the PALM WINE DRINKARD guy) sent a story from Nigeria§—and very wisely said, "I will send more when you send money." It's all in long hand and most fantastic, so I'm saving the script for Yale.

---

* Hughes completed the manuscript for *Famous Negro Music Makers* (Dodd, Mead, 1955) in ten days. ("Don't tell anybody," he begged a friend.)

† Hughes was still sending his papers systematically to the James Weldon Johnson Memorial Collection of Negro Arts and Letters founded by Carl Van Vechten at Yale University. (See the following letter, dated August 22, 1955.)

‡ The letter includes a handwritten note: "Repaid by check 2502, $100.00, May 25, 1955."

§ The complete title of this seminal novel by the Nigerian author Amos Tutuola (1920–1997) is *The Palm-Wine Drinkard and His Dead Palm-Wine Tapster in the Dead's Town* (1952).

TO ARNA BONTEMPS   [TLS]

[On Langston Hughes, 20 East 127th Street, New York 35, N.Y. *stationery*]

August 22, 1955

Dear Arna, You being more experienced in these matters, since you're a Curator and Librarian yourself, kindly give me your opinion on this: I've finally gotten around to sorting and filing by name or category some several hundred letters for Yale of persons in public life mostly: writers, artists, actors, NAACP personalities, etc. most of them still living. None of them contain anything which I myself would object to anyone seeing. But since no one wrote with a Library collection repository in mind:

1. Do you think these letters should be restricted in any way? (They can be locked away for any number of years I<,> as donor<,> wish).

2. Do you think perhaps any publication of them or any parts of them should be prohibited without the writer's permission, although they would otherwise be open to researchers?

3. In the case of your own letters (at the moment I've come across a hundred or more from the '30s to now) which carry a thread of the history and personalities of our times—nothing that I see objectionable to anyone's eyes. Would you wish them restricted in any way? Or would you rather they be not given at all now? (With hurricanes, leaking roofs, bursting pipes, they ought to be somewhere safe for posterity's delectation and enlightenment)?

I've boxes more to sort in the basement. But would value your opinion as to propriety in regard to museums and other people's mail, before sending the present boxes off. So when you get rested from your vacation, let me know, please.*

Georgia Douglas Johnson, I hear, is not well.

Sincerely,

Langston

PS: Having sent thousands of ordinary folks' letters to Yale already, now I get concerned about "name" personalities—Zora for example!X&%$#! Claude

---

* In response, Bontemps suggested restricting access to letters written by persons still alive, and also letters that revealed intimate details about living persons. In fact, Hughes made almost no stipulations of this kind in his gift to Yale.

|McKay|, Walter |White|, Wallie |Thurman|, Mrs. Bethune have gone to Glory so could hardly object! Maybe hant!

TO NOËL SULLIVAN   *[TLS]*

[*On* Langston Hughes, 20 East 127th Street, New York 35, N.Y. *stationery*]

November 14, 1955

Dear Noël,

I'm doing you like some of my fans do me—sitting down and answering you right back. But you're not to take answering me seriously—for who knows better than I what letter writing entails. And I've seen your desk, too! Of course, I'm always glad to hear from you. But don't feel you're remiss when I don't.

Coincidentally, your name came up at a meeting at the John Hay Whitney Foundation this morning (I didn't bring it up, either) and when I got home, here's your letter! I got up at 7 A.M. believe it or not! for a 9 o'clock conference of scholars and writers and a publisher to help plan a series of Centennial volumes to be published in the 1960s celebrating the One Hundred Years of Freedom of the "race." And in considering possible honorary sponsors of the project, when it came to the West Coast you and Wallace Stegner[*] were mentioned. But all of this is very long range, and at this preliminary meeting nothing much was decided upon except that all of us should submit memos and ideas to be perhaps incorporated into a general publishing plan to be considered at the next conference in December.

I'm certainly sorry to hear that you're temporarily laid up, and hope you're not in pain—or bored. And if you need me, I'll get on a plane and come out there. I've been sort of planning in the back of my head to come out in the late winter for a week or two just to say hello again, or sooner if I can finish the two current projects I have on hand for late Spring publication. (At the moment, I'm weeks behind, so one or two more wouldn't make much difference. All year I've been rushing to be late, and feel sort of weary myself. But I still find sleep a great restorer—and sometimes go into another world for twelve hours and wake up all right.) As you know, I'm a great travel sleeper,

---

[*] Wallace Stegner (1909–1993), a writer and conservationist who founded the creative writing program at Stanford University in California, published more than thirty books. His autobiographical novel *The Big Rock Candy Mountain* (1943) was widely admired; he also won the Pulitzer Prize for Fiction for *Angle of Repose* (1972) and the National Book Award in fiction for *The Spectator Bird* (1975).

and can sleep my way to the Coast and be out there tomorrow, if my presence would be of any value to you. This <u>quite</u> <u>seriously</u>, as I'm sure you know—so you have only to let me know: LEhigh 4-2952, or otherwise. In any case, I shall see you after the holidays, and I'm holding all the good thoughts in the world for you.[*] (And hope you've given up Christmas cards—as I <u>say</u> I'm going to do this year. Maybe make it an every-other-year pleasure.)

Dorothy I haven't seen since her concert. But am happy to hear from you that she is headed your way. Some things she sang so beautifully she made folks cry at her concert—a kind of art from the heart.[†]

The TIMES has just sent me James Baldwin's new book of essays to review.[‡] I've long thought him a very talented fellow, writing provocatively and beautifully. I met him briefly last summer. He's back in Paris now, I hear. . . . . Leonard de Paur[§] invited me to dinner to tell me how wonderful you were, and what a happy summer he had with the Williams and his other Highland neighbors, and apparently didn't go out much. I have the same feeling you do about him—and his chorus that sings beautifully, but don't really move me.

Take it slow now! You've got to be here in 1963 to see <u>us</u> 100 years free!

Yours,

Langston

---

[*] Hughes visited Sullivan in January 1956; Sullivan died later that year.

[†] Dorothy Leigh Maynor (1910–1996), an African American soprano, studied music at Hampton Institute (now Hampton University) and became a successful concert performer who toured internationally. In 1947, she founded the St. James Community Center, Inc., in the basement of the Presbyterian church where her husband, Rev. Dr. Shelby Rooks, was pastor. The center was renamed the Harlem School of the Arts in 1964.

[‡] Hughes's review of *Notes of a Native Son*, a collection of essays by James Baldwin, appeared in *The New York Times Book Review* on February 26, 1956. The review described Baldwin as a "thought-provoking, tantalizing, irritating, abusing, and amusing" essayist.

[§] Leonard de Paur (1914–1998), an African American arranger and a conductor of choruses and orchestras, was a music director with the Federal Negro Theatre from 1936 to 1939. De Paur conducted more than 2,300 performances between 1947 and 1968.

TO JAN MEYEROWITZ   [TL]

January 23 P.M., 1956

Mr. Jan Meyerowitz,
27 Morningside Avenue,
Cresskill, New Jersey.

Dear Jan,

Art thou Ahasuerus? A mere piece of paper on my part does not constitute
a decree. So, by what manner of reasoning do you waken me out of my sleep
at the ungodly hour of 10 A.M. to shout imprecations on the phone, without
even a "goodmorning?" Especially after I have been up all night working on
ESTHER so that I might post additional scenes to you in ample time—your
mails being so slow.* I finished the corrections about 8 A.M. and took the
material over to the Post Office to mail to you (perhaps you have it by now)
and so did not get to bed until after 9 and had seemingly just gone to sleep
good when the phone rang. Unfortunately, I had forgotten to unplug it, so
kindly forgive me for unplugging it then. I am sure you know one cannot
discuss anything intelligent in one's sleep. So, for your sake, not to waste your
time talking to a zombie, I suggest in the future, you call me much later in the
day. Otherwise, naturally, I forgive you.

Concerning the letter of collaboration, you are perfectly free to draw up
your own, as I suggested you do weeks ago. Send yours to me and I will forward it on to my agent for his approval, since you know that I do not handle
my own business matters.

Gifts of Purim to you! Sincerely,

---

* This letter, over the opera *Esther*, documents one of the sharpest clashes ever between
Hughes and a collaborator. The Fromm Foundation had commissioned Hughes and the
temperamental Meyerowitz to compose an opera to celebrate Purim, the Jewish feast day
that marks the ancient deliverance of Persian Jews from a threatened massacre. The opera,
Esther, is based on the biblical story of Esther, her cousin Mordecai, and Ahasuerus, the
king of Persia and the husband of Esther.

TO ARNA BONTEMPS   [TLS]

[On Langston Hughes, 20 East 127th Street, New York 35, N.Y. *stationery*]

5 A. M.
April 26, 1956

Dear Arna,

I've been out nightclubbing with Jack Robbins & Yvonne Bouvier—Inez Cavanaugh at the Valentine, and Mabel Mercer at the Byline*—and came back to cut a dozen more pages from my LIFE. From 783 pages I've got it down to about 500 and am working on the last sequence now from which I hope to extract 20 or so more pages. Unfortunately, in the cutting our Alabama Christmas and the meatless roasts got cut out. But the tale of Watts and the white lady who came a-begging remains—when we wrote BOY OF THE BORDER which I wish you'd add to while I'm cutting this, please![†] Let there be a stampede or a chase or something kicking up lots of dust.

My No. 2 LIFE is going to be good. I never really read it before until this week. I've now cut out all the impersonal stuff, down to a running narrative with me in the middle on every page, extraneous background and statistics and stories not my own gone by the board. The kind of intense condensation that, of course, keeps an autobiography from being entirely true, in that nobody's life is pure essence without pulp, waste matter, and rind—which art, of course, throws in the trash can. No wonder folks read such books and say, "How intensely you've lived!" (The three hundred duller months have just been thrown away, that's all, in this case; as in THE BIG SEA, too. And nobody will know I ever lived through them. They'll think I galloped around the world at <top> speed.) Well, anyhow,

I remain,

Sincerely,
Langston

---

* Jack Robbins was a music publisher for MGM. Yvonne Bouvier was also connected to the movie industry. The singer Inez Cavanaugh (1909–1980) became one of the first African American jazz journalists. Mabel Mercer (1900–1984) was a popular British-born cabaret singer.
† This story appears in *I Wonder as I Wander*. "Boy of the Border," a children's tale written with Bontemps around 1939, never found a publisher in their lifetimes. It finally appeared in 2009.

TO W. E. B. DU BOIS

[TL]

May 22, 1956

Dr. W. E. B. Du Bois,*
31 Grace Court,
Brooklyn 2, New York.

Dear Dr. Du Bois,
I have just read again your <u>The</u> <u>Souls</u> <u>of</u> <u>Black</u> <u>Folk</u>—for perhaps the tenth time—the first time having been some forty years ago when I was a child in Kansas.† Its beauty and passion and power are as moving and as meaningful as ever.

My very best regards to Shirley‡ and continued good wishes to you both,

Sincerely,
Langston Hughes

TO MAXIM LIEBER

[TL]

SEPTEMBER
SEVENTEENTH
1
9
5
6

Dear Maxim:
I am delighted to have your recent letter and thought that I had written you but it might be that I did not since I have been behind the literary eight ball for the past several months and am more of a writer-sharecropper than ever.

---

* This letter reflects Hughes's sensitivity about how Du Bois, once one of his admirers as well as icons, now saw him. In 1958, Du Bois would publicly criticize him by name for publishing a children's book, *Famous Negro Music Makers* (1955), in which Hughes "deliberately omitted [Paul] Robeson's name." Hughes probably had succumbed to pressure not to include Robeson, by then a pariah in mainstream America.

† In *The Souls of Black Folk: Essays and Sketches* (A. C. McClurg, 1903), Du Bois proposed that "the problem of the Twentieth Century is the problem of the color-line"; he also explored the historical, social, religious, and musical traditions of black Americans in a book that profoundly influenced African American intellectual life.

‡ Shirley Graham Du Bois (1896–1977), a prize-winning author, a composer, and a civil rights activist, married W. E. B. Du Bois in 1951.

But at last things seem to be clearing up a bit and the two major jobs that took so much time are now at the printers; A PICTORIAL HISTORY OF THE NEGRO IN AMERICA (Crown),* and the second volume of my autobiography, I WONDER AS I WANDER (Rinehart). Both will be out in November, and a new juvenile, THE FIRST BOOK OF THE WEST INDIES (Franklin Watts) has just appeared.† But with all this work, bills rather than royalties fall out of publishers' envelopes. I have just gotten a bill from Simon and Schuster for $1080. and another from Watts for some $700. for books that I purchased in the past. So it is my intention never to sell or give away another book, only to write them from now on and let the volumes fall where they may.

Arna |Bontemps| was in town last week, and said he would be delighted to receive whatever royalties you have for him. He may be addressed at the Fisk University Library, Nashville 8, Tenn. He never did finish his big book on Douglass, Washington and Du Bois. But I read some of the earlier portions and they were beautifully written. He seems to be increasingly burdened with academic duties and is a sort of right hand man to the President of Fisk, and he never did write very rapidly anyhow. But I shall pass on to him what you said about the book and its possibilities in Europe. I certainly hope he will finish it.

I would be delighted if I could get in American money whatever royalties are due me for Russian translations of my books, as the New York Times sometime ago stated that such royalties were now payable in Valuta.‡ I find Ivan von Auw an excellent agent and am most grateful to Minna for having suggested him.§ The only thing is that if something is not sold, he does not bother to give it away for sheer pleasure of publication as we used to do.

Have you heard that |Joseph| McCarthy has lost 43 lbs recently and is slowly dying? In the third volume of my autobiography, since I am now through I WONDER AS I WANDER, I will record my TV show with him when he was certainly in full possession of his faculties. He asked me if I would consent

---

* After gathering suitable photographs, the historian Milton Meltzer (1915–2009) looked for someone to write an accompanying text about the history of black America. In 1955, he approached Arna Bontemps, who suggested Hughes. The book appeared from Crown in 1956.
† Hughes published five volumes in the Franklin Watts "First Book" series. His final contributions were *The First Book of the West Indies* (1956) and *The First Book of Africa* (1960).
‡ Earlier Hughes's royalties in the Soviet Union were paid in rubles, which could not be transferred abroad.
§ Lieber's wife, Minna, had led Hughes to Ivan von Auw, Jr., of the Harold Ober Agency before she left for Mexico to join Maxim there.

to appear on TV and I said—"Delighted!" I figured I photographed as well as he did.

All my good wishes to Minna and the children, as ever,

Sincerely yours,

Langston Hughes

LH/g

TO ZELL INGRAM   [TL]

September

Twenty-Eighth

1

9

5

6

Dear Zell:

The book has now gone down to the publisher and the editor says he would like very much to see the drawings, so if you have any more done, or do any over the weekend, bring them by on Monday or Tuesday and I will see that they get downtown.* Here are a few suggestions for more of the chapter heads, but of course you do not need to follow them if they do not excite your imagination:

THE FIX (10)—Rather than show a whole policeman receiving graft, we might show a hand with an official looking cuff and Laura's hand slipping a $10 bill into it and maybe the other hand with a billy club be worked in on the side.

ETHIOPIAN EDEN (11)—A Sarah Vaughan-like Eve clad partially in vine leaves and maybe looking at a dollar; the S of which is a snake with an apple in its mouth, or the snakelike bill alone might be used as headpiece for another chapter—APPLE OF EVIL. Perhaps for the mural, Sarah Vaughan and Joe Louis as Adam and Eve without the snake.†

---

* Hughes's *Tambourines to Glory: A Novel* (John Day, 1958). Zell Ingram created a series of pen-and-ink illustrations for the novel that do not appear in the published book; they are housed in Special Collections, Lincoln University.
† Sarah Vaughan (1924–1990) started singing in the early 1940s in bands with jazz legends such as Earl Hines, Dizzy Gillespie, Charlie Parker, and Miles Davis. Soon the

STRAY CATS STRAY DOGS (18)—There might be an alley cat, a
mongrel and a pair of feet that look as though they belong to a stray
person.

WATCH WITH ME (32)—There should certainly be some jail bars with
a placid but solemn face behind jail bars (Essie).

These suggestions are not obligatory at all—just ideas. I tried a couple of
times to get you on the phone but found no one at home so I am sending this
note instead.

Regards to Garnett.

Sincerely,
Langston Hughes

TO ROY BLACKBURN   [TLS]

[On Langston Hughes, 20 East 127th Street, New York 35, N.Y. stationery]

November 6, 1956

Dear Roy,

Thank you so much for so kindly sending me so promptly the clippings about
Noël.* Marie |Short| and others sent me the Carmel and Monterey notices
and tributes, so I was able to show them to friends of Noël's here in New York
who were not so fortunate in such thoughtful friends on the Coast in that
regard. . . . . Me. I am behind several assorted 8-balls as usual—one being a
book due yesterday that I haven't even started, so I told the MAN <I'd have it>
on the 15th<,> on the phone today, so have to WRITE it in about a week. Fortunately, it's for teenagers, so not too long†. . . . . But this is just a hasty note to
tell you I've ordered sent you from Rinehart's my 2nd autobiography, I WON-
DER AS I WANDER, and to explain to you re the Carmel section that you
were included therein in the 780 page version that had to be cut down to 400,
<but> in the condensing, since I was pushed for time (working on the PICTO-
RIAL HISTORY then going to press in sections as I turned them in) whole
chapters had to be jerked out (almost 20) and I had no time to weave any of

---

renowned vocalist Ella Fitzgerald hailed her as the "greatest singing talent." Joe Louis,
nicknamed the "Brown Bomber," successfully defended his heavyweight boxing title
twenty-five times and held the title for more than eleven years.
* Roy C. Blackburn worked as Hughes's secretary in Carmel in 1934. He had sent Hughes
newspaper notices about the death of Noël Sullivan.
† Perhaps *The First Book of Africa* (Franklin Watts, 1960).

the material into other portions. A description of Willa's parties, a wonderful bullfight in Mexico, and several of my friends <u>disappeared</u> from the book in the process of hasty but absolutely necessary cutting before it went to press. But I can use much of it in the 3rd LIFE I'll do in a couple of years or so. . . . . The same thing happened with the PICTORIAL HISTORY OF THE NEGRO. I told Lester Granger's wife the other day <u>his</u> picture was in the book, only to discover when I got copies yesterday, it <u>WASN'T</u>.* Some 30 photos had to be dropped at the last minute at the printers. So will I be embarrassed when I run into the guy!<*> . . . . . . Both these big old books cost $6 bucks, so I can't buy hardly nary one myself. Since I'm only co-collaborator on the Pictorial, it's not mine no how! Best to Marie,† Roy, and Marty. Hastily, but Sincerely,

Langston

<I haven't even been to Brooklyn to see Edwards or other friends since I saw you—but aim to make it across the river one of these days. Dorothy |Maynor| and Shelby |Rooks| invited me to the country this summer, but I never got to go! Nothing but WORK.>

<*nice photo of Dorothy in it, though, & Marian |Anderson|.>

TO ARNA BONTEMPS   [*TLS*]

[On Langston Hughes, 20 East 127th Street, New York 35, N.Y. stationery]

January 31, 1957

Mr. Arna Bontemps,
919 - 18th Avenue, North,
Nashville 8, Tennessee.

Dear Arna:

The Book of Negro Folklore seems now in the bag. Mr. Dodd made a memo to start drawing up contracts while I was there.‡ We had an hour's conference with Mr. Bond and Allen Klots (Dodd's Editorial Assistant) also present.

Mr. Bond (with whom we talked when you were here) is Vice President and seemingly head sales advisor, and he did most of the talking. I was interested in what he came up with. Although not stated in so many words, it

---

* Lester Granger (1896–1976) was executive director of the New York–based National Urban League from 1941 until 1961.
† Most likely Marie Mitchell Blackburn, Roy's wife.
‡ Hughes and Bontemps adapted part of a manuscript they completed in 1949 on Negro humor (which publishers had rejected) for their *Book of Negro Folklore* (Dodd, Mead, 1958).

amounted to a <u>socially</u> <u>slanted</u> book of folk lore—a sort of "people want to know what the Negro is thinking, and has thought in the past, about life in this country—not so many animal verses and things like that." He liked the integration jokes, etc., and the urban stuff, house rent party cards and ads. And thinks the book should be—in his own words now, "One that an Englishman could pick up and find in it something of how the Negro lives, thinks, and reacts to life in the U. S. A."

Mr. Dodd agreed to this, but added that, of course, the book should contain <u>some</u> examples of all the various categories of folklore we had outlined, and certainly the famous songs like JOHN HENRY, etc., and a representative group of spirituals, including the well known ones like SWING LOW that teachers and students might be looking up. But he approves the general social slant, too, and feels in this age of interest in race problems, <it> gives the book more vitality than merely a collection of folklore per se.

I found their viewpoint amenable—thinking to myself all the while that if I had proposed it, they would have thought me a leftist! I assured them there was certainly enough such material available to make an exciting book, mentioning the Fisk plantation material, the Jack Conroy industrial material, chain gang songs, boll weevil verses, etc., plus the current racially slanted jokes like the drunks and the bus. I read them your bit about mama never reaching California which they liked. And we all parted happy. Suggested length for the book—300-350 manuscript pages. Deadline November 15, which would give us the summer to assemble it, and probably you'd be North for a week or two when we could complete the details, section intros, etc., long about August. Meanwhile, we can be selecting, gathering, and typing up material. Is that date O. K. by you to put in the contract? If you've any contractual suggestions, better airmail them to me and/or Ivan |von Auw, Jr.|.

The only mention of the Centennial project was that they said they'd written Cresswell some time ago, but had no answer as yet.[*] And I said we were still preparing the outline, but would have it soon. So was glad to find your note when I came home saying it's on the way. . . . Nice clipping from the Birmingham paper!. . . . . Oddly, Mrs. S. Barr was up to see Aunt Toy |Harper| today.[†] Rain kept Dorothy home. . . . It <u>was</u> Miss Waters. First rumor

---

* Arna Bontemps published *100 Years of Negro Freedom* (1961) to help mark the centennial of the Emancipation Proclamation.
† Probably Mrs. Stringfellow Barr. Stringfellow Barr (1897–1982), editor of *The Virginia Quarterly Review,* was an outspoken opponent of the House Committee on Un-American Activities. Barr and Hughes corresponded between 1954 and 1958.

was another Ethel.* Seems she's cut several hogs (verbally) lately. <Too bad!>
Lang

<Carlo |Van Vechten| and Fania |Marinoff| sent me two big boxes of champagne jelly for my birthday!>

TO JAN MEYEROWITZ   *[TLS]*

April 2, 1957

Dear Jan, Thank you for your letter today, and your memo on my suggested improvements for our opera, ESTHER.† I note that you are just like a composer: you will accept no suggestions at all. No doubt the Lord made you that way, so I trust He will accept the responsibility. . . . . I still think the very end would be <im>proved, and less abrupt, with addition of a line like: "Handmaid of God, Esther, lovely Esther!" But if adding it means the death of you, don't do it. Maybe someday you will explain to me why composers expect lyricists and librettists to make ALL the changes a composer wants, but maestros are seldom, if ever, willing to change a NOTE. Even those with less talent than yourself are equally adamant. May God help you all! (So, you see, you still have my prayers.)

As to my money for the trip, I sure would like to have it. But since all correspondence with the Fromm Foundation, and promises, were made through you, for that reason I asked you to call it to the attention of the Foundation, since I have heretofore not been in negotiations with them in any way personally, and you have up to now attended to all money matters relative to ESTHER—who fortunately had a rich uncle.

Let me know how much the tape will cost and I will send you (or the recording folks) my check.

I'm so glad EDEN went well, and wish very much I could have heard it.‡

---

* In an earlier letter, Hughes wrote to Bontemps, "Hear tell a colored actress got cut off TV the other day as she was saying a white man raped her mama, so she didn't like white folks." Here he identifies the actress as Ethel Waters.
† Hughes and Meyerowitz continued to spar even after their three-act opera *Esther* had a successful premiere on March 17, 1957, at the Lincoln Hall Theater of the University of Illinois in Champaign–Urbana.
‡ Probably *Eastward in Eden* (1951), Meyerowitz's opera about the poet Emily Dickinson with a libretto by Dorothy Gardner.

With cordial regards ever, and thanks for "lovely ESTHER," I remain comme toujours,

L.H.

P.S. Thanks for that FINE sermon!

TO STELLA HOLT   [TL]

April 10, 1957

Miss Stella Holt,*
325 West 87th Street,
New York City.

Dear Stella:

I'm enclosing a carbon of a note I just wrote Josh.† As you can see, I still have a very strong feeling that we are skating on quite thin ice in regard to the current Simple as cast last night—but I hope the ice holds up. Just in case it does not hold up, I think we ought to have a tough old professional swimmer on hand who can swim under water in case the young White Hope gets drowned.

Incidentally, I went through the same sort of hassle with Michael Myerberg regarding Lawrence Tibbett in the Broadway production of the opera of mine, THE BARRIER‡—pointing out as strongly as I could that (for about the same reasons as I oppose the choice of our current Simple) Tibbett was wrong. Subsequently, my judgment was proven quite correct—Mr. Tibbett proved a headache to all concerned, and to the critics who reviewed the production as well. It ran four days! So, for the record, DON'T SAY I DIDN'T WARN YOU and Josh! (And in writing for your files.)

---

* Blind from the age of eighteen, Stella Holt (1914?–1967?) left her job as a social worker in 1952 to become managing director of the Greenwich Mews, a theater sponsored by the Village Presbyterian Church and the Brotherhood Synagogue. Holt produced Hughes's *Simply Heavenly* in 1958.
† Joshua Shelley (1920–1990), the director of *Simply Heavenly*, had cast the inexperienced black actor Melvin Stewart (1929–2002) to play Simple. This choice disturbed Hughes, who instead wanted the veteran comic Nipsey Russell. At the opening on May 21, Stewart gave an excellent performance, and Hughes revised his opinion about Stewart's ability (see letter dated September 26, 1957).
‡ Michael Myerberg (1906–1974) had been one of the producers of Hughes's opera *The Barrier* on Broadway in 1950.

I'd greatly appreciate knowing your action regarding a professional under-study for SIMPLE as soon as you can conveniently give it to me.

Best regards ever,

Sincerely,

2 enclosures
Letter to Shelley
Receipt from Bell

TO LÉOPOLD SÉDAR SENGHOR   [TL]

August 1, 1957

Dear Leopold Senghor:*

Please forgive me for being so long in thanking you for your beautiful book of poems, ETHIOPIQUES, which arrived sometime ago. It is a stunning book to look at, and an exciting book to read. I am most grateful to you for sending it to me and for your kind inscription.

I have been for the past months deeply engaged in theatre. A musicale play of mine, SIMPLY HEAVENLY, which had a successful run in a little the-atre|,| is now about to open on Broadway on August 20th. Nothing takes more time than a show and so my correspondence has suffered greatly. But I repeat that the arrival of your book gave me great pleasure and I am very happy indeed to have it.

With admiration and all good wishes, I remain

Sincerely yours,
Langston Hughes

M. Leopold Sedar Senghor
Editions Du Seuil
27 Rue Jacob
Paris 6, France

* Léopold Sédar Senghor (1906–2001), an African poet and theorist who was influenced by Hughes, was a key developer of the Negritude movement. His books include *Éthiopiques* (1956). When Senegal became free from France in 1960, he became the country's first president. He held this position until stepping down in 1980.

TO RICHARD WRIGHT [TLS]

August 11, 1957

Dear Dick:

Sometime ago, Knopf forwarded to me your request to use the last four lines of LET AMERICA BE AMERICA AGAIN in your book of four lectures.* I am happy to grant you permission to use these lines.

I must beg your forgiveness for not writing sooner but I was on the Coast when the letter came and when I returned, I found myself in the midst of rehearsals for my folk comedy, SIMPLY HEAVENLY. I am sure you know there is nothing like a theatre project to take up twenty-four hours of one's day and I am still deeply involved as we are now rehearsing for the Broadway opening on August 20th.

Ever so often I have news of you from someone who has been in Europe, and I am hoping <sometime> to get to Paris again myself. In recent years I have been so tied up with one book contract after another and running so far behind on deadlines that I have not been able to go anywhere. This summer I haven't even been to the beach although New York has had the hottest summer in years. Along with the show I have been reading proofs of my third Simple book, SIMPLE STAKES A CLAIM†—meaning a claim in Democracy. It will appear in September. Also I managed to complete this summer a translation from the Spanish of the beautiful poetry of the late Chilean poet, Gabriela Mistral.‡ This will be published in November by the Indiana University Press. I am nothing but a literary sharecropper!

I was delighted to read the fine reviews which your book about Spain received and only intense pre-occupation with things theatrical has kept me from reading it.§ But I shall read it very soon.

---

* Richard Wright published a series of lectures on race he had given recently in Europe as *White Man, Listen!* (Doubleday, 1957).
† Rinehart published Hughes's *Simple Stakes a Claim* in 1957.
‡ Gabriela Mistral (1889–1957), the pen name of Lucila Godoy Alcayaga, was a Nobel Prize–winning Chilean poet. Hughes translated and published *Selected Poems of Gabriela Mistral* (Indiana University Press, 1958).
§ *Pagan Spain* (1957), a book of cultural analysis, followed Wright's visit of fifteen weeks to that country, which was then ruled by the dictator Francisco Franco (1892–1975).

All my good wishes to you, Ellen and the children.

Sincerely yours,
Langston Hughes

Mr. Richard Wright
14, rue Monsieur le Prince
Paris VIe, France

TO INA STEELE   [TL]

September 26, 1957

Dear Ina: I've been trying to write you ever since I got back from the Coast ten days or so ago, but every day something comes up to take ALL one's time, what with the show running and a new book just out: interviews, TV (Portraits), radio (Tex and Jinx), recording sessions, a new song to write for the show, etc. etc. (New York's nothing but a workhouse)!. . . . Anyhow, they saved a piece of the cake for me that came while I was away—wrapped in tin foil, so still DE-licious. Merci beaucoup. . . . And Sam Allen* sent me a pretty painting that I haven't acknowledged yet. But will soon, I hope. . . . And today my namesake cousin (a teenager) came from Chicago for a long promised visit, so I've got to show him around. And this weekend there are two autographing parties for the new book. So I don't have time to let the devil "find work for idle hands" etc., because the fast pace of modern life has got me in the go-long! Anyhow, I LOVED Simple's Birthday card, and your letters I found on my return to Harlem. And if you like Simple, I know he must be half-way alright anyhow. And I'm lucky to have such a good actor playing him. And that is good news, too, that Youra |Qualls| is going to be at Maryland State along with you this year. Me, imagining her back in Dixie 'ere now! Tell her HAIL and not Farewell! And I hope you-all will come up and see the show again. And I'd love to get down there if the Lord ever lets me get anywhere not connected with work. That show I flew out to the Coast to see, A PART OF

---

* In 1949, Samuel W. Allen (b. 1917), also known as Paul Vesey, published his first poems in Alioune Diop's *Présence Africaine*. Allen's influential 1959 essay "Negritude and Its Relevance to the American Negro Writer" also appeared there. He was virtually unknown in the United States until the 1960s, when Bontemps and Hughes included him in their anthologies.

THE BLUES,* was so theatrically interesting I forgot it was derived from my work, or had anything to do with me, which was a relief after so much WORK on SIMPLY HEAVENLY. Its adaptor is another sort of Orson Welles, I'd say. Very talented. . . . Best ever

TO HERBERT WEINSTOCK   [TL]

November 30, 1957

Mr. Herbert Weinstock,
Alfred A. Knopf, Inc.,
501 Madison Avenue,
New York 22, New York.

Dear Herbert:
I am delighted, of course, that Alfred A. Knopf intends to publish THE SELECTED POEMS OF LANGSTON HUGHES, according to the information received from Ivan von Auw, Jr., recently. If you would send me your suggestions for any omissions or additional inclusions, I would be happy to consider them.

And, since Carl Van Vechten did the Preface for my first book of poems, THE WEARY BLUES, I think it would be quite appropriate if he would consent to write a foreword for this one. I would like it very much.†

With cordial regards,

---

* Walter Brough (b. 1935), a young white actor, wove excerpts from *The Big Sea* and *I Wonder as I Wander* with selections from Hughes's poems, blues, and songs to create the play *A Part of the Blues*. The Stage Society, a nonprofit professional actors group, presented it successfully on weekends in Hollywood.

† Herbert Weinstock of Knopf replied: "I really do not think that at this time it would be a good idea to ask Van Vechten to write one." Hughes then told Van Vechten only that Weinstock thought the proposed book was "so big that . . . it needs no introduction." *Selected Poems* appeared without an introduction.

TO NNAMDI AZIKIWE   *[TL]*

February 28, 1958

The Hon. Nnamdi Azikiwe,
Premier
Eastern Nigeria
Lagos, Nigeria

Dear Zik:

Many years have passed since our paths crossed at Lincoln |University|, and eventful years indeed for Africa. I write to you at this time in connection with a project on which I have been working a few years now—an anthology of indigenous African writers. It was originally conceived as a collection of fiction, but the publisher has recently indicated to me his wish to extend the anthology to include poetry and articles of current interest. Naturally, I could not think of such a book that did not include a contribution from you. I know that you are a very busy man with many demands on your time and so I do not expect to receive a very long piece from you. Perhaps a statement of two or three typewritten pages in which you touched on the future of Nigeria as an independent nation would be most apropos. At any rate I leave this to your judgment.*

As you are aware, present-day interest in Africa is tremendous and though the book shelves here are stacked with books covering practically every aspect of Africa and its peoples, few are being published which have been written by Africans themselves.

I visited our alma mater a few weeks ago to lecture there during Negro History Week. There have been many, many wonderful changes and it was good to see a few of the old faces again.

Know that I send to you and to your Nigeria all of my very best wishes for a bright future.

Yours very sincerely,
Langston Hughes

* Azikiwe did not contribute a piece to *An African Treasury*.

TO ARNA BONTEMPS   [TLS]

[On Langston Hughes, 20 East 127th Street, New York 35, N.Y. stationery]

August 30, 1958

Mr. Arna Bontemps,
919 - 18th Avenue North,
Nashville 8, Tennessee.

Dear Arna: The New York Omegas, who last year awarded me their Manhattan MAN OF THE YEAR plaque, now wish to nominate me for the National Award at the coming conclave. In getting together information for them (as you can see from the enclosed carbon) I recalled that last year you were kind enough to suggest nominating me for the Spingarn Award, and I asked you to hold off until my SELECTED POEMS were published.* Now that they will be coming out in January, and I think it is in late January or February that the NAACP Awards Committee begin their deliberations (as I recall from once being a member of the Committee myself) if you |would| like to make the nomination within the next few months, I'd say go to it. And (if you want to work at it that hard) get a few other folks around the country to also send in nominations: maybe Ivan Johnson in California, Truman Gibson (who's a great Simple fan) in Chicago,† and C. V. V. |Carl Van Vechten| in New York, or others if you think of them.

I suppose the categories of achievement to consider would be, among others:

- POETRY: 9 books, and almost 40 years of magazine publication,
-     beginning with THE CRISIS in 1921.
- PROSE: 15 books of my own, not counting collaborations, such as our
-     POETRY or FOLK LORE.
- TRANSLATIONS by myself of other writers: 3 books—GABRIELA
-     MISTRAL, JACQUES ROUMAIN, and NICOLÁS GUILLÉN and
-     numerous poems and stories from the Spanish and French.
- LECTURES: This season will be my 8th Cross Country tour, not
-     counting hundreds of other engagements covering practically all the

---

* In June 1960, Hughes received a telegram from his friend Henry Lee Moon of the NAACP telling him that he would receive the forty-fifth annual Spingarn Medal.
† Truman Gibson (1912–2005), a Chicago lawyer and government employee, had also served as an informal advisor to Presidents Roosevelt and Truman.

- major American colleges, and a great many high, grammar, and even
- kindergarten schools, reform schools, penitentiaries, and hospitals.
- Most Negro U.S.O. Clubs during the war and many Army Camps.
- PLAYS, MUSICALS, AND OPERAS: 12 from the Karamu Theatre to
- Broadway—MULATTO, STREET SCENE, TROUBLED ISLAND, THE BARRIER, SIMPLY HEAVENLY. MULATTO has been performed in Italy, the Argentine, Brazil, and currently in Japan. THE BARRIER is being given a major production on the Rome radio in November for which Meyerowitz is flying over.

TEACHER OF CREATIVE WRITING: The Laboratory School of the University of Chicago; Atlanta University.

BOOKS PUBLISHED ABROAD: in every major language, including Japanese, Chines<e>, Bengali, and Hindi.

UTILIZATION OF NEGRO FOLK MATERIAL: In poetry, prose (SIMPLE) and song. Our BOOK OF NEGRO FOLK LORE.

Enough!. . . . . Gracias!. . . . . Sincerely yours, Lang Litt.D. (Um-huh!)
SPECIAL AWARD: P.S. Have lived longer than any other known Negro solely on writing—from 1925 to now without a regular job!!!!! (Besides fighting the Race Problem)

!

!

!

!

TO CARL VAN VECHTEN   [TLS]

September 18, 1958

Carlo, mon cher:

Amigo mio:

Man: I got 30 letters today, which took me all day to read, answer, and get ready for Yale—which is why it is hard to go back 30 years and read mail—when I can't hardly keep ahead 30 minutes with contemporary correspondence! But I see in the papers where Mrs. Roosevelt answers 100 letters a day—so I am taking heart from that! You and she are human dynamos or something, I reckon—and not cullud. Anyhow, your letters will really go to Yale SUBITO if you say so. (I gather SUBITO means with "all deliberate speed".) But what I had actually rather do some day next week is have a drink with you one afternoon, rather than spend it looking for your letters still not unearthed in the basement! Or maybe I can do both.

What is PLACE WITHOUT TWILIGHT? And is it as good as PRANCING NIGGER was?* Which I still love.

We'll probably NEVER get ahold of Sidney Poitier now.† But he told me he was going to do RAISIN IN THE SUN this winter in New York, so maybe then. Perhaps I'll see him on the Coast in October, as I head that way on lecture tour in a couple of weeks, and since Mr. Goldwyn invites me to dinner, I'll probably visit the PORGY AND-YOU-IS-MY-WOMAN-NOW set.‡

Is Bruce Kellner the guy whose coat I wore off by mistake?§ And did you ever see or hear Bertice Reading?¶ I didn't so far as I know, but she certainly stole the London show. It is now about to be done in Prague. Maybe it will have better luck there—in a state supported theatre. And the BARRIER is to |be| done on the Rome radio in November, with Meyerowitz flying over to assist in rehearsals. And MULATTO is now on the boards in Tokyo. And I'm still in Harlem un-caught-up with my mail.

Anyhow, Lincoln 4¢ stamps to you! Langston

<"TAMBOURINES TO GLORY" has a real lively black-yellow-red jacket (proofs)!>

---

* Hughes refers to two popular novels: *A Place Without Twilight* (World Publishing, 1958) by Peter S. Feibleman (b. 1930) and *Prancing Nigger* (Brentano's, 1924) by the British novelist Ronald Firbank (1886–1926). The latter includes an introduction by Carl Van Vechten.
† Sidney Poitier (b. 1927), then an up-and-coming actor from the Bahamas, had just appeared in *The Defiant Ones* (1958), his first motion picture to give him star billing. Van Vechten was eager to get him to sit for photographs.
‡ The Samuel Goldwyn Company filmed *Porgy and Bess* (1959), based on the Gershwin opera, at its studios in Hollywood. Directed by Otto Preminger, the musical starred Sidney Poitier and Dorothy Dandridge.
§ Bruce Kellner (b. 1930) is the author of *Carl Van Vechten and the Irreverent Decades* (1968), among other volumes. He later served as an executive of the Van Vechten estate.
¶ Entertainer and actress Bertice Reading (1933–1991) was nominated in 1959 for a Tony Award as Best Supporting Female Actress (Dramatic) for her Broadway debut in William Faulkner's *Requiem for a Nun*.

TO LAWRENCE LANGNER   [*TL*]

August 12, 1959

Mr. Lawrence Langner,*
The Theatre Guild,
27 West 53rd Street,
New York 19, N. Y.

Dear Lawrence:

The revisions on TAMBOURINES TO GLORY are coming along fine.† All of your suggestions have been taken into account, and the play is greatly strengthened thereby. I have reworked the entire script, added two new scenes, and inserted into others some new and, I think, highly dramatic material that should play well. Laura's character has been further built up and made both more humorous and more sympathetic in places, placing her over Essie as the show's lead. The Buddy-C. J. fight scene is exciting, and the Essie-Laura conversation that follows, closing the scene, should be very moving. As is the jail house scene. And for the finale of the show, I've devised a surprise twist on Laura's part which makes it appear that Essie and Deacon Crow-For-Day are about to be married until at the very curtain, Marrietta and C. J. are revealed as the bridal couple. Laura, of course, has been taken back into the fold—with a front page picture of her in the DAILY NEWS—for, through her killing of Buddy the whole underworld racket in Harlem has been exposed, and she is currently the heroine of the District Attorney's office. Says Essie, "God works in mysterious way, His wonders to perform." Song: "Tambourines! Tambourines! Tambourines to glory!" The new script is about ready to deliver to Anne Myerson for typing on Monday. . . . . . Incidentally, at the White Barn Theatre near you on August 29-30 they<'re> doing an adaptation of my poems, SHAKESPEARE <IN H>ARLEM‡. . . . . . . Sincerely,

---

* As a producer with the Theatre Guild, Lawrence Langner (1890–1962) supervised more than two hundred productions. He also built the Westport Country Playhouse in Connecticut and wrote several plays, including *The Pursuit of Happiness* (1933), and an autobiography, *The Magic Curtain* (1951).
† Hughes collaborated with the North Carolina–born singer and composer Jobe Huntley (1917–1995) on *Tambourines to Glory*. Hughes proudly called it the first musical play based on the black gospel musical tradition.
‡ Robert Glenn, a young white dramatist and director, adapted *Shakespeare in Harlem* into a one-act play with the main theme of "a dream deferred." The play was later produced off-Broadway in 1960.

TO ARNA BONTEMPS [*TLS*]

[On Langston Hughes, 20 East 127th Street, New York 35, N.Y. *stationery]*

October 11, 1959

Mon cher ami:

My least idea of pleasure is—as you put it—"browsing" in a basement full of 20 years junk! And what bugs me is Yale never did tell me one could make income tax deductions on stuff given. (I only learned it from the Library of Congress.) Now they come saying they thought I knew it all the time. Arthur Spingarn says he deducts from 50¢ to $5.00 a letter, especially when they're handwritten and from famous folks; also the cost price of all books. And I've given Yale hundreds of letters, and God knows how many books, my own and others inscribed to me! Records, music, and all kinds of things that would have helped a bit on income taxes for 10 years or more!

Well, anyhow! Did I tell you the State Department's asked me if I want to lecture abroad? Ah regrets. Trinidad in November and Midwest in February (all booked up already) is about all I can do this season without giving the rest of my advances back. . . . . I've really done a little work on the Harlem book. But none on the promised teenage novel yet.* TAMBOURINES TO GLORY has been taking up lots of time lately—but the Guild suggestions are all so sound that it is now a much better play than originally—and fuller than the novel. (After all, the novel was written in a week—from Sunday to Sunday—and the play which was done first, didn't take much longer. What you call "tour de forces" I reckon. But fun, since I had no deadlines on either, or con-tracts, and really should have |been| doing my Hollywood script.)†

Well, anyhow! I am really disillusioned with quiz shows! Seems like no cullud involved.

I hear a mighty whooping and hollering out the back window (1 AM) but can't make out if it is a fight or a frolic. Got to see. Lang

---

* The "promised teenage novel" might be "The Nine O'Clock Bell," a proposed book for young readers about the civil rights struggle in the South. Hughes soon abandoned the project.
† Samuel Goldwyn, the movie producer, had contacted Hughes about the possibility of a movie version of *Simply Heavenly.* Nothing came of the idea.

TO CARL VAN VECHTEN [*TLS*]

<I was so glad to see you the other night. I guess absence makes the heart grow fonder.>

October 12,1959
Columbus Night

Dear Carlo: Unbearded Patriarch—

I haven't gotten such a long letter from you since the days of the Cullud Rennaissance! And I would answer you in kind were it not that I have a toothache and have to get up early and go have it pulled out.

Of course, I understand how you feel about the JWJ Collection. I feel that way, too.[*] But, in my long life, I have noticed no general excitement among large numbers of the colored race about ANY collection—from the Schomburg to the Metropolitan, JWJ to the Library of Congress, Cluny to the Cloisters. They are just not collection minded. And (as I have heard you say about other things many times)—"that's the way it is." So, those of us who do know and do care will just have to redouble our efforts, I reckon, and include in those efforts (as did Nora) the bestirring of others.[†]

Concerning Sidney |Poitier| and the photos, he has never said he wouldn't be photographed. I've spoken to him both here, on the Coast, and in Chicago about it, and each time he's said, "Soon as my next picture is over," or "Soon as the play settles down," or something like that. He is certainly a very busy (and very tense) young man and also very hard to get a hold of, or talk with quietly. And probably can't quite cope with all the things that go into career making with the success, say, of Miss Eartha Kitt.[‡] And he has no Essie to his Robeson, or Lennie to the Horne.[§] Or so, it seems to me "that's the way it is." About

---

[*] On October 11, Van Vechten wrote to Hughes: "For the past ten years I have devoted at least fifty per cent of my waking hours to this perpetuation of the fame of the Negro and it saddens me to realize how few Negroes realize this and how still fewer make any attempt to assist the collection." He signed the letter "Carlo the Patriarch!"

[†] On June 22, 1955, Nora Holt joined Van Vechten at Yale University for the opening of an exhibition of material from all the collections that Van Vechten had obtained for the Yale Library (including the James Weldon Johnson Collection and, among others, the papers of Gertrude Stein).

[‡] At sixteen, Eartha Kitt (1927–2008) won a scholarship to the Katherine Dunham School, and then toured with its dance group. In Paris she became a leading nightclub singer and dancer before gaining even greater fame in the United States. In 1956 she successfully published *Thursday's Child,* an autobiography.

[§] The singer and actress Lena Horne (1917–2010) was married to the composer and drummer Lennie Hayton (1908–1971).

which I do not know what to do. He does not seem as yet to have managed to surround himself with efficient and helpful people—as Harry Belafonte* and some of the other younger Negro stars seem to have achieved—which might leave him a little more time to be courteous and photographable.

Anyhow, have you photographed the colored beatnik poet of the Village, LeRoi Jones? He seems to me to be talented. I've never met him. But when I first read his poems, I asked someone to find out for me if he was colored, and in some fashion the inquiry reached him. So he called me up to tell me he was. I wasn't home, but he left the message. (I thought he was colored anyway, named LeRoi.) He edits a magazine called YUNGEN and, I believe, has his own print shop.† <(And he <u>doesn't</u> like my work—which I don't mind. I like his.)>

Which is all my observations for the moment as I have to put a clove in my tooth and go to bed. But, so you can <u>lament</u> better the faults of the *race ——➤

Sackcloth dipped in eau de vie and <u>just</u> a soupçon of ashes in champagne— that wonderful big-bottle kind like you had at the party the other night (which was a wonderful party)—

Langston

*We both should use a capital R—Race!

---

* Harry Belafonte (b. 1927) achieved fame as a folksinger (of Caribbean music especially) and a film actor. Also a social activist, he worked closely with Rev. Dr. Martin Luther King, Jr., in the 1950s and 1960s and currently serves as a Goodwill Ambassador for the United Nations Children's Fund.
† LeRoi Jones (1934–2014), born in Newark, New Jersey, was a poet, playwright, essayist, and music critic who changed his name to Amiri Baraka in 1968. From 1958 to 1963 he coedited the avant-garde literary magazine *Yugen* (not *Yungen*, as Hughes wrote) in Greenwich Village with his first wife, Hettie Cohen. His first collection of poetry, *Preface to a Twenty-Volume Suicide Note*, appeared in 1961 from Corinth Books. In 1964, Jones's *Dutchman* won the Obie Award for the Best American Play. Jones was probably the most influential leader in the transformational Black Arts movement that started later in the 1960s.

TO REVEREND DR. MARTIN LUTHER KING, JR.   *[TL]*

December 12, 1959

Salute to A. Philip Randolph Committee
Rev. Martin Luther King*
165 West 131st Street
New York 27, New York

Dear Rev. King:

I am happy to write a poem in salute to A. Philip Randolph and I am enclosing a copy which you may print in the souvenir program, have read at the testimonial, and use in any other way feasible. My regret is that immediately after the holidays I am going to California and unless some urgent commitment brings me east again, sooner than I expect, it is unlikely that I will be in New York on the night of January 24th. But perhaps, if you wish, Fred O'Neal†️ or some other skilled performer might be invited to read my poem, if accepted for use on the program.

Thank you very much indeed for you|r| kind words about my poetry and certainly I am most pleased that you have used it in your speeches and sermons so effectively. As I have attempted to express to you before, and through my column in the CHICAGO DEFENDER, I have the greatest admiration for you and your work.

With kindest regards,

Cordially yours
Langston Hughes

LH/gb
Encl: POEM FOR A MAN
By Langston Hughes

---

* Rev. Dr. Martin Luther King, Jr. (1929–1968), appealed to Hughes for a poem honoring the veteran labor leader A. Philip Randolph, to be read at a Carnegie Hall tribute to Randolph. In response, Hughes wrote "Poem for a Man."

† Frederick O'Neal (1905–1992), an African American actor, co-founded the American Negro Theatre in 1940.

PART V

I Heard the Horn of Plenty Blowing

1960 to 1967

At the Spingarn Medal award ceremony, St. Paul,
Minnesota, 1960. Arthur B. Spingarn is behind Hughes.

Durban, Birmingham,
Cape Town, Atlanta,
Johannesburg, Watts,
The earth around
Struggling, fighting,
Dying—for what?

A world to gain.
—"QUESTION AND ANSWER," 1966

In 1960, when the NAACP bestowed on Hughes its highest honor,
the Spingarn Medal, he declared: "I can accept it only in the name
of the Negro people who have given me the materials out of which my
poems and stories, plays and songs, have come." This link between his
art and black Americans remained essential to him. With the United

States on the brink of historic political and cultural changes, it led Hughes to works such as *Ask Your Mama,* an innovative volume of poetry with roots in the blues and modernist jazz, and *Black Nativity,* a Christmas gospel show that would remain a favorite with African American audiences. Inspired by Africa as various countries there emerged from colonialism, he traveled in 1961 to Uganda and Egypt and later made other visits to the continent. Although some younger black Americans, with the rise of Black Power militancy in the mid-1960s, would increasingly find his verse on the whole too tame, most readers continued to celebrate Hughes as a towering figure who had moved people to understand better and eventually to celebrate not only African American culture but also the human condition itself.

TO ARNA BONTEMPS   [TLS]

[On Langston Hughes, 20 East 127th Street, New York 35, N.Y. *stationery*]

January 21, 1960

Dear Arna: Was way over in Brooklyn tonight for rehearsal of the Poetry-Choir program.* Back at 1:30 and revised part of SHAKESPEARE IN HARLEM for which I hear they've got the money and go into rehearsal next week for off-Broadway opening mid-February.† Then on my way to bed I started to read the COOL WORLD, novel version, and just finished it now at 8:30 in the A. M. so am <u>really</u> on my way to bed.‡ (Someone at rehearsal lent it to me.)

<u>Play script</u> |of *Cool World*| is much <u>more</u> repellant than novel, although it uses most of the dialogue. But, lacking the asides and overtones, it comes out (in my opinion) a holy horror with nobody at all sympathetic or likable— just a script full of unpleasant kids, each one depicting a vice of one sort or another—a kind of colored juvenile BEGGARS OPERA without that play's

---

* On January 31, at the Antioch Baptist Church of Brooklyn, Hughes participated in the program *Spiritual Spectacular,* a performance of religious songs and poetry.
† *Shakespeare in Harlem,* which opened at the 41st Street Theatre in New York City on February 9, closed after thirty-two performances.
‡ The novel *The Cool World* (1959) by Warren Miller (1921–1966), a white writer, is narrated by the fourteen-year-old leader of a Harlem street gang. The Broadway staging of its adaptation ran for only two performances (February 22 and 23, 1960).

sardonic humor and social commentary. (Or am I becoming over-sensitive racially, and NAACP-ish? I just hate to see a whole stage full of Harlem kids at a big Broadway theatre—in front of white folks—depicted that way—without a single decent one in the bunch.) None are <u>that</u> bad.

Oh, well, set back 50 years again! <The Race!> But the last setback—when it comes—will be the boomerang that will set back the setter-backers! Some old slingshot somewhere in the world is going to throw the rock that slays Goliath. Selah! A 14 year old strumpet and a 15 year old pimp and a 16 year old junkie whose brother goes to Fisk is just <u>un peu trop</u>! Didn't Lillian Smith's loose young lady go to Fisk, too?* Why do they pick on <u>you-all</u> so much— suppose to be our most polished college? (It turned out Du Bois, but nobody puts him in a play.) I think they're out to do us in, myself. I know you have a more protective feeling than I toward liberals. Didn't somebody say, "I can take care of my enemies, but God protect me from my friends."

And I hear it's got a movie sale, already!

You're colleged. If I'm over-sensitive, tell me. I tries to be objective.

But, honest, I never saw or read a white play about so many assorted bad people <u>so young</u> on any stage. Even in THE BAD SEED and TEA AND SYMPATHY and HATFUL OF RAIN and BLACK ORPHEUS and THE RESPECTFUL PROSTITUTE, somebody is trying to do right.†

Respectfully yours,

J. L. Hughes

James L. Hughes

(My full and legal name)

---

* Hughes most likely refers to Nonnie Anderson, a young mixed-race woman who becomes pregnant by her white lover in the novel *Strange Fruit* (1944) written by Lillian Smith (1897–1966). Nonnie is a graduate of Spelman College, not Fisk University.

† The novel *The Bad Seed*, by William March (1893–1954), about an eight-year-old girl willing to kill to get her way, was the basis of a Broadway play by Maxwell Anderson (1888–1959). Robert Anderson (1917–2009) adapted his play *Tea and Sympathy* (1953) for a 1956 film of the same name, in which a teenaged boy is bullied about his perceived sexuality. *A Hatful of Rain* (1953), by the playwright Michael V. Gazzo (1923–1995), presents the struggles of a young man addicted to morphine. Set in Rio, the film *Orfeu Negro* (*Black Orpheus*) (1959) is loosely based on the Greek myth of the star-crossed lovers Orpheus and Eurydice. The play *The Respectful Prostitute* (1946), by Jean-Paul Sartre (1905–1980), was the basis for a 1952 French film about a New York prostitute who witnesses the murder of a black man.

TO WOLE SOYINKA   [TLS]

[On Crown Publishers, Inc. 419 Fourth Avenue, New York 16, N. Y. letterhead]

January 31, 1960

Dear Wole Soyinka:*

As you may know, for many years now I have been compiling an anthology of African writing, which will be published by Crown Publishers under the title of AN AFRICAN TREASURY. It will consist of articles, essays, stories, poems, and miscellaneous items by indigenous Africans, and one of the distinguishing features of the collection is that all of the contributors are writers of color. I think this will make for not only a rich and stimulating reading experience but also an important expression of what African writers are thinking and saying.

In keeping with the high standards we have set for this anthology, I would very much like to include the material listed below, the rights to which, I understand, are controlled by you. If you do not control the rights, would you please pass this letter on to the person or publication which does. Since there is a time consideration, I would appreciate it if you could return the form below to me Airmail. We will of course give you appropriate credit in each instance, so would you please indicate exactly how you would like that credit to read. Since this is a small book which we are trying to put out at the lowest price possible to reach the widest market, our budget necessarily is limited; but if you do give us permission to include your material, we will pay you $10.00.

Thank you very much for your attention to this matter.

Sincerely yours,

Langston Hughes

Langston Hughes

Selection(s): 2 POEMS

THE IMMIGRANT

.... AND THE OTHER IMMIGRANT

from "Black Orpheus"

---

* The future Nobel Prize–winning Nigerian writer Akinwande Oluwole "Wole" Soyinka (b. 1934) allowed Hughes to include his poems "The Immigrant" and "And the Other Immigrant" in *An African Treasury: Articles / Essays / Stories / Poems by Black Africans* (Crown, 1960).

TO JULIAN BOND   [TL]

TO: Julian Bond,[*]
672 Beckwith Street, S. W.,
Atlanta, Georgia (14)
Apt. 4.

March 21, 1960

Dear Julian:

Please send me the poems, man! I liked the three I saw very much, so would like to have copies of those, plus a half dozen or so more, if you have them, from which I might make a tentative selection for the anthology of new poets[†]—before I go away next week on a North Carolina lecture tour until Easter.

I have already some thirteen very interesting younger colored poets' work—quite enough to make what I think will be a very good collection of mostly—as yet—unpublished work. And I'd certainly like to include some things of yours among them in submitting the manuscripts to the interested publisher shortly. There will be a payment for each poem used, if accepted.

Please tell the family I enjoyed seeing them all—and the dinner—very much. And I will be writing your father shortly. At the moment I am BUSY finishing up details on my AFRICAN TREASURY, and preparing for the Theatre Guild auditions for TAMBOURINES TO GLORY coming up in a few days. Della Reese is going to have the lead[‡]—but we lost Odetta to the movies, so have to find another singing actress for the second role.[§]

Cordial regards,

Sincerely,

---

[*] Horace Julian Bond (b. 1940), son of Horace Mann Bond, a former president of Lincoln University, was one of the younger leaders of the civil rights movement. In 1960, he helped to found the influential Student Non-Violent Coordinating Committee (SNCC).

[†] In *New Negro Poets: USA* (Indiana University Press, 1964), Hughes included two of Bond's poems, "Year Without Seasons" and "Beast with Chrome Teeth."

[‡] The singing star Della Reese (b. 1931) did not appear in the Westport Playhouse opening of *Tambourines to Glory* on September 5, 1960. The lead female was the pianist and sometime singer Hazel Scott (1920–1981). Hughes found her performance weak. When *Tambourines to Glory* opened on Broadway in November 1963, Hilda Simms (1918–1994) enacted the role.

[§] Odetta Holmes (1930–2008), known professionally as Odetta, was an actress and folksinger with ties to the civil rights movement. Clara Ward (1924–1973), a famous gospel singer, performed the part of Birdie Lee in the Broadway production.

TO AMY SPINGARN   [TL]

April 18, 1960

Dear Amy Spingarn,

At last I have come out ahead of the Income Tax man, with something left over at the end of the year—instead of having to start entirely from scratch again! So I am enclosing for you my check for the remaining $100.00 due you on the loan you so kindly made me some seven years ago now. I'm so sorry to have been so long. Trying to run a major career on a minor income is something! My very great thanks to you. . . . . And I am looking forward to seeing you at dinner on the 27th.*

   With cordial regards, as ever

Sincerely yours,
Langston Hughes

TO JAN MEYEROWITZ   [TL]

August 27, 1960

Dear Jan:

After "Port Town" performance, I really am not interested in writing any more opera librettos for anyone.† As operas are done in America, the words had just as well be nonsense syllables. I see no point in spending long hours of thought, and weeks of writing seeking poetic phrases and just the right word—and then not enough of the librettist's lines are heard for anybody to know what is being sung. There is another factor, too, which seems to me to make libretto writing a waste of time: so few performances of an operatic work are given—and NO money is made. Each time I go to hear an opera of mine (whose words I cannot hear) it costs me more in transportation, hotel bills, and tickets for friends than I will ever make from the work. So, when there is no artistic joy in hearing (or rather NOT hearing) one's work, and no financial income, either, why bother? I am sure if you were a writer of words, you would agree with me that when a great deal of hard work goes

* Presumably Hughes refers to the annual banquet of the NAACP in St. Paul, Minnesota, where he received the Spingarn Medal.
† Differences between Hughes and Jan Meyerowitz reached a critical point after their one-act opera, *Port Town*, had its premiere at the Tanglewood Music Festival in Massachusetts on August 4, 1960.

into putting those words together, you would like them to reach an audience clearly, and certainly you would like to be able to hear and understand a few of them yourself. No, mon cher? Anyhow, just for the record, I make my position clear. And, of course, none of this is your fault. It's just the way things are, I reckon—or were, since they won't be for me again. Folks who write librettos must be simple! Your music doesn't need words, anyhow. It sounds fine all by itself. I wish I could write music. I'd leave words alone. .. .. . . Cordial regards ever,

TO LOFTEN MITCHELL [TL]

September 26, 1960

Dear Loften:*

Thanks so much for your VERY helpful letter. Just the kind of comments and suggestions I need at this stage! One of yours had already occurred to me and been worked in, and the others all influenced the revisions I've just completed. The script† now has a brand new singing opening PROLOGUE, a new Scene 1—eviction with ESSIE founding her church on top of a pile of old furniture on the curb; two old scenes deleted entirely; the jail scene built up as you suggested, too; and a brand new ending with ESSIE taking over the church in a more POSITIVE fashion than before and delivering herself of a very moving little sermon, instead of the wedding ending. And all three of the leading characters illuminated in depth a bit more than they were. And the whole now down to 2 hours running time, compared to the $2^{1}/_{2}$ it was on opening at Westport. Who said, "Plays are not written—but re-written?" Whoever did sure was right! But this one, I hope, gets better each time. And |Lawrence| Langner's suggestions seem to me nine times out of ten good. He's theatrically astute without tampering with the basic meanings. The Guild swears it will come to Broadway this season, maybe around the holidays, if and when the theatre log-jam lets up a bit both in town and on the road, where they hope

---

* Loften Mitchell (1919–2001), an African American playwright, was nominated for a Tony Award in 1976 for his book for the hit musical *Bubbling Brown Sugar*. In 1957, he and the producer Stella Holt staged his play *A Land Beyond the River* at Greenwich Mews Theatre in New York.

† The play discussed is *Tambourines to Glory*, produced at the Westport Playhouse in Connecticut starting in August 1960. The play was to have been the third production that season of the Theatre Guild in New York, but some observers, black and white alike, worried that its comic elements were out of tune with the harsh realities of the current civil rights movement.

to give it further chance at polishing. Anyhow, for the moment, I'm through, having done almost nothing else since last Spring. ALL the rest of my work is so FAR behind I don't know where to pick up at. . . . . Saw the CONNECTION tonight. Found it fascinating in some ways, and very well acted, I thought. Certainly it and the BALCONY are about the most unique!*. . . . Best to the family, and thanks again.

Script just sent to Anne Myerson for copying again—10th time—some $600 worth of typing all told! Plays not only the MOST work, but MOST expensive!

TO MARGARET WALKER (ALEXANDER)   [TL]

October 7, 1960

Dear Margaret:

I've been so busy with my Theatre Guild show, TAMBOURINES TO GLORY, for the past few months, that I am not quite sure what I have or haven't done! But maybe I wrote you, I submitted as a part of the manuscript of NEW NEGRO POETS your NEGRO SOLDIERS, LINES FOR WILLIE McGHEE, and NOTICE. . . . ATTENTION.† It seems university presses are noted for slowness in making up their minds. But recently I got a summary of their various readers' reports, and the consensus seems to be to limit the proposed book (if finally O.K.ed) to about a dozen of the more "avante guarde" poets like the current beatnik crop—which they feel represents the trend nowadays—as I guess it does. Loud and angry race cries such as you and I are accustomed to give are not at the moment "comme il faut" or "a la mode" as a poetic style. (But don't worry, I expect they will be again in due time!) Anyhow, if I may, I'll keep your above poems in my files, as other publication sources may come up. Meanwhile I'm returning the enclosed manuscripts. And thanks a lot for giving me the pleasure of reading them. I liked some of your sister's poems very much, too, as I think I wrote her.

---

* *The Connection* (1959), the Obie Award–winning drama by Jack Gelber (1932–2003), ran for 722 performances at the Living Theatre in New York. *The Balcony* (1956), by the French writer Jean Genet (1910–1986), won the Obie Award for Best Foreign Play in 1960.
† Walker's poetry is not included in *New Negro Poets: USA*. The poems noted in the letter do not appear in her volume *This Is My Century: New and Collected Poems* (University of Georgia Press, 1989) or in her other published books.

Adele is looking for a place to move the Market Place.* And I'm looking for an ivory tower!

Cordial regards always,

Sincerely,

TO FRANK GREENWOOD [TL]

October 27, 1960

Dear Frank:†

Thanks a lot! I've given programs a couple of times at Scott Methodist in Pasadena, nice church. And have appeared elsewhere there, too. But each time it is white or mixed sponsorship, out come the 200% Americans to picket or in general bug the sponsors—first it was Aimee Semple McPherson; another time the Minute Women; so I'd just as leave not be bothered with Pasadena, especially with "liberal whites" involved who usually get scared if one single letter is written to the paper—and leave the Negroes holding the bag in the end . . . . . . What I would prefer is a Negro-sponsored date in Los Angeles proper, if one comes along. If not, O.K., too, since I'll have only a few days there all told, and can use the time seeing relatives and friends—now that Mills College has switched its dates to the 14-15-16, taking the whole middle of NEGRO HISTORY WEEK up North‡ . . . . . . Fee $150 to $200 depending on size of group, non-profit or not, etc. (More for white folks!)

I've got to go speak in Philly tomorrow night, and have just caught a cold!§ What a drag! So am drinking fruit juices, wines, codeine, and lickers all day today—trying to soak it out.

Regards,

* Adele Glasgow, a close friend of Hughes, ran the Market Place Gallery in Harlem and also the Negro Book Society. A member of his Harlem Suitcase Theatre in 1938, she sometimes worked for him as a typist.
† Frank Greenwood worked for a lecture-booking agency that Hughes retained after he left the Colston Leigh Agency, which had arranged his bookings for many years.
‡ Hughes's February 1961 lecture tour included a visit to Mills College in Oakland, California, where he received exactly the kind of unwanted attention that he describes in this letter. However, Mills did not bow to this pressure. All of his lectures and class meetings were held as scheduled.
§ Hughes went to Philadelphia to celebrate the twenty-fifth anniversary of the ministry of Franklin B. Mitchell, Jr. (1910–2000), a Lincoln University classmate.

TO JAN MEYEROWITZ   [TL]

[On B.O.A.C. stationery]

Back home again,[*]
December 8, 1960

Dear Jan:

I find your note on arrival and am delighted to hear the BARRIER tapes will be aired soon. Better I don't promise to do a narration (unless it is taped beforehand) as I'll be out of town lots on lecture trips and might not be in New York that Sunday. Certainly I'll be in California ALL of the month of February and maybe part of March. The last two Sundays of March I have programs with a Choir. In April there is a Midwestern tour—Detroit, Cleveland, etc., so I am loath to add anything else to my calendar. But if the radio station would like to tape a brief introduction, O. K., that I could do.

My week in Nigeria was exciting, and my day in Rome restful, Paris and London both lovely. Paris I found the same as ever—such an endearing city. I think I'll go back and stay.

I was Richard Wright's last visitor at home and as I left, he left to go to the hospital, seemingly not very ill. But three days later while I was in London, he died.[†]

Since my SIMPLY HEAVENLY has been a hit in Prague, there is interest in possibly doing other things of mine there. I suggest concerning THE BARRIER that Marks[‡] contact:

Mr. Josef Kalas,
D I L I A,
Vysehradska 28,
Prague 2, Nove Mesto,
Czechoslovakia.

---

[*] Nnamdi "Zik" Azikiwe invited Hughes and thirty other Lincoln University graduates and professors to attend (with all expenses paid) his inauguration on November 16, 1960, as governor-general and commander-in-chief of newly independent Nigeria. Other guests of Azikiwe included W. E. B. Du Bois and Martin Luther King, Jr. After a week in Nigeria, Hughes visited Rome, Paris, and London.

[†] Richard Wright died on November 28, 1960. After contracting amoebic dysentery in Africa in 1957, he suffered several apparently related setbacks to his health before succumbing at the age of fifty-two to a fatal heart attack in Paris. He is buried in the Père-Lachaise Cemetery there.

[‡] Probably the noted music publisher Edward B. Marks.

(DILIA means Czech Theatrical and Literary Agency. They pay royalties in American money. I've gotten some quite nice checks from them.)

Cordial regards to Marguerite,

Sincerely,

Langston Hughes

TO ARNA BONTEMPS   [*TLS*]

[*On* Langston Hughes, 20 East 127th Street, New York 35, N.Y. *stationery*]

January 28, 1961

Dear Arna:

Don't think you have to sit down and write right back, just because I reply to your welcome letters with promptitude occasionally. I know you are BUSY. Me, too. But get tired of being BUSY about 4-5 A. M. as now, so take pen in hand. . . . . Been wrestling with the preliminaries to income tax tonight. . . . Also trying to figure out if I have <u>LOST</u> my mind. Just signed contracts for <u>TWO new books</u> today, and haven't even started the last TWO I've spent the advances on.* But I've heard tell the Lord DOES help children and authors—and I DO need the money paid on signing. (I got back from Africa with <u>less</u> than a hundred dollars in the bank—after 52 years of what Mrs. Bethune called "SERVICE." But then she also said, "The reward for service is MORE service." Do |you| reckon that is ALL?))) Anyhow, I am nothing but a literary share cropper. Swing low, sweet chariot and rescue me!

The King of Ragtime called up from Florida (he's white) and says Missouri is giving a big thing March 15th in honor of Blind Boone and his music, and wanted me to do some new lyrics for some of <Boone's> outmoded "darkie" lines.† (Which I've been thinking ought to be done to some of the old but good stuff written in the minstrel tradition—maybe once mentioned it to you.) Unfortunately, as I'm about to go on tour, can't do this particular job in time for the big Missouri concert which is having the Lincoln U. Choir, a big symphony, and this ragtime man, Bob Darch, as soloist. Wish I could.

Thanks for the comments on MAMA/. The first time, to my knowledge,

---

* One of the contracts Hughes signed that day was for *Fight for Freedom: The Story of the NAACP* (Norton, 1962). The NAACP commissioned the volume.
† "Ragtime" Bob Darch (1920–2002), a pianist, was the featured performer at a benefit concert in historical tribute to John William "Blind" Boone held at the University of Missouri–Columbia on March 15, 1961. Boone (1864–1927) was a revered black composer and pianist of ragtime who had lost his sight as an infant.

the Dozens have been used in poetry.* I'm reading it for the NAACP with Buddy Collette's combo in California.† That ought to be fun!

See Jimmy Baldwin's piece on King in current Harper's. Some wonderful sentences on Negro leaders. <Also Worthy on Muslims in "Esquire;" Peter A. on Puerto Rico in "Holiday.">‡ I sent C.V.V. his Memoirs of Dick, and C.V.V. writes that his version and Chester Himes' are quite different as to why they all fell out, which jives with what you say.§ How come we never fall out with NOBODY? Or do you? I don't believe I ever did. Maybe it's about time. My most vivid memor<y> of Dick is relative to Margaret and his fleeing from her in New York and she running after the 5th Avenue bus and never caught up with him again.¶ He went to Paris. But she's in HIS Mississippi.

Hope C. R. stays sober in his State Department job.** Tipsy tales about him come from all around the world. . . . Nice about Leontyne busting the

* In *Ask Your Mama: 12 Moods for Jazz* (Knopf, 1961), Hughes fused jazz and other black music with the form called the "dozens," a ritual of genial insult rooted in African American culture. Each of the twelve sections of the poem is attended by musical cues that are integral to its poetic meaning. On January 26, Bontemps wrote to Hughes: "*Ask Your Mama* is undoubtedly a milestone in your writing career. It indicates, for one thing, that you are not ready to play it safe, but prefer to try new rhythms and styles for new effects. . . . Moreover, it challenges the current trends in beat poetry with something more subtle and at the same time more solid." Most reviewers dismissed the work.
† The culmination of Hughes's February 1961 lecture tour was an NAACP-sponsored event at the University of California–Los Angeles. He read excerpts from *Ask Your Mama* for the first time publicly, backed by Buddy Collette's jazz group. Collette (1921–2010) was an influential African American jazzman, teacher, and social activist based in California.
‡ The recommended articles are James Baldwin's "The Dangerous Road Before Martin Luther King" in *Harper's*; Peter Abrahams's "The Puerto Ricans" in *Holiday*; and William Worthy's "The Angriest Negroes" in *Esquire*. Each piece appeared in the February 1961 issue of these magazines.
§ A convicted felon who served several years in the Ohio Penitentiary for armed robbery, Chester B. Himes (1909–1984) started writing and became one of Richard Wright's protégés. Van Vechten helped him find a publisher for his second novel, *Lonely Crusade* (Knopf, 1947). A feud developed between Baldwin and Wright, which Baldwin recalls in his essay "The Exile" (*Encounter,* April 1961). This essay and two others appear together as "Alas, Poor Richard" in his collection *Nobody Knows My Name: More Notes from a Native Son* (1961).
¶ In 1939, Margaret Walker (Alexander) traveled from Chicago to New York apparently in pursuit of Richard Wright. They fell out after Walker, who had known Wright in Chicago, accused him of having too close a friendship with the playwright Ted Ward. Amused, Hughes wrote a ditty he called "Epic" about the incident. It goes: "Margaret Walker is a talker / When she came to town / What she said put Ted in bed / And turned Dick upside down."
** In 1961, the veteran journalist Carl Rowan was appointed deputy assistant secretary of state for public affairs by President John F. Kennedy. He became ambassador to Finland in 1963 and director of the United States Information Agency (USIA) in 1964.

wall of the Metropolitan wide open last night.* Negroes and Italians do sing the most! . . . My Selected Poems (of a sort) just came out in Italy: IO SONO UN NEGRO (Il Gallo, Collana omnibus 58, Edizioni Avanti, Milano—in case the Library would like to order it. They only sent me one copy, so can't present you with one). . . . I've recently gotten another letter from Germany from a researcher who can't find hardly anything by cullud authors in Amerika Haus. I hope Mr. Rowan takes up this dilemma o<n> our cultural front.† Or you, or somebody respected. They'd pay me no mind. Their MAMA! Lang

TO LEROI JONES   [TLS]

<["Horn of Plenty" enclosed]>
<"Floating Bear">

April 27, 1961

Dear LeRoi:

Perhaps the enclosed sequence from ASK YOUR MAMA might be of interest to THE FLOATING BEAR—since the dozens are still news to lots of people.‡ But don't mind returning it, if not suitable to your needs. (I've got more rejection slips then if you live so long). Stamps enclosed.

Either you are getting square, or the Whitney folks are getting hip. . . . . . . Which? At any rate, I hear they are giving you "earnest consideration." (I hope it turns into "<u>due</u>" consideration.)§

Comme toujours,
Langston

---

* Leontyne Price (b. 1927), singing with the Italian tenor Franco Corelli, shared in an ovation of at least thirty minutes at the end of a performance of Verdi's *Il Trovatore* on January 27, 1961, at the Metropolitan Opera House in New York. Corelli and Price, who sang the role of Leonora, made their debuts at the Met that evening.

† Bontemps responded: "As soon as Carl Rowan is settled down in his job I will definitely take up with him the question of Negro authors in USIA libraries, etc. I'm sure he will be sensitive to the fact that his books were just as *absent* as yours or mine."

‡ The poet Diane Di Prima (b. 1934) edited the mimeographed literary newsletter *The Floating Bear* from 1961 to 1969. LeRoi Jones (with whom she had a daughter, Dominique Di Prima) was her coeditor from 1961 to 1963.

§ Jones was awarded a John Hay Whitney Fellowship in 1961.

TO JAMES BALDWIN
[Draft of a postcard]

POSTAL CARD TO JAMES BALDWIN AFTER READING
GALLEYS OF "NOBODY KNOWS MY NAME"——

May 4, 1961

Jimmy:

I fear you are becoming a "NEGRO" writer—and a propaganda one, at that! What's happening????? (Or am I reading wrong?)

Anyhow, NOBODY KNOWS MY NAME is fascinating reading, wonderful for many evenings of discussion for the talkative uptown and down—and surely makes of <you a> sage—a cullud sage—whose hair, once processed, seems to be reverting.*

Hope it makes the best-seller list. You might as well suffer in comfort.

Sincerely,
Langston

TO JUDITH JONES   [*TLS*]
[On Langston Hughes, 20 East 127th Street, New York 35, N.Y. *stationery]*

July 23, 1961

Dear Judith Jones:†

The editor of THE CRISIS, James Ivy, has answered me as follows:

THE CRISIS is glad to reassign the copyright of your poem, TWO WAY STREET, to you in order that it may be used by your publisher, Knopf. The poem will appear in the August-September issue of THE CRISIS.

So kindly add THE CRISIS to the list of acknowledgements on the page proofs.

I've sent the ballet version of ASK YOUR MAMA to Alvin Ailey (now danc-

---

* Baldwin's essay collection *Nobody Knows My Name* (1961), a best-seller in the United States, became an influential volume in the civil rights movement.

† An editor at Knopf, Judith Jones worked with Hughes on *Ask Your Mama* and other projects in the 1960s. Blanche Knopf, Hughes's former editor there, had become president of the firm in 1957. Widely known in the publishing world for having rescued the diary of Anne Frank from a pile of rejected manuscripts, Jones also edited books by other renowned authors such as the chef Julia Child and the novelist John Updike.

ing at Jacob's Pillow)* and the jazz composer, Randy Weston,† has expressed interest in doing a score for it.

Tonight (Monday, July 24, at 8:30) at NYU's last Summer Concert in the new aircooled Student Center on Washington Square, Maurice Peress‡ is conducting my Meyerowitz opera, THE BARRIER, interestingly staged with no sets, no props, but dramatically, on platforms, 6 levels, lighted, and beautifully sung. The preview audience on Friday gave it a big hand, and folks think the new soprano, Gwendolyn Walters,§ is a "discovery." THE BARRIER grew out of the poem, CROSS, in my first Knopf book: the poem became the play, MULATTO, which in turn became the short story, FATHER AND SON (in Knopf book) which in turn became the opera libretto, THE BARRIER, done at Columbia in 1950, and since then everywhichawhere.

Langston

TO ARNA BONTEMPS   [*TLS*]

[*On* Langston Hughes, 20 East 127th Street, New York 35, N.Y. *stationery*]

September 19, 1961

Arna: On Labor Day there was an old race track man here after Saratoga ended, and |he| knows all the living old jockeys. Says about the most famous colored one is:

Samuel J. Bush, Apt. 53,
676 St. Nicholas Avenue,
New York 30, N. Y.

whom he phoned to see if he was in town. It seems he goes back and forth to Europe a lot, keeping a little stable of his own in France, friend of Aga Kahn, etc. Bush won the Grand National, 1917 and 1918—only jockey to repeat, says John Ewing, our informant. So I relay this to you in case it's of value. . . . . And

---

* Alvin Ailey (1931–1989) founded the Alvin Ailey American Dance Theater in 1958. The Jacob's Pillow Dance Festival, started in 1933 by the acclaimed choreographer Ted Shawn on a farm in western Massachusetts, is the longest-running and probably the most prestigious dance festival in the United States.

† Hughes asked the jazz pianist Randy Weston (b. 1926) to compose a score for *Ask Your Mama*. The men had collaborated on Weston's 1960 recording *Uhuru Afrika!* ("Freedom Africa!"), for which Hughes wrote the poem "African Woman."

‡ Maurice Peress (b. 1930) is an orchestra conductor and educator. In 1961, he was an assistant conductor of the New York Philharmonic.

§ Gwendolyn Walters was a winner of the Marian Anderson Award for musical excellence.

Hughes considered the design and layout of *Ask Your Mama* "stunning."

I found in my basement files a BIG Sports File full of old clippings. If you think you need it, I'll box it up and send you.[*]

George got his deferment and is back in grad school, this time at NYU.[†] His Voices, Inc., did an excellent series of song-documentary programs on CBS PROTESTANT HERITAGE, closing this Sunday with Thurgood Marshall as guest. (Me, Spaulding, Carol Brice were the others—Literature, Business, Music).[‡]

[*] Arna Bontemps was then working on his book *Famous Negro Athletes* (Dodd, Mead, 1964). According to records of the Grand National, an annual steeplechase held in Liverpool, England, Samuel J. Bush was not the winning jockey in 1917 or 1918.

[†] George Houston Bass (1938–1990), a Fisk University graduate, moved to New York to attend the business school at Columbia. Recommended by Arna Bontemps, who had known him at Fisk, Bass served as Hughes's secretary from June 1959 to July 1964. Hughes later appointed him executor-trustee of his estate. Eventually Bass became a professor in the fields of theater and African American Studies at Brown University.

[‡] George Bass was then a leader of Voices, Inc., an a cappella octet that performed a series of song-documentary programs for CBS Television in New York. As a leading lawyer for the NAACP, Thurgood Marshall (1908–1993) helped to win the landmark desegregation case *Brown v. Board of Education* in 1954. In 1967, he became the first African American justice on the U.S. Supreme Court. "Spaulding" is probably one of the sons of Charles C. Spaulding (1874–1952). The grandson of a former slave, Spaulding had been a noted entre-

I'm on the last 50 pages of my NAACP book |*Fight for Freedom*|—but about beat down. Eyes wore out from reading so much, and typing all night. So had to lay off a day yesterday. Besides a namesake I had not seen in 20 years woke me up after only two hours sleep, arriving in town with lots of song lyrics he hoped to place! About the same time a Dutchman showed up, but I couldn't see him, too. Couldn't hardly see anyhow!

Both SIMPLE and MAMA look fine, sample copy of each has arrived. Others due next week. MAMA is stunning, in fact, should win a Graphic Arts prize for format and unique design.

Lang

TO JAMES A. EMANUEL [*TLS*]

<Langston Hughes>

September 19, 1961

Mr. James A. Emanuel[*]
195 Hoyt Street
Brooklyn 17, New York

Dear Emanuel:
It is not easy for me to analyze my own work. But since you did NOT ask me to do so, I am sending you some comments on my short stories, anyhow, while you are engaged in a study of them. Perhaps these are aspects you may not yet have considered, I don't know.

> WOMEN IN MY STORIES: Most of them, if main characters, are
> looking for love in an ultimately satisfying way, but somebody or
> something is making it hard for them to pin love down, even when
> it is a non-physical, non-sexual love in the sense of simply being
> appreciated, maybe even understood.

---

preneur, especially as a cofounder of the North Carolina Mutual Life Insurance Company. His sons, Charles, Jr., John, and Booker Spaulding, worked in the thriving business their father created. The African American contralto Carol Brice (1918–1985) had sung at a concert to mark Franklin Roosevelt's third inauguration in 1941.
* The poet and scholar James A. Emanuel (1921–2013) wrote a study of Hughes's short fiction as his doctoral dissertation at Columbia University. In 1967, Emanuel's *Langston Hughes* (based on that study) was published by Twayne in its "United States Authors" series. He became a professor of English at City College of the City University of New York. Later, after he moved to France, he published more than a dozen books of poetry.

MEN IN MY STORIES: Mostly seeking, or trying to hold onto, some sort of security, some sort of stability, trying to make the circle revolve around them, instead of revolving around the circle themselves without ever touching its center.

WHITES IN MY STORIES: You may have noticed that I feel as sorry for them as I do for the Negroes usually involved in hurtful or potentially hurtful situations. Through at least one (maybe only one) white character in each story, I try to indicate that "they are human, too." The young girl in CORA UNASHAMED, the artist in SLAVE ON THE BLOCK, the white woman in the red hat in HOME, the rich lover in A GOOD JOB GONE helping the boy through college, the sailor all shook up about his RED-HEADED BABY, the parents-by-adoption in POOR LITTLE BLACK FELLOW, the white kids in BERRY, the plantation owner in FATHER AND SON who wants to love his son, but there's the barrier of color between them. What I try to indicate is that circumstances and conditioning make it very hard for whites, in interracial relationships, each to his "own self to be true."

DEATH IN MY STORIES: It is always resented—by Cora in CORA UNASHAMED; the other Cora in FATHER AND SON; by the son in ON THE WAY HOME; by the healer in TAIN'T SO who has her own way of keeping people alive.

MYSELF IN MY STORIES: Of course, I am in all of them. But I am most consciously in those based upon situations in which I have actually found myself in the past:

The object of over-much attention by white friends, racially speaking, as in SLAVE ON THE BLOCK. I am in part Luther.

The object of interference by patronage with my objectives as in THE BLUES I'M PLAYING. I am in part Oceola.

The son of a father who seemingly wanted to love—but it never happened—as in FATHER AND SON. I am Bert.

As a Negro American abroad, as in SOMETHING IN COMMON. I am Samuel Johnson.

As a Negro student in predominantly white schools prevented by color from achieving some of the things white students might achieve, as in ONE FRIDAY MORNING. I am Nancy Lee.

As one afraid to fully face realities, as the sailor of RED HEADED

BABY; the young man in ON THE WAY HOME or the father in
BLESSED ASSURANCE. They are me.

As the spied-upon in LITTLE OLD SPY which really happened to me
in Havana in somewhat the same fashion as in the story. This is
perhaps my most verbatim story.

As the frustrated Logan in TROUBLE WITH THE ANGELS, since
I felt the same way when THE GREEN PASTURES played
Washington, although I was not actually present.

As the boy in BIG MEETING since this is really an autobiographical
narrative out of childhood memories of a series of religious
revivals held in Pinkney Woods, Lawrence, Kansas, about 1914.

Among my favorite characters in my short stories, neither of
whom are consciously based on myself, are Miss Pauline Jones
in TAIN'T SO (a joke made into a story) and Sergeant in ON
THE ROAD, probably because they are so completely self-
contained—as I would like to be.

You may quote from this letter, if you wish, or use it in its entirety in your
thesis, should it be of any value to you.

Sincerely yours,
Langston Hughes

TO ARNA BONTEMPS [TLS]

[On Langston Hughes, 20 East 127th Street, New York 35, N.Y. stationery]

November 7, 1961

Mon cher ami: The menu at the White House was all in French (in honor,
no doubt, of Senghor); and last night at the Arts and Letters dinner for Sir
and Lady C. P. Snow, in French also.* (Why, I don't know.) But when it came
to talking for or against to whom the 1962 Gold Medal for Lit is to go, I was
forced to rise and state in plain English why I wouldn't give it to the leading
Southern cracker novelist if it were left to me, great "writer" though he may

---

* On November 3, 1961, Hughes attended a White House luncheon hosted by President
Kennedy in honor of the poet Léopold Sédar Senghor, president of Senegal. On November
6 in New York, the National Institute of Arts and Letters (which had elected Hughes a
member that year) hosted a dinner he attended in honor of the British intellectual C. P.
Snow (1905–1980).

be.* I was sitting next to Carson McCullers and we had fun translating the French menu into jive English for her cullud cook to try some of the dishes. Carlo |Van Vechten| was there. . . . . Mrs. Estelle Massey Riddle Osborne had cocktails for Zelma Watson George on Sunday;† and the Lincolnites had same for our new president, at the Waldorf. So my social season started off in a big way—so big I've about had enough already—at least till I come back from Africa—if I get gone‡. . . . . . Mrs. |Toy| Harper is still in California. . . . . Spite of all I've finished another deadline. Now only have one more really urgent one to go—a promised magazine piece. So I hope to see a few shows, and a few friends, and take a breather in a week or so. But I don't believe I'll go to Hot Springs—I were there once and found it real simple. . . . . Zelma is on a lecture trek—Omaha preceding N.,Y., now to Beloit, Wisconsin—she being with Colston Leigh, which is the way they jump folks around—and take 35%. She says they have one other cullud lecturer on their list this season, but I forgot to find out who it is. Anyhow, I'm glad it's not me! Two more African parties coming up this week—Alioune Diop of PRESENCE§ and Mphahlele, the good writer.¶ (His I think I'll go |to|, but can't make them both—not and make my deadline and get my sleep, too—with two radio interviews and a book party for MAMA this weekend.) Too much!. . . . Did I tell you some white man with a big manuscript (whom George |Houston Bass| told I was

* "Leading Southern cracker novelist" refers to the Mississippi-based author William Faulkner (1897–1962), who won the Nobel Prize in Literature in 1949. In 1962, he won the Gold Medal for Literature of the American Academy of Arts and Letters (the elite inner circle of the National Institute of Arts and Letters) despite Hughes's objections. In the 1950s Faulkner vigorously opposed racial segregation, but in 1956 *The Sunday Times* of London reported him as saying that he would "fight for Mississippi against the United States, even if it meant going out into the street and shooting Negroes." Faulkner denied saying so but also urged moderation in the national response to the concerns of most Southern whites.
† Zelma Watson George (1903–1994) was a civil rights activist, musicologist, and college teacher. Managed by the W. Colston Leigh Agency, she lectured widely in the 1960s on behalf of organizations such as the Danforth Foundation and the American Association of Colleges.
‡ On December 13, 1961, Hughes traveled to Africa with a delegation of performers, including Randy Weston, Nina Simone, and Odetta, organized by the American Society of African Culture (AMSAC). The main purpose of the trip was to take part in an arts festival in Lagos, Nigeria. He remained there until January 7, 1962.
§ In 1947, the Senegalese writer and editor Alioune Diop (1910–1980) founded *Présence Africaine*, the major journal of the Negritude movement.
¶ The South African writer and scholar Es'kia Mphahlele, born Ezekiel Mphahlele (1919–2008) was one of the founders of modern African literature. Best known perhaps for *Down Second Avenue* (1959), an autobiography, he grew up in Pretoria. Later he earned a doctorate from the University of Colorado and also taught there and at the University of Pennsylvania.

out) sat on the stoop till 3 A.M. waiting for me to come home—so I couldn't get out! L.H.

P.S. Emanuel's Ph. D. thesis on my short stories (see excerpt in PHYLON) runs to over 300 pages. I'm to read it this weekend before he turns it in. !!!!

Your DIGEST piece is really good.

****

J. Saunders Redding's father died.*

****

Channing Tobias, too, I see in tonight's paper.

****

Rosey Pool is also invited to Nigeria.†

TO ARNA BONTEMPS   [TLS]

[*On* Langston Hughes, 20 East 127th Street, New York 35, N.Y. *stationery*]

November 21, 1961

Dear Arna: Did Macmillan send you a copy of the Czech POPO AND FIFINA? I've asked them to send one to E. Simms in Switzerland, too‡...... You remember the white lady who called on me in Watts wanting a large sum of money<?>§ Well, the same thing happened a few days ago, only this time it was a white man (who sat on the steps all night one night, came back several times, and finally got in on the heels of a visitor who had an appointment). He said he'd given away $100,000 helping others. Now, being down and out and having a book to finish, he thought I might advance a few thousand! He finally came down to a few hundred, then $50, then $25. I gave him $3.00

---

* J. Saunders Redding (1906–1988) was a professor (at Morehouse College, Hampton Institute, and Cornell University), and a literary scholar noted especially for his study *To Make a Poet Black* (1939).

† The Dutch-born Rosey E. Pool (1905–1971) was a translator from English into Dutch. A popular figure, she translated several of Hughes's poems and also works by various African writers who lived, like her, in London.

‡ E. Simms Campbell (1906–1971), a successful African American cartoonist, had illustrated Hughes and Bontemps's *Popo and Fifina* in 1932. He moved his family to Switzerland in 1957 and lived there until 1970.

§ In the section "Invitation to Philanthropy" in his second autobiography, *I Wonder as I Wander,* Hughes tells the droll story of a strange woman who asks him for money on behalf of an obviously nonexistent foundation to improve race relations.

since he said he was down to his last penny. The other visitor had brought a tape of a play he had written—which he played in full—poetic and highflown, but almost put me to sleep. So my day was shot! Took me 24 hours to get my nerves together again. At the moment, neither white folks nor Negroes get past the front door. . . . . A more amusing visitor was the Nigerian poet and playwright, Wole Soyinka, whom George |Houston Bass| helped to teach the Twist and Soyinka in turn taught him the JuJu. He's about to have a play done in London. Bright boy. . . . . |Alioune| Diop of PRESENCE is here, too. But I just can't see everybody. Africans are a whole career in themselves nowadays once one gets started. Mphahlele was just here last week. |Léopold Sédar| Senghor the week before. There's got to be a limit—unless one is endowed with both time and money—as I told the State Department lady last year—if I'm to be the official host of Harlem.

Quand meme,

Langston

<I'm standing in the need of prayer! My Xmas show goes in rehearsal next week.>*

<P.S. 2nd SPORTS file posted you today.>

TO ARNA BONTEMPS   [TLS]

[<i>On 20 East 127th Street, New York 35, N.Y. stationery</i>]</div>

February 16, 1962

Dear Arna:

In getting ready to do another script for the producers of <u>Black Nativity</u> (who now have all kinds of plans, and think <u>they</u> discovered the format of dramatizing the gospel songs <u>themselves</u>)|,|† I was looking through our BOOK OF NEGRO FOLKLORE (which I haven't done for <a> long <time,> and so with an objective eye) and it is a GREAT book, and if we were white we would be

---

* Hughes's gospel play *Black Nativity* (1961) is probably the most frequently produced of his dramatic works. Critics hailed its opening performance on December 11, 1961, at the 41st Street Theatre in Manhattan. In 2013, a film version of the musical play, also called *Black Nativity*, was released. (*Black Nativity* was probably inspired by the success of Gian Carlo Menotti's one-act opera *Amahl and the Night Visitors*, reputedly the most frequently produced of all operas following its premiere on NBC Television in 1951. *Black Nativity* was staged in 1962 at Menotti's popular Festival of Two Worlds in Spoleto, Italy.)

† Eager to build on the success of *Black Nativity*, Lawrence Langner encouraged Hughes to update the script of *Tambourines to Glory*, also a gospel musical.

recognized as doctors and authorities and professors and <u>such</u> because of having assembled and put it together. All of which helps me to understand and appreciate Dr. W. E. B. |Du Bois| who went off to Africa and said, "Kiss my so-and-so!" For which I do not blame him.*

As Margaret Walker |Alexander| once said, "They're low! They're low! They're low! They're lower than a snake's belly."

You've probably read where white gospel singing groups are beginning to appear on the scene. In another six months, they will claim to have originated the idiom—and maybe get away with it in the public prints. As Eva Tanguay tried to do with the Charleston, and Gilda Gray did with the shimmy.†

"They've taken my blues and gone . . . . . ."

George |Houston Bass| tells me he has an offer of a $200 a week job. Do you have at Fisk anyone else looking for a New York apprenticeship?

There's a wonderful book by a <wh>ite lady coming out called HER NAME WAS SOJOURNER TRUTH. (Hertha Pauli, Appleton Century).‡

Lang

TO ARNA BONTEMPS [*TLS*]

[*On* Langston Hughes, 20 East 127th Street, New York 35, N.Y. *stationery*]

March 17, 1962

Dear Arna:

I am sending you, addressed to the Library, a packet of material that may <be of> interest to your L. H. files. Included in it is the final script of THE GOSPEL GLORY, A Passion Play to be enacted to the Spirituals (the <u>first</u> Negro Passion Play, so far as I know).§ Has there been a previous one authored by the Race?????? The Library copy is autographed to Fisk.

---

* In 1961, W. E. B. Du Bois joined the Communist Party of the United States and left the United States to live in Ghana. In 1963, after the U.S. government refused to renew his passport, he renounced his citizenship and became a Ghanaian. He died there later that year.
† Eva Tanguay (1878–1947) was a vaudeville performer. Gilda Gray (1901–1959) was a Polish-born actress known for doing the Shimmy dance in films in the 1920s.
‡ *Her Name Was Sojourner Truth,* by the Austrian actress and writer Hertha Pauli (1906–1973), was published in 1962.
§ Hughes refers to his musical play *The Gospel Glory: A Passion Play* (1962), about the Crucifixion. Later that year, he and Alfred Duckett (1917–1984), a veteran writer but an inexperienced producer, launched the work at the Temple of the Church of God in Christ in Brooklyn. After a particularly ragged staging of the play in Westport, Connecticut, Hughes ended his arrangement with Duckett.

I have, however, enclosed an <u>unsigned</u> copy of this song-play which I would like you to <u>give</u> to whomever at Fisk might be interested in staging it there—if only in a concert version—perhaps the head of the Jubilee Singers. I would send it direct, except that I don't know to whom it might best be addressed. I think the Music Department would probably find it of more interest than the Drama folks—since the Crucifixion story is told largely in and through songs.

Re Jean Toomer—I don't feel I ever knew him well enough, either, to intrude upon his privacy by writing or phoning him at this late date in life—especially since he never answered any of my notes in the days when we were preparing POETRY OF THE NEGRO—and I was told he'd gone over entirely into the white (and Quaker) world. Not even Georgia Douglas Johnson, of whom he used to be quite fond, and she of him, had had any contact for years. . . . . Waring Cuney has also disappeared from sight. Nobody's seen him for more than a year. I've written him—no answer. I hope he's not ill. I'll try asking Breman in London if he's in <u>touch with</u> him.[*]

Langston

Georgia has new little booklet of poems out. Get it. Please![†]

P.S. Are you making any headway on your SPORTS book? . . . . I saw Jackie Robinson and his quite charming wife riding down Broadway the other night in a great <u>long</u> car[‡]. . . . Duke |Ellington| has moved out of Harlem! Who's left? Just me—and Ralph |Ellison| (if you include Riverside Drive in Harlem). Hall |Johnson| is back in Cal.

---

[*] The Dutch-born bookseller Paul Breman (1931–2008) edited and wrote the introduction to Waring Cuney's volume of poetry *Puzzles* (DeRoos, 1960). He operated a small press in London, where he published the "Heritage Series of Black Poetry," featuring African American poets, from 1962 to 1975. Arna Bontemps's first poetry collection, *Personals* (1963), was part of this series.

[†] In 1962, Georgia Douglas Johnson published *Share My World*, her first book of poems in more than thirty years.

[‡] Jackie Robinson (1919–1972) broke the color barrier in modern Major League Baseball in 1947 when he played for the Brooklyn Dodgers. In 1963, he and his wife, Rachel Robinson (b. 1922), began hosting jazz concerts on the grounds at their home in Stamford, Connecticut, to raise funds for civil rights and other worthy causes.

TO GWENDOLYN BROOKS [TL]

March 24, 1962

Dear Gwendolyn,

After watching on TV the other night the appalling finale of the Griffith-Paret fight at the Garden,* the only thing I thought of doing was playing Oscar's recording of your NOTHING BUT A PLAIN BLACK BOY—more moving than ever then.† It has always been one of your favorite poems with me. I think the recording is beautiful.

Regards to Henry‡—and you, too.

Sincerely,
Langston Hughes

TO WILLIAM "BLOKE" MODISANE [TL]

May 14, 1962

BLO-kie:§

What is HELLO in Bantu? Bakubona to you! And just to embarrass you, since you haven't written me for so long, I am sitting down to answer you RIGHT back. Greetings!.... What union dragged you out on WHAT strike?¶ And no need to hide from New Yorkers. We can't see all the way to London (gracias a dios!) Folks who <u>know</u> they are going crazy, aren't. It is the ones who <u>don't</u> know who are, crazy already..... I did NOT get any magazine with any essay of yours in it. You probably just <u>thought</u> you sent it..... As beautifully as you

---

* On March 24, 1962, on national television, Emile Griffith (1938–1913) and Benny "the Kid" Paret (1937–1962) fought for the world welterweight boxing title at Madison Square Garden in New York. Enraged by Paret's taunts asserting that Griffith was gay, Griffith knocked him out after a severe beating. Paret never regained consciousness. He died on April 3.
† The Chicago-based entertainer Oscar Brown, Jr. (1926–2005) set Brooks's poem to music under the title "Elegy (Plain Black Boy)."
‡ The African American poet and writer Henry Blakely (1917?–1996) was Gwendolyn Brooks's husband.
§ William "Bloke" Modisane (1923–1986), a South African writer and actor, moved to England in 1959 to escape apartheid. His autobiography, *Blame Me on History* (E. P. Dutton, 1963), tells of his life in South Africa. Writing to Hughes, Modisane had greeted him in Sesotho and isiZulu. Hughes responds with an attempt at Bantu.
¶ Modisane had written to inform Hughes that he faced eviction because his union had gone on strike. Hughes responded with a check ("the enclosed").

type, you can't be dead. Why don't you get a job as a typist, copyist for writers, or something like that? Such folks are not easy to find here. If you were in New York, you could copy and COPY and copy for me. As my one lone assistant is hard put to keep up. . . . . And, hey, Bantu, you are not really BLACK. Me, neither. Wish I was—so, like SIMPLE says, I could scare the white folks to death. (Not Rosey Pool, who is a Dutch bonbon bar). . . . . Hey, don't you sign your letters? Or maybe there's a page missing. Where is the rest of it— B-l-o-k-e—wrote out long hand good like you can write?. . . . . . . Bloke, don't be simple-minded. Just be simple. Why didn't you write me a long time ago if you were having it rough? I could have sent you a little something—like the enclosed.<⟨ x ⟩> And no obligations. You don't even need to say, <u>Thank you,</u> or anything except <u>safely</u> <u>received</u>, maybe, so one will know it is not lost. Not really necessary, either. It's a bore to HAVE to do anything. . . . . My plan is to leave London for Entebbe (Kampala, Makerere) on BOAC Flight No. 161 on Wednesday, June 6th.* I reach London on Flight 500 about 9:30 A. M. I'll have 5 hours at airport. If you're not on my flight, come out and have luncheon with me. Or I'll see you.

BLOKE: Let's come back on 19th or 20th via Cairo, Athens, Rome, and you can see my show at Spoleto.† (And the Sphinx, and Parthenon, and Vatican.) O.K.? No problem. . . . . . <⟨ x ⟩> Sent by cable instead, as maybe you can use it NOW.

TO ARNA BONTEMPS   [TLS]
[On 20 East 127th Street, New York 35, N.Y. *stationery*]

May 28, 1962

Dear Arna: Thanks for that fine quote you gave me to use in Uganda. I'd also very much like to have a copy of your <u>full</u> Harlem Renaissance talk, if one should be typed up before I leave next Tuesday, or if it could be airmailed to me:

c/o Writers Conference,
Makerere College,
Kampala, Uganda.

---

* Hughes and Modisane later went to Kampala, Uganda, to attend the M'Bari Writers Congress at Makerere College (later University) from June 11 to 15. Other writers in attendance included Wole Soyinka, Ezekiel Mphahlele, and Chinua Achebe.
† From Uganda, Hughes stopped at Cairo and Rome en route to Spoleto in Umbria, Italy, where he saw *Black Nativity* performed at Gian Carlo Menotti's Festival of Two Worlds.

An announcement of some of those participating in the Conference came today: your Robie Macaulay is one.* But who is J. T. Ngugi of Uganda,† and Grace Ogot of Kenya‡—if you know from your visit there? Also today USIS confirmed my trip to Ghana§ and also wish me to go to Nigeria, as does M'bari that is celebrating, right after the Kampala gathering, its First Anniversary at Ibadan—so with two invites now to Nigeria, reckon I'll fly on down there, too. It is less than an hour from Accra. Sam Allen tells me he is also going to Ghana and Nigeria for USIS at the same time. Negritude, in that case, will be amply represented¶. . . . . George |Houston Bass| is reading the Baldwin novel.** (It's for sale here for the past two weeks.) A hasty look on my part—seems like he is trying to out-Henry Henry Miller in the use of bad BAD bad words, or run THE CARPETBAGGERS†† one better on sex in bed and out, left and right, plus a description of a latrine with all the little-boy words reproduced in the telling. (Opinion seems to be, he's aiming for a best seller.) With John Williams turning down an Institute of Arts and Letters grant, cullud is doing everything white folks are doing these days!‡‡ Even

---

* Robie Macaulay (1919–1995), a writer and critic, succeeded the poet John Crowe Ransom as editor of *The Kenyon Review*. In 1966 he became fiction editor at *Playboy* magazine.
† Ngugi wa Thiong'o, formerly J. T. Ngugi (b. 1938), is an internationally known Kenyan author and American-based university professor. His first play was staged when he was a student at Makerere College in 1962, around the time that he first met Hughes. His first novel, *A Grain of Wheat*, appeared in 1964.
‡ Grace Ogot (b. 1930) published her first novel, *The Promised Land*, in 1966. Drawn to politics, she became the first Kenyan woman to serve as an assistant cabinet member. She did so in the government of Daniel Arap Moi, who later imprisoned Ngugi for political reasons.
§ Invited by the U.S. government, Hughes went to Ghana to speak at the dedication of the new United States Information Service (USIS) Center and Library in Accra. (The U.S. ambassador was William P. Mahoney. Hughes had known his wife, Alice, a niece of Noël Sullivan, since she was a little girl, and had been a guest of the Mahoneys at their Phoenix home before Mahoney's appointment.) In late June, after his trip to Cairo and Italy, he returned to Africa for this event. The USIS, as units of the United States Information Agency centered outside the U.S. were known, was a branch of the Department of State. The latter took over its functions in 1999.
¶ Negritude was a literary movement in the 1930s and 1940s among French-speaking authors that focused on "black consciousness." Its key developers included Léopold Sédar Senghor and Aimé Césaire (1913–2008), who acknowledged the influence of Hughes's work on their thinking.
** Hughes refers to James Baldwin's best-selling novel *Another Country* (1962), which includes graphic descriptions of interracial sex as well as gay and bisexual male liaisons.
†† Harold Robbins (1916–1997) achieved notoriety with his sexually explicit novel *The Carpetbaggers* (Simon & Schuster, 1961).
‡‡ John Alfred Williams (b. 1925) is a prolific novelist whose books include *The Angry Ones* (1960) and *The Man Who Cried I Am* (1967). In 1962, the American Academy and National Institute of Arts and Letters in New York (of which Hughes was a member) chose Williams for one of its annual writing residencies at the American Academy in Rome. In an unprecedented response, the organization in Rome refused to accept Williams. When the New York body then offered Williams a writing grant, he declined it.

getting their hair cut in white barber shops, and being buried by Campbell's on Park Avenue—latest vogue in Negro funerals with all-white undertakers and pallbearers. (Integration is going to RUIN Negro business.<*> <*> With the DEFENDER able to get Leonard Lyons and Bennett Cerf's syndicated columns for $5 a week, why pay me my former fee for mine, is just about what Sengstacke said.<)>* Oh well—Lang

TO ARNA BONTEMPS [TLS]

[On Langston Hughes, 20 East 127th Street, New York 35, N.Y. *stationery*]

March 11, 1963
<u>\<Important\></u>†

Mr. Arna Bontemps,
919 - 18th Avenue North,
Nashville 8, Tennessee.

Dear Arna:

Since you have known me nigh on to forty years, and since you have<,> in my numerous letters to you<,> information possessed by no one else, this grants you permission to write whenever you may choose my officially authorized biography, as you state in your letter to me of March 8, 1963, that you might like to do.

Regarding a volume of my COLLECTED POEMS, this note also grants you access to all of my poetry to be found at any time in manuscript or unpublished in my files or in the James Weldon Johnson Memorial Collection at the Yale University Library.‡ Donald Dickinson at Bemidji College in Minnesota should eventually have a complete bibliography of my published work in

---

* Leonard Lyons (1906–1976) wrote his syndicated column *The Lyons Den* for the *New York Post* from 1934 to 1974. Bennett Cerf (1898–1971), cofounder of Random House, wrote a daily humor column called *Try and Stop Me* for the King Features syndicate. John Sengstacke (1912–1997) was publisher of *The Chicago Defender*, where Hughes's weekly column, *Here to Yonder*, had appeared since 1942. With nationally syndicated (white) columnists available much more cheaply, the *Defender* wanted to alter Hughes's contract and reduce his salary.

† The word "important" was probably written by Arna Bontemps after he read the contents of this letter.

‡ *The Collected Poems of Langston Hughes*, edited by Arnold Rampersad and David Roessel and published by Knopf, finally appeared in 1994.

magazines, newspapers, and elsewhere.* The rights to all the poems included in my three volumes of poetry now in print as of this date, namely, THE DREAM KEEPER, SELECTED POEMS, and ASK YOUR MAMA, belong to Alfred A. Knopf, Inc., but all other poems including those in previous Knopf books but not in the three above mentioned, are my property, and may be used without Knopf permission in case there is a COLLECTED POEMS. All my previous books of poems published by Knopf are now out of print and the rights have reverted to me. These matters may be cleared with my literary representatives, Harold Ober Associates, whom you know.

Since a COLLECTED POEMS need not include bad poems, or specially written occasional verse, etc., I am willing to trust your literary judgment to exclude all manuscript or magazine verse you may judge to be not up to par. Such poems should be destroyed to prevent their being used elsewhere or, if given to Yale or any other collection, marked: NOT FOR PUBLICATION AT ANY TIME OR IN ANY FORM ANYWHERE.†

As you know, James Emanuel is doing a brief biography of me in his study of my work for the American Authors series, with my permission.‡ Constance Maxon, whom I do not know, declares herself to be doing an unauthorized biography of me, and I have written her that it is unauthorized by myself, and was begun without my knowledge or consent.§

I myself plan to do perhaps a third autobiographical volume in due time; maybe even a fourth. You may, of course, make use of any of my published books for your proposed biography. Much unpublished manuscript material omitted from I WONDER AS I WANDER may be found at Yale, since that book originally was much too long and had to be cut considerably.

With cordial regards to you,

Langston Hughes

---

* In 1964, Donald C. Dickinson (later a professor of library science at the University of Arizona, Tucson) published his doctoral dissertation, *A Bio-bibliography of Langston Hughes, 1920–1960.* In 1972, Archon Books published a revised edition to include Hughes's work up to his death in 1967.
† On March 13, Bontemps responded: "Your letter of Monday (11) covers the matter of the *Collected Poems* and the *Authorized Biography* of L. H. with your usual thoroughness and feeling for essentials. I propose to do both, and I regard my authorization as a sacred trust."
‡ See also Hughes's letter to Emanuel of September 19, 1961.
§ Constance M. Maxon, a freelance writer, was said to be working on an unauthorized biography of Hughes. The biography was never published.

TO FAITH WILSON   [TL]

April 9, 1963

Dear Faith:* Was it Wordsworth (?) who wrote, "The world is too much with me, late and soon" which I remember often and wonder if he meant late night and soon in the morning, too?† In any case, one reason I sleep late is once up so much starts happening that when midnight comes and things maybe quiet down a bit, I say, "Peace!" Yesterday I thought (since I had nothing at all on my calendar) I will have a nice clear uninterrupted quiet day and do some of the things I've been putting off (but unavoidably) for weeks and answer some of the mail I really want to answer (not just business) and put winter clothes down in the basement and things like that. But hardly had I awakened then (my student-secretary being out) I made the mistake of answering the phone myself. It was a foreign voice reminding me that I had agreed to an appointment weeks ago and tomorrow he was going to England and he was at that moment just around the corner from me. I couldn't say no, so I said come by for a few minutes. He stayed an hour or so—but singing most delightful West Indian songs he had collected and wanted me to hear and help get published or on the air. In the midst of his concert, same mistake, I answered the phone again. It was another stranger, a young man the Whitney Foundation had asked me |to| see with a Fellowship in Photography, just back from the South. So I said, "Come on." He came, bringing some quite wonderful photographs of lovely children and people and trees and bits of bark and semi-abstractions and insisting on displaying them one by one against a plain background. And I phoned around a lot of folks he wanted to meet in New York who might help him in his work, and by that time the afternoon was gone (3 or 4 other assorted folks and my little after-school Puerto Rican errand boy—"Chief Assistant Junior Grade" and the fellow who washes windows, too, had been in and out) and it was dinner time—between 7 and eight with us. And next thing I knew it was 10 going on 11—and the whole day

---

* A housewife in Windom, Kansas, Faith Wilson (who was white) began writing Hughes in November 1951 after she casually took one of his books out of her local library. "I had no idea who you were," she admitted to Hughes. They corresponded for more than ten years, with their letters offering an unusual perspective on race relations at the time. They finally met some years after the letters began, when Wilson and her husband visited New York.
† Hughes adapts the first line of William Wordsworth's well-known sonnet "The World Is Too Much with Us." It was first published in *Poems, in Two Volumes* (1807).

gone and not a lick of work done or letters answered or winter clothes sorted out. But by midnight, "Peace!" and that is why I find no use in trying to work, creatively or otherwise in the day time. Each day I think might be different and calm, but no, "The world is too much with. . . . etc. . . . ." But no chance to be bored, at any rate. . . . . And then my secretary |George Houston Bass| gets home from night classes at NYU full of the problems of trying to do disciplined TV (student) shows with undisciplined kids (who, he thinks|,| are only going to college for fun) who create problems for the serious students trying to put actors and cameras and scripts together into a production involving numbers of folks, and half of them "just playing around." So I listen to that, and condole and sympathize—and advise how almost anything in the entertainment field, professional or amateur, involves being able to put up with many other people's foibles and ways and contrariness. Better to write a book, than a play or a script. But books are probably on their way to Limbo— the "communication media" being the thing nowadays—and probably what young folks interested in expression had best better study. . . . . . . And those poor little kittens drug in out of the rain, you speak of—so many of them in this world!. . . . I once brought home a few years ago a real kitten out of the rain one autumn night. The little thing had to be dewormed and veterinized and cost me about $50—and when he came home went gleefully around scratching up all my Aunt Toy |Harper|'s furniture—including the piano—so I had to give it away. . . . I love your portrait of the two girls—and I hope they last and don't wear themselves out, and get just a little more sleep. . . . . Me, I sleep 8-9-10 hours at the drop of a hat. Did I tell you an unknown fan came by one day and staged a sit-in? He said every time he tried to meet me, I was either asleep or out, so this time, he told my Aunt, "I will just stay until he is available. I'm a sit-inner." So he sat from noon until after four o'clock. Said he just wanted to lay eyes on me—he likes my books—so he did!

I'm so glad you like the lady of the blue suede shoes.

Years ago in Alamosa, Colorado, seemingly there was only one or two colored families there, and one of them was named Qualls. Seems the family had so many children they ran out of names, so the later kids were called, I'm-a (Ima Qualls), Youra (You're) Qualls, Hesa Qualls, Shesa Qualls, etc., so they say. Anyhow, the girl twins I know really are named Youra and Ina (she changed the m to an n) and Ina writes charming letters (not unlike yours) and before she moved to Maryland, she used to write me from the Southwest (Texas after she left home), about the beauties of Alamosa in the Spring. Have you seen Alamosa? Seems it might be a bit like Longmont?

I'm so glad your fall wasn't so bad, after all—and that you're sewing, I reckon, for Easter! And that Earl liked your new dress!

Happy Easter to you both,

Sincerely,

TO ARNA BONTEMPS   [TLS]

[On Langston Hughes, 20 East 127th Street, New York 35, N.Y. *stationery*]

5:45 A. M.,
April 23, 1963

Dear Arna: CONGRATULATES on your Milwaukee haircut! I am glad it were not your haid! . . . . . . I sat next to Emily Kimbrough* and across from Marc Connelly† at the Lloyd Garrison Dinner‡ (though we being "surprise guests" dined privately and "intime" with beaucoup cocktails and wine and hilarity) and we got to talking about lecture tour adventures. Emily said once she went out to take a walk in the cool of the evening before her lecture, but neglected to remark the name of her hotel, got lost, panicked, and could not even remember the name of the town she was in or for whom she was speaking, so stopped to buy a paper, thinking she would at least get the name of the town and her sponsor therefrom, but it turned out to be an OUT OF TOWN NEWS STAND and the paper she bought was Indianapolis or someplace she wasn't so when she asked passersby for the name of the biggest hotel in Indianapolis, they thought she was crazy! She was almost due on the stage before she got straightened out . . . . . . Then they got to talking about Texas. I a<sk>ed if anybody there had met Billie Sol Estes.§ None had, but said, "Let's talk about somebody else we haven't met." I suggested Elizabeth Taylor. It turned out half the table had met her, and she was a schoolmate of Emily

---

* The writer Emily Kimbrough (1899–1989), who contributed pieces to *The New Yorker*, *The Atlantic Monthly*, and other magazines, also published fourteen books.
† Marcus Cook Connelly (1890–1980) won a Pulitzer Prize for his play *The Green Pastures* (1931).
‡ The dinner was in honor of Lloyd K. Garrison, who had advised Hughes in his 1953 encounter with Senator Joseph McCarthy. In private practice as a lawyer, Garrison was also a veteran counselor of the NAACP and past president of the National Urban League.
§ A flamboyant Texas financier, Billie Sol Estes (1925–2013) was convicted on March 28, 1963, of four counts of mail fraud and one count of conspiracy involving $24 million in fraudulent mortgages. He was sentenced to fifteen years in prison.

Kimbrough's twin daughters. So there followed many a tale about her, Mike Todd, and all, as our table host was the head of MGM or whatever company made AROUND THE WORLD IN 80 DAYS.* By the time we did our surprise appearance at the main dinner, there wasn't much fun left to be had. But since <we> "topped the bill" and I was the last speaker, it was O. K. Except for Adlai Stevenson[†] and Garrison himself—who quoted about half my BIG SEA in his speech!

George |Houston Bass|, me and the sorting student have been up all night preparing for the Yale truck to come tomorr<ow>—which, I think, is getting its most precious haul yet: several hundred letters of the Harlem Renaissance period. I came acro<s>s an enormous big dusty box full of 1920-30 letters, that must have been boxed up before I went to Russia and unopened until now: underbody in it—you, Zora |Neale Hurston|, Wallie |Thurman|, |W. E. B.| Du Bois, Aaron |Douglas|, Bruce |Nugent|, even Jean Toomer, a hundred or so C. V. V. cards and letters including the whole Zora-MULE BONE episode from both sides with him as an arbitrator who finally washed his hands and declared he wanted no further parts of it; Alain Locke, and a real treasure trove of Jessie Fauset letters<,> from the one accepting my first poem <to> 10 or 12 years thereafter; lots of James Weldon Johnson and Walter |White|. I guess I never throw anything away ever. Wonderful letters from you<!> You will HAVE to go to Yale to ever write a book <a>bout me—or about yourself, either. (These make up 39 separate manila folders in a BIG transfer file. Plus various small boxes of categories too large to fit into single folders.) I don't know how I ever read so many letters. It will take posterity quite awhile!. . . . . . I also found some letters I never had opened or read. Some<,> I just left that way and sent on to Yale. I am sure I told you I have a bad habit of not opening letters I feel at the time I do not want to read—worriation letters and such. Usually I get around to opening them eventually—unless they get buried in piles, as some of these of the 20s and 30s evidently did . . . . . . I have a half dozen <unopened> from March-April of this year, right now 1963, until I feel better toward the projects, persons, or causes they represent, or can maybe

---

* Mike Todd was married at one time to the movie star Elizabeth Taylor (1932–2011). The film *Around the World in Eighty Days*, which Todd's company produced in 1956, won the 1957 Academy Award for Best Picture. Their marriage ended in 1958 when Todd died in a plane crash in New Mexico.
† Adlai Stevenson (1900–1965) was then U.S. ambassador to the United Nations. A former governor of Illinois, he ran unsuccessfully as the Democratic Party nominee for president in 1952 and 1956.

cope with what I am sure some of them want, or am less pressured by dead-lines . . . . . . Once I opened <one> some years ago months late—and found a check—fortunately still good. . . . . My namesake godson brought me his junior high graduation photo today. I am proud of that boy, getting through school and cannot read a lick. But, being most amiable, teachers all like him. Also seems like he plays good basket ball. . . . . Sincerely, Langston

Hughes with Carl Van Vechten, February 16, 1963.
Photograph by Richard Avedon

Go slow, I hear—
While they tell me
You can't eat here!
You can't live here!
You can't work here!
Don't demonstrate! Wait!—
—"GO SLOW," 1963

In August 1963, Hughes was in Paris on the day of the historic March
on Washington, when Martin Luther King, Jr., delivered his "I Have
a Dream" speech. (The speech draws, as Hughes privately noted, on a
motif he had long popularized through his verse.) Although he did not
march in Selma, Alabama, or at other dangerous places in the South,
Hughes rededicated his pen to the civil rights movement. Nearly all of

his writing between 1963 and his death in 1967 served this cause. His musical play *Jericho-Jim Crow* (1964), for example, brought the civil rights movement to the stage. It won the strong approval of organizations such as the NAACP, CORE, and SNCC.

TO NANCY CUNARD   [*TLS*]

April 28, 1963

Dear Nancy:

Such a wonderful letter from you! Bringing back so many old memories. . . . . Henry's book,* your marvelous NEGRO (listed at $60.00 last time I saw a mention of it in an old Rare Books catalogue), your lovely poems are all in sight as I write<,> on my studio bookshelves. . . . . One of Pickens' grandsons† turned out to be a very brillian<t> (and handsome) young man, top mathematician or something, with a high paid job although still quite young . . . . . . Arthur Spingarn, at 86, is heading for Greenwood, Mississippi (where all the current voting trouble and riots are) next week—to prove he is with the Freedom Riders and other kids—one of whom he met at my house last night who was just out of jail down there for teaching a voters registration class. (Negroes have to learn to read the whole constitution—and even then they've registered only 10 in the past six months!)

I'm so sorry to hear you're ill, so don't use up precious strength answering this, or acknowledging books. (My short stories ordered sent you, and POEMS FROM BLACK AFRICA will be on its way soon. But needn't write.) Just send me a line about mid-July to the: c/o American Express, Paris, as I hope to be there by the Quatorze Juillet day.‡ But maybe can only stay a couple of weeks, as it looks now as if my Theatre Guild play will be going into rehearsals (at

---

* Nancy Cunard published a book of music by her African American companion Henry Crowder, entitled *Henry-Music* (Hours Press, 1930).
† Cunard included three essays by William Pickens in her *Negro: An Anthology* (1934): "The American Congo: The Burning of Henry Lowry"; "The Roman Holiday"; and "Aftermath of a Lynching."
‡ Quatorze Juillet or July 14, is Bastille Day in France, celebrated to mark the French Revolution of 1789. On July 2, 1963, Hughes left for Paris. He spent two months abroad.

last) in August. But do let me know where <you> might be found at midsummer—and if I can come and say Hello, I <u>will</u>.

Affectionately,

Langston

<There are only about 3 people I want to see in all of Europe—and you're one.>

TO CASSIUS CLAY *[TLS]*

<Harlem U. S. A.>

<March 3, 1964>

<Dear Cassius>*

I HEAR YOU ARE INTERESTED
IN HISTORY.
WELL, HISTORY IS NO
MYSTERY.
WHY, OUT OF THE FACT
THAT SOME MEN ARE BLACK,
OTHERS TRY TO MAKE A
TWISTERY
IS THE ONLY MYSTERY.
TAKE IT FROM ME—

See page 333.†

Langston <Pic History given>

Hughes called Cassius Clay's attention to page 333 of the second, revised, edition of *A Pictorial History of the Negro in America* (Crown, 1963). The page appears in a section called "The Black Muslims."

* Later that year, 1964, the American boxer Cassius Marcellus Clay (b. 1942) changed his name to Muhammad Ali after converting to membership in the Nation of Islam. Clay loved to employ humorous rhymes in his public remarks; hence Hughes's use of doggerel here.

† Along with this note, Hughes probably sent Clay an inscribed copy of the 1963 revised edition of his and Milton Meltzer's *A Pictorial History of the Negro in America,* which was first published in 1956. Hughes acted shortly after Clay beat Sonny Liston in a shocking upset on February 25, 1964, to become the heavyweight champion of the world.

TO JIMMY DAVIS

[TL]

April 28, 1964

Dear Jimmy: *

I'm saving stamps, I reckon. BLACK NATIVITY closed on the road owing me
$10,000 back royalties and TV fees. (So am suing).† My column syndicate
got behind $600, so have taken my column back from them, and it is now
running only in New York POST which I can handle myself.‡ JERICHO-JIM
CROW ran in hole while Stella Holt was in Hawaii setting up theatre project for Ford Foundation.§ But she is now back and almost has deficit wiped
out, although it closed Sunday, but is still doing outside church and lodge
engagements, so I stand a chance to get back sums due there. And Rible
Blakey and partner are negotiating to bring it to Paris in the fall. So I may get
over your way then. Am invited to a writers conference, anyhow, in Europe
in September, expenses paid . . . . . . Over here the white folks are wondering
what to do with the Negroes. CORE pretty well tied up the Worlds Fair on
opening day—even tried to sit-in on top of the Orange Ball atop the Florida
pavilion¶. . . . . Mr. |Emerson| Harper had a double hernia operation but is out
and doing O. K. Mrs. |Toy| Harper getting older and crosser by the minute,
and her sight no longer very good. . . . . I'm recently back from a program in
St. Croix, Virgin Islands, and a few days in Puerto Rico. I had to return to lecture platform, having lost $$$$$ on TAMBOURINES which was a $125,000
flop on Broadway, due to management fights. Cast behaved beautifully, only
white folks fighting like cats and dogs. Last week of run, show had no ads, no
management. And we missed the Ed Sullivan show on weekend the President died. So this is my bad-luck-in-theatre season. LIFE took a big spread
on JERICHO, but held it up to combine with the James Baldwin BLUES FOR
MISTER CHARLIE—which postponed its opening till this week. Meanwhile

---

* Jimmy Davis, a Juilliard-trained American pianist then living in Paris, was a close
friend and frequent correspondent of Hughes.
† In a settlement, the producers of *Black Nativity* paid Hughes $6,900.
‡ With *The Chicago Defender* way behind in paying him, and seeking to cut his salary,
Hughes jumped at the chance in 1962 to move the column to the mainstream *New York
Post*. The *Post*, at that time a liberal newspaper, paid more and reached a much wider audi-
ence. He later returned as a columnist to the *Defender*.
§ *Jericho-Jim Crow*, Hughes's gospel musical about the civil rights movement, opened at
the Greenwich Mews Theatre on January 12, 1964. It closed in late April that year.
¶ Supporters of the civil rights organization Congress of Racial Equality (CORE) and
other groups picketed the opening of the 1964 World's Fair in New York to protest as
demeaning to blacks the staging of a minstrel-styled satire against bigotry.

JERICHO closes, so our photos may never appear!!!. . . . . Naturally, I am OFF the theatre for all time! Back to poetry!

Talked to Jobe |Huntley| on |the| phone last night. He's reducing—and taking time off to do it.

My secretary says he has got to go to NYU where he's getting his MA in TV this spring, so I'll end this epistle and let him mail it off. Answer to your note.

You may be gone, but not forgotten!

Drink Vin Postillon!

Sincerely,

TO INA STEELE   [TL]

Memorial Day,
1964

Dear Ina:

I was fascinated by your description of you and Youra |Qualls| and all the brave in the face of the fire hoses.

And delighted with you in red suit receiving a citation.

And just happy to hear from you on general principles.

Sam Allen was in town Sunday for the autographing party for NEW NEGRO POETS: U. S. A.

And poetry, it seems, will carry me to Europe in September for the Berlin Arts Festival. At least, I'm officially invited as a poet. And maybe JERICHO JIM CROW will be there, too.

After next week I will no longer be Dr. 2, but Dr. III—raised to the third power—this time by white folks, no less!* (Unless they get hip between now and then.)

If you come to town, see LeRoi Jones' DUTCHMAN (photo in current LIFE). It is the MOST. He's the cullud Eugene O'Neill.

The house next door to us has opened a GARDEN OF EDEN outdoor barbecue pit for public eating in the backyard. I sent them an opening night wire—because it smells good as I write.

Cheerio!

* In 1964, Hughes was awarded an honorary Doctorate of Literature degree by Western Reserve University (now Case Western Reserve) in Cleveland, Ohio. He had received honorary degrees from Lincoln University (1943) and Howard University (1960).

TO ARNA BONTEMPS   [TLS]

[On 20 East 127th Street, New York 35, N.Y. stationery]

July 17, 1964

Dear Arna: I see where you're scheduled for the Asilomar Conference at Monterey.* The run down looks interesting. (I wonder if Baldwin will show—or Horace |Cayton| who used to be like Baldwin is now—easily lost). Will you and Alberta drive to the Coast? Do you still have relatives out there? If my most amusing friend, Marie Short, were in Carmel, I'd give you a note to her. But she's not been well recently, and is sort of in a rest home in San Francisco. Hollow Hills Farm is now some sort of church center, I believe, non-Catholic.

Johnny Davis finally got me!† I've promised him the manuscript next week. Just when I start working good two girl cousins are descending upon me Monday from Chicago for the Fair. And several of Mrs. Harper's relatives are arriving from Los Angeles later in the week. I need a tree house in Kenya!

"Life for me ain't been no crystal stair."
"Life for me ain't been no crystal
"Life for me ain't been no
Life for me ain't been"
Life for me ain't"   Lang
Life for me"
Life for"
Life"""‡
O
"

---

* The 1964 Negro Writers Conference held on the Asilomar Conference Grounds in August brought together in California several African American and white writers and critics from across the United States. Horace Cayton, then a professor at the University of California–Berkeley was an organizer of the event.
† John Preston Davis (1905–1973), a lawyer and civil rights activist, founded *Our World* magazine in 1946. In 1964 he produced the substantial *American Negro Reference Book* with a grant from the Phelps-Stokes Fund. Hughes contributed an essay, "The Negro and American Entertainment," to the volume. Davis had been one of the writers published in *Fire!!* (1926).
‡ Hughes is riffing on his popular poem "Mother to Son," which first appeared in 1922 in *The Crisis*.

TO BOBB HAMILTON [TL]

<u>COPY</u>

(Langston Hughes to Bobb Hamilton)*

January 18, 1965

Dear Bobb:

Thanks a lot for sending me a copy of your letter to the POST re my column on LeRoi Jones—whose talent and position will hardly be harmed by a bit of controversy. In fact, I hope it helps box office. . . . . Pardon my putting this paper in crooked. It's now 3 A.M. and I've spent the evening reading through some hundred or so letters from white cabbies who are MADDER about my TAXI column† than you are about LeRoi's—who won't, I believe, be mad at all. He knows I like the bulk of his work very much. I loved DUTCHMAN (and said so in the POST) and have frequently expressed my admiration for his talent in print, on the air, and elsewhere. But I don't like the current plays at St. Mark's, and see no harm in saying so, do you?‡ Just as you or LeRoi have a perfect right to dislike (and say so) any writing of mine. (By the way, I didn't see the review of a "booklet" of mine you mention, but I'll phone LeRoi and see if he can tell me where to find it). . . . . In my long years of writing, I've found that adverse (and particularly controversial) comment which arouses discussion, does more GOOD than harm. I've been called since the Twenties everything from a "sewer dweller" (Negro press) to a "Communist traitor" (white press). Result: book sales grew, lecture audiences increased, folks wanted to see for themselves what the excitement was all about. So I hope my comments won't hurt LeRoi. I'd like to see him become (if not an O'Neill success-wise—to which you object) at least a Shaw or an O'Casey or Brecht—or just a great big <u>Jones</u> in marquee lights. And more power to you,

---

* Early in 1965, the cultural nationalist Bobb Hamilton (1928–?) became one of the cofounders of *Soulbook: The Revolutionary Journal of the Black World,* based in Berkeley, California.

† Hughes's controversial column "Taxi, Anyone," about taxi drivers in New York who refused to pick up black customers, appeared in the *New York Post* on January 8, 1965.

‡ LeRoi Jones's one-act plays *The Toilet* and *The Slave* opened at St. Mark's Playhouse on December 13, 1964. Hughes's column "That Boy LeRoi" appeared in the *Post* on January 15, 1965. *The Toilet* is set in the lavatory of a boys' school. It opens with a black boy using one of the seven urinals and ends with the battered head of a white boy in another. *Time* magazine called the plays "spasms of fury" aimed vengefully at whites, and reflective of Jones's "venomous intensity."

too, for so frankly expressing your opinions. It would be a sad day if the young writers all agreed with the old. Best ever,

Sincerely,

(SIGNED)

Langston Hughes

<Copy sent
LeRoi
Madden
Gloria
Arna
Yale>

TO JIMMY DAVIS   [TL]

February 24, 1965

Dear Jimmy, mon cher:

It's a rather tense week in Harlem, what with bomb threats etc. going around as Malcolm X lies in state.*

Anyhow, I was glad to have your note, and trust you're saved by the bell and not homeless and houseless.

I'm hoping my BLACK NATIVITY programs will be along soon. Boats take so long. Negro press here carried a Wiggins release from Paris about a glorious closing with ushers and firemen taking part in the hand-clapping the last night at the Champs Elysees. The Australian company is going well, too, I hear. And the Alvin Ailey dancers are there, as well.

My Nigerian godson, Sunday, got sent to the Congo, I guess as part of the UN task force, so I'm worried about him.† My JERICHO lead here (that I discovered) Gilbert Price, is a BIG hit in out-of-town tryouts in ROAR OF THE GREASE PAINT headed for Broadway in April.‡ He's only 21, a very sweet kid, and looks like he'll be a star. Claudia McNeil became a star, too, after I found

---

* Malcolm X, born Malcolm Little (1925–1965), the charismatic Nation of Islam minister and a radical champion of the ideals of black dignity and power, was assassinated by gunmen at the Audubon Ballroom in Harlem on February 21, 1965.
† After Hughes met a young policeman, Sunday Osuya, during his trip to Nigeria for the inauguration of Azikiwe, the two men became friends and exchanged several letters. Osuya was sent to the Congo as a peacekeeper. Eventually Hughes would name Osuya as one of his beneficiaries in his last will and testament.
‡ Classically trained, the baritone Gilbert Price (1942–1991) toured with Harry Belafonte and the Leonard de Paur chorus and also performed in two off-Broadway shows prior to appearing in *Jericho-Jim Crow*.

her working in a gift shop.* So Broadway ought to make me a talent scout! N'est-pas?

No word from Nina on your song. But my former secretary's SEA LION WOMAN she is featuring live on every concert, and it is on her latest album.† (I wish she'd do one of yours—or mine!) Her versions of Kurt Weill's PIRATE JENNY is absolutely great, but too "Civil Rights"—as she paraphrased it—for the juke boxes. In fact, it's hair raising, when all the black "pirates" take over a Southern town.

I'll probably be seeing you in May.

Avec mes compliments, etc . . . .
Langston Hughes, moi meme

TO ARNA BONTEMPS   [TLS]

Arna:

March 20, 1965

I'm catching up on a few minor deadlines, at least, holed away in a downtown hotel across the street from where you're due to be again soon, aren't you?‡ Lemme know. Right now I'm listening to Odetta records (on Cicely Tyson's borrowed machine from across the hall) to try to select some songs for an Easter TV show for her on the Coast§. . . . . Phoned today to see how Dorothy |Peterson| came out of her operation. O. K. . . . . Juanita Miller told me Mrs. Lester Granger was buried recently. And today was Dupree White's funeral here—Nate's former wife. And I read where Nancy Cunard died in Paris. This is the DYING season. I hope I get back to Paris one more time once. Seminars there are now scheduled for May. Dakar for next April and Harris and I have put your name on the proposed list—which seems like will be limited to five writers. The music, jazz bands, and dancers are getting the big budgets. We

---

* The African American actress Claudia McNeil (1917–1993) won praise for her performance in Hughes's *Simply Heavenly*. In 1961, with limited stage experience, she had emerged as a star on Broadway in Lorraine Hansberry's *A Raisin in the Sun*.

† This song, recorded as "See-Line Woman" on Nina Simone's album *Broadway-Blues-Ballads* (Verve, 1964), was written by Simone and George Houston Bass. Nina Simone was the stage name of Eunice Kathleen Waymon (1933–2003).

‡ To avoid distractions as he worked, Hughes sometimes took a room at the Wellington Hotel on Seventh Avenue at 55th Street in mid-Manhattan.

§ Cicely Tyson (b. 1933), an accomplished actress of the stage and screen, grew up in Harlem.

ought to <u>also</u> play a trumpet. . . . Wm. Melvin Kelley's new novel just came,[*] also proofs of Tolson's book,[†] who will be in New York Monday. This volume has no footnotes, but a lot of BIG words: (says Tolson)—O Cleobulus / O Thales, Solon, Periander, Bias, Chilo, / O Pittacus, / unriddle the pho|e|nix riddle of this? . . . . . I say, MORE POWER TO YOU, MELVIN B., GO, JACK, GO! That Negro not only reads, but <u>has read</u>! . . . . . . Sincerely,

Langston

With all I've got to do, looks like my PRODIGAL SON will up and go into rehearsal next week, too, as companion to a Brecht one-acter at the Mews.[‡] They want to start casting tomorrow. So much to do, NO time!

TO JIMMY DAVIS   [TL]

New York City,
October 9, 1965

Dear Jimmy: <[Davis]>

My PRODIGAL SON show departed these shores last night for Glasgow, Scotland. After a brief tour of the British provinces the show comes to London, then so I am told, Paris in late December. If you see anything about it in the French press beforehand, please send me the clips.

I'm back from Hollywood, and my Belafonte TV script is finished, to be video taped in December.[§] Harry, at the moment, is in Africa.

Karamu Theatre is celebrating the 50th anniversary in November, so I'm invited out there. Then probably on to San Francisco for a performance of a commissioned cantata of mine at the Opera with, so they say now, Jennie Tourel, and a star baritone whose name I can't recall at the moment, in it.[¶]

---

* William Melvin Kelley (b. 1937) published his third novel, *A Drop of Patience*, in 1965.
† Melvin B. Tolson's *Harlem Gallery* (Twayne, 1965) is a complex, erudite poem of twenty-four cantos (one for each letter of the Greek alphabet).
‡ Hughes's play *The Prodigal Son* shared a billing at the Greenwich Mews Theatre with *The Exception and the Rule*, Bertolt Brecht's Marxist drama about a merchant and his servant.
§ Hughes collaborated with the folksinger and actor Harry Belafonte on Belafonte's *The Strollin' Twenties*, a television variety show set in Harlem in the 1920s. Sammy Davis, Jr., Diahann Carroll, Duke Ellington, and Sidney Poitier also starred in the show.
¶ Hughes wrote the text of "Let Us Remember," a cantata with music by David Amram (b. 1930) commissioned for the biennial meeting in 1965 of the Union of American Hebrew Congregations. According to Amram, Hughes calmed one rabbi's fears about his ability to convey Jewish feeling by asserting that he had a Jewish grandfather. Actually, Hughes mentioned elsewhere that he had a Jewish great-grandfather. The noted mezzo-soprano Jennie Tourel (1900–1973) was the principal soloist, and Edward G. Robinson, a Hollywood star, the narrator.

Music by David Amram, a serious composer who also plays jazz at Village night spots—in other words, a hip long hair.

Jobe |Huntley| got mugged on Lenox Avenue—but not hurt. A few days later the guy, one of them, turns up in Harlem Hospital shot by an intended victim who happened to have a gun. Jobe recognized him. Now both the culprits are caught. At least 4 folks I know have been robbed or mugged in the last two weeks. N. Y. is getting BAD. My advice, STAY in Paris. . . . . . Best ever,

On the shores of Senegal, 1966. Photograph by Bracher
Dakar

They done tried to make me
Stop laughin', stop lovin', stop livin'—
But I don't care!
I'm still here!
—"STILL HERE," 1943

In 1966, Hughes led a large delegation sent by President Johnson
to represent the United States at the First World Festival of Negro
Arts in Dakar, Senegal. Once reviled as a communist sympathizer
or worse, he was now politically rehabilitated in a nation much less
dominated by the extreme right and by the worst excesses of racism.
Invigorated, he seemed poised to begin exciting new ventures. Near
the end of 1966, however, Hughes's life became even more complicated than usual. "Aunt" Toy Harper, now past eighty, fell seriously ill
and entered a Harlem hospital for what became a prolonged stay. In
the new year, urgently needed repair work mandated by city inspec-
tors began throughout the old brownstone on East 127th Street. Then

in May, with the renovations dragging on and Mrs. Harper fading, Hughes himself fell ill. A series of tests at New York Polytechnic Hospital on West Fiftieth Street in Manhattan revealed the presence of a large prostate tumor. Although it was noncancerous, his doctors recommended immediate surgery. Canceling an eagerly anticipated trip to Paris for the launch of *L'Ingénu de Harlem,* a French translation of *Simple stories,* Hughes underwent an operation on May 12.

TO MR. MILTON LARKIN　　　　　　　　　[TL]

March 5, 1966

Dear Mr. Larkin:*

I appreciate receiving your most interesting note, and thanks very much for the nice things you say about NEGRO HUMOR.†

As to THE STROLLIN' TWENTIES, first I must tell |you| that in the entertainment field (involving as it does so many people other than the author or playwright, directors, producers, actors, the backers who put up the money, all of whom have opinions) a writer is lucky if 50% of what he writes gets transferred to the stage, screen or airwaves. However, in the case of the TV show, Harry Belafonte's intent was to show another side of Harlem, mainly the entertainment side in the 1920s—in contrast to the seamy side which has been really over-presented in recent years—since almost everything on the radio or TV lately has been in the nature of THE COOL WORLD, |James| Baldwin, or James Brown‡—which is not entirely true either. Of the half million people (almost) who live in Harlem most are quite decent hardworking folks who are not bitten by rats everyday. There has been little balance in the Harlem picture lately—the liberal and well meant intent seemingly being to present the worst aspects in order to arouse sympathy and action. It sometimes boomerangs and makes folks think all is hopeless. So the TWENTIES

---

* After *The Strollin' Twenties* aired on television, some viewers were indignant. One such response came from Milton Larkin (1910–1996), an African American jazz trumpeter, bandleader, and singer. Larkin wrote to Hughes on February 25: "Why did you show Harlem as such a happy place? Why didn't you show the poor schools, tenements, rats, roaches, crime, lack of community interest, the cop on the block (who isn't black), the number runners, the junkies, the street gangs, the exploitation by the local merchants, the slumlords and the kids hopefully looking for a way out?"

† Hughes edited *The Book of Negro Humor* (Dodd, Mead, 1966). He called the volume "the *first* definitive well-rounded collection of American Negro humor."

‡ James Brown (1933–2006) was often called "the Godfather of Soul."

consciously tried to present something of beauty and fun—in contrast. And in 51 minutes, a producer cannot put everything. Duke's entire band was not available, and Duke himself on the verge of going to Europe, could only be gotten for 1 day, so his music was canned in advance—as is often done these days.*

Cordial regards,

Sincerely,

TO ARNA BONTEMPS   [ALS]

[On 1st. World festival of negro arts, 1-24 – Avril 1966, Dakar stationery]

April 27, 1966

Dear Arna—

It was something! Almost everybody you ever knew was here—from New York, Chicago, Cleveland, Alabama, Mississippi—even California—and Bill Demby from Rome,† Josephine Baker from Paris, Rosey Pool. Never saw the like. Too much to tell now, as I'm off to the Sudan in an hour. Congratulations to Hayden on top Dakar Poetry Prize.‡ Rosey Pool and I "went to town" in his favor!! Final vote was unanimous. Write USIA, Wash. for French edition of TOPIC with you in it.

Langston

(over)

[TLS]

Khartoum Continuation:§

May 1, 1966

---

* Duke Ellington's band provided some of the music for *The Strollin' Twenties.*

† William Demby (1922–2013), a Fisk University graduate, was then living in Rome. He wrote and published his novels *Beetlecreek* (1950) and *The Catacombs* (1965) during his time there.

‡ Robert Hayden (1913–1980) won the Grand Prize in Poetry at the first World Festival of Negro Arts. Born Asa Bundy Sheffey in Detroit, he was educated at Detroit City College (later Wayne State University) and the University of Michigan, where the British-born poet W. H. Auden encouraged him. His volumes include *Words in the Mourning Time* (1970) and *Angle of Ascent* (1975). In addition to serving as a professor at Fisk, from 1976 to 1978 he was consultant in poetry at the Library of Congress. He was the first African American to hold this position.

§ After spending April 1966 in Dakar, Hughes left Senegal to begin his reading tour of Africa at the request of the U.S. Department of State.

Didn't get a chance to address this in Dakar—was kept on the go right up to plane time. . . . Changed planes in Lagos and had luncheon there with the Joe Hills. Arminta Adams,* and Godfrey Amacree with me on plane to Khartoum. Seem to run into folks I know EVERYWHERE. Etta Moten looking like a million dollars in Dakar. Margaret Danner,† Sidney Williams,‡ Zelma Watson George renting a car and driving all over Dakar just as if she'd lived there forever. . . . Lagos is more like the old Chicago of gangster days than ever. Held up and robbed two folks on the main street in their car, made them get out, and the bandits drove away <the day I was there>. Folks are buying automatic locks for |their| cars that refuse to budge for anybody but the owners. . . . <Here in Khartoum> <u>All</u> Sudanese dress alike in white turbans and nightgowns. At a garden party last night for me, I mistook the Speaker of the Assembly for the head waiter, and asked him for a plate! Khartoum looks like a Texas-Mexican border town, blazing sun, dust, and the Nile here about the size of the Rio Grande. One blessing, no snakes—it is TOO hot!. . . . About a dozen Negroes from the States here in gov posts, etc. Population 80% black—but not as dark, DARK, DARK as the Senegalese who are the absolute blackest in the world. Most exotically clothed of all Africa—Dakar is colorful no end. Nigeria, too, and West Africa in general much more eye-catching in color than Sudan and East Coast, everybody here agrees. French African cities are gay, British ones gray. And given to rather stiff garden parties—Sudanese writers are giving another one for me today—most speak English, have been to Oxford. Have had a fine trip so far, and will arrive in Addis on May 5, Liberation Day, big fete! <USIA asked me to write a poem for the Emperor. Write me to Dar-es-Salaam.>

Langston

---

* Arminta Adams played the piano at the Dakar Festival.
† The poet Margaret Danner (1915–1984) traveled to Africa in 1966 on a Whitney Fellowship. In Dakar, Senegal, she read some of her poems at the Festival.
‡ Sidney Williams was the activist executive secretary of the Chicago Urban League from 1947 until 1955, when conservative board members removed him.

TO RAOUL ABDUL   [TL]

June 8, 1966

Dear Raoul:*

Just finishing up my African trek—from Senegal to the Indian Ocean, Dakar to Dar-es-Salaam and the Kenya game parks—full of giraffes taller than Lindsay!† Had a wonderful trip, except for Addis—which I LOATHED in spite of the fact the Emperor gave me a medal in a beautiful red case—in exchange for a poem!‡

They kept me so BUSY on this tour I did not hardly have a chance to breathe—meeting Presidents and Beys and whatnot and being entertained red carpet fashion and canaped and cocktailed to DEATH! I never want to see an hors' d'ouvre again. I've sent boxes of books and clothes and statuettes home, so hold till I arrive in July.

Sorry to be so long in sending checks, but NO time at all until now, where I'm resting a week, then on to Paris. Write me there, c/o American Express, 11 rue Scribe, and tell me all the news. Just read today where Mrs. Knopf died.§

Please pay American Express Credit Card bill right away, as I'm using it to the hilt!. . . . Ask Jean Blackwell about the Dakar Festival.¶ She were there, plus almost everybody else. And there are lots of "us" all over Africa—some living in mansions and serving caviar!

Love to the family.

* Raoul Abdul (1929–2010), Hughes's secretary at this time, was a formally trained con-cert singer, an actor, and a promoter of classical music concerts in Harlem.
† A reference to John V. Lindsay (1921–2000), who became mayor of New York City in January 1966. At six feet four inches, Lindsay was at the time probably the tallest man to have held that position.
‡ Hughes wrote the poem "Emperor Haile Selassie" for the Ethiopian ruler. It was later published in *Negro Digest* (November 1966).
§ Blanche Knopf, Hughes's main editor at Alfred A. Knopf for most of his career, died in her sleep on June 6, 1966, in New York after a struggle of many years with cancer.
¶ The librarian Jean Blackwell Hutson (1914–1998), a longtime friend of Hughes, was curator and then chief of what became the Schomburg Center for Research in Black Cul-ture, at the main branch (on 135th Street) of the New York Public Library in Harlem.

TO ARNA BONTEMPS   [*TLS*]

[*On* Langston Hughes, 20 East 127th Street, New York 35, N.Y. *stationery*]

August 5, 1966

Dear Arna:

I decided not to go to California after all. October will be here before I could turn around—and I've <u>GOT</u> to get my (and our) books done. Also, I'm not too fond of the bigot backlash out there—remembering how they tied up the Mills College switchboard with hate calls all day LONG when I was Convocation speaker there a couple of years ago—so the President could not even call his wife! So why cope with that again?

I finished my Intro for the BOOK OF NEGRO SHORT STORIES, but it will not come out now until late winter. The galleys read well, and there are some very good stories in it—including yours.*

Now I've just cleared my desk to finish the ENTERTAINMENT book over the weekend, as it HAS to be <in> next week in order to make a now delayed Spring deadline.†

When can we confer with Dodd, Mead about the Davis project? With that and other interesting things pending, I must stick to my resolve NOT to take any more lectures, etc. since they take so much time—and I like writing much better, anyhow. One's words don't go in one ear and out the other so quickly. Besides, on paper, you can be heard around the world.

Selah!

Langston

---

* In 1967, Little, Brown published Hughes's *The Best Short Stories by Negro Writers: An Anthology from 1899 to the Present.* It included Bontemps's best-known story, "A Summer Tragedy."

† Hughes and Milton Meltzer published *Black Magic: A Pictorial History of the Negro in American Entertainment* (Prentice Hall, 1967).

TO ARNA BONTEMPS   [TLS]

[On Langston Hughes, 20 East 127th Street, New York 35, N.Y. stationery]

5:45 A. M. Monday
Morning, Oct. 31, 1966

Dear Arna:

In looking for the poetry of Jack Micheline (a Village beatnik poet published in the little magazines who has been sending me manuscripts off and on for several years, and who may have something worthy of our book) I suddenly remembered I had a <u>BIG</u> box of poetry in a closet somewhere I'd forgotten about.* I hauled it out—and found not only Micheline, but an overflowing folder of <u>old</u> Negro poetry and manuscripts (some by hand and many signed) including dozens of Waring Cuney poems sent me to keep for him when he was in the South Pacific in the Army, letters and poems from Richard Wright—some I'm sure unpublished—dozens of Frank Horne's†—and a whole sheaf of YOUR poems from <u>way</u> <u>back</u> all signed by you and some I'm sure you've probably forgotten you ever wrote! (Maybe you gave them to me when you were living in Watts. Unfortunately, they're not dated.) Also found a large folder of poems written about (or to) me; the Fenton Johnson poems you once sent me;‡ Georgia Douglas Johnson's poems on cards she used to send friends; and various other poetics, including some Jessie Fauset verses she had long ago sent, <too>. All of which has taken me ALL NIGHT to sort out and put in some semblance of order in manila folders—in the process finding a few items which I'd put in that box a year or two ago especially for our P. of NEGRO and forgotten about—but which seem good on rereading. Micheline has <u>too</u> much to look into before going to bed, so I've put him aside until waking up a-fresh. Lloyd Addison manuscri<pts> I also found, too dif-

---

* Hughes and Bontemps were working on the second edition of their 1949 anthology, *The Poetry of the Negro*. This edition would be published in 1970. No poem by Jack Micheline (1929–1998) appears in the later volume.

† The poetry of Frank Horne (1899–1974) was published in *The Crisis* and *Opportunity* as well as various anthologies. In 1925, his "Letters Found Near a Suicide" took second place in that year's *Crisis* literary contest (Countee Cullen won first place, and Hughes was third). Later a member of Franklin Roosevelt's "Black Cabinet," Horne held several positions within the U.S. Housing Authority.

‡ Fenton Johnson (1888–1958) is considered a key forerunner of the Harlem Renaissance. A graduate of the University of Chicago, he published his first volume of poetry, *A Little Dreaming*, in 1913, followed by *Visions of Dusk* (1915) and *Songs of the Soul* (1916). His work also appeared in Harriet Monroe's *Poetry* magazine.

ficult to read when sleepy, sent when he was at University of New Mexico. He's on order of Russell Atkins, strange typography, etc., but some folks think he is good.* Notation on corner of one of his typescripts says I sen<t> "And Some—" to you once. What did you think of it?????

Anyhow, cheerio, Langston

<P.S. ① |Paul| Breman is back in town. . . . Calvin Hernton is in Sweden†. . . . Julia Fields is pregnant.>‡

< ② P.S. — — — — — — — —
I made a dummy of the revised book for our editor, marking and cutting up the copy she sent me for that purpose. Will list cuts|,| changes, inserts for you this week, for Raoul |Abdul| to type.>

<"Simple" book in Italian came yesterday.>

TO JUDITH JONES   [TL]

November 26, 1966

Dear Judith,

Since I am inserting 5 additional poems into THE PANTHER AND THE LASH,§ and have revised and recopied a couple of others, as well as retyping the revised ACKNOWLEDGMENTS and CONTENTS, rather than sending these new pages down to you, it would be simpler and easier for us both if you would return the manuscript you have to me for a couple of hours on Monday—today—BY MESSENGER; and I will return it to you by my errand boy before 5 P.M. with all the new material inserted. You would then have a complete copy.

Enclosed herewith is a fresh copy of the suggested description of the book typed on the blue sheet returned to you by post this weekend. Also some addition|al| possible blurb or publicity material, and some quotes on my work

---

* Hughes and Bontemps did not include Lloyd Addison's poetry in their anthology. In London, Paul Breman later published a small volume by the avant-garde writer Russell Atkins (b. 1926).

† Calvin Hernton (1933–2001), a professor and frequent commentator on racial, social, and literary issues, was probably best known for his volume *Sex and Racism in America* (1965).

‡ "Alabama," by Julia Fields (b. 1938), appears in *The Poetry of the Negro, 1746–1970*.

§ Knopf published Hughes's *The Panther and the Lash: Poems for Our Times* (1967) after his death that year.

from recent sources, that might be useful for the jacket or releases on the book.*

Monday along with the new inserts, I will send you three photographs. See which one, if any, you like. And we can then have some glossies made from it. I think I like the Dar-es-Salaam one by John Taylor best—a young Negro photographer now in Ethiopia.

If we achieve a format for the book anywhere near as handsome as ASK YOUR MAMA, wouldn't that be wonderful?

I'll phone you on Monday.

Sincerely,

TO ARNA BONTEMPS   [*TLS*]

[*On* Langston Hughes, 20 East 127th Street, New York 35, N.Y. *stationery*]

December 9, 1966

Dear Arna:

A minor <u>miracle</u> has been achieved! After 50-11 phone calls, cards, letters to old friends of hers, TIMES and AMSTERDAM morgues, etc. (after failure of Schomburg and CRISIS—NAACP to be of any help) we finally tracked down the lawyer for the Alain Locke estate, who tracked down Arthur Fauset (whom some said was dead; others "institutionalized;" others hadn't seen in years, etc.) but we found him very much alive and running a school for the teaching of English and Americanization to Puerto Ricans in N. Y.† From her death certificate, he gave us what I believe nobody else on God's earth has <u>BUT US</u>:

JESSIE REDMOND FAUSET (1882-1961)
Born in Fredericksville, New Jersey‡

---

* Hughes offered Knopf the following statement for possible use in publicizing the book: "<u>The Panther and the Lash</u> is a collection of poems by Langston Hughes in which is distilled the essence of the emotional undercurrents that have rocked America in our present decade of racial dilemmas, freedom marches, sit-ins, speeches, prayers, violence and nonviolence, loud longings and silent hopes that now involve the entire nation."
† Arthur Huff Fauset (1899–1983), a trained anthropologist and published author, was the half-brother of Jessie Redmon Fauset.
‡ Hughes was misled here in this spelling of Fauset's middle name as "REDMOND." It was "Redmon." The mistake made its way into both editions of *The Poetry of the Negro* (1949 and 1970), as well as into publications by several other editors and writers.

Now if <u>you</u> can get VILMA HOWARD*<;> and ASNLH in Washington† or the Howard folks (Sterling |Brown|, etc,) to whom we've written can supply LEWIS ALEXANDER death date,‡ we'll come pretty near having a DEFINITIVE biographical section. Help!

Trust you're back at your hearth and fireside.

Lang

(P.)-(S.)

Saw the opening of YERMA tonight at the Lincoln Center complex, with Gloria Foster in lead, Ruth Attaway in cast.§ It's Art with a capital "A" (more posturing and posing than poetry). Americans have no flair for the poetic on stage. It just sounds high flown, rhetorical, and speechified—in a stilted translation, to boot, I thought. MEWS had a much more beautiful production in Spanish last month by a Puerto Rican-Cuban studio group. . . . But as I write, the radio suddenly blares out a review praising the current YERMA (so maybe I am wrong) saying at last Lincoln Center has achieved "the shining power of theatre." Never no telling what white folks will like! Let's see what the papers say tomorrow. Audience applause was only polite, mildly so at end. Sidney Poitier was there. He has the friendliest smile in show biz—so it was nice seeing him—late like me, so we had to watch the first scene on lobby TV—a new deal for late comers (who are NEVER seated while a scene is on at the Center). A good rule for folks like you who get places on time (I reckon, <u>good</u>?).

L. H.
(<u>A</u>rtist)

* Vilma Howard's poem "The Citizen" was included in *New Negro Poets: USA*. Associated with *The Paris Review* in the 1950s, she lived for many years in Europe.
† The Association for the Study of Negro Life and History (ASNLH) is now known as the Association for the Study of African American Life and History.
‡ Also a playwright and an actor, Lewis G. Alexander (1900–1945) of Washington, D.C., was one of the poets featured in 1926 in the sole issue of *Fire!!* He also published work in *The Messenger* and *Opportunity*, and in Countee Cullen's special number on black poets for *Palms* (October 1926).
§ Federico García Lorca's tragedy *Yerma* was written and first staged in 1934. (See also letter dated August 30, 1938.)

TO ARNA BONTEMPS [TLS]

[*On* Langston Hughes, 20 East 127th Street, New York 35, N.Y. *stationery*]

December 22, 1966

Dear Arna:

Since LITANY AT ATLANTA by Du Bois has been anthologized so much, what would you think of possibly substituting for it in our updated edition, the poem enclosed from DARKWATER which is little known, THE PRAYERS OF GOD.* Let me know.

Hughes placed this sticker near his signature in this letter to Bontemps.

In parentheses beneath the title of THE PINCHOT MANSION might we not put where or what the mansion is? I have no idea what the poem is about, or where or what Buddenbrook or Forsyte refers to, or what Puchinello symbolizes. So a clue would do no harm.†

Also in the same poem, you probably have a misprint in the third line from the bottom:

Or Forsyte stepl three tiers . . . etc.

What should the third word be, step, or what? Let me know, so I can make copies for the manuscript.

I saw Roy Wilkins at the Taconic party and had fun quoting him the LeRoi Jones poem:

"Roy Wilkins is an eternal faggot. . . ."

---

* Despite this comment, "A Litany at Atlanta" and not "The Prayers of God" was included in the second edition of *The Poetry of the Negro* (1970).
† No poem entitled "The Pinchot Mansion" or any with these references appears in the volume.

which amused him*..... All the establishment was at the party: Kenneth Clark,† James Farmer,‡ Urban League folks, etc. But SNCC is now nix.§

L. Hughes

<u>P.S.</u> Little Alice Walker came to see me yesterday.¶ She is really "cute as a button" and real bright. She brought her young Jewish NAACP lawyer fiancé with her. They're getting married in the Spring and will live and work in MISSISSIPPI, Jackson Branch. Mine is her first important publication (and her first story in print) so I can claim her discovery, too, I reckon..... As well as Bethune, Patterson, King—first publication, too, also Milner**..... Be SURE to read the John Williams story. Most evil of all!††

TO ARNA BONTEMPS   [TLS]

[On Langston Hughes, 20 East 127th Street, New York 35, N.Y. stationery]

January 5, 1966-7-7-7
(Got to get used to it)

Dear Arna: I reckon you're back up North in God's (?) country by now. How're things in the deep dark Southland?..... Do you ever see <u>ETC.</u>? Don Haya-

---

* Hughes quotes the first words of LeRoi Jones's "Civil Rights Poem," which was included later in Jones's *Black Magic . . . Collected Poetry, 1961–1967* (Bobbs-Merrill, 1969). Wilkins was then executive director of the NAACP.
† A study involving the conflicted responses of African American children when offered a choice between black dolls and white dolls, prepared by the psychologists Kenneth Clark (1914–1983) and his wife, Mamie Phipps Clark (1917–1983), stressed the harm done by segregation to the self-esteem of black children. This work influenced the landmark U.S. Supreme Court decision *Brown v. Board of Education* (1954).
‡ James L. Farmer, Jr. (1920–1999), was a founder of the Congress of Racial Equality (CORE).
§ The Student Non-Violent Coordinating Committee (SNCC), formed in April 1960 at Shaw University in Raleigh, North Carolina, organized sit-ins and was also involved in the Freedom Rides of 1961, the 1963 March on Washington, and the Mississippi Freedom Summer of 1964.
¶ Hughes published the first story to appear in print by Alice Walker (b. 1944) when he included "To Hell with Dying" in *The Best Short Stories by Negro Writers: An Anthology from 1899 to the Present* (Little, Brown, 1967). Walker later won a Pulitzer Prize for her novel *The Color Purple* (1982). In 1967 she married Melvyn Leventhal, a lawyer, and moved with him to Mississippi.
** *The Best Short Stories* includes Lebert Bethune's "The Burglar," Lindsay Patterson's "Red Bonnet," Woodie King, Jr.'s, "Beautiful Light and Black Our Dreams," and Ronald Milner's "Junkie-Joe Had Some Money."
†† John A. Williams's "Son in the Afternoon" also appears in the volume.

kawa's magazine.* He just sent me the September issue with a provocative article of his on WATTS. I always think of him and Horace |Cayton| and the wild Rosenwald gang in Chi in one breath—Vandy Haygood, etc.—and somehow Karamu—maybe wilder in some ways, if the truth be known. Shades of DOLCHE VITA, U. S. A.† . . . . Somebody ought to (NO!) write a book on the good<->time side of do-gooding. (Or am I out of my mind?)

Did I tell you that the night after Aunt Toy |Harper| was rushed back to the hospital in an ambulance, her oldest friend, our house guest for the holidays <(>for the past twenty years<)>—> (Will Vodery's widow, Rosana from Saratoga)‡ went to the clinic at Harlem for a headache at 9 A. M. and by 5 hadn't come home so we got worried about her and went looking—and she had been LOST in Harlem Hospital! They'd kept her, but nobody could find her for 24 hours (and she weights 250). Mignon Richmond from Salt Lake<,>§ who was going home the next day<,> was allowed to go all through the wards looking for her. No luck, no records. Absolutely LOST. New York hospitals are so crowded they'd put her and lots of other patients on cots in a corridor until beds were available, but nobody knew what corridor where? What with Aunt Toy being gravely ill, and Emerson's nephew-in-law dropping dead just around the corner, we've had quite a holiday week between Christmas and New Year's. . . . And now up comes a community committee INSISTING on giving me a testimonial for my Birthday—and me saying now (of all times) is not the time.<X> Wait a little while, till I'm 75 anyhow, and the days are less hectic. I haven't recovered from the Detroit and Brooklyn ones yet—and have enough scrolls and plaques to last me a life time. . . . Anyhow, HAPPY NEW YEAR to you-all! Lang

<X> I do NOT now want NO testimonial—although they claim I will not have to be involved AT ALL. (But, having gone through them before—)<.Help!>
P. S. One cheerful note: Just got today the loveliest simpliest very small very

* Samuel Ichiye "Don" Hayakawa (1906–1992), an English professor, a university president, and a U.S. senator from California, edited (1943–1970) ETC, the journal of the International Society for General Semantics. He lived for several years in Chicago, where his close friends included Horace Cayton. Hughes refers to the article "Reflections on a Visit to Watts" by Hayakawa and Barry Goodfield about the Watts Riots in Los Angeles that left thirty-four persons dead between August 11 and 17, 1965.
† A reference to the film director Federico Fellini's masterpiece La Dolce Vita (1960).
‡ Will Vodery (1885–1951), an African American composer, created vocal and choral arrangements for the original Broadway production of Show Boat (1927).
§ Mignon Richmond, a graduate of Utah State Agricultural College, was active in the NAACP and YWCA.

handsome gold fleur-de-lis single insignia on vermillion-red holiday card from Josephine Baker whose elegance is still superb and who seemingly is still in her chateau at Les Milandes in spite of hell and high water and 14 children. So maybe from somewhere came the half million francs to pay off the mortgage.* I hope so.

\<Help!\>
\<¡d¡ǝH\>

P. S. 2—Aunt Toy is constantly under oxygen—and sedation.†

TO ARNA BONTEMPS [TLS]

[On Hotel Wellington, Seventh Avenue At Fifty-Fifth Street,
New York, N.Y. 10019 *stationery]*

CURRENT ADDRESS
April 22, 1967

Dear Arna,

I believe I asked Raoul |Abdul| to drop you a card requesting that you revise, as you like, your own biog, and add to it what you wish, to bring it up to date for THE POETRY OF THE NEGRO and send it to me post haste as I'm now ready to type those sheets up for Doubleday, having all the material—but Lewis Alexander's birth date—which I intend to find if it KILLS me. Ran into Kurtz Myers of the Hackley Collection in Detroit, who says he thinks he can get it for me through a library researcher who finds things for him in Washington.

The house is still ALL torn up,‡ and Emerson is going around in circles, not being good at "law and order" and quite lost without Aunt Toy, who is wasting away by the hour to a wisp of her former self, now too weak to sit up,

---

* Josephine Baker (1906–1975), born Freda Josephine McDonald in St. Louis, Missouri, was a singer, dancer, actress, and patriot who was awarded the Croix de Guerre, a military honor, for her work in the French Resistance in World War II. Arriving as an unknown in Paris in 1925 with *La Revue Nègre*, she soon built an enormous following. Eventually she became a French citizen and a revered figure. In the 1960s she was also known for her "Rainbow Tribe," a group of a dozen or more children she adopted from all over the world. They lived together at her Château des Milandes in the Dordogne. About this time she was dogged by reports of financial insolvency.
† Toy Harper collapsed in 1966, between Christmas and New Year's, and was taken to Sydenham Hospital in Harlem.
‡ The house at 20 East 127th Street was undergoing major repairs.

but wants to come home—which really would put an end to her if she saw the house as it is now—full of paint fumes, dust and debris. You never saw the like.

With such confusion there, I shall stay here at the hotel until I go to Europe (maybe not till July now). So you may best write me here, ROOM 41, at the above address. Impossible to work at home.

Meltzer's second draft of his book, LANGSTON HUGHES, is good.[*] And I've just added a little chapter for him about my African trip. But this is the LAST book or thesis I can take time out to help anybody with. Enough anyhow—four—with |James| Emanuel's and the two in France-Belgium[†]. . . . . SIMPLE got off to a good start in Paris, so they write me, and still urge me to fly over right now for interviews.[‡] Wish I could. But not for just a week, not for just a year. . . . . as the song says . . . but—

Toujours,[§]
Langston

---

[*] Milton Meltzer, Hughes's collaborator on *Black Magic: A Pictorial History of the Negro in American Entertainment* (1967), wrote *Langston Hughes: A Biography* (Crowell, 1968).
[†] With a large section on Hughes, Jean Wagner published *Poètes nègres des États-Unis; le sentiment racial et religieux dans la poésie de P. L. Dunbar à L. Hughes (1890–1940)* (Librairie Istra, 1963) in France. The study appeared in the United States as *Black Poets of the United States: From Paul Laurence Dunbar to Langston Hughes* (University of Illinois Press, 1973). Raymond Quinot's *Langston Hughes, ou l'Étoile Noire* (Ed. du C.E.L.F., 1964) was published in Belgium.
[‡] Editions Robert Laffont, the French publisher of *L'Ingénu de Harlem*, the first French book based on Hughes's Simple stories, invited him to visit Paris to help launch the volume.
[§] Quoting from Irving Berlin's classic song "Always" (1925), Hughes replaced the final "always" with its French equivalent, "Toujours," to bid goodbye to his best friend. On May 1, Bontemps replied: "I think one whose career in writing has reached the point of warm reflection and the reading of biographies of himself has earned residence in Paris, prior to residence in glory." Hughes entered the hospital for tests a few days later.

CURRENT ADDRESS

Hotel Wellington

CIRCLE 7-3900

SEVENTH AVENUE
AT FIFTY-FIFTH STREET
NEW YORK N.Y. 10019

April 22, 1967

Dear Arna:

    I believe I asked Raoul to drop you a card
requesting that you revise, as you like, your own
biog, and add to it what you wish, to bring it up
to date for the POETRY OF THE NEGRO and send it
to me post haste as I'm now ready to type those
sheets up for Doubleday, having all the material--
but Lewis Alexander's birth date---which I intend
to find if it KILLS me. Ran into Kurtz Myers of
the Hackley Collection in Detroit, who says he
thinks he can get it for me through a library
researcher who finds things for him in Washington.

    The house is still ALL torn up, and Emerson is
going around in circles, not being good at "law and
order" and quite lost without Aunt Toy, who is
wasting away by the hour to wisp of her former
self, now too weak to sit up, but wants to come
home---which really would put an end to her if she
saw the house as it is now---and full of paint
fumes, dust and debris. You never saw the like.

    With such confusion there, I shall stay here
at the hotel until I go to Europe (maybe not till
July now). So you may best write me here, ROOM 41,
at the above address. Impossible to work at home.

    Meltzer's second draft of his book: LANGSTON
HUGHES, is good. And I've just added a little
chapter for him about my African trip. But this is t'
the LAST book or thesis I can take time out to help
anybody with. Enough, anyhow---four---with Emanuel's
and the two in France-Belgium.....SIMPLE got off to a
good start in Paris, so they write me, and still urge
me to fly over right now for interviews. Wish I
could. But not for just a week, not for just a
year.....as the song says...but-----

        Toujours,   *Langston*

On May 22, 1967, Langston Hughes died in the New York Polyclinic Hospital in Manhattan from infections contracted following his operation there.

Following his written instructions closely, George Houston Bass supervised Hughes's funeral on May 25 at Benta's, probably the leading funeral home in Harlem. His instructions were spare. No minister was to be included in the proceedings, a jazz band would perform the only music allowed, and Arna Bontemps would speak. A trio led by the pianist Randy Weston played selections chosen by Weston, and Arna Bontemps gave the eulogy. Finally, as specified by Hughes, the service ended with the trio playing Duke Ellington's "Do Nothing Till You Hear from Me."

Later that day, in a ceremony attended by a few chosen mourners and supervised again by George Bass, who led them in a spirited recitation of "The Negro Speaks of Rivers," Hughes's body was cremated in Hartsdale, New York, north of Manhattan.

Acknowledgments

"Hope the journey is a long one," Constantine Cavafy advises us in his poem "Ithaca." The journey to complete this book was indeed long but it was also gratifying, full of happy discoveries that offset our moments of distress over missed deadlines.

Along the way we incurred many debts. Above all, we owe much to Judith Jones, who commissioned this book from us, just as she asked us several years ago to prepare what became *The Collected Poems of Langston Hughes* (1994). As Hughes's last editor at Knopf during his lifetime, she earned his admiration for her efforts on two volumes of his poetry. She is now retired from Knopf but her brilliance as an editor lives on. She has served Hughes and his legacy well. This is why we dedicate this book to her.

In editing Hughes's books at Knopf, Ms. Jones directly succeeded Blanche Knopf, who awarded him his first publishing contract in 1925 and then worked with him for more than thirty years. When Ms. Jones retired, Deborah Garrison succeeded her in managing this project. We also owe much to Ms. Garrison for her patience and understanding, and for continuing Knopf's commitment to Langston Hughes.

We also thank various libraries and the librarians who responded so diligently to us as we searched for Hughes's letters, or searched for information about persons and topics mentioned in his letters. Our indebtedness here begins with the Beinecke Rare Book and Manuscript Library at Yale University. The Beinecke houses the Langston Hughes Papers in the James Weldon Johnson Memorial Collection of literary material rooted in African American culture, a landmark collection founded by Hughes's friend and ally Carl Van Vechten. We are especially grateful to E. C. Schroeder, Director of the Beinecke Library; and to Nancy Kuhl, Curator of Poetry, and Melissa Barton, Curator of Prose and Drama, in the Yale University Collection of American Literature.

We are also indebted to the staffs of the Amistad Research Center, New Orleans; the Bancroft Library, University of California, Berkeley; Special Collections and Archives, the John Hope and Aurelia E. Franklin Library, Fisk University, Nashville; the Special Collections Research Center, Bird Library, Syracuse University, Syracuse; the Moorland-Spingarn Research Center, Founders Library, Howard University, Washington, D.C.; the Tamiment Library and Robert F. Wagner Labor Archives, New York University, New York City; the Manuscript Division, Library of Congress, Washington, D.C.; Special Collections and Archives, Langston Hughes Memorial Library, Lincoln University, Pennsylvania; the Schomburg Center for Research in Black Culture, New York Public Library, New York City; the Harry Ransom Center, The University of Texas, Austin; the Van Pelt-Dietrich Library, University of Pennsylvania, Philadelphia; Rare Books and Special Collections, Firestone Library, Princeton University, Princeton; the Charles L. Blockson Afro-American Collection, Temple University, Philadelphia; the Paul Robeson Library, Rutgers University, Camden; and the Archibald S. Alexander Library, Rutgers University, New Brunswick, New Jersey.

In addition to librarians, many other individuals helped to improve the quality of this book. Near the end of our journey, Professor Arna Alexander Bontemps of Arizona State University provided invaluable assistance in identifying certain figures by drawing on his memories of Langston Hughes, with whom his father, Arna Wendell Bontemps, corresponded for almost forty years. We know that we stand on the shoulders of other scholars and critics who have probed—and are probing—the complexities of Hughes's life and work, and the circles in which he moved. Some of these scholars and critics are no longer with us but our debt to them remains real. Our task was made easier by the efforts of individuals such as Charles H. Nichols, who published the first edited volume of Hughes's letters (to Arna Bontemps); George Houston Bass, Hughes's choice as executor-trustee of his estate; and other pioneering figures such as Richard K. Barksdale; Faith Berry; Thomas Cripps; Donald C. Dickinson; Arthur P. Davis; James A. Emanuel; Nathan I. Huggins; Onwuchekwa Jemie; Bruce Kellner; David Levering Lewis; John F. Matheus; Milton Meltzer; Edward J. Mullen; Kenneth P. Neilson; Therman B. O'Daniel; Hans A. Ostrom; Webster Smalley; Darwin Turner; Jean Wagner; and Thomas H. Wirth.

We also acknowledge our debt to other figures who, in varying degrees, have advanced and are advancing our understanding of the wide world of Langston Hughes. They include Elizabeth Alexander; Giselle L. Anatol; Kwame Anthony Appiah; Valerie Babb; Kate A. Baldwin; Kimberly J. Banks; Juda Bennett; Emily Bernard; Harold Bloom; Marcellus Blount; Michael Borshuk; Dennis Chester; David Chinitz; Martha Cobb; Carrie Cowherd; Rosemary K. Curb; Letitia Dace; Anthony Dawahare; James DeJongh; Christopher C. De Santis; Susan Duffy; Ira Dworkin; Brent H. Edwards; Nicholas M. Evans; Nikky Finney; Karen Jackson Ford; Paul Gardullo; Henry Louis Gates; Sandra Govan; Maryemma Graham; Shane Graham; Sandra M. Grayson; Donna Akiba Sullivan Harper; Carolyn R. Hodges; Dolan Hubbard; George Hutchinson; Richard Jackson; Dianne Johnson; Meta DuEwa Jones; Carla Kaplan; David Krasner; Vera M. Kutzinksi; Brian Loftus; Dellita Martin-Orgunsola; Joseph McLaren; Thomas A. Mikolyzk; W. Jason Miller; R. Baxter Miller; Seth Moglen; David Chioni Moore; David M. Nifong; Thomas H. Nigel; Anita H. Patterson; Jay Plum; Martin J. Ponce; Cheryl R. Ragar; Jahan Ramazani; Donald A. Ritchie; Leslie C. Sanders; Larry Scanlon; Elizabeth Schultz; Jonathan Scott; William Scott; Amritjit Singh; James E. Smethurst; Isabel Soto; H. Nigel Thomas; Michael Thurston; John Edgar Tidwell; Steven C. Tracy; James C. Trotman; Alan M. Wald; Maurice O. Wallace; John Walters; Carmeletta M. Williams; Regennia N. Williams; Gregory Woods; and Robert Young.

Certainly there are others who deserve to be mentioned for their contributions to our knowledge and understanding of Langston Hughes. We are thankful to them all. Lisa Donato served as our first research assistant on this project. Edward Horan, Ciara Barrick, and Kate Brown checked letters at different times. Fred Mench took time away from his own research projects to aid ours. Pamela Beatrice read through the manuscript several times and Bryan Hoffman proofread the manuscript when deadlines loomed large. The Richard Stockton College of New Jersey helped to bring the project to a speedier conclusion by providing sabbatical support to David Roessel for the 2010–2011 academic year. Robert Gregg, formerly Dean of Arts and Humanities at Stockton College, championed the effort, as have Dean Lisa Honaker, Provost Harvey Kesselman, and the Hellenic Studies community of Stockton. Stanford University was also generous in supporting our efforts.

Above all, we are grateful to Langston Hughes himself. In his letters, as in his other writings, he showed those rare qualities of personal grace and steely but principled determination, as well as abundant literary skill, that helped him to create enduring works of art out of the sorrows and joys of his remarkable American life.

Index

Page numbers in *italics* refer to illustrations.

A NOTE ABOUT THE EDITORS

ARNOLD RAMPERSAD, the Sarah Hart Kimball Professor Emeritus in the Humanities at Stanford University, has also taught at Princeton, Columbia, and Rutgers Universities. His books include *The Life of Langston Hughes* (two volumes); biographies of W. E. B. Du Bois, Jackie Robinson, and Ralph Ellison; and, with Arthur Ashe, *Days of Grace: A Memoir*. Among his numerous awards and honors are a MacArthur Foundation fellowship in 1991 and the National Humanities Medal, presented at the White House in 2011.

DAVID ROESSEL is the Peter and Stella Yiannos Professor of Greek Language and Literature at the Richard Stockton College of New Jersey. He is the associate editor, with Arnold Rampersad, of *The Collected Poems of Langston Hughes*, as well as the coeditor of *The Collected Poems of Tennessee Williams*. Among his other books is the acclaimed *In Byron's Shadow: Modern Greece in the English and American Imagination*, which in 2002 won the prize awarded annually by the Modern Language Association for the best book published by an independent scholar.

A NOTE ON THE TYPE

This book was set in Scala, a typeface designed by the Dutch designer Martin Majoor (b. 1960) in 1988 and released by the FontFont foundry in 1990. While designed as a fully modern family of fonts containing both a serif and a sans serif alphabet, Scala retains many refinements normally associated with traditional fonts.

Composed by North Market Street Graphics,
Lancaster, Pennsylvania

Printed and bound by Berryville Graphics,
Berryville, Virginia

Designed by Cassandra J. Pappas